Brothers in Arms

Brothers in Arms

The Great War Letters
of Captain Nigel Boulton R.A.M.C.
& Lieut Stephen Boulton, A.I.F.

Compiled & Edited By Louise Wilson

Brothers in Arms: The Great War Letters of Captain Nigel Boulton R.A.M.C. and Lieut Stephen Boulton, A.I.F.

Copyright © 2015 Louise Wilson

All rights are reserved. The material contained within this book is protected by copyright law, no part may be copied, reproduced, presented, stored, communicated or transmitted in any form by any means without prior written permission.

Printed and bound in Australia by BookPOD
Typeset layout by BookPOD
P.O. Box 6015, Vermont South, VIC, 3133
www.bookpod.com.au

A Catalogue-in-Publication is available from the National Library of Australia.

ISBN: 978-0-9804478-5-9

Available from Louise Wilson, PO Box 3055, South Melbourne VIC 3205,
or by email to louisewilson@tpg.com.au,
or online at www.bookstore.bookpod.com.au

Every effort has been made to trace and acknowledge original source material contained in this book. Where the attempt has been unsuccessful, the author would be pleased to rectify any omission.

More details at www.louisewilson.com.au

Dedicated to my mother, Julia Woodhouse.

Contents

1914

Commonwealth Offices, 72 Victoria St, London S.W., 18 Aug 1914 19
Strathmore, Camborne Terrace, Richmond, 2 Sep 1914 23
Military Hospital, Western Heights, Dover, 19 Sep 1914 28
Dover Castle, 13 Oct 1914 30
From M.O. i/c Effective Troops, Dover Castle, 22 Oct 1914 31
Letter from England 34
Section Hospital, Dover Castle, 28 Oct 1914 37
Section Hospital, Dover Castle, 5 Nov 1914 40
Section Hospital, Dover Castle, 19 Nov 1914 42
Section Hospital, Dover Castle, 26 Nov 1914 44
Section Hospital, Dover Castle, 3 Dec 1914 46
Section Hospital, Dover Castle, 10 Dec 1914 48
Section Hospital, Dover Castle, 17 Dec 1914 50
Section Hospital, Dover Castle, 31 Dec 1914 51

1915

Connaught House, The Parade, Dover, 7 Jan 1915 53
Section Hospital, Dover Castle, 13 Jan 1915 55
Section Hospital, Dover Castle, 20 Jan 1915 57
Section Hospital, Dover Castle, 2 Feb 1915 60
Commonwealth Offices, 72 Victoria St, London, 11 Feb 1915 62
Postcard from Newcastle, NSW, Sunday, 21 Feb 1915 64
Letter, Newcastle, Monday 64
Postcard, Newcastle, Tuesday, 23 Feb 1915 65
Drayton Lodge, Cargate Av, Aldershot, 2 Mar 1915 66
At Sea, March 1915 68
S.S. 'Minnewaska', 8 Mar 1915 71
Still at Sea, Transport A 21 73
Mustafa Pacha, Alexandria, Egypt, 19 Mar 1915 74
Transport 21, At Sea [c 22 Mar 1915] 78
Postcard, On Active Service [Suez], Postmarked 27 Mar 1915 78
Mustafa Pacha, Alexandria, Egypt, 28 Mar 1915 79

No 15 General Hospital, Abbassia Schools, Alexandria, 4 Apr 1915 81
Mena Camp, Mena, Cairo, 4 Apr 1915 84
Postcard postmarked Cairo, 5 April 1915 86
Mena Camp, Egypt, 9 Apr 1915 87
No 15 General Hospital, Abbassia School, Alexandria, 11 Apr 1915 89
Undated Postcard from Cairo, 13 Apr 1915 91
Undated Postcard, Mena Camp, 13 Apr 1915 92
Postcard, postmarked Alexandria, 18 April 1915, 3.30pm 92
Postcard, postmarked Alexandria, 18 April 1915, 8.30pm 92
No 15 General Hospital, Abbassia Schools, Alexandria, 19 Apr 1915 93
Postcard dated 23 April 1915, postmarked Alexandria 24 April &
Port Said 25 April 95
No 15 General Hospital, Abbassia Schools, Alexandria, 25 Apr 1915 96
No 15 General Hospital, Abbassia School, Alexandria, 2 May 1915 99
'Minneapolis', 4 May 1915 102
No 15 General Hospital, Alexandria, 9 May 1915 104
Postcard dated 11 May 1915 107
S.S. 'Minneapolis', 15 May 1915 108
No 15 General Hospital, Alexandria, 17 May 1915 110
No 15 General Hospital, Alexandria, 26 May 1915 112
Cleopatra Camp, Alexandria, 27 May 1915 114
No 15 General Hospital, Alexandria, 31 May 1915 116
Cleopatra Camp, Alexandria, 7 Jun 1915 118
Cleopatra Camp, Alexandria, 9 Jun 1915 120
No 15 General Hospital, Alexandria, 13 June 1915 122
Cleopatra Camp, 20 Jun 1915 124
No 15 General Hospital, Alexandria, 22 June 1915 125
Cleopatra Camp, Alexandria, 30 Jun 1915 127
No 15 General Hospital, Alexandria, 6 July 1915 128
Egypt, 12 July 1915 131
No 15 General Hospital, Abbassia Schools, Alexandria, 14 July 1915 132
No 15 General Hospital, Alexandria, 21 July 1915 134
Dardanelles, Gallipoli Peninsula, 24 Jul 1915 136
Postcard, Gallipoli, Undated 138
No 15 General Hospital, Abbassia Schools, Alexandria, 29 Jul 1915 138

Anzac, Gallipoli, 30 Jul 1915 140
Divisional Ammn Park, Anzac, Gallipoli Penn, 30 Jul 1915 142
No 15 General Hospital, Alexandria, 4 Aug 1915 143
No 15 General Hospital, Abbassia Schools, Alexandria, 11 Aug 1915 ... 146
Divisional Ammunition Park, ANZAC, 16 Aug 1915 147
No 15 General Hospital, Abbassia Schools, Alexandria, 22 Aug 1915 ... 151
Nigel Renews Contract, 29 Aug 1915 154
Divisional Ammn Park, ANZAC, 3 Sep 1915 154
No 15 General Hospital, Alexandria, 8 Sep 1915 156
Island of Imbros, 11 Sep 1915 159
Hospital, Island of Imbros, 15 Sep 1915 160
No 15 General Hospital, Alexandria, 16 Sep 1915 162
25th Casualty Clearing Hospital, Island of Imbros, 19 Sep 1915 164
No 15 General Hospital, Abbassia Schools, Alexandria, 22 Sep 1915 ... 165
25th Casualty Clearing Hospital, Imbros Island, 25 Sep 1915 167
No 15 General Hospital, Alexandria, 29 Sep 1915 168
At Sea, Hospital Ship 'Grantully Castle', 4 Oct 1915 170
St. Johns Military Hospital, Sliema, Malta, 7 Oct 1915 172
St. Johns Military Hospital, Sliema, Malta, 16 Oct 1915 174
No 15 General Hospital, Alexandria, 18 Oct 1915 175
St. Johns Military Hospital, Sliema, Malta, 23 Oct 1915 178
No 15 General Hospital, Alexandria, 25 Oct 1915 179
St. Johns Military Hospital, Sliema, Malta, 30 Oct 1915 181
Union Club, Alexandria, Egypt, 4 Nov 1915 183
St. John's Military Hospital, Sliema, Malta, 6 Nov 1915 185
St. Johns Military Hospital, Sliema, Malta, 14 Nov 1915 187
No 15 General Hospital, Alexandria, Egypt, 15 Nov 1915 189
St. Johns Military Hospital, Sliema, Malta, 19 Nov 1915 192
St. Johns Military Hospital, Sliema, Malta, 26 Nov 1915 195
Ghain-Tuffieha Convalescent Camp, Malta, 3 Dec 1915 196
Ghain-Tuffieha Convalescent Camp, Malta, 9 Dec 1915 198
No 15 General Hospital, Alexandria, 12 Dec 1915 200
Ghain-Tuffeiha Convalescent Camp, Malta, 17 Dec 1915 203
Ghain-Tuffieha Convalescent Camp, Malta, 18 Dec 1915 205
No 15 General Hospital, Alexandria, 31 Dec 1915 206

Ghain-Tuffieha Convalescent Camp, Malta, 31 Dec 1915 208

1916

Luna Park, Heliopolis, 13 Jan 1916 211
Partial Postcard to Thea, Egypt, Jan 1916 212
Postcard to Grandmother, Heliopolis, 22 Jan 1916 213
No 1 Auxiliary Con. Depot, Luna Park, Heliopolis, 27 Jan 1916 213
Postcard, No 1 Auxiliary Conv Depot, Luna Park, Heliopolis, 30 Jan 1916 214
Postcard from No 1 Aust Conv Depot, Luna Park, Heliopolis, 30 Jan 1916 215
No 1 Auxiliary Hospital, Luna Park, Heliopolis, 7 Feb 1916 215
No 1 Auxiliary Hospital, Luna Park, Heliopolis, 17 Feb 1916 216
1st Divisional Ammunition Column, Egypt, 27 Feb 1916 218
No 15 General Hospital, Alexandria, 29 Feb 1916 220
1st Section, 1st D.A.C., Zietoun, 1 Mar 1916 222
No 15 General Hospital, Alexandria, 10 Mar 1916 223
Tel-el-kebir, 14 Mar 1916 225
Postcard, Postmarked 21 Mar 1916 227
The ANZAC Heroes 227
At sea, H.M.T. 'Knight Templar', 25 Mar 1916 228
Somewhere in France, Sunday night, 2 Apr 1916 230
Somewhere in France, 10 Apr 1916 232
No 15 General Hospital, Alexandria, 18 Apr 1916 233
Somewhere in France, 30 Apr 1916 235
Somewhere in France [Caëstre], 8 May 1916 239
No 15 General Hospital, Alexandria, 21 May 1916 240
In the line, Somewhere in France [Fleurbaix], 22 May 1916 242
In a Farm, Somewhere in France [Fleurbaix], 13 Jun 1916 245
In a farm, Somewhere in Flanders, 21 Jun 1916 246
In a farm, Somewhere in Belgium [Ploegsteert], 8 Jul 1916 248
Somewhere in France [Somme], 14 Jul 1916 251
In a German Trench, Somewhere in France [Pozières], 23 Jul 1916 253
In a Bosch Trench, Somewhere in France [Pozières], 28 Jul 1916 255
Somewhere in France [St Léger], 13 Aug 1916 259
Somewhere in France, 26 Aug 1916 261
Somewhere in Flanders, 2 Sep 1916 262

Somewhere in Flanders, 9 Sep 1916 264
All Saints Camp, Malta, 11 Sep 1916 265
Somewhere in Flanders, 16 Sep 1916 266
Somewhere in Flanders, In the field, 23 Sep 1916 268
Somewhere in Flanders, In the field, 27 Sep 1916 269
No 17 Field Ambulance, B.E.F. France, Oct 1916 271
Somewhere in France, Oct 1916 273
Somewhere in France [Gueudecourt], 7 Nov 1916 275
Somewhere in France, In the field, 1 Dec 1916 277
Somewhere in France, In the field, 4 Dec 1916 278
Somewhere in France, In the field, 14 Dec 1916 279
Somewhere in France [Havernas], 31 Dec 1916 280

1917

Somewhere in France, 6 Jan 1917 281
Imperial Hotel, Russell Square, 9 Jan 1917 282
Kennet House, Harrow, 11 Jan 1917 283
Somewhere in France, In the field, 19 Jan 1917 284
G Ward, No 14 Casualty Hospital, Boulogne, France, 27 Jan 1917 286
No 1 Convalescent Camp, Boulogne, France, 14 Feb 1917 288
Base Camp, Somewhere in France, 3 Mar 1917 289
Hotel Windsor, Victoria Street, London S.W., 4 Mar 1917 290
Somewhere in France, 11 Mar 1917 292
Base Camp, Somewhere in France, 17 Mar 1917 293
Advanced Dressing Station, Somewhere in France, 28 Mar 1917 295
Advanced Dressing Station, Somewhere in France, 7 Apr 1917 298
Advanced Dressing Station, Somewhere in France, 20 Apr 1917 299
In the Field, 17 Jun 1917 302
R.F.A. Officer Cadet School, Lord's, 29 Jul 1917 304
R.F.A. Officer Cadet School, Lord's, 12 Aug 1917 307
R.F.A. Officer Cadet School, Lord's Cricket Ground,
St. John's Wood N.W., 19 Aug 1917 309
In the Field, 20 Aug 1917 311
Undated Postcard from France 312
R.F.A. Officer Cadet School, Lord's Cricket Ground,
St. John's Wood N.W., 30 Aug 1917 313

R.F.A. Officer Cadet School, Lord's, 15 Sep 1917 315
St John's Wood, 26 Sep 1917 317
Durrington Camp, Salisbury Plain, 28 Oct 1917 318
Durrington Camp, Salisbury Plain, 30 Oct 1917 319
Bedford Hotel, London, 13 Nov 1917 321
Somewhere in France, 27 Nov 1917 323
Somewhere in France, 18 Dec 1917 327
Somewhere in France, 24 Dec 1917 329
No 10 Convalescent Depot, B.E.F. France, 28 Dec 1917 330

1918

Somewhere in France, 20 Jan 1918 333
Somewhere in France, 4 Mar 1918 335
In the field, 29 Mar 1918 337
No 10 Convalescent Depot, B.E.F. France, 31 Mar 1918 338
In the field, 7 Apr 1918 340
No 10 Convalescent Depot, B.E.F. France, 12 Apr 1918 342
In the Field [near Hazebrouck], 19 Apr 1918 344
No 10 Convalescent Depot, B.E.F. France, 23 Apr 1918 346
In the field [Caëstre], 28 Apr 1918 348
In the field, 8 May 1918 350
In the field, 19 May 1918 352
In the field, 27 May 1918 353
No 10 Convalescent Depot, B.E.F. France, 4 June 1918 355
In the field, Somewhere in France, 11 Jun 1918 359
June and July near Hazebrouck 360
August 1918 on the Somme, the Battle of Amiens 362
No 10 Convalescent Depot, B.E.F. France, 17 Aug 1918 363
Torbay Hotel, Torquay, 21 Aug 1918 366
France [Boulogne], 29 Aug 1918 370
In the field [Sailly-Laurette], France, 6 Sep 1918 373
In the field [Jeancourt], France, 22 Sep 1918 376
2nd Aus F A Bgde [Jeancourt], 6 Oct 1918 378
Condé-Folie, France, 14 Oct 1918 380
Condé-Folie, France, 26 October 1918 381

France, 29 Oct 1918 383
Cablegram, 31 Oct 1918 384
Somewhere in Belgium, 5 Nov 1918 384
Somewhere in Belgium [Harlebeke], 12 Nov 1918 387
C/o Sir W. Napier, Cherton Hangar, Chart, Farnham, Surrey, 17 Nov 1918 388
Somewhere in Belgium, 18 Nov 1918 389
C/o Sir W. Napier, Cherton Hangar, Chart, Farnham, Surrey, 20 Nov 1918 390
Somewhere in Belgium, 26 Nov 1918 392
130 Horseferry Road, London, 3 Dec 1918 393
Near Verviers, Belgium, 3 Dec 1918 394
Fernleigh, Kiama, 24 December 1918 396

POST WAR

Solingen, Germany, 15 Feb 1919 399
The Legacy 400
1925 404
Greenwich Rd, 28 October 1928 405
Lest We Forget 406

Illustrations

Stephen & Nigel Boulton, c December 1890	18
Stephen, Dora & Nigel Boulton, c 1893	18
Philip Boulton, c 1895	18
Mona & her Mother, Mrs. Little	21
Cleon Dennis, Aunt Julia & Cousin Bessie, early 1919	24
Kennet House, Harrow	24
Cousin Blanche & Aunt Eleanor, c 1890s	25
Stephen, Thea and Nigel Boulton in England, c 1903	26
Thea & Dora Boulton with their Pet Dogs, c 1915	27
Wolsley Valise	32
Captain Nigel Boulton, R.A.M.C., Dover, Oct 1914	33
Nigel's diagram of Dover Harbour	38
Holiday Group, Bulli, Christmas 1909	39
Engr Lieut Cleon Dennis, R.A.N.	39
Officers on HMAS *Sydney*, after the Emden Battle, 1914	46
Aunt Mog (Margaret Lilian Flockton), c 1914	47
Casualty Evacuation System	59
Dora Mary Boulton (Dolly), c 1915	63
HMAT *Marere* A21, c 1915	63
'Coolah', Ross Street, Gladesville c. 1914	65
Gran (Isabel Mary Flockton), c Jan 1915	67
S.S. *Minnewaska*	72
Mustafa Pacha Camp, Alexandria, April 1915	75
General View of Cairo, 1915	76
Alexandria, 1915	77
Uncle Frank (Francis Egerton Bryant)	78
General Hospital, Abbassia Schools, Alexandria	82
Mena Camp, Cairo	84
Mrs. Lee (Nora Barton) & Dr Harry Lee	89
Gunner Stephen Boulton in Egypt, April 1915	92
Alexandria, Postcard sent as Steve leaves for Gallipoli, 1915.	93
Capt J H Dancy & Lieut Nigel Boulton at Mustafa Pacha Camp, April 1915	94
R.A.M.C. Doctors, Stanley Beach, Alexandria, March 1915	95
Max Barton & friends, Egypt, March 1916	99

HMT *Minneapolis*, Alexandria, 1915	102
Gunner S P Boulton, 28 Feb 1915	105
Dancy, Boulton, Campion etc, Mustafa Pacha Camp, April 1915	129
Capt Carson, Lieut Dolling & Capt Kennedy-Taylor, Alexandria, 1915	135
Beach at Anzac Cove, 1915	141
Clarke Cousins, Bulli, Christmas 1909	158
Hospital Ship *Grantully Castle* off Salonika, 1915	171
St Clare College, used as St John's Military Hospital, Malta, in WWI	173
Patients, St. Johns Military Hospital, Malta, Oct 1915	175
Anzac Buffet, London, c Nov 1915	191
Loading the Mules, Beach at Anzac Cove, 1915	194
Ghain-Tuffieha Camp Hospital, Malta	196
St Paul's Hospital Camp, Malta	198
Dora Boulton at 'Ermo', 1915	200
Thea and Dora at 'Ermo', 1915	201
Thea & Dora at 'Ermo', 1915	201
Captain Waddy with Some Eye Patients	202
Hospital Ship, *Essequibo*	210
Unloading a hospital train	210
Luna Park, Heliopolis	210
Patients, Luna Park	210
18 pounder gun near Ypres, Oct 1917	225
Harold Boulton & wife Nan, 1928	234
Nigel Boulton, Egypt, 1916	234
Gas Masks, Ypres, Sep 1917	240
Vignacourt	249
Pozières Village, before and after the battle.	256
Captured German trench at Pozières	256
Source AWM-e00007	256
Conscription Posters, 1916	257
Unveiling the Pozières Memorial, 8 July 1917	258
Flockton Sisters & 'The Moles', c 1916	262
Biscuit Trench, Gueudecourt, Dec 1916	276
Mud on the Western Front	276
Cpl S P Boulton, Jan 1917	283

Moving the Artillery Guns, Western Front	287
22nd Battery, March 1917	295
Nigel Boulton & Officers, France, c Feb 1917?	296
Nigel with Pip, March 1917	297
Creeping Barrage Map	306
Nigel Boulton & Officers, France, c August 1917	312
Cadets, Royal Field Artillery School, London, Sep 1917	316
Cpl Stephen Boulton & Capt Nigel Boulton, Sep 1917	317
Cpl Stephen Boulton, Capt Nigel Boulton, Mona & Pip, Sep 1917	317
Larkhill & Durrington Camp Buildings	318
Cousin Kate (Kate Mansfield) at her home 'The Warren', c 1915	321
Nissen Huts, WW1	340
2nd Lieut Stephen Boulton, Harrow, Nov 1917	348
2nd Lieut Stephen Boulton at Harrow, Nov 1917	349
2nd Lieut Stephen Boulton, Harrow, Nov 1917	349
Camouflaged Gun, Western Front	363
Pip Boulton with toys, July 1918	367
Aunt Phoebe's Home, Hillside, View St, Chatswood, c 1916	369
Burial Site, Roisel Cemetery, 5 October 1918	379
Nigel, Pip & Mona Boulton, mid 1918	386
Identity Discs	401
A for Anzac Badge, for service at Gallipoli	401
Example of a Black Kit Bag	402
Rising Sun Badge	402
Lieutenant's Shoulder Pips or Stars	402
Officer's Trench Whistle	402
Australia Badge	402
List of Contents of Kit Bag	403
List of Contents of Valise	403
Roisel Communal Cemetery Extension, France, 2001	404
Inscription, Roisel, Plot 1, Row M, Grave 4, 2001	404
Amelia (Millie) Dennis, Roisel, 2012	406
Mona & Nigel Boulton with Thea Dennis, Sydney, c 1920	408
P H Boulton, at The King's School, c 1928	408
Mona, Peter & Pip Boulton, c 1925	408

Nigel Boulton & second wife, Marie Tofield née Memory......................409
Philip Hugh Boulton (Pip), England, Winter 1939................................409
Eileen Boulton née Sellars, c 1939..409
Nigel's third wife, Thelma Attwood..409
Eileen Boulton and her son, c 1951..410
Peter Martin Boulton, c 1944..410
Nigel Boulton & Great Niece Jennifer, 1947...410

Maps

Map 1: Western Front, 1918 36
Map 2: Route Taken by Transport A21 Marere, 1915............................ 69
Map 3: Egypt, 1915 75
Map 4: Cairo and Environs, c 1915 85
Map 5: Gallipoli Peninsula, 1915 97
Map 6: The Great War in Europe & Middle East 109
Map 7: Aegean Sea, 1915... 115
Map 8: North East France, 1916-1918 236
Map 9: The Somme, 1916-1918.. 250
Map 10: Pozières, 1916 254
Map 11: Breaking the Beaurevoir Line, 1918 374

Stephen & Nigel Boulton,
c December 1890
(Picture Courtesy Julia Woodhouse)

Stephen, Dora & Nigel Boulton, c 1893
(Picture Courtesy Julia Woodhouse)

Philip Boulton, c 1895
(Picture Courtesy Julia Woodhouse)

1914

Dr Nigel Boulton arrived in Dunkirk aboard the *Port Macquarie* on 29 January 1914 and next day signed off as the ship's surgeon, the duties which had earned him his free passage from Sydney to Europe. Aged 25, he was planning to study paediatrics in London, having completed his medical and surgical studies at the University of Sydney. His photo album records a brief period of tourism in Europe before he crossed the Channel to England.

For the past 18 months he'd been working as a young doctor in Wollongong, where he met Mona Little, the daughter of the proprietress of the 'South Coast Times and Wollongong Argus' newspaper. Proclaiming she was engaged to Nigel, Mona followed him to London with her widowed mother in May 1914. Nigel's family was less charitable: Mona had chased her 'good catch' to London.

England declared war on Germany on 4 August, following Germany's invasion of Belgium. By now Nigel was busy at the East London Hospital for Children, which enjoyed an international reputation as a teaching hospital for paediatrics. Then, and still, young men were enticed to serve their country by relatively generous pay offers, and this struck a chord with Nigel. His mother had been a widow for most of his life and she'd trained him to operate on a tight budget.[1] Nigel had a close relationship with his mother and he felt the usual pressures faced by an eldest child to perform well and to be responsible.

COMMONWEALTH OFFICES, 72 VICTORIA ST, LONDON S.W., 18 AUG 1914

Dearest Mother

This letter will be pregnant with news so I do hope you will receive it, altho' at the present time communication must be very uncertain.

Since I last wrote to you War has been declared by England and the whole of Europe is practically involved, 7 nations being at war at present. No doubt you

---

1   His mother, Dora Mary Boulton née Flockton, known as Dolly, left London in 1882 to migrate to Australia. In 1885, in Queensland, she married bank manager Philip Boulton, another migrant from London. He died in Melbourne in 1895.

in Australia have been pretty well posted by cablegrams, etc, of what has been going on, altho' news from the front only dribbles thro' and one is never quite sure how much is rumour and how much genuine.

As a consequence of this War there has been a tremendous stir in England and volunteers are pouring in from every direction.

There has been a great demand for army and navy doctors, and if I hadn't been left dirtily at the Hospital it's quite possible I should have managed to get across with the First Expeditionary Force as Waugh has! I was to have left the hospital on the 31st of July, having given a month's notice to that effect. However, Waugh[2], who had been a year at the Hospital, wanted his annual holiday and asked me as a great favour to stay on till he came back, which would be about the 14th of August, to enable him to have his full holiday. This I didn't mind doing. When War was declared an advertisement appeared in the paper very shortly, offering billets for either the Army or Navy for civil surgeons not over 35 years of age, on the following terms:- To take rank of lieutenant, pay 24/- a day with all travelling expenses, and £60 bonus at end of service, and a 12 month's agreement. This would have suited me down to the ground and I was dying to apply.[3] However, I couldn't leave the hospital to the tender mercies of Jones[4], a chap just qualified and Fowler[5], an awful lad from the Sydney University and no casualty officer.

I was wondering what had happened to Waugh and intended to ask him to come back before his time was up, as I wanted to get off, my time being up and the War having altered my arrangements, when he rang up the next morning to say he was leaving for Aldershot that day, to say goodbye to them at the hospital and to pack his things up and send them home!

Pretty cool, wasn't it?

I suggested to him that in the event of my wanting to go to the War, what was to happen to the place? "Oh, well, just take the matter in your own hands and leave. They'll have to do something."

It was all very fine but, owing to everybody volunteering and scurrying off, the hospital authorities hadn't a hope of filling my place and with babies dying on the doorstep, it being the middle of the summer diarrhoea season, my hand

---

2   Dr Arthur John Waugh, a graduate of the University of Cambridge, was killed on the Somme in 1916.
3   His hospital salary at the time was £75 p.a.
4   Dr J D Jones, MRCS, LRCP
5   Dr Cosmo William Fowler. For more details, see the 'Beyond 1914' website of the University of Sydney.

was practically forced. Jones and Fowler spent most of their days at the War Office or about the city collecting their kits, and left the place practically for me to run alone.

It was wonderfully good experience, but far too much. I represented to the Hospital committee that I couldn't go on: my time was up, the other fellows had left me in the lurch and that I was most anxious to go to the War too, as it meant a very great deal to me. They were much distressed and were very sick with Waugh and would try and do their best. Owing to the magnanimity of two of the former R.M.O's at the hospital agreeing to take over the work of the hospital temporarily till something could be done, I was able to get off. The committee were very grateful indeed to me for running the place practically on my own for a fortnight and wrote me a letter thanking me for the splendid work I had done for the Hospital and expressing their gratitude to me for the way I had brought them thro' a period of great difficulty. It was very nice of them and constitutes the best reference I have as yet. I think they thought a good deal of me there, at any rate I seemed to be pretty well liked - still my chance of a good job at the front was gone, and I was pretty sore I can tell you.

I applied as soon as I left and the War Office seemed pretty confident that they would find me an appointment. I think having had 5 years training with the University Scouts was in my favour, as very few of the other lads had similar advantages. I suppose I shall get attached to the Territorials somewhere in this country. I don't suppose I shall have the luck to get abroad. However, the screw is a very tempting one. It is a question of how long the War lasts, the longer the better from my point of view as I should be able with care to amass a small capital. I am now expecting a communication every day from the War Office, notifying me of my appointment. I have been measured for my uniforms, etc. I can't tell you where I shall be going as that is always kept secret.

Mona & her Mother, Mrs. Little
(Picture Courtesy Julia Woodhouse)

Mona[6] is very distressed at my going, but is quite willing as she realizes it will be for both our welfares. As no one knows quite what is

---

6   Mona Edith Little, daughter of Martin J Little (dec'd), former proprietor and editor of the South Coast Times newspaper at Wollongong.

going to happen here, things are in a very parlous state and the excitement is tremendous. Trade is dislocated and many people are becoming panic stricken. This, of course, does no good and probably things will settle down soon.

This war, of course, is the largest the world has ever seen and the nature of its termination conjectural. Mona and her mother are stranded here practically till the war ends, as shipping is disorganized and passenger services largely suspended.

I wonder if the next piece of news will come as a great shock to you, Mother - I am afraid it will. It was bound to come, whether it comes now or later is merely a matter of expediency. I married Mona 4 days ago by Special Licence in Holy Trinity Church, Paddington. It was all decided after I applied to the War Office for service. If the war lasts 6 months, which is not an improbability, I should have at least, with care, £182 + £60 bonus, which will be a nice little nest egg and should enable me to start in Australia. Also Mona would be able to stay here till I return, which she is very anxious to do, whereas her mother is getting rather lonely and is becoming restless and anxious to get back. She has no interests or friends over here so it must be a little miserable for her. Mrs. Little[7] has been rather cut up since we married as she loses her only daughter and a lonely old age is not altogether a pleasing prospect. I am afraid you will feel it too, Mum, but I hope you won't take it hardly and look on things in as pleasant a light as possible.

I know what I'm about, and have got a most excellent wife. I am even finding that out already. One's future happiness is everything. I never should have married but for this war till I returned to Australia and I don't think Mrs. Little would have been agreeable. She was disappointed in the wedding as it was very quiet, and she had hoped for a great splash when it took place in N.S.W.

The service was very nicely conducted by the Curate of the Parish, the Vicar being away for his holiday, and there only being 5 of us there, was very impressive, far more so than it would have been in the presence of a large crowd, at least I think so. Mrs. Little, 2 friends - English people, who travelled over with her on the boat, and ourselves. We had a very nice afternoon tea afterwards, being married at 2.30 p.m. We went to Tunbridge Wells after that, it being Saturday, and returned on Tuesday morning. And now I am waiting daily for a letter from the War Office.

---

7   Nigel's widowed mother-in-law, Edith Elizabeth Little, current proprietor of the South Coast Times newspaper.

As long as there are only 2 of us I think we shall be able to scrape along and there's not going to be 3 for a bit at any rate. Well, Mum, I trust everything will go well with me, I don't see why it shouldn't. I have always been a very fortunate boy. Don't know whether I shall be able to write to you as regularly when I go to the War, as communication will be uncertain. However, I shall do so whenever I get a chance. Give my love to all at home. You have been saved the expense of wedding presents at any rate.

Goodbye for the present, dearest Mother,

Yours ever,

NIGE

I wonder what you think of this war. Is it the beginning of the end? It looks very much like it. I expect you are watching things very closely as you have been following the prophecies pretty closely latterly, haven't you?

Strathmore, Camborne Terrace, Richmond, 2 Sep 1914

Dearest Mother

I have not left for the war yet, altho' I am expecting to hear any hour now. I have been much worried at being kept waiting and have been to the War Office 5 times to shake them up. They tell me the same tale each time: "Have patience, your turn will come". There have not been any appointments made for the last week or so, and I have squared the head clerk whom I shall have to tip to engineer my name to the top of the list when the next series of appointments are made as there are a whole host of chaps waiting to get off.

This he has promised me faithfully he will do, and is going to send me a wire before I receive official notice in writing. So that is the best I can do. I have just got to wait. I asked the authorities there whether influence played a large part in your getting a job, and they vehemently assured me it was not so. It makes me very sore to think of Waugh and Jones having got away, Waugh actually abroad with the Expeditionary Force, both of them with no knowledge at all of things military, and here I am kicking my heels about here doing nothing. They did the dirty on the Hospital, and incidentally on me, but I don't suppose that worries them.

Whiteley's have made all my uniforms which amount to £25. This the War Office have promised to advance out of my pay when I am appointed, but I haven't been appointed yet so I expect Whiteley will be becoming impatient soon and start to wonder whether they are going to be paid. However, I daresay things will turn out all right; I am always impatient and apt to look on the gloomy side of things. One of the big bugs at the War Office I saw the other day explained to me that I was bound to be kept waiting as they were not appointing doctors to the various regiments till the latter were fully organized and equipped, as there would not be anything for us to do.

I shall probably be attached to one of the units of Lord Kitchener's army.[8] I saw Lord Roberts[9] at the War Office. Passed within an inch of him and had a good look at him: a small insignificant looking little man with a grey moustache and a grey imperial and a steely eye.

Aunt Julia[10] and Cousin Bessie[11] wrote me a kind letter the other day, at least Bessie wrote and asked me what I was doing during this awful time, and would I like to go and stay with them. Nearly all the male representatives of their family are serving their Country, either in the

Cleon Dennis, Aunt Julia & Cousin Bessie, early 1919
(Picture Courtesy Julia Woodhouse)

Kennet House, Harrow
(Picture Courtesy Alasdair Kirk)

---

8   A senior British army officer and government official who foresaw the likelihood of a long war and organised a huge volunteer army. He was famous for his face on England's 'Your Country Needs You' recruiting poster for World War 1.
9   Famous British soldier, who had warned of the likelihood of war against Germany from 1912. He died in November 1914 aged 82.
10 Nigel's great aunt. Julia Charles was his mother's paternal aunt. She lived at Kennet House, Harrow, now part of Harrow School near London.
11 Julia's unmarried daughter Bessie Charles, who lived with her mother at Kennet House.

Navy or Army. I wrote and told them I was hoping to be appointed any day to the R.A.M.C.

Aunt Eleanor[12] also wrote to me and invited me down. Mrs. Ashley Hall[13], who is living in Buckinghamshire now, wrote to me a week or so ago asking me down to Tennis one Saturday, or to go down on a Sunday if more convenient. Both her boys are doing something: Jack is legal adviser to a General at Chatham which she is greatly proud of, and Phil is doing something else - pretty safe jobs!

Cousin Blanche & Aunt Eleanor, c 1890s
(Picture Courtesy Julia Woodhouse)

Mrs. Little has given up the flat at Bayswater. We left on Monday, this is Wednesday. I have got Mona and her here in rather a nice boarding house on the river. The flat was so deadly quiet, they not knowing a soul, and I think they will be happier here as there is quite a houseful of people – Mona and I have been wonderfully happy since we married and I don't see any reason why we shouldn't be till the end of the chapter; altho' I realize life is a grim struggle, I don't think I shall go under. Mona has been terribly disappointed at not having a trousseau, but she intends to get together a nice one while I'm away. Mrs. Little is rather worried now this war is on as everything is very unsettled and her ideas of a trip to the Continent and roundabout have become impracticable.

Also she is feeling a little uncertain about whether she will be able to get any money over from Australia in the event of her wanting some more. She would like to return to N.S.W. if travelling were safer, but does not care to risk it at present. A large number of Australians seem to be returning to Australia which surprises me as Europe is a far more exciting place to live in just now. Mona has not decided what she will do if her mother decides on returning, she very much wants to remain over here till I'm ready to go back, altho' she doesn't altogether like her mother making that long journey by herself.

---

12 Nigel's great aunt. Eleanor Flockton, a younger unmarried sister of Julia Charles, also lived at Harrow, near her sister.
13 Mrs Ashley Hall, a widow and his mother's old friend, née Marion Louisa Careless.

I see by the papers that Australia has become greatly excited by the War and has promised men and money. I wonder if any of her troops will come over. It is an appalling war and the casualties will be frightful. England will win through - the question is how long it will last.

Did I tell you that Aunt Bee[14] wrote to me some time ago after she had heard from Mary Dixon[15] of my arrival over here? She is living in the Isle of Wight and so was too far off to ask me down for a week end. However, she hoped she would see me before I went back. Just the polite I suppose.

I have taken Mona out on the river here several times, also her mother. It is very beautiful, the Thames, at this part. Mona and I had a picnic last Sunday, went for the day and took our lunch. We hired a sweet little dinghy and rowed up as far as Teddington Lock. It was a very happy day, it being an English summer day. I also, a week or so ago, took Mona and her mother to Thames Ditton, and hired a skiff there, and rowed them up past Hampton Court. We had lunch at the "Swan Hotel" and afternoon tea on our return.

Stephen, Thea and Nigel Boulton in England, c 1903
(Picture Courtesy Julia Woodhouse)

I thought of you and Steve[16] and Thea[17], how 10 years ago (what ages it seems) we all were to be seen in a boat on this part of the river. I did not go past the Rogers' house, I wonder if they are still there.

Thames Ditton is just the same. We walked thro' the old Churchyard where you and I went to Church several times. Some of the little cottage gardens were sweetly pretty and so tidy and well cared for. I wonder if ever you will see these things again. It is rather sad coming back to places after such a long spell. You feel a sort of Rip van Winkle.

---

14 Nigel's great aunt. Beatrice Shaw née Flockton was his grandmother's sister and mother's maternal aunt.
15 Mary Dixon née Ashby was his mother's first cousin on the maternal side, and was a niece of Beatrice Shaw.
16 His younger brother
17 His younger sister.

I went in to the War Office again this afternoon and saw Major Blackwell[18], a lad I'd seen before. He sympathized with me and said he knew it was beastly being kept waiting, but thought I should be sent for soon now as a good many doctors had been captured at the front and their places would have to be filled up. Who knows? I may get a job at the front yet. How exciting it would be! I should score over the doctors in Australia.

Well, dearest Mum, goodbye. I haven't received a letter from you for 10 days now; the mails will be uncertain now. I do hope you get this letter all right, it is quite a long one.

Best love to all at home

Yours ever,

NIGE

Thea & Dora Boulton with their Pet Dogs, c 1915
(Picture Courtesy Julia Woodhouse)

Nigel's official enlistment date was 9 September, as a member of the R.A.M.C. He was posted to the strategically important town of Dover, always a major embarkation point for crossing the English Channel, and also of key significance to the homeland defence of England.

---

18   Major W R Blackwell was involved with organising, mobilising, and preparing medical services for war.

Military Hospital, Western Heights, Dover, 19 Sep 1914

Dearest Mother

Here I am at Dover, not far from Calais, is it? However, I doubt if I shall be for overseas service for a bit yet, altho' I am hoping an order for me to go will come eventually. Two of our chaps here at the hospital left today for Southampton en route for the Continent.

There are 4 chaps senior to me so I have to wait my turn. I have been gazetted and am drawing 24 bob a day, which is not too swelling, is it? It is not all profit, however, as I am at present at a boarding house in Dover paying 37/6 a week. This is what we are all doing as the hotels are too expensive, and we all being together in the one boarding establishment makes it very nice.

Dover is a fortress town and will be probably the first place the Germans will attack if our Navy gives them half a chance. But I think there is little fear of that at present as they don't seem to be at all keen at risking a naval encounter, and the whole of their fleet is sheltering under the protection of their fortress guns.

We have about 4 cruisers in the harbour here, and 12 to 16 torpedo boats. The latter boats are most useful and are scouting and reconnoitering up and down the coast ceaselessly, but chiefly at night time. It is very pretty to watch them one by one lift anchor about 5 p.m. and leave the harbour and go scurrying about their various duties at anything from 20 to 35 knots an hour. The harbour is well lit up at night and search lights going from all the piers, every vessel within miles being most thoroughly searched. It is marvellous the power of the light.

Dover being a fortress town is under martial law, and so far we have not been receiving any wounded, as in the event of our being attacked they would be in the way. Also we have rather a limited accommodation at our command, the hospital here being pretty small. There are several 1,000 troops stationed here, and we are responsible for their health and welfare, and also have to supervise the sanitation of their camps and barracks, no small order. This place is wonderfully well fortified, and the coast here is rather a treacherous one so we are pretty safe.

We are inoculating all the troops with anti-typhoid vaccine which is a very efficient safeguard against typhoid. I have been done today. It makes your arm pretty sore for a few days and you feel like an attack of influenza for about 3 days. Its efficacy lasts about two years, at any rate ought to see you thro' the War.

I heard from Cousin Bessie today, who is greatly interested in me. She saw in the paper a notice of my Gazettage, and wants to know what has happened to me. Her various relatives are so far safe, altho' have been in some of the fighting. Arthur, Charles or Mansfield, I'm not sure which[19], was on board the *Speedy* which was blown up by a mine, luckily only one man lost his life - I expect she will tell you all about it. Two transports left here today taking away 2 or 3 thousand marines and some other regiment for service abroad. It is the first time transports have left here in the day, most of them leaving in the middle of the night. It is an index of our extreme confidence in their safe despatch to their destination.

A destroyer acts as a convoy. It must be very galling for the Germans to know that we can land any number of troops where we like and when we like, and to have all their shipping locked up in the various harbours of the world, not game to come out. Our Navy, of which we have heard such a lot in peace time, has quite justified all the praise, etc., it has received, and Britain is still Mistress of the Seas!

It means an enormous deal. Germany is deriving a certain amount of foodstuffs thro' Holland, a neutral country. This can't be very well stopped, it's not supposed to be going on, but all the same it is going on. These laws re neutrality are an infernal nuisance at times. However, the Germans are not getting much and I believe the price of things is going up tremendously already, and she is feeling the pinch very much.

How glorious it is to feel one is a Britisher at a time like this. What a wonderful country England is, and what a wonderful nation. I quite agree with you, Mum, I thank God I was born of English parents every time I think of it.

Mona and her mother arrived here yesterday. I am afraid Mrs. Little will be very much bored as there is nothing for her to do and Dover is emptying of civil folk a good deal. Scotland will be too cold now, she was contemplating visiting there - my time is not my own now, so I can't see very much of them, but Mona is quite content to be near me and see me every now and then. It's a pity Mrs. L. is so common, she doesn't appreciate things at all over here as she should; the sights and wonders of England are largely wasted. Ever since she landed she has been worrying about getting back to Australia. Of course,

---

19 Arthur Charles was his second cousin, being a grandson of Aunt Julia. H.M.S. *Speedy* was sunk in the North Sea on 4 Sep 1914.

poor thing, I can sympathise with her, as she doesn't know a soul, and English people are very cold, and she hasn't many ideas, etc., so cannot converse with any freedom. Mona and I take her about a good deal and do the best we can.

It's very improper of me to talk of my mother-in-law thus, still -----!

Goodbye, Mum, shall try and write again ere long. The mails are erratic now.

Love to all at home,

Yours

NIGE

P.S. Has Billy[20] joined the contingent yet? The Corps to which I belong, the Royal Army Medical Corps, or R.A.M.C. is a very crack one apparently, and ranks high over here. The Colonel told us the other day that we have the biggest list of casualties and the biggest list of V.C's for our numbers. So I'm in luck to be in it.

Dover Castle, 13 Oct 1914

Dearest Mother

I hope you won't be greatly disappointed at only a letter card this mail. I thought, however, that even a few lines would be better than missing the mail.

You see I have a very aristocratic address now. I have been at the Castle now 2 days. I have been put in charge of the garrison there, i.e. the M.O. in charge of troops, Dover Castle.

I am going to live up there, and consequently shall not be able to see as much of Mona as I have been doing up till now. She is much distressed, but still it can't be helped. I shall be able to get off in the afternoons to see her, I feel sure.

My quarters there are not very grand, still one must not grumble. I have been spoilt till now. Consists of a dusty old room, with no furniture. As I have a folding bed, chair, table and a pillow, canvas bath, wash stand and bucket I shall be all right. This gear is made after the War Office pattern, and would prove a tremendous boon for camping in Australia; everything so wonderfully compact and portable.

---

20   Nigel's nickname for his younger brother Stephen.

The Germans have captured Antwerp and Ghent, and on the verge of annexing Ostend, so it won't be long, I expect, before we are visited by a few of their bomb-dropping airships. The Castle here is the place that will be picked out before all others, as it is a magnificent place and one of the most, if not the most, historic castles in England. It is a truly wonderful place. One part of it dates back to A.D.65. It has been marvellously preserved and has always been maintained as a fortress. The public are allowed over it in peace time.

I have been very busy getting the hang of my new job, hence this miserably short letter. Forgive me, I will endeavour to do better next time.

I trust all is well with you at home. Give them all my love, shall probably be at the Castle now till my time comes to go abroad. Up at 5.45 every morn. Winter coming on.

Best love, dearest Mum,

Yours ever, NIGE,

Have not got your mail this week yet.

From M.O. i/c Effective Troops, Dover Castle, 22 Oct 1914

Dearest Mother

Here I still am at Dover. I have a bit of a swanky title at present, haven't I? Am getting hold of the Government red tape methods bit by bit. The Army is nothing but Government red tapeism. I find it a bit of a drawback not having had much office training. Have got a good deal more to do up here than I had at the Western Heights Military Hospital. I have a clerk, a dispenser, an orderly of my own, and 2 hospital orderlies to look after.

This hospital has only 4 beds, really a detention ward, to take cases in temporarily till they are transferred to wherever they are to go. Have about 70 sick to see starting at 7 a.m., various inoculations to do and vaccinations and the sanitation of the Castle. Nothing of an exciting nature, still I am earning money. I shall not be able to save so well here as I have an orderly to pay 5/- a week and a mess bill, which will mount up I expect. Still I am doing things on the cheap as far as possible. I expect I shall be here till my turn comes to go, if it ever does!

Have got my room fixed up pretty comfortably here. Have purchased a sleeping bag which is a great idea.

We are not provided with sheets or counterpanes so one has to sleep in blankets. The sleeping bag material is beautifully soft and woolly. I purchased also a cheap blanket for 6/-, a most appalling coloured thing, still warm, which I have had sewn inside the bag, to go over to the top of me if the weather is cold, or underneath if warm. I have also a rug on top; so far I have not found all 3 too much. If I go across the water I am to buy a Wolsley Valise, which is a waterproof bag, like a hold-all on a big scale, into which you put your sleeping bag and then you can lie down in the wet anywhere and go to sleep.

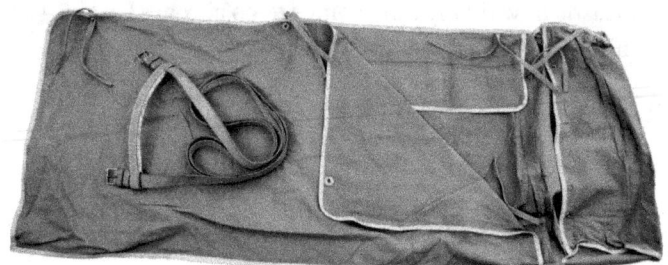

Wolsley Valise

Received your letter a day or two ago and very pleased I was to hear from you, altho' you were rather pushed for news.

I expect you hear all there is to hear about the War, we are kept pretty much in the dark over here. Occasionally one of Sir John French's despatches[21] is published days after things have happened. Still I suppose it's only right. News has been much more encouraging and refreshing recently. We are certainly holding our own in the Western theatre of the war. The Germans have had a great deal of luck with their submarines so far. Altho' they have only sunk practically obsolete boats, viz. *Aboukir*, *Cressy*, *Hogue* and *Hawke*, still it is the great loss of gallant lives that is the blow. The sinking of four of their torpedo boats, however, day before yesterday was more cheering. If we can only get a fair and square above board go at them we seem to settle them pretty quick, don't we?

It is maddening having the German Fleet bottled up in the Kiel Canal, where we can't get at them. It's a pity they can't be dug out. That German cruiser

---

21 Field Marshall Sir John French was Commander in Chief of the British Armies in France and Flanders, and was required to report progress to the War Office via regular despatches, which were subsequently published in the London Gazette. Individual servicemen were sometimes singled out for 'mention' in these despatches.

Emden seems to have done a great deal of harm - what a pity we can't afford the boats to settle her.[22] She has done wonderfully well.

We are being deluged with refugees here. Nearly all from Belgium. It's a pitiful sight. Poor creatures absolutely homeless, with only the clothes they stand up in, and stranded in a foreign country with no means of livelihood or earning one. Babies being born on the way over, in lots of cases fatherless! Belgium has practically been wiped out with all its wonderful art treasures. The Germans have wrought irreparable havoc. Their plan of campaign seems to be one of intimidation. Their hatred for the English people is extraordinary and our prisoners in a very large number of cases have been treated brutally. England, of course, has taken the utmost care of all her German prisoners and is feeding them on the fat of the land and providing them with every comfort. German spies over-running the place everywhere - it's a maddening policy. The German system of espionage has been marvellous. They have been at work for years and the information they have gathered that is revealed day by day is immense.

Wonder if I shall see anything of the Australian troops when they arrive? They won't be here I shouldn't think till the New Year pretty well, by which time I hope to have been in France some time.

I had my photograph taken in military rig the other day. Fairly successful from the proof. They have, however, stuck me in a position to emphasize my champagne bottle shoulders. Wonder whether you are going to have yours taken as you promised me, Mum? It is rather remarkable not having a photograph of one's own Mother, when she happens to be 15,000 miles away!

Captain Nigel Boulton,
R.A.M.C., Dover, Oct 1914
(Picture Courtesy Julia Woodhouse)

Best love to all at Bifrons.[23] How's Billy? Mona and Mrs. L. quite well.

Goodbye for the present, Mum,

Yours ever,

NIGE

---

22 HMAS *Sydney* 1 was about to pull off a huge coup by sinking the *Emden* in the Indian Ocean.
23 Bifrons or Bi-frons is presumed to be the name of the rented home in Linsley Street, Gladesville where his mother lived with his younger brother & sister, grandmother & aunt.

Nigel's earlier comments about his 'common' mother-in-law seem at odds with this letter she wrote from Dover. It was subsequently published by the newspaper she still owned back in Australia, the 'South Coast Times and Wollongong Argus'.[24]

LETTER FROM ENGLAND

A letter from Mrs. E. E. Little (of Wollongong), from London, is as follows:—

'We are having a very anxious time, as no doubt you are, although you do not see so much of the sorrows of the war. Yesterday and today have been most exciting for us, as thousands of Belgians are being landed here, also wounded. It is oh, so sad to see those poor things, chiefly women and children, coming off the boats with bundles of clothing, mostly tied up in sheets or old tablecloths. Where they are going to put the poor things I do not know. They are being taken to different places in trains sent down from London, specially. A great number of the wounded soldiers are only suffering from slight wounds and shock, but some are horrible cases, better be dead, I think.

While we were out this morning we saw a man taken away who had been caught (a spy). He was disguised as an ambulance man with a Red Cross on his arm, and turned out to be a German who had come across with the refugees. Each day they are cropping up, but everyone is on the lookout for them. The Germans have had some victories, but ours is coming, without a doubt.

Mona and I are working hard at making clothes for the soldiers and sailors, which, I think, every woman who has time is doing. Social life over here has completely changed, and each woman, instead of frittering away her time over pleasure and fashions is now doing good work for those who are fighting to keep our homes over our heads and for the women and children they have left behind. So, although this war is a dreadful thing, it has done much good in bringing out the better part of thousands of men and women who only lived in the past for the idle pleasures of life, and is doing away with so much snobbery. The Kaiser is a brute, but his brutality has wakened us all up.

We had a trip through some of the country last week, and it is very beautiful. The Autumn tints are just coming on, and doubtless on a fine day will be worth seeing. The days are getting cold, so I expect when you get this we shall be experiencing some English winter weather.

We have some Australians staying in the house we are in just now and it is most interesting to Mrs. Boulton and myself to chat with them and exchange our

---

24 On Fri 27 Nov 1914, p 14

different bits of Australian news. They are most interested in the contingent which is coming over, as some of their relations are coming with it. We also are interested, as like all Australians we feel proud of our men and their willingness to come and fight for our freedom. I only wish that I was a man and could get a shot at the Germans.

I see by the papers that you are all doing your share to send relief to those suffering over here. It is all needed, as there shall be no end of suffering and want before Peace is proclaimed. Everything that can be done is being got ready for trouble on our own shores. Let us hope it will not come, but one never knows.

Across the Channel, a fierce battle was underway around the Belgian city of Ypres, or "Wipers". The town was an important strategic landmark blocking the route for the Imperial German Army through to the French coastal ports. According to official records quoted on the Great War, 1914-1918 website, the danger of the Allied line being broken at Ypres in October and November 1914 was:

> one of the most momentous and critical of the war, and only by the most desperate fighting did the Allies succeed in maintaining their front. Had the British forces lost Ypres, the whole of Belgian territory must have been lost, and the Germans would have reached Dunkirk and Calais - which were, indeed, their objectives, to stop the flood of British forces across the Channel. If these ports had fallen to the enemy the effect on sea communications and on operations generally might well have proved fatal not only to the British Empire, but to the whole of the civilized world. Many thousands of Allied troops died in the years 1914-1918 in order to maintain the Allies' possession of this place. They died in the rubble of its buildings and the shattered farmland around it, fighting in ferocious battles and surviving daily life in inhuman conditions. On the German side of the wire, many thousands of German lives were also lost in the landscape north, east and south of Ypres during the German Army's four years of offensive and defensive battles.

That website further explains:

> Throughout the war, the city was continuously shelled by German artillery. By the end of the war there was no building left untouched. Only a tiny number of buildings, walls or façades were still intact ... The medieval town with its historic buildings, centuries of traditions and its pre-war prosperity had been demolished.

Its famous Menin Gate War Memorial is now the symbol of that time, where the Last Post tribute began in 1928 and has been played every night at 8pm since 11 November 1929, except for the period in WWII when the Germans occupied the town.

Map 1: Western Front, 1918

(The Front was different in 1914, but this map shows the location of Ypres.) Map © John Newland, 2015

Section Hospital, Dover Castle, 28 Oct 1914

Dearest Mother

Here I am still at Dover. None of our fellows have been sent away to France yet since the 1st two went. We have not heard from either of them, so don't know what they have been up to. I may be here all the winter; there is very little evidence of my getting a move for a bit at any rate.

I do hope I shall be over in France before the Australian troops arrive. Campaigning will be pretty severe during the winter, which is certainly not the best time to go; still one wouldn't mind that, as the experience would be that of a lifetime.

I am getting into the way of things a bit better now, and I shall be a regular 'army man' before long! Mona and her mother are still here. I think they intend wintering here. The walks are very limited, and it is not long before one knows Dover from one end to the other. Still there is always a certain amount of excitement going on, and now the Germans are putting forth such terrific efforts to reach Calais, Dover is certainly gaining in importance.

I had my photograph taken the week before last, I think I told you. The results were fairly good. I am sending you one, and hope you will like it. I am also sending one to Cousin Bessie and Mrs. Lee.[25] These are 15/- for ½ dozen, which is pretty solid. I only procured the ½ doz. I hope you will get them safely.

The boarding house Mrs. Little and Mona are staying at is crowded with military lads and naval chaps. I manage to get off usually for lunch, afternoon tea, and dinner, so I don't do too badly. I have a big climb up to the Castle which overlooks the cliffs from the town which is on the sea level.

Dover, I believe I told you in a former letter, is surrounded by hills all round. It has a long broad promenade or sea front with a long row of houses fully a mile long, stretching from one end to the other. When this promenade is lit up at night time as it is in peace time it is a very pretty sight.

There are 3 piers, the Admiralty Pier with 2 batteries upon it mounting 6" guns, the Prince of Wales pier and a small pier, the Town pier. Here is a diagram [on next page] to give you a rough idea of the place -

Mona is fairly happy down here, but is looking forward to the time when we settle down in Australia again, and all this War and depression is over. She

---

25 The wife of the doctor with whom Nigel worked prior to departing for England.

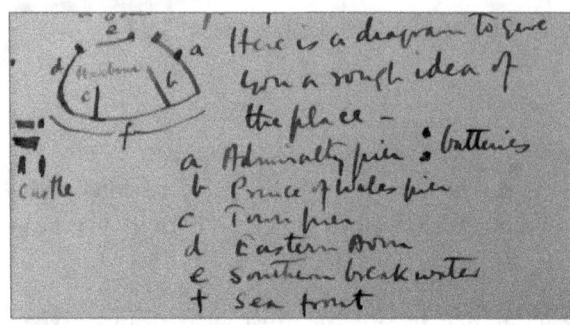

Nigel's diagram of Dover Harbour

is absolutely dreading my going to the front and waits in gloom for the call to come. She will feel it terribly, I'm afraid, but so are 1,000s of women everywhere, one might comfortably say 1,000 000s. She has knitted me 2 pairs of nice warm socks, her first pair are excellently knitted, a shade tight, but considering she has never knitted a pair in her life before, she has done wonders. Her second pair are beauties, she is an expert knitter after a few days practice, and cannot be stopped, she is knitting every spare minute she gets.

This is my birthday, 26 years today. Somehow I don't feel a bit older. Mona and Mrs. Little have decided to give me a very fine military overcoat which will cost them 4 guineas. It won't be money wasted as it will come in for an ordinary great coat after the war is over if I take the buttons and badges off - it will do splendidly for a motor coat if I ever acquire the motor.

Mrs. Little has just completed a beautiful khaki comforter hand-knitted, which no doubt will prove a great boon on cold nights. She has also knitted me a pair of mittens, things Gran shines at, so you see they are both looking after me and spoiling me.

R.A.M.C. men are regarded as non-combatants, and are not allowed to take part in any of the fighting, so we are not supposed to carry arms. You may carry a sword but it is really an emblem of rank and is of no use. A lot of the fellows are taking revolvers which they carry in holsters in their belts. Our Colonel advised us not to do this as it would attract the Germans attention and they would consider us combatants and fire without provocation. I am purchasing a small Browning pistol for £2.7.0, which is an automatic weapon and quite handy, goes comfortably in one's hip pocket. Altho' very small, quite deadly if the occasion should arise.

I am also to get a pair of field glasses before I go. I shall endeavour to get a pair of prismatics, as they are very fine and they should last a lifetime. I am getting my various wants gradually so as not to feel it so much.

Well, Mum, this is a very scratchy letter. I'm afraid I have forgotten your birthday, mine coming along today has reminded me of it. I'm very sorry,

Mum, but it is rather risky sending things at this time. I shall try and manage a small offering for Xmas and risk it.

Give my love to all at home. I wonder how long it will be before I see you all again.

Bestest love, dearest Mum,

Yours,

NIGE

On the other side of the world, on 1 November 1914, the first convoy of ANZAC troops set sail for the war from Albany in Western Australia. The 38 transport ships were accompanied by a naval escort of four vessels, including the brand new cruiser *HMAS Sydney*. Aboard *Sydney* was Nigel's prospective brother-in-law Engr Lieut Cleon Dennis, a friend of Nigel's from Sydney University days and now a young career naval officer.

As they crossed the Indian Ocean, everyone worried about the likely presence of the German raider *SS Emden*, the famous ship which had wreaked havoc in the first few months of the war by sinking many Allied ships and bombarding Madras in India. Off England at this early stage of the war, the threat to shipping came mainly from mines.

Holiday Group, Bulli, Christmas 1909

(Stephen Boulton is standing second from the right at the rear, next to his brother Nigel. On the left is Cleon Dennis, and next left is Nigel and Stephen's mother, Dora. Their sister Thea is reclining on the ground. Picture Courtesy Julia Woodhouse)

Engr Lieut Cleon Dennis, R.A.N.

(Picture Courtesy Julia Woodhouse)

Section Hospital, Dover Castle, 5 Nov 1914

Dearest Mother

Many thanks for your letter to hand the day before yesterday. Also one from Steve and one from Thea to Mona.

You see I am still here, and am afraid I am likely to remain here for a very long while yet, as there have been no moves for weeks. It seems a mistaken policy of England's to keep such a lot of troops on this island, when they are so badly needed on the continent. They apparently are preparing for the possibility of an invasion. This, in my opinion, is rather remote as long as our Navy is intact, as provided they could land a force it could not be a very large one, and they could not support it, and the defences all along the coast have been very thorough. Our small army of 750,000 men, these are the regular troops have been sadly depleted, as the casualties altho' terrific on the German side have been terrific on our side too. Our men can't endure fight after fight without need of a rest, whereas the Germans are daily bringing up numerous reinforcements.

I don't see why the territorials should not be made use of. Of course, they are not trained to anything like the same extent as the regular forces, still they will be able to give an account of themselves as the London Scottish, a territorial regiment, have proved just recently. The territorials are what we know as volunteers. The Germans are not hesitating to use every man and boy that can march and carry a rifle.

It is sad our losses from mine disasters. However, England is slowly waking up now and with Lord Fisher at the helm the English Navy we hope will not 'take her gloves off' to fight, as one of the papers here aptly puts it. I see tonight the Germans have lost one of their cruisers as a result of a mine which is more cheering.

Turkey has entered the fray after vacillating for a long time, at the instance of Germany. I don't think she will do very much harm, as her action was contemplated.

Egypt, of course, is what we are anxious about. It is practically suicide on her part. She has had 2 wars recently. One with Italy, when she lost her African possession, Tripoli, and one with the Balkan States when she lost her European possessions. Now she has only Asia Minor left.

England has been terribly slow at waking up to the seriousness of the situation. She has just finished rubbing her eyes and perhaps she will now realize things in their true light, and put her whole soul and body into everything. Everyone made a fatal error thinking this war is going to be a short one. Germany is fighting for her very existence and means to make it a fight to a finish.

The peace party or pacifists have done a tremendous amount of harm before the War, unarming the country, till they thought the possibility of a war with Germany remote. The results of their labours have required some destroying. England did not want War, and Germany caught her unprepared, but she will find we hope before long not hopelessly so.

I do wish they would send us over soon; I am getting very impatient being kept over here, while the other fellows are having such a gruelling time of it. Two of our fellows (civilian surgeons) not the regular men, but men like myself who have been given temporary commissions in the Regular forces as officers in the R.A.M.C., were mentioned in General French's last despatches for distinguished service. I expect they were two of the lucky chaps who applied right at the jump and got a move up to the Front right early.

I am kept very busy and am getting up at a ¼ to 6 in the mornings which is very good for Pigee[26] in an English winter! I have more work to do than the other fellows, not because I am a better man at all (wish it were so!) but because I always seem to stop work when I'm given a job. (This sounds Irish!!) The other chaps have a fairly easy time of it, with most of their afternoons off, but I'm at it nearly all day and always have to be at the end of a telephone. Still I would much rather be busy than idle. They are allowed 24 hours leave occasionally, but I'm not, as they can find substitutes, but I can't. Wish I could see more of Mona especially at night time, but it is not possible. I have been sleeping in a sleeping bag since my advent to the Castle, and have quite got used to it. It is very warm and specially suited to this country. I shan't know what sheets feel like soon, altho' I have no doubt I shall relish them again.

Mona has had a very nasty attack of gastric influenza, with diarrhoea and vomiting. Poor little girl, she had a nasty time of it, but some powders I prescribed worked wonders. Now she is picking up again and will be her own self again very shortly. I have a nasty cold; it is full blast at present. However, I shall shake it off as soon as possible, as colds in England don't want encouraging. This letter ought to reach you about Xmas, so I have done my best to make it a long and interesting one. I am getting Mona to pack up my photograph and send it to you. I wonder whether you will like it.

---

26 A family nickname for Nigel. Presumably Nigee Pigee came from the same tradition as the Georgie Porgie nursery rhyme.

Best love to all at home, hoping you will all have as happy a Xmas as is possible considering the gloom this war casts over things. Wonder whether I shall be near you next Xmas, Mum. One never knows one's luck.

Goodbye, dearest Mum,

NIGE

P.S. Thank Billy for his letter. I have very little time for writing, but must try and make an effort someday to let him have a line.

Section Hospital, Dover Castle, 19 Nov 1914

Dearest Mother

Yesterday was your birthday; I wonder whether you had a good one. I am so sorry I had not sent you anything but it is very risky sending anything by post at present, one never knows whether it will reach its destination. What ripe old age have you arrived at this time? You will be approaching the 60 limit ere long. Birthdays are very sad things as life goes on, one realizes the best part of one's life has gone and that the sere and yellow does not promise an attractive vista ahead. One would think me a regular Methuselah!

Well, Mum, I must drop this dismal strain. I wonder whether I shall be able to spend your next birthday with you, I must make an effort if it is possible. It all depends on how long this grim war goes on for - I don't see how it is going to be settled for several months yet. I am still hard at it; I am getting busier every day. This getting up at 6 a.m. every morning in an English winter is no joke. The weather is getting very cold now - we had a small fall of snow today. Altho' Dover is on the S. Coast, it can be very cold here with a N.W. wind. I hear it is a perisher. The poor chaps the other side must be having a terrible experience.

The trenches are half full of water in many cases, and with this cold it will be appalling for them. We have another R.A.M.C. chap attached to us here, a Captain who was invalided back from the front for dysentery. He was over there 10 weeks - was in the retreat from Mons and in the battle of the Marne and the battle of the Aisne. He tells most interesting experiences and makes me more anxious than ever to get over. He says the French and Belgians aren't up to our fellows at fighting. The French are no good up against a wall or in a trench. They are too impatient and nervy and won't keep still. At the same time they are excellent when there's a chance for a charge or in anything where they can let off steam. He is of opinion, which seems to be becoming a true one now facts are leaking out, that if it weren't for us the Germans would have walked straight into Paris. That the French couldn't have stopped them. In the Retreat from Mons the British Army was absolutely left by the French and that it was the nearest squeak that they weren't wiped out entirely. They fought a rear guard action, a staff officer told him, which was so successful & hit the Germans so hard that they thought our Army was three times the size it was and retreated 4 miles which saved us. If they had grasped how few of us there were they would have wiped us out!

He says from what he saw that the Germans Artillery impressed him tremendously. They were devilishly accurate. Seemed to know the positions exactly and poured in shells with deadly precision. Found subsequently that they derived all their information from spies, etc. Their system of espionage is most marvellous apparently. We were hopelessly behind in our artillery.

Our aeroplanes and air craft were wonderful. Quite superior to the Germans who were afraid of us. Our transport and Army Service Corps work was an eye-opener. All motor.

He says that the Germans owe their success to their huge masses, and absolute indifference to loss of life apparently. They advance in line after line, as fast as one line is mowed down up comes another gaining, of course, all the time. He says he counted 600 German dead in one field alone! Our fellows were wonderfully steady and deadly with the rifle. The Germans are mortally afraid of our rifle fire.

That some of them run like rabbits and are terribly pleased at being captured. Several Germans who advanced to surrender were shot before they reached our trenches by their own men. He was attached to the Artillery and had a very good time and altho' the life was very strenuous it made you as hard as nails.

One of our fellows went abroad today which brings me one closer to a chance of going. I have still five chaps ahead of me. I wonder if I shall get over before Xmas. I doubt it. It would be pretty beastly to start in the heart of the winter; however, one can't pick and choose. I have over 3,000 troops to look after now and am kept hard at it. It makes me rather sore to see the other fellows having a pretty easy time of it while I grind my inside out. Still I'm getting the strength of Army routine, if that is of any value abroad. I doubt it.

Well, Mum, this is rather a rambling letter. I wonder if it will be in time to wish you all a very happy New Year. I do trust things will go well with you in 1915. Best love to all at home. Mona sends hers. Mrs. Little is getting more used to things over here and is not quite so depressed. This letter ought to have been to Billy. I still owe him one.

Goodbye, Mum,

Yours ever, NIGE

By now Nigel was aware of a hugely newsworthy Australian victory in the war, the destruction of the *Emden* by HMAS *Sydney*. It had happened on 9 November. As the ANZAC convoy neared the Cocos Islands, wireless telegraphy officers on various ships heard suspicious signals and the telegraph station on Direction Island in the Cocos group sighted a strange ship. *HMAS Sydney*, the nearest warship to the Cocos Islands, proceeded at full speed to investigate and several hours later found the *Emden*. The German ship had already despatched a landing party to destroy the cable and wireless station on Direction Island, crippling Allied communications in the Indian Ocean, and was waiting for its collier to arrive and refuel the ship before seeking new targets. The *Sydney* engaged with the enemy in a major naval battle, and crippled the *Emden*. Engr Lieut Cleon Dennis, who had been in Portsmouth in 1912 installing the powerful engines on the *Sydney*, was helping to extract every last ounce of performance from those engines when his ship destroyed the *Emden*. The feat was celebrated widely in Australia, but Nigel almost forgets to mention it here.

Section Hospital, Dover Castle, 26 Nov 1914

Dearest Mum

Many thanks for your long letter. I trust in time your views as to my hasty marriage will be modified. It would never have occurred if this War had not broken out. I fully endorse your hopes that things will work out well in the end. I think they will.

I am still here, and probably shall be till after Xmas. There has been a great scare here the last few weeks, and 5 battleships are in the harbour at present. This is most unusual as up till now we have had nothing but armed scouts, cruisers and torpedo boats.

The opinion held is that the Germans are contemplating an attack somewhere along the S. coast of England, consequently every preparation and precaution is being made. If they come they will find us ready.

An idea which I heard today, and there is the possibility of truth in it, is that the Kaiser is beginning to realise that the attack on Calais will fail. But because of the promises that have been made to the German people of an attack on England, this must take place.

Accordingly he has arranged that an expeditionary force of some size must land somewhere whether there is a chance of its being successful or not. The scheme of attack suggested is that the German fleet is going to venture out with the ostentatious reason of giving battle to our fleet, but really to cause a concentration of our ships in the North Sea. He is then going to seize this chance to rush across all the transports he can muster in a vain attack on the unprotected South shores. Let's hope it will be in vain. I think there is not much doubt about it as our coast defences are very thorough.

I think we shall all go to the front in time, in fact are bound to go all in good time, but must be patient. At present everyone is being kept here while this scare is on; when things become quieter again we shall most likely go.

Our Colonel went a fortnight ago, and we have another who is not half so popular and not so decent and competent. I have had a chap attached to me the last day or two to help me which is rather nice as I have had about as much as I can swing lately in the way of work. I had 600 men to examine for a draft for service overseas yesterday, and even with this lad, an Irishman called Lane[27], to help, it took us 4 hours and a half solid to get thro' them.

The experience I have been having is valuable in a way, but very monotonous. I do wish I could get to a base hospital, or somewhere where I should have plenty of wounded to handle, but at present that seems unlikely. However, as I'm getting 24 bob a day I suppose I mustn't grumble.

Yes, I wonder when we shall all meet again. It will indeed be an exciting time. I do hope it will be next year as English winters are very depressing. The absence of sunlight is difficult to get used to, altho' there are lots of compensations. This War, I fear, will go on well into next year, and my chances of returning are nil till the war ends. Let's hope it won't be too long. I don't know how it is you have had so few letters; I only missed one mail at the time of my marriage. It is rather disappointing writing letters that don't reach you.

Well, Mum, I must stop. I trust you will get this missive.

Love to all from us both,

---

27 Identity unknown: many doctors named Lane served in R.A.M.C.

Yours, NIGE

P.S. There is really not very much news to give you this time. I've been so busy. Let me wish you all a very happy and prosperous New Year, and the Child[28] a very happy birthday. How excited you all must have been over Cleon's and the *Sydney*'s brilliant efforts.

Officers on HMAS *Sydney*, after the Emden Battle, 1914
Engr Lieut Cleon Dennis standing in top row, second from left. Source AWM EN0163.

Section Hospital, Dover Castle, 3 Dec 1914

Dearest Mum

Many thanks for your two letters which both arrived by the same mail, with one from Gran and Aunt Mog.[29] I have written pretty lengthy letters to Aunt Mog and Steve this time, so you will forgive me if mine to you is pretty short this mail.

---

28 Nigel's sister, Thea, 6 years younger than him, was often referred to as 'the Child'.
29 Aunt Mog was Nigel's maternal aunt, his mother's middle sister. She was the well-known botanical artist Margaret Flockton, the subject of the forthcoming book 'A Fragrant Memory' by Louise Wilson. Aunt Mog lived with Nigel's mother, sister and grandmother at Gladesville and travelled to the city each day to her dream job at the Royal Botanic Gardens, Sydney.

I am still here at Dover and as far from the front as ever! They keep sending new medicos down here, 3 arrived last week and another one today. There are 20 of us now! Goodness knows what is going to happen to us all. The Colonel will be worrying what jobs he can find us all. We first arrivals have all got our billets, but as the garrison is increasing in numbers by degrees I suppose work will be found. Every man is being given a special regiment of his own to look after and remain with in the event of an attack. I have the Royal Garrison Artillery. They are permanent troops always stationed here. I have the sick of the 3rd and 10th Battalions of the Royal Sussex Regt. in addition to the R.G.A. They number well over 2,000, so I'm kept pretty busy. I see by tonight's paper that the Australian troops have landed in Egypt where they will complete their training and deal with any attack the Turks might venture before embarking direct for the front. The Canadians are still hard at work with their training on Salisbury Plain.

Aunt Mog (Margaret Lilian Flockton), c 1914

(Picture Courtesy Julia Woodhouse)

Being attached to the Artillery here as Regimental Surgeon, I have had one or two lessons on guns. They are very interesting and to the uninitiated very complex. The anti-aircraft guns are very cleverly constructed and are technically "an inverted Hotchkiss" whatever that means, giving a 3 inch shrapnel shell.[30] The 9.2's are massive chaps and have to have special cradles and lifts to put the shells into the breech. So far we have had no Zeppelin raid and people here don't seem to be at all alarmed at the prospect. They really are only to create panic, etc.

Mona has joined the Red Cross Society. She has been at it a fortnight. She could not join before, as when she applied the course had started and they won't let anyone start except at the beginning. I don't know whether it will be useful to her for this War, I think not, as fully trained nurses, of which there are 1000's offering, must have priority of appointment. However, a knowledge of 1st aid never comes amiss, and it will provide her with a hobby. Officers

---

30 Shrapnel shells contained pellets which were released by a timed explosion in the air and carried forward to the ground by the momentum of the shell.

at the front are being brought across the Channel for weekends off and short holidays, which is an excellent scheme. They return fresh and eager to rejoin the fray. Our Navy seems to have complete mastery of the sea, as King George would not have been allowed to go across the Channel unless things were safe.

Well, Mum, I must stop now. Bestest love. I do hope 1915 will provide you with a good deal of happiness and prosperity. I wonder if it will bring us together again.

Ever yours,

NIGE

Section Hospital, Dover Castle, 10 Dec 1914

Dearest Mother and Gran,

Here goes for another letter, I wonder whether you will get it safely. I am beginning to get rather dubious now whether some of my letters reach their destination. They are being censored. I wonder whether any of my previous ones have been so treated. One of Mrs. Little's that arrived last week had the Censor's stamp upon it, so I expect yours in future will be similarly dealt with.

Two of our fellows received wires this week to report themselves for service overseas at Southampton on Monday. This means that there are only 2 more chaps before I go! It is quite possible I shall leave before Xmas, as the popular opinion among our men seems to be that a lot of our fellows at the front will be given a few days off for Xmas, and we are being sent over gradually to relieve them. They have been fighting now 4 months and I guess will relish a spell. It's a splendid idea and officers of all units are being accommodated in this way as far as possible. Everyone is beginning to realize at last that this is going to be a very long war, and now preparations are being made with this end in view.

Even the Kaiser's death will not suspend hostilities as the German General Staff seem to be the vis-a-tergo that is directing things. It will be a great thing if I get over soon, as I have been waiting patiently for my turn to come, or perhaps I should say impatiently. I have had little experience with wounded so far, and that is really the thing I'm after. If I get posted at a base hospital I shall be in clover, and shall have all the work I can possibly wish for.

I see typhoid has broken out in the Belgian Army, and will if left to develop, so report has it, sweep the remnants of the Belgian Army from the field, together with a large part of the civil population of Western Flanders, and N.W. France. I am very pleased I have been inoculated and trust I shall escape it. I hope I shan't be put in a typhoid hospital and left to wrestle with them. However, one hopes this scourge will not develop as it did in the S. African war, which was responsible for 57,684 cases with over 8,000 deaths. Anti-typhoid inoculation has been more thorough this war, and much more perfectly understood.

Poor little Mona is feeling very glum now the prospects of my going become more certain. She will feel it terribly I am afraid, still I am certain I shall come back quite safe and sound. 1000's of women, 100's of 1000's would be nearer the mark, are having to bear the suspense and anxiety of waiting in this little island. The women have a harder task than the men to bear; still they unflinchingly bear it, and would not have their men folk stay behind. One finds that out among British folk, that when they are up against it they will put up with all sorts of sacrifices smilingly. It is in times like this that one feels a thrill of pride at being born a Britisher.

Altho' the latter part of the last century and the present part of this has been seeing a general decadence in the manhood of England, I think this crisis and ordeal has just come in time to stop it gaining ground, and after this war England will be purged to a great extent of its feminine mankind. At least we hope so at any rate. There are still 1000's of vapid young men who have not enlisted, but perhaps gradually they will join the colours, as their numbers become fewer and fewer.

How interesting for the Australians being stationed at Egypt, what an experience for them. The climate there will suit them admirably, and by the time they have finished their training, spring will be at hand, when Europe is a very pleasant country.

Well, Mum, this letter will have to be to you and Gran, as I have just written a fairly long letter to Aunt Phoebe[31], and it is getting late. Best love to all at home, trusting Gran is hale and hearty, with best love to yourself,

Yours ever,

NIGE

---

31   Nigel's mother's youngest sister Isabel Phoebe Clarke née Flockton, who lived at Chatswood in Sydney.

Section Hospital, Dover Castle, 17 Dec 1914

Dearest Mother

I still keep writing you letters regularly once a week, but each mail I hear from you that my letters are few and far between. It is very disappointing, but still all I can do is to keep going strong and trust some of my later ones will be more fortunate in reaching their destination.

Am very glad to hear all is going well with you. The war must affect you all soon, I am afraid. The income tax in England has been practically doubled, and I shall come in for some of it I expect. I do hope, dearest Mum, you won't feel it very much; things are hard enough for you without war prices, etc. tacked on.

We have all been very much stirred up by the attack of the Germans on our Yorkshire coast, they did some damage, but as none of the towns were fortified that was to be expected. It is apparently quite easy to get thro' to our east coast in the unfortified parts, but they cannot stay any length of time and as soon as any of our patrols appear, skedaddle for all their worth. They can't get away quick enough. An attack like this is quite a sop for the German public, but is really of no military significance. Their chance of landing a force is very remote. The Admiralty are rather sick at letting the German battle cruisers slip thro' their fingers, but they only escaped by a very small margin and were greatly assisted by fog which is a thing one finds it difficult to cope with. It literally saved the situation for them.

It makes me wild to hear people slanging the Navy, for allowing such terrible things like this to happen. The killing of poor children, women and babies, harmless non-combatants! Still altho' it is not a nice thing to occur, they are of less fighting value to their country than able active trained men. It's a cold blooded way of looking at it, but it's nevertheless true. The Navy are not omnipotent, they have done marvels, and every credit is due to them. One usually finds the praters among people who are doing next to nothing in the way of defence for their country.

I am off to the front at last; leastways I expect it will be some time before I get there if I do. One never knows exactly what one's job is going to be till one crosses the water. There are base hospitals, which are quite good to get to for experience, but perfectly safe. Then there are the clearing hospitals, which have a tremendous lot of work to do, and are midway between the firing line and the last hospital. Then there is the actual front or firing line. One's job here is really a glorified first aid, not much experience beyond a certain point, but plenty of excitement. One can't pick and choose what one wants. I have been warned by the War Office to hold myself in readiness for embarkation for service overseas at the end of this month, so shall have Xmas here first. I am very much excited I can tell you. It will be an experience of a life time.

Poor little Mona is feeling it greatly. It is very hard for those who are left behind. She says she is going to do her darnedest to get over to France and get some sort of job or other. If I am in a base hospital I daresay this might be a practicable idea, but if I'm not it would be no use her going over. I don't think she will go however.

I had a letter from Mrs. Lee wishing me happiness, etc. during my married life. It was an appear-to-be-cordial letter, still one could read between the lines pretty definitely. After all it is nothing to worry about, as it is no business of hers at all whom I marry. I also received a photograph of herself taken at Freeman's; you may have received one too. It was most flattering, so much so that I couldn't spot who it was at first. However, I did the polite and wrote and said all the things I ought to say and what I didn't think, etc.

It will be rather an exciting Xmas here for me this year, knowing all the time that I am on the eve of departing for the War. I shall be thinking of you all at home and shall drink your healths and future well beings in whatever's going. I think Mona means it to be champagne. Well, I shall stop now. I don't think there is much in this letter the Censor can object to, if he should consider it worth his while to peruse it. Best love to all at home, trusting this reaches you eventually.

Yours ever, NIGE

Section Hospital, Dover Castle, 31 Dec 1914

Dearest Mother

This is the last of the old year; and what a year it has been! I little dreamt when I saw it in, in the heart of the Indian Ocean on the *Port Macquarie,* what it held ahead. It is a year that will be eternally remembered in the history books. I am afraid 1915 could not be entering upon its reign with more forbidding auspices. I do hope it won't be more appalling in its associations. But there is not much hope of this being the case. It may be more appalling!

The war from an unbiased outlook really has not progressed very far. After 5 months hard fighting the opposing armies are still hammering away at each other on their frontiers. The advances made seem to be inappreciable. It will really become a matter of endurance. Our army has fought magnificently, upheld and more than upheld the glorious traditions of the British Army. Outnumbered always by at least 3 to 1 it has held its own and actually assumed the aggressive. We are now in a position to take the offensive along the whole front, but we have not got sufficient men!

The French have done excellently, but they were hopelessly unprepared for war, more hopelessly unprepared than the Germans ever realized, in spite of their wonderful secret service. If they had only known how weak a resistance France would have offered, they would never have violated Belgium, but would have walked across the French frontier at Verdun, reduced France's forts to piles of bricks and mortar and stepped into Paris. The German General Staff have grasped this now and are terribly sick at their diplomatic blunder. Our Government would never have interfered. England as it is was practically forced to fight, and hesitated and hesitated till at last Churchill[32] precipitated things on his own initiative.

I am hourly waiting for notice to go across the Channel. I don't think I shall have much longer to wait. I am terribly fed up of the monotonous grind that I have been doing for weeks, but still what little knowledge I have acquired of Army ways and means will probably prove useful.

The casualty lists have been huge recently. The losses must be over 100,000 now. The absolute pick of England's manhood. The losses in officers has been awful. The R.A.M.C. lost pretty heavily at first, but have been particularly free from casualties lately. There is not the same risk as in the line regiments. Still we are all ready to take any that are necessary.

Your Xmas letters came safely to hand, a little late, but still in time for the New Year.

I wrote to Cousin Bessie 2 or 3 weeks ago and told them of my marriage. They were much surprised at my not letting them know before! I thought however it would appear as if I was after wedding presents.

Well, Mum, I shall wind up now. The weather has been terribly wild here this winter so far. The storms have been terrific. The worst for years. Fortunately not many wrecks so far. Mona is writing to you too I think so I will stop. Best love to all at home from us both,

Yours ever, NIGE

---

32   Winston Churchill, then First Lord of the Admiralty.

1915

CONNAUGHT HOUSE, THE PARADE, DOVER, 7 JAN 1915

Dearest Mother

Here I am writing from the boarding house where Mrs. Little and Mona have taken up their abode since their arrival in Dover many weeks ago. I am still waiting for the call to go to the opposite shore, but it is a long time making itself heard. Everyone says they would be patient if they were me, as it is the very worst time of the year to go over. Certainly the weather has been appalling, rain, rain, rain, with howling winds and gales and biting cold, all mixed up together. Christmas day was the last fine day we've had. One talks about English drizzle, but it is more than drizzle, real heavy downpours. I believe it is the heaviest rainfall England has experienced for some years. Floods have occurred all along the Thames valley.

I am gradually getting together my kit and equipment. It is an expensive proceeding. It will run up to £40 or £50 before it is all complete. I have got most of my things now. I shall hope to bring back a goodish part of my outfit when I return to Australia if I am lucky and don't lose it when I am over the other side. Mona is a very clever little girl and has knitted comforters, mittens, socks galore, head covers, ties, and everything practically a knitting needle can do. Considering she had never knitted in her life before she married she is rather a oner at it. I believe she would give you a good go at it, Mum.

The mail is going much earlier this week, so I'm afraid my news will be rather short. There have been rumours of Zeppelins off Calais the last day or two. I don't know whether there is much truth in the reports. Dover is anxiously almost feverishly awaiting their arrival here - we have a good number of anti-aircraft guns, and the artillery people are most keen on having a go at them. These guns are more or less of an experiment only introduced since this war - so they have had very little practice with them, but want some! Turkey seems to have been pretty thoroughly crushed by the Russians doesn't she?

I don't fancy hostilities between Germany, Russia, Austria, France and England will make much progress during the winter. They all seem to be getting themselves into nick for a devil of a go in the spring. The roads and country are inundated with water, and make progress most difficult, our casualty lists have been huge, practically very few of the first lot that went over from here will return, I'm afraid.

This war will cause the greatest reformation the world has seen as far as I can conjecture. The excess of women will become tremendously increased and open up still wider that difficult social problem - it's a pity the suffragists can't raise an army. They would certainly fight with fury if properly aroused! One doesn't hear much of them nowadays, I think they have turned loyalists and are doing their darnedest for their country in their own light. Let's hope so, at any rate.

I see today that the Germans claim they sank the *Formidable*.[33] It is rather difficult to believe as there was a sea running tho' no submarine was supposed to be able to live in.

Well, Mum, I shall stop now. Thank Steve for his Xmas letter to hand yesterday, one also from Aunt Phoebe, sending Mona a small book mark ribbon.

Best love to all at home, wonder when I write next whether I shall be any nearer leaving.

Fondest love,

Yours ever,

NIGE

On 12 January 1915 Nigel's brother Stephen Philip Boulton (Steve, a.k.a. "Billy"), a 25-yr-old bank official, enlisted in Sydney in the Australian Imperial Force (A.I.F.), Australia's volunteer soldiers of the Great War. He joined about 20,000 men in Australia's 1st Division, originally formed in New South Wales but later reinforced by men from other states. They wore the famous insignia of the A.I.F., the Rising Sun badge.

Steve chose the artillery, which formed part of the infantry. The long-range guns of the artillery were generally used to soften up and destroy enemy targets (men

---

33 The battleship HMS *Formidable* sank in the English Channel on 1 Jan 1915 after being struck by two torpedoes.

and equipment) ahead of the work of the infantry. Artillery was to become the signature statement of the Great War: the battle winner, the wreaker of fear and carnage, the killer and maimer on a horrendous scale.

Steve signed up as a Gunner, equivalent in rank to a Private in the Infantry. His enlistment papers make no mention of any previous form of military service. Later, nice guy Steve admitted that he'd been a 'mug' for rushing off to war and not holding back, as did many others, to train as an Officer before going overseas. Steve was initially assigned to the Divisional Ammunition Column, the men hauling ammunition to the forces in the field, using horses as the means of transport.

Nigel remained unaware of his brother's action for some months.

Section Hospital, Dover Castle, 13 Jan 1915

Dearest Mother

I am still at the old Castle and am getting quite fond of the venerable pile of architecture. Altho' I have been here so long I haven't poked into all the treasures of this wonderful old English citadel. There are lots of secret passages and places the public are never allowed to see. However, I stand as good a chance of getting to see everything there is to be seen as anyone and must make enquiries as I may never have such an opportunity again.

The winter is practically half over and I have spent it in comfort on this side of the channel, so I should not be impatient. This war must be a long one, the more one looks at it the more one comes to realize it. It will be a war of endurance and persistence. The condition of the Exchequer will largely influence the result and ability to carry on - England fortunately is far wealthier than Germany, and this as Lloyd George asserts must tell in time.

The spring will be a time for tremendous activity and tremendous onslaughts. As it is now, owing to the flooded and swamped condition of the fighting area, things are quite at a deadlock. I shall probably be over before the gates of Hell (!) are opened when the weather clears up. There will be a tremendous amount of work for those of my profession. Altho' the casualties have been enormous up till now on all sides, it will be nothing to the carnage that is to come. I see Von Moltke is counselling the Kaiser and the German people to fight to the bitter end. And what a bitter end it will be for Germany. Still one must realize if one looks ahead a bit that the sweets of victory, which must be ours, will be robbed of sweetness by innumerable sorrows, remembrances, and future hardships. Wives without husbands, mothers bereft of their sons and father, left stranded to fight for their existence thro' the remainder of their lives. It is wonderful how human nature forgets, in many ways merciful, and I dare say the next generation will be pursuing its way, laughing, joking and talking, secure from a similar struggle for a century to come.

The winter here is a season of feverish preparation, the getting ready of men, guns, rifles, ammunition, in fact every material necessary for war. These, of course, should long ago have been at hand if old Lord Roberts had been listened to. We are turning out 30,000 rifles a week, which altho' it sounds a lot, authorities say is far too small a number. Our arsenals are working at top pressure fashioning all sorts of siege guns to oppose the Germans and to be used to batter our way through to the German frontier and past it.

The 9.7 inch howitzer is the gun we are going to put our trust in. I learn from gunnery experts at the Castle, where we have the Royal Garrison Artillery stationed, that they will be just as effective as the enormous siege guns of the Germans, easier to conceal and what is more important, more mobile. They will have to be drawn by traction engines. Motor traffic has absolutely revolutionized warfare in the way of transport of troops and supplies.

The Army Service Corps has been wonderfully organized and is really a marvel of efficiency and expediency. After the war is over our Army Service Corps and Transport work will be a revelation. The French have absolutely stood agape at some of our methods in this direction. Kitchener, I dare say, is responsible largely for this branch of our service being so wonderfully good, as he is a colossus at organization.

We had a little fracas here last night. Shortly after 11 there was heard a huge explosion and dead silence. One immediately thought of bombs, as Dunkirk has had 2 aerial raids this week. However, on looking out to sea a short time afterwards one saw another flash followed by a loud report coming from the breakwater battery. We learnt afterwards that a submarine was seen entering the western entrance, and had been fired at. It therefrom turned about and made off out to sea, but when it was seen again the breakwater battery loosed off their 6" gun and the shell burst almost on top of it. Altho' one does not know whether it was hit, it pretty effectually scared the beggar, I bet. The German submarines have been wonderfully daring and have had all the luck of the game so far. This must be so as we, having command of the seas, have our ships constantly on it and therefore always more or less of a target, whereas the German ships are all bottled up in the harbours of Wilhelmshaven, Cuxhaven, Kiel, etc. secure from attack, except by aircraft. That Cuxhaven raid was a daring piece of work, and a lot more damage resulted I have reason to believe than we were led to hear.

Well, Mum, this is a dry sort of letter. There's not much of interest, just my opinions on subjects, which I daresay are largely rot! Mona has had a nasty headache today; she wants Thea to excuse her writing this mail. Well, dearest Mum, I must stop now. I received a letter from Steve a week ago; I must answer it some time. Thank Billy for it. It is nice of him to write. Best love to all at home. Trust you are not all worn out by the summer. Well, till next mail,

Yours ever, NIGE

Section Hospital, Dover Castle, 20 Jan 1915

Dearest Mother

This may be the last letter I shall write from the above address - I have been told by the War Office to hold myself in readiness for service overseas at short notice. This means that I shall probably only get 24 hours or so to report myself to the Embarkation Commandant at Southampton. I am getting quite excited, and it is great to feel at last that I am going to get across the channel to the scene of hostilities.

One never knows what one's job is going to be. I shall probably get a billet as regimental. surgeon, and be attached to a regiment, either cavalry, artillery or infantry. I don't expect there will be many cavalry ones going as the cavalry regiments are limited. As a matter of fact the cavalry are mostly fighting as infantry. I shall not be sent up to the front for a bit, but may get there gradually as the regiment to which I am attached moves up. On the other hand, I may be given a position at a base hospital or at a receiving depot, usually on the coast, or a clearing hospital at which there is a tremendous amount to do. At the latter place all the cases are seen and drafted off in various groups, seriously wounded, slightly wounded, etc. One gets a lot of emergency surgery here, in the way of amputations, etc. Still again there is the field hospital, where cases are taken direct from the trenches and battle field. This hospital is nearest the front, usually in a fairly protected position, altho, of course, it occasionally happens that a shell comes thro' the canvas roof.

The casualties among the R.A.M.C. have been quite small the last 2 or 3 months, in fact this branch of the service is coming to be looked upon as one of the safest. So you don't want to worry, Mum, your Pigee will be pretty safe.

It's only in retreats that the R.A.M.C. is apt to suffer, and there hasn't been a retreat since Mons, and I don't think there is going to be again.

The weather now is very cold and has been lately. Some cutting easterly winds from the North Sea, which is our worst wind in Dover. We have not had anything in the way of a fall of snow yet, only one or two attempts at one. Snow in Dover is rather rare, I learn from the inhabitants, altho' the winds make it very trying in the cold weather. We are continually having air raid scares. A flight of Zeppelins seen approaching Dover, etc, up to the present nothing has happened. The raid over Yarmouth last night was practically certain by aeroplanes.

I see in today's paper that all lieutenants in the R.A.M.C. holding temporary commissions for the war are to have £30 allowed them for their equipment. That is a great help, and altho' it won't quite cover all I've spent on my rig out for foreign service, it will go a good way towards it. England is treating her fighting men, or military men I should say, very well so far this war, and has been pretty liberal with separation allowances and pensions, etc. which is praiseworthy of her and rather unusual going by her past behaviour towards the men who have made her name.

I had a letter from Aunt Eleanor yesterday, thanking me for the Xmas cards. She was surprised to hear of my marriage. It was in *The Times*, but apparently had escaped all their notices. She supposed I hadn't told them I was engaged when I was at Harrow, being "shy". They had not heard from you but would not doubt before long. I suppose I should have told them at the time, but I thought they would think I was hanging my tongue out for wedding presents.

Mona is dreading my going very much as the time draws closer and sometimes wishes she were in Australia, but will not hear of returning as long as I am over here. It will be very miserable for her when I go, and she will feel it terribly, I'm afraid. However, there are 1,000's and 1,000's of women in similar positions and it will be a slight comfort to know that the ordeal of being left behind is being shared by others everywhere.

Poor old Billy, I haven't written him a line for some time. I must try and manage to let him have one from the front!

Give my best love to all at home. Trusting you are quite well all of you. Bestest love, Mum,

Yours ever, NIGE

Casualty evacuation system

This diagram outlines the theoretical wartime structure of medical services alluded to in Nigel's various letters. Operational difficulties often forced the casualty evacuation system to be hastily modified. The term RAP stood for Regimental Aid Post.

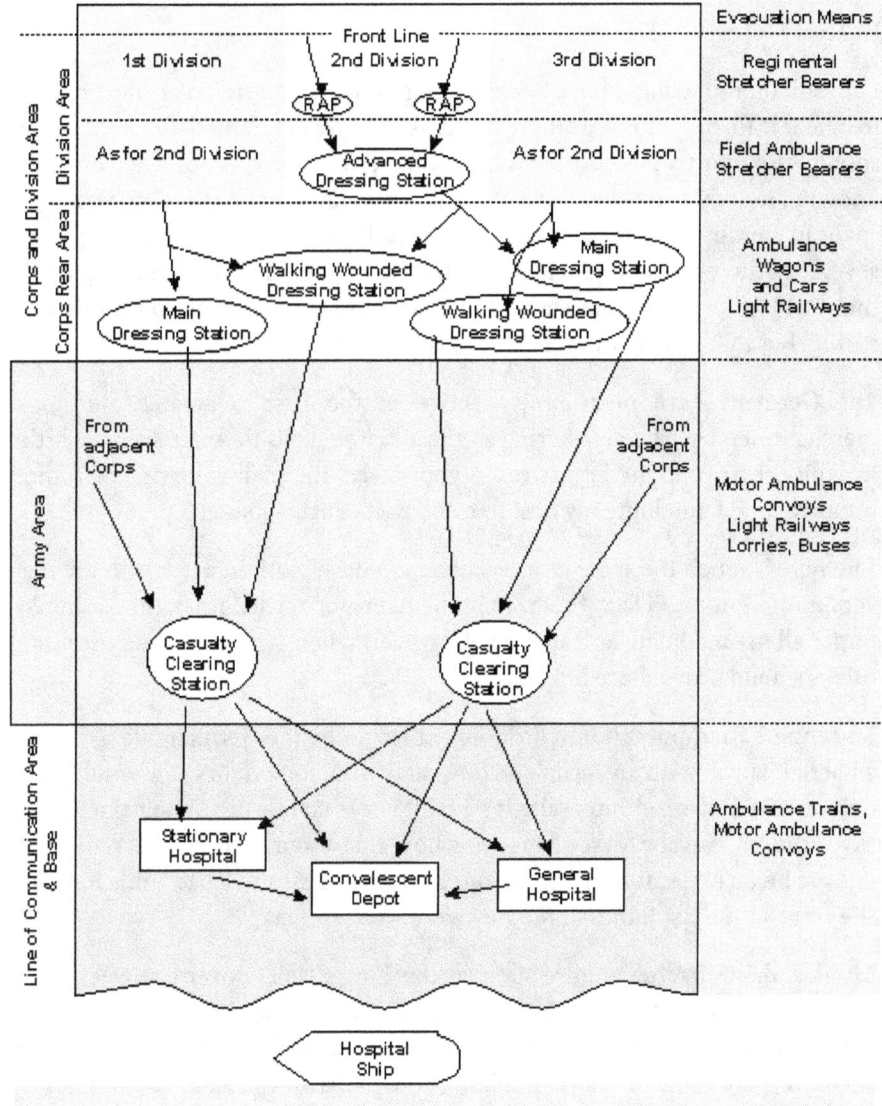

Casualty Evacuation System
Source http://www.anzacday.org.au/digging/hospitals.html, accessed 20 Feb 2015

A German bomb fell close to Dover Castle on Christmas Eve: the first air raid attack on Britain in World War 1. Sea-borne attacks also saw 23 shells landing on the town during the war. Nigel fails to mention that air raid until this letter. His love affair with aircraft started around this time.

SECTION HOSPITAL, DOVER CASTLE, 2 FEB 1915

Dearest Mother

I am still on the string. I have been waiting for the notice to go at short notice for the last fortnight, but nothing has crystallized yet of any definite nature, I should hear shortly now. Altho' it is very irksome feeling so unsettled and not knowing exactly when one is to go, still every day spent here is more or less spent in comfort, whereas when I go over to France conditions will be pretty severe, as the winter has been one of the worst they have had in this part of the world for years, I understand. It would be, of course, nicer to wait till the spring, but that is hardly practicable under the circs.

The Germans have been pretty active in the Irish Sea lately and our merchantmen have been suffering as a result. The mails to Australia are a little irregular; I trust all my letters reach you safely. The mail is leaving at 7 a.m. tomorrow, so I am doing my best to catch it. It usually goes at 7 p.m.

Life here is much the same as it has been. Medical work in a garrison town is very monotonous. In fact if I stayed in the Army for any length of time I should forget all my medicine and surgery. However, when I get over the other side things should prove more interesting.

Since the 2 attempts at bomb dropping at Dover by the Germans we have had an aerial patrol, with an aeroplane on sentry duty for 2 hours at a time, being duly relieved at fixed intervals. It's really very wonderful. When one looks skywards one can always see a machine hovering about. They are very graceful and are being built more and more on the lines of a bird. We had 7 machines in the air at a time last Sunday and they were worth seeing.

Mona and I went to a picture show at the King's Hall, Dover last week. The pictures were nothing out of the way. But there was a violinist there who simply played marvellously. He was a small frail dark man with long black hair, but he was a veritable demon on the violin. The wonderful tones he got out of the instrument fairly bewitched you - he was encored twice and very generously gave us long pieces. He mixed up a series of tunes from the most classical stuff to ordinary homely ones. I think he must have been a refugee, as one seldom if ever hears music like he gave us at a picture show. I wish you had heard him,

Mum, as you so love the violin. It certainly is the finest instrument in the world when played well.

The climate of Dover is beastly, every man, woman and child has a cold, or a throat or a cough or a chill of some sort. The old Colonel here, Col. Tothill[34] has contracted bronchitis and has had quite a parlous time, and I have been looking after him. He is a very peppery old gentleman, and is greatly feared by his subordinates. He literally has them crawling about on their stomachs before him! His poor servant could scarcely locomote while he was ill, from fright. He is on the road to recovery now, I am glad to say.

I went to the dentist a few days ago to have my teeth fixed up before going abroad, and expected to have a tremendous amount want doing. I had 3 stumps extracted, and four small stoppings at a sitting which wasn't too bad. So I got the whole thing fixed up in about an hour. It was very satisfactory. My teeth must be pretty good as I haven't been to a dentist since I went to Dainty at Windsor while I was at Slough.[35]

Nigel & Stephen Boulton, British Orphan's Asylum, Slough, Christmas 1900
(Picture Courtesy Julia Woodhouse)

Well, Mum, I am going to stop now as I must get this posted with as little delay as possible. Give my love to all at home. I wonder whether I shall be here next mail still. I shall let you know in my next letter at any rate. Trusting you are all well, and that Billy's neck is behaving itself. Best love,

Yours ever, NIGE

---

34 Francis William Galbraith Tothill. His 22-yr-old son Geoffrey was killed on the Western Front in 1916.

35 From 1900-1903 Nigel attended the British Orphan's Asylum at Slough. It offered free tuition and board to the children of 'gentlemen' where the father had died leaving the family to suffer a declining standard of living. Entry to the school required sufficient 'votes' from its financial supporters. Evidently the English relatives did a fine job promoting the cause of the Boulton boys, because both were accepted into the school. Aged only ten, Nigel set sail in Sep 1899 to travel alone to England, no doubt entrusted to the care of someone known to his mother. Likewise, in July 1900 10-yr-old Stephen also embarked alone on the long sea voyage.

Commonwealth Offices, 72 Victoria St, London, 11 Feb 1915

Dearest Mother

My call has come at last. I am writing from Aldershot, where I arrived last night from Dover. I have been detailed for No 15 General Hospital, which leaves for France tomorrow morning. My notice has been very short, but as I had been expecting something of the sort I was not taken unawares.

I am taking the place of a man who was suddenly taken ill, and who had been previously warned, hence the shortness of the notice. The War Office is trying as far as possible to give every man 3 clear days leave before he leaves for abroad, but I have had to dispense with this allowance.

Mona and I arrived last night, as till I reached here I had heard nothing about how long I was to be stationed here, and was led to think it might be 10 days or a fortnight. Poor little Mona will feel the parting a great deal, I am afraid but she, of course, knew it was bound to come. We had a most awful time trying to secure accommodation here, all the hotels are crammed, and boarding houses, in fact every place that can put anyone up, as the soldiers are all billeted on the township.

Aldershot is rather an uninteresting place. We arrived at 4 p.m. or so and did not get fixed up till 8, spending the 4 hours wandering about from pillar to post in a vain search for a lodging for the night and following day.

However, we struck a kindly woman, who possessed 8 houses, which she was running at Aldershot (a bit of an undertaking in the boarding house line!) and altho' every cranny was occupied she made extensive enquiries and found us a place which was just starting. We were introduced to a very swagger house called "Drayton Lodge" and found it to be furnished most luxuriously and expensively and occupied by a lady of means who was anticipating throwing the house at the disposal of officers who wanted to recover from nerve strain and overwork occasioned by the war. At any rate she rather graciously permitted us to be put up for the night. We were very grateful, as it apparently was the only place in the town where a room was to be had. She is very stiff and English, and wants it thoroughly to be understood that it is not a boarding house.

Many thanks for your photograph, which I think quite a good one and wonderfully cheap. I shall treasure it highly and appreciate having it with me. The 2 snaps were quite a good effort on the Child's part; I hope she will continue to direct her energies in the snapshot direction.

Well, Mum, I must stop now; everything is excitement and bustle and worry especially when my time and place of departure is to be kept such a mystery.

I shall hear tonight at 6 p.m. I trust. I believe there are 34 of us and we are to go to a base on the coast of France for a beginning. I shall write you again soon.

Best love to all at home. Hoping all is well with you.

Yours ever, NIGE

Dora Mary Boulton (Dolly), c 1915
(Picture Courtesy Julia Woodhouse)

On Friday 19 February 1915 Gunner S.P Boulton boarded HMAT *Marere* A21 in Sydney, among the Reinforcements for the 1st Division's Ammunition Column. The ship also carried a limited number of Artillery reinforcements for the first convoy of ANZAC troops which had sailed off to war in October 1914, and some Cavalry men of the Australian Light Horse. *Marere*, a horse boat, departed on Saturday, heading north to collect more than 400 of the all-important horses. These were the 'Walers', iconic creatures celebrated in poems such as 'The Man from Snowy River'. Evolving in harsh outback conditions from the range of horses brought into New South Wales in the early days of white settlement of Australia, these tough riding-horses were able to endure extreme stress from lack of water and food.

HMAT *Marere* A21, c 1915
Source SLNSW a638400h

Postcard from Newcastle, NSW, Sunday, 21 Feb 1915

Dear Gran

Hope the cold is better. Am having a pretty good time at present. Tomorrow the work begins when once we get the horses on board. Had my first night in a hammock last night but will sleep better when I get used to it. We are very cramped for room on board – eat, sleep and live in the same room. Things will be rather unsettled until we leave Newcastle. We have had leave this afternoon and most of the men went for a swim in the surf. It was very refreshing but the beach is no good. Love to all from Steve

Letter, Newcastle, Monday

Dear Old Mum left 'hind

Just got your letter. Am having a good time so far. No work to do yet as we haven't got the horses on board yet. We had 2 hours leave on Saturday night and went ashore to look round.

Enjoyed the trip up and wasn't sick. Had a good dinner into the bargain. Church parade on Sunday morning at the Cathedral. Leave again all Sunday afternoon till 9.30 p.m. Walked all round Newcastle and had a good dinner at the George Hotel. On Monday morning we prepared all the stalls for the horses, ready for them to come aboard. They are all jammed alongside one another in stalls just wide enough for them. They can't turn or lie down. When fine they are exercised up and down the deck which is covered with cocoanut [sic] matting.

The men are all crowded into a room in the fo'csle - 86 of them. They eat and dress and sleep there, but are allowed on deck to sleep when fine and most of us bring our hammocks and sling them there. I am in the sergeants' mess and get better food than the men and have a separate space partitioned off to eat and sleep. There are 6 sergeants so it is not so bad. I didn't sleep too well the first night, but last night the sergeants had mattresses served out of them. I put mine in the hammock and didn't move all night. It may have been due to the swim we had in the surf on Sunday afternoon. We have just had a bathing parade this afternoon and marched over to the surf. It was very good. I wish the horses didn't come along for another week.

We have formed a Sports Committee on board and have collected £12 odd amongst the Officers and men to spend in Newcastle on games and songs and all sorts of amusements on the voyage. It is going to be a much longer trip than most of us expected. Five weeks at least.

Well Mum it is tea time so I must stop if I don't want to miss it. We are getting very good food and plenty of it. Ships cooks are doing all the cooking and so we are enjoying the meals. Please give my best love to Gran, Aunt Mog and tell her it's a good job she is not on board to see the horses especially when they begin to feel sick. Tell the Child to write and heaps of love to you both from Tootie[36] who has escaped. Hope peace is not declared for a while yet until we get well away. Better get all the family on the letter writing racket. It has been terribly hot here the last 2 days and must have been a corker in the oven.[37]

Love from TOOTIE to his Ma

'Coolah', Ross Street, Gladesville c. 1914
(Picture Courtesy Julia Woodhouse)

Postcard, Newcastle, Tuesday, 23 Feb 1915

Off today around 4pm. Good Bye and love to Matee-Boos.[38]

---

36 Tootie was Steve's way of referring to himself.
37 The family now lived at 'Coolah', Gladesville, a house which belied its 'cooler' name. Being very hot in summer, it was referred to as 'the oven'.
38 Parents were often referred to as 'the pater' and 'the mater' at this time, and Matee-Boos was the affectionate nickname Steve gave to his mother.

Drayton Lodge, Cargate Av, Aldershot, 2 Mar 1915

Dearest Mother

This will be my last letter written from England to you for a good while I really believe. We were to have left 3 weeks ago, but our destination has been twice changed. At any rate I am pretty sure we are off this time. We are leaving the day after tomorrow at 5 a.m. to embark at Southampton for the eastern end of the Mediterranean, where exactly is unknown at present.

As I told you in my last letter, there was a chance of our going to Serbia; but in the end No. 16 General Hospital was despatched thither and we were held back. The reason for this is obscure, as we being No.15 General were due to go first. However, in the long run I think we shall get the best of it, as it is most probable we are eventually bound for Turkey, to take part in the military operations connected with the forcing of the Dardanelles. Of course, nothing has been breathed to us of our future movements, but in my opinion we are being either sent to Cyprus, Crete, Syria, or perhaps Egypt for a short while to be handy when the time is ripe for the landing of troops on the shores of the Dardanelles, i.e. when the Navy have sufficiently cleared the shores of any opposition.

The opening up of the Dardanelles will have far reaching effects, and altho' it will be a most difficult task, quite within reason, and if successful will constitute one of the most brilliant pieces of military and naval work under the present order of modern warfare. It will give Russia a free way for the export of the large quantities of grain she has at present no means of disposing of, for the import of equipment, arms, etc. wherewith to supply her innumerable troops, and to re-establish her trade and commercial activities, which, of course, have been practically squashed since Turkey came into the war. It will also have a tremendous moral effect on all the States of the Balkan Peninsula, which have been very restless and very undecided as to which side they should support. What naval supremacy means has not been brought home to these countries, and a piece of work like the forcing of the Dardanelles and the Bosphorus will be a striking illustration. Undoubtedly if it is my luck to take part in these operations, this will be the most interesting theatre of the war. Altho' I have been cursing my luck at being left so long in England, it is quite on the cards that I shall have as good a job as any of the others who have already gone to France and Flanders.

Thank you for your last letter, Mum, to hand 2 or 3 days ago. I was delighted to get it, also the snaps taken by the Child of Gran, Aunt Mog, and Aunt Mog's cottage.[39] I am afraid I shall not get your letters so regularly after this, nor will you get mine. Still I will endeavour to write to you regularly every time I get a chance, altho' as I said before both your letters and mine will be censored. You had better always address my letters to the Commonwealth Offices, 72 Victoria St. S.W. and I will let them know where to forward them to.

Gran (Isabel Mary Flockton), c Jan 1915
(Picture Courtesy Julia Woodhouse)

Mona has been flourishing since she came here and Aldershot air is certainly very health giving. Her mother is still at Dover, where Mona will return when I leave here for abroad. Poor little girl, she is not looking forward to my going, especially as my destination is so far off and uncertain. However, when she learns exactly where I am and that the voyage has been safely accomplished she will be somewhat relieved. She is worrying greatly what she is going to do after I have gone, and dreads the possibility of inactivity. It is so difficult to find things for girls and women to do just now, as there are such 1000's in search of the same thing. She wants to get some job where she will have a chance of earning a little money if possible. This, however, is the difficulty.

Well, Mum, I will end now, dinner is just going in and I must wash and brush my hair.

Best love to all at home. I expect you will wait for my next letter with some degree of excitement. I shall write as soon as I can, but it will probably be a week on the voyage. My life has been full of interest so far, but I seem to be entering on the most exciting of all. Who knows? Best love, Mum and a big hug,

Your NIGE

---

39   The photo of Gran has survived.

At Sea, March 1915

My dear Matee

You will have waited a long time for this the first letter. However as we have not called anywhere at all it cannot be helped. After leaving Newcastle we do not stop until we get to (censored) a terrible long run without a break of any sort. It wasn't so bad whilst coming round the coast of Australia when we could see land, but now it is deadly with nothing but the sea all round day after day.

Have only seen about 4 ships since we left and two of these were at night time. We have wireless on board and I could have sent you a marconigram but I could have only put 2 words and the address for about 7/6. I didn't think it was worth it. We are travelling alone as are all the transports now and whilst near Australia we could use the wireless. We are now supposed to be in unprotected waters and so cannot speak to anyone.

The horses are looking well. They are practically the whole business on a horse boat, and make a tremendous lot of work. We get up at 6 a.m. and have coffee whilst dressing. At 6.30 we water the horses, i.e. give them some water to drink. Then get up chaff and bran and lucerne from the hold and mix it and feed them. This generally takes till 8 a.m. when we have breakfast, consisting of porridge, chops and bread and jam with tea or coffee. At 9 we start again and clean out all the horses' stalls, which means taking a horse out and moving all the others up one. Mats and matting are put down all over the deck when the horses are to be moved so as to prevent them slipping. The stalls are just made big enough to hold them. They cannot sit down and have to stand the whole time. Their legs get a bit puffed and swollen after a time. This cleaning out or "mucking out" as it is called takes up to 11.30.

Each man I forgot to say has 7 horses to look after. At 11.30 we water and feed them again. At 12.30 we have dinner – soup, meat and pudding. At 2 o'clock when the weather permits and the ship pretty steady we take the horses out and exercise them up and round the decks. The horses are of course a bit groggy at first, especially as there are so many obstacles to trip over, and also a good deal frightened and nervy. At 4.30 we water and feed them again. At 5.30 we have tea, chiefly meat and vegetables and bread and jam. After that there is nothing more to do unless you happen to be on picquet duty which means you have to take a watch of 4 hours during the night over some of the horses. You see we have plenty of work, and most of it is good solid manual stuff. Our horses came down from the Muswellbrook district and had a long train trip before embarking, which didn't do them any good. We have lost about 7 so far, chiefly from pneumonia and strangles.

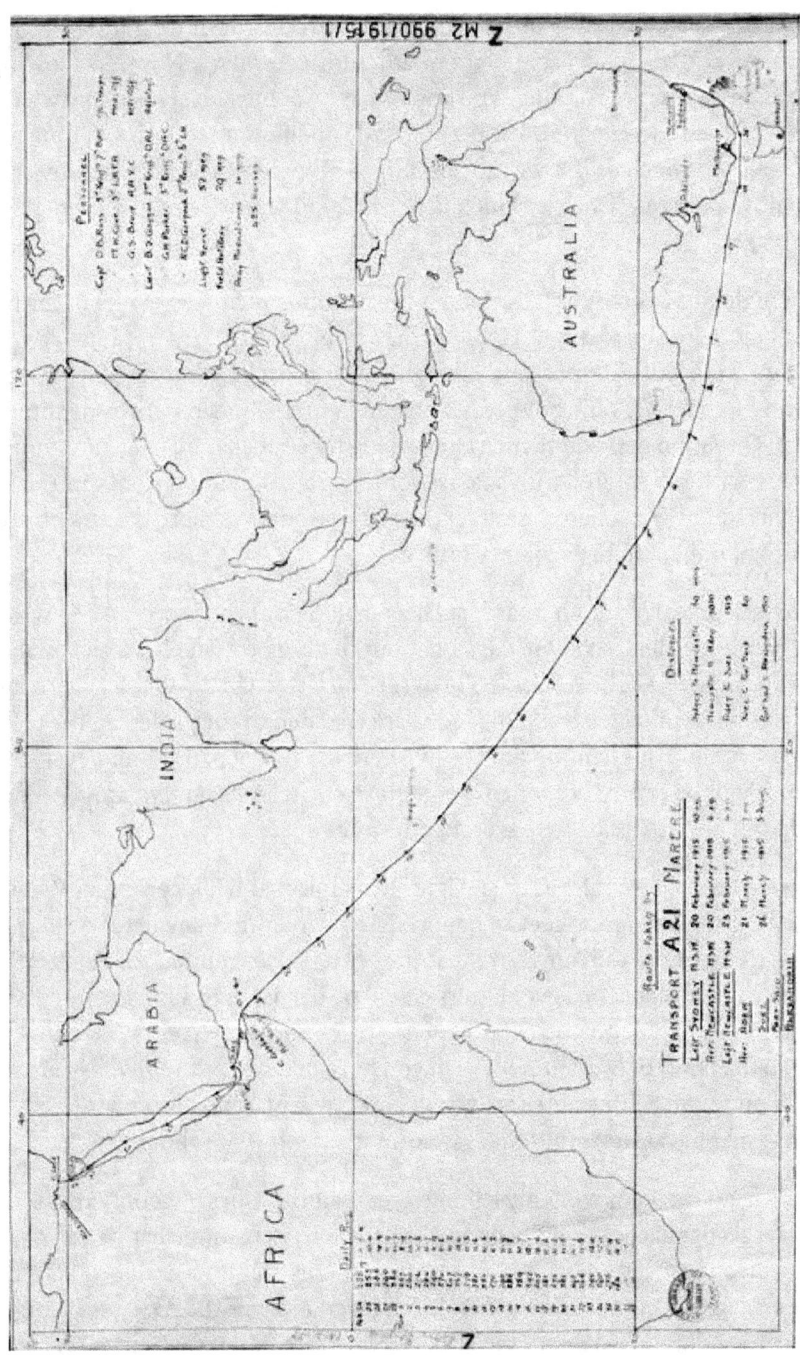

Map 2: Route Taken by Transport A21 Marere, 1915
State Library of New South Wales ZM2 99019151

The first week out from Newcastle was pretty rough until we got through the Bight. After that we had some fine weather for a few days. Now it is blowing a gale and big seas are running. The horses have not been exercised for two days as it has been too rough. Luckily the wind is behind us so it doesn't make us roll about as much as if it was ahead. I have been very well without any aches or pains, not even sea sick, which is pretty good considering the place where we live.

Although I don't know as much about the handling of horses as a lot of the men who belong to the 6th Light Horse & drivers of the artillery, yet I get through the mucking out & exercising all right. Any horse that starts playing up & kicking I generally take hold of his head & let the "horsey" coves manipulate them. One soon gets confidence after seeing these chaps and even now you can see me with my shoulder up against some outlaw's hindquarters shifting him into his stall. We get better food on these horse boats as there is so much more work to do than on the ordinary transport.

I do the clerical work on board, such as making out the pay books & writing any routine orders, so some days I get out of doing the stables which makes a bit of a change. All the troops (85 of us) are quartered in the foc'sle where there are a number of tables erected. Hooks are fastened to the girders in the ceiling where we sling our hammocks. We live here & eat, sleep, dress and everything else. It will be pretty hot when we get into the tropics but we are allowed to sleep out on the deck where we can find some space.

I hope you will get this letter all right. It will probably be censored. We were told only to write one sheet of paper & not to mention any dates or places. I don't think I have said anything that they can take exception to. Post cards of course have precedence over letters & will be despatched almost immediately. All our letters will be posted at [Aden – blacked out by censor]. Write & tell me all the news of everyone & when you have finished with Billy's letters send them on to me.[40] This letter is only all about what happens on board, & is just like so much war news, but there is nothing else to write about.

I am alright and enjoying myself in spite of all the work. I get my meals with the sergeant's mess, being orderly clerk, and so get somewhat better stuff to eat which makes it easier. We all eat tremendous amounts and I expect I have put on a little weight since I enlisted. I am glad I joined the Army as I wouldn't have missed it for anything. We are pretty certain to be stopping at Egypt and will have at least 3 or 4 months of training solidly before they think of sending us on to Europe. There are lots of old soldiers with us on board chiefly amongst

---

40 Very confusingly, both brothers referred to the other as Billy.

the L.H. They probably will get any vacancies or chances to get back to their old Regiments & so go to the Front.

Well Good-bye Mum, give my love to Gran, I hope she is well again and still going strong; Aunt Mog and all her dogs; The Child and all at Coolah and heaps and heaps for yourself, hoping that Concord and Ermo are not giving any trouble.[41]

What about coming over and joining Mrs. Guest and "Tookie". I may perhaps be seeing something of "Took" in Egypt. You had better tell Boja that I have got the V.C. or tell Mrs. Howard which is as good.[42]

Love from TOOTIE.

Nigel is now at sea, heading to Egypt and unaware that his brother is also at sea, en route to Egypt.

S.S. 'Minnewaska', 8 Mar 1915

Dearest Mother

Here we are at sea. Left Avonmouth on Friday, the 5th. Avonmouth is on the Bristol Channel just near Bristol. We are bound for some place to the east of Malta - where, we don't know, not even the Captain. There are numerous conjectures. Some say the Dardanelles, some Crete, some Cyprus, some Syria. My idea is we are to take some part in the military operations connected with the forcing of the operations, and we are going to be put in some place nice and handy so that we can be landed when the navy have made it possible for a landing to be made on a large scale. At present we are running along the Portuguese coast, and expect to make Gibraltar tomorrow morning. The vessel is a big beauty of some 16,000 tons. She is a trans-Atlantic liner and is averaging 16 knots. She is faster than the Orient boats. I am awfully comfortable. Have a glorious state room (cabin) which I am sharing with an Oxford chap called Collier.[43] The vessel is built to take 1st Class passengers only, and the officers have the entire run of the best part of the boat, a very large saloon, deck and a

---

41 His mother owned a small house in the Sydney suburb of Concord and tried to generate income from a small farm at Ermington (Ermo), but was currently living at 'Coolah' at Gladesville, helping to look after his grandmother.
42 All the people mentioned in this short paragraph appear to be friends of Stephen's mother, who was born in England and moved to Australia as a young woman in 1882. Boja was a nickname for someone in his grandmother's family.
43 Oxford University's Roll of Service lists W T Collier, 1908, B.M., M.A. (Feb. 10, 1915). Capt. R.A.M.C. Egypt, Palestine, and Hedjaz. M.C., Jan. 1, 1918. Died Palestine, 1918

promenade deck above this. All the men are accommodated in hammocks on the deck below. We are taking a large number of mules.

S.S. *Minnewaska*
Photo Courtesy Jonathan Kinghorn

The weather has so far been excellent. The first 2 days we met with a bit of a swell usual in the Atlantic, but this vessel, being of such large dimensions, made nothing of it. However, a goodly number of the fellows tho' not actually ill, were in various phases of 'seediness' during the day. I have been as right as rain, and I think it will have to be pretty rough before it will upset me. The food is excellent and we are being done proud. There is a chance of getting this letter posted at the Gib,[44] in which case you should hear from me earlier than I supposed.

There was some excitement the day before yesterday when an object popped up on our starboard side, just abeam. It was held to be a periscope by most people who beheld it. At any rate we swung round suddenly. Nothing more was seen of it. If it was a submarine the chances are it was a French one as at this time we were within radius of the French submarine base - Brest. But it is not at all certain it was a periscope and the Captain apparently discounts it.

Don't worry about me, Mum. I am far safer on a job of this sort than if I was detailed for France. We have several fellows on board who have been to France, 2 or 3 of them wounded, and they are all delighted at being on this expedition instead of being put over to France again. We have a General[45] on board with us. Seems a decent old chap.

---

44   Gibraltar
45   General William Birdwood, ANZAC Commander.

Today we have a truly beautiful day. When one leaves England one apparently leaves rotten weather behind. We had a fire practice yesterday and a church service afterwards. The skipper took it and the General read the lessons. This vessel is a huge one as I have told you and eminently suitable for transport work. Our run yesterday was 383 miles. The boat altho' full is pretty empty (sounds Irish!) What I mean to say the cargo is light and movable and she is vibrating a good deal which makes writing difficult.

I will stop now, Mum, best love to all at home. Little Mona will miss me terribly, altho' I left her very well. Hoping you are all well at home.

Fondest love, dearest Mother.

Yours ever, NIGE

Before I sailed I visited Bristol, saw the Cathedral and Clifton Suspension Bridge. It is a fine English city and was well worth the visit.

Still at Sea, Transport A 21

My dear Matee

Still on our way and are now right in the Tropics. We cross the Line in a day or so and it is a fair corker day and night - reminds me of the "The Oven" on a summer's day.

Am keeping well and working like a navee all day long; it is outdoor work so quite bearable although the heat is a bit trying. Had a bit of a cold a week ago, but it did not last more than a week owing to some good eucalyptus oil I got the veterinary sergeant to give me which he was using on the horses. We were inoculated for the first time against typhoid two days ago. Have not felt any effects yet except for a stiff and sore arm where the injection was made. We are to be done again twice more yet, each dose increasing proportionately.

This is Sunday afternoon, about the only little bit of leisure we get during the day time. We start again at 4 p.m. No time for any church parades as we work solidly all the morning. Did you get another letter I sent and posted a little bit after this one? Let me know if it arrived eventually.

I am like you, haven't got any news since I left Australia, so will be glad to get some letters at our first stopping place. All our letters whilst we are on board are censored before leaving the ship and we are advised not to mention where we are going or what the date is, so you won't be able to gather any information as to where we are, or where we are going.

There is no news to tell you as there would be if I was on a tourist trip, but under these circumstances we have our daily work to do and it's done with clockwork precision and beyond that there is no time to do anything else and nothing happens ever. We get paid every 10 days at the rate of 1/- per diem. There is a canteen on board for the use of the troops where we can buy lemonade, chocolates etc.

Give my love to Gran, Aunt Mog and the Child. I hope everyone is well. I wonder if you have moved to Ermo yet and started the farm. I have written to Billy and told him where I am going. Will be interested to hear if he has got across into France yet. If we go to England and he is still there he ought to be able to get leave to see me soon after we get there.

Well Good-bye Matee Boo with my best love, hoping there are not too many blows descending just now and that you are well supplied with maids. Don't forget to send Billy's letters on to me as soon as you have finished with them.

Love from

TOOTIE

The equipment, stores, and personnel of No 15 General Hospital reached Alexandria from England on 15 March. In his next letter, Nigel's attitude to the discipline of the Australian troops, here and later, reflects the British perception of discipline – correct handling of guns, discipline on parade, saluting of officers in the correct fashion and so on. The Australian attitude to discipline revolved around unquestioning obedience to orders from superior officers and the carrying out of the intentions of battle orders. The 'false legend about lack of discipline, born out of a feeling of jealousy, pursued the A.I.F. throughout the whole war'.[46]

MUSTAFA PACHA, ALEXANDRIA, EGYPT, 19 MAR 1915

Dearest Mother

Here I am in Egypt, arrived at the beginning of the week. We are camped about 3 miles outside Alexandria, which is a truly remarkable place. This is what is

---

46   Joynt, *Saving the Channel Ports 1918*, p 209-210.

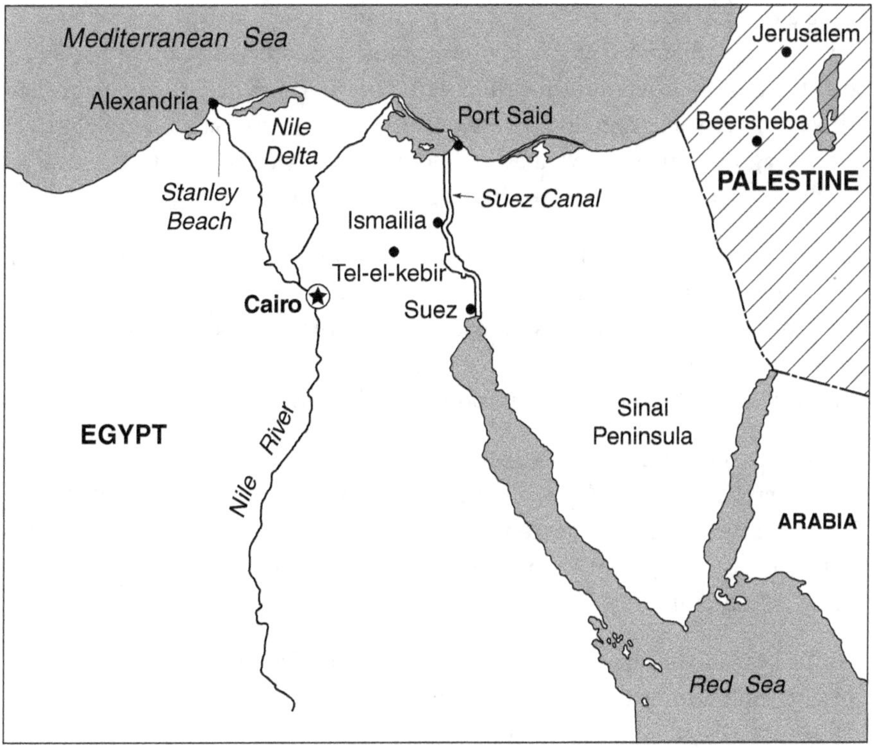

Map 3: Egypt, 1915
© John Newland, 2015

Mustafa Pacha Camp, Alexandria, April 1915
(Picture Courtesy Julia Woodhouse)

called a rest camp, i.e. we are not here permanently but are just here standing by till we are wanted. Our destination is quite a mystery. We are probably to be at the base of operations for the forcing of the Dardanelles, wherever that is likely to be. Some suggest Cyprus, others Lemnos, an island in the Grecian Archipelago. At any rate, we may be here for 2 or 3 weeks yet. The division to which we are attached is not ready apparently to embark.

Most of the Australians are at Mena Camp, about 7 miles outside Cairo, so I haven't seen many of them, only a few stray ones here on special duty, but no one I know. I believe the Australians of which there are about 30,000 are to form part of the expeditionary force to be despatched against Turkey. I learn that there are to be about 80,000 troops sent thither.

Alexandria is typically oriental, very dirty and smelly, but absolutely teeming with interest. The population is very cosmopolitan and consists of Arabs, French, Greeks, Italians, a few Spaniards, Armenians, Syrians, Nubians, Barbarons, English, etc. Excepting the troops, the English are in the minority quite, I should think.

The Arabs form the nucleus of the population. They dress in most extraordinary colours, and the streets are a veritable blaze of colour, which altho' so extraordinarily blended seem to harmonize perfectly. Aunt Mog and Gran would positively dote on the street scenes, market places, cafes, etc., which provide endless material for an artist's brush.

Some of our fellows have got leave to go to Cairo this week end, and should have a wonderfully interesting time, seeing sights they have never seen before and will never see in any other part of the globe. They, a large number of them, have scarcely ever left English shores, so it is a phenomenal excitement for them. I am to go to Cairo next week and am looking forward to it enormously I can tell you. I often think of you and wish you could be here with me as I know how you would revel in everything. A lot of the fellows fail to appreciate the extraordinary chances that have been thrown in their way of seeing such wonders. The trip to Cairo will be pretty expensive, I fear,

General View of Cairo, 1915

Source AWM RCDIG0000210-entire-20-

however it seems a pity not to avail oneself of an opportunity one probably will never get again.

And we are getting special military reductions, which is a great idea. The Australians are very fortunate indeed in being sent here, as they would never have anything like the good time they're having here in France. Their discipline when they first arrived I hear was very poor and accordingly they were not fitted for trench warfare, which requires very highly disciplined troops. I learn that they are greatly disappointed at not being sent to France, but I think it was a very wise move on the part of the War Office in stationing them here to finish their training.

Alexandria, 1915
Source AWM RCDIG0000210-entire-7-

They will certainly be doing most valuable work, in assisting at the forcing of the Dardanelles, which will have a tremendous effect in providing an inlet for munitions of war and ammunition to equip the vast hordes of Russians who cannot be properly armed at present. Russia in point of fact is just as isolated as Germany from the outside world and it is imperative to have the Bosphorus and Dardanelles clear. I wonder whether I shall get to Constantinople. I'm doubtful but I am hoping to, as I understand it is one of the most remarkable cities in the world. Worth 5 Cairos.

Wonder whether Billy will be able to get over here with the Commonwealth forces. This war has opened up unprecedented opportunities for the young men of the British Empire.

I am to visit some Egyptian catacombs in a day or two and Pompey's Column and will tell you about them when I write next. I haven't heard from Mona yet, as a letter has not had time to come from England yet. Poor little girl she will find it very dull in England, being a grass widow, I'm afraid. She would enjoy being here just as much as you Mum, I expect. Shall stop for the present.

Best love to all at home, shall write again soon, dearest Mother.

Ever yours, NIGE

Transport 21, At Sea [c 22 Mar 1915]

Dearest Mother

We have another chance of sending some letters. We eventually arrived at Aden, but only stayed 6 hours, time enough to take on some coal. None of the men went ashore, but as usual the natives of the town came alongside and did their best to take us all down. Most of the fellows bought cigarettes and singlets and dates and hoisted them up in a basket. I got a singlet for 9d. after the nigger asking 2/-. The interesting part of the voyage has now arrived as we are generally in sight of land and there is always some ship passing including some armed merchantmen.

We are in touch with Paris with the wireless and are getting some war news. Heard about the Dardanelles bombardment 2 days ago. We don't know yet where we are bound for. I am well and having a good time, but won't be sorry to arrive at our destination and settle down to work.

I hope Ermo and Concord are still going strong without causing any trouble. Am sending Uncle Frank[47] a p.c. from Aden.

Give my best love to Gran and Aunt Mog and the Child and will write again as soon as possible. Heaps of love from

TOOTS.

Uncle Frank (Francis Egerton Bryant)
(Picture Courtesy Julia Woodhouse)

Postcard, On Active Service [Suez], Postmarked 27 Mar 1915

Dear Matee

Have reached the next port after Aden. Am well and the weather is very mild. Very cold at night and morning until the sun gets up. Sleep on deck in a hammock with two blankets well wrapped up. Directly the sun gets over the horizon the air changes immediately and is warm at once. Am anxious to get to our destination & get leave to look round at the sights etc. Four N. Zealand

---

47 A courtesy title for family friend, Francis Egerton Bryant, an old friend of his father's and now a senior manager with the Union Bank of Australasia in Sydney.

transports got in after us this morning packed with more soldiers. Had my hair done à la the military cut and am sporting a "mow". Much love from TOOTS.

In this letter Nigel shows he is unaware that his brother's transport ship is about to dock in nearby Port Said.

Mustafa Pacha, Alexandria, Egypt, 28 Mar 1915

Dearest Mother

As a mail leaves tomorrow at 10 a.m. I am hoping that this letter will catch it.

As you will see we are still here, and are likely to be for a week or so longer. Some French troops arrived yesterday; they are supposed to be the advance guard of many more to follow. Egypt apparently is being used for the mobilization of our troops who are to take part in the Dardanelles operations and elsewhere not yet known. We are starting a hospital to accommodate 200 to start with tomorrow at the Abbassia Schools.

Some of us have been detailed for it, but I am not one of them. As the hospital is to be expanded I may be required before long. I shall be glad to have some medical work, as I want to have a good deal to do. One doesn't mind being away from home then, but if one has time to think of things one feels a bit homesick, I can tell you.

Our crowd of fellows are a cosmopolitan crowd, and a number of them have travelled a good deal, so they can narrate interesting experiences. There is another Australian with us, a chap called Campion[48], whom I met at the Varsity doing Arts. His father was manager of the A.J.S. Bank in Sydney and was transferred to the managership of the branch in London eight years ago. He brought his family with him and Campion the fellow with us has qualified as a dentist, taking a medical degree as well. He is practising dentistry in London and doing quite well, I believe. We also have a S. African, a chap from Madeira, several Scotchmen, 2 Irishmen.

We have been here a fortnight now and have not had any letters yet. The mail came in 3 days ago from England, but it brought none for us. Probably all our

---

48 Rowland Burnell Campion, Lieut, R.A.M.C., 1914, also served in World War 2. His work at the No 15 General Hospital is described in detail in the book 'A Consulting Surgeon in the Near East', by A H Tubby, published in 1920 & available online. See pics page 95 & 129.

letters are lying at the War Office waiting for censorship. It's a jolly shame the way they keep back your letters, but I believe one has to put up with it as it has been so since the war started. Some of the fellows in France had to wait a month for their first mail. I haven't had a letter from you, Mum, for a month and shall much relish hearing from you again. Your letters will be a trifle out of date when they arrive, I fear.

Our trip to Cairo was cancelled. Half the fellows have been, but the other half were prevented from going by Hd. Qrs. However, our Colonel, who is a dear old chap, is going to do his best to arrange that we go somehow, by twos if necessary. The fellows who have been were overwhelmed with the wonders of the place, and were tremendously impressed. I do hope I shall be able to get there, I probably will if I am patient as we shall probably be here for some time yet.

We are having glorious swims here. The water is nice and warm and there are no sharks to be afraid of, and there is quite a nice little sandy beach. I have bought a No.2 Folding Brownie with me and will send you some photographs when I get a chance.

I haven't heard from Mona yet, I expect the little girl is worrying a good deal as she did not know where I was going to. However, she probably has got one of my letters by this time, and has cheered up a bit. It will be very lonely and depressing for her being left at home, for months probably. If she could only get something to do to occupy her thoughts and distract her mind it would be a great boon - herein lies the difficulty.

Enclosed are some Egyptian stamps I bought at the Post Office. They are for Steve. I thought he might like to have them. They are rather pretty and not fudges. Alexandria is still very interesting, altho' the novelty of the place is wearing off a bit. This is rather a nice place where we are encamped. There are some catacombs here that I have not visited, also Pompey's Column. I must try and get along some time during the week as I understand they are worth seeing.

Well, Mum, I shall stop now. The mail to Australia only goes once a week. The post closes at 10 a.m. tomorrow in Cairo. I hope this catches it, it should. Love to all at home, trusting you are all well. Best love, Mum,

Yours ever, NIGE

By early April, No 15 General Hospital had commandeered and set up in the Abbassia Secondary Schools building in Alexandria. Run by Lt. Col H.E.R. James, it was the first of the military hospitals established in Egypt and said to be the best arranged and best administered, setting a good example to other hospitals.

No 15 General Hospital, Abbassia Schools, Alexandria, 4 Apr 1915

Dearest Mother

This is Easter Sunday. How are you all at home? I have just had breakfast after being to the early service at St. Marks, the English church here. Quite a nice service, and quite a number of fellows in uniform attending. Wonder whether you and Aunt Mog and Thea went and were administered to by "Hoppy"?

This time last year I was at East London[49], and the year before at Wollongong. It's a very long time since I spent Easter with you, Mum, I must when I return to Australia; I expect Mona went at Dover. I heard from the little girl this week and she tells me Steve is on his way over here. Poor Mum, I expect you are feeling very lonely having lost both your boys, but cheer up, Mum, we may all come back together.

It is nice Billy having joined. I trust all will go well with him, which is pretty sure to happen. I expect he will be kept here for 2 or 3 months to complete his training, as few of the troops here are highly trained, and they are all going thro' their training while everything is being got ready for the military operations against the Turks. I wonder if I shall see anything of Billy. He will probably go to Mena Camp next door to the Pyramids, where nearly all the Australians are encamped. He will meet a lot of chaps he knows and will have a great time, altho' the work will be pretty hard at first. It will probably do him a wonderful amount of good after the bank life, and when he returns you won't know him. I shall be as black as a nigger soon, we are all getting well-tanned.

I haven't had a letter from you since I left England, and am eagerly looking forward to one, Mum, I can tell you. Mona has one from you for me, but she hasn't sent it on yet till she is more certain of my address and is assured it will reach me. I wonder what Billy is in? Probably an infantry battalion, as infantry seem to be most needed nowadays in modern warfare. Also I expect there are enough mounted troops here to go on with.

---

49   He was working at the East London Hospital for Children at Shadwell

We moved in here from Mustafa Pacha the day before yesterday. These schools are very large buildings and admirably adapted for a hospital. We shall be

General Hospital, Abbassia Schools, Alexandria

Source http://www.qaranc.co.uk/british_military_hospital_egypt_bmh_alexandria.php

able to accommodate 700 in the hospital and another 300 in marquees. Also can provide for 40 officers in the headmaster's house, which will bring our full complement up to 1040. It looks as if we are to be here for a long time, maybe till the end of the war. We hear, however, that in the event of a base hospital being moved from here, we are to go, which is something. At present we are quite in the dark as to what is going to happen. As troops keep pouring into Egypt daily, something is afoot, and probably in 2 or 3 weeks or so military operations will be started against the Turks.

Whether we are to land near the Dardanelles and assist the Navy, or whether we are to land in Asia Minor somewhere and march on Constantinople, is absolutely a mystery at present. I think England is waiting to see if Greece is coming in, which the latter country is considering very carefully, as she would probably have a good deal to gain in the event of the Allies being successful. If Greece does throw in her lot with us it would help us tremendously as we could then land troops on Balkan Peninsula, pour them into Turkey on the European side.

We have at present only 200 beds going, but shall expand as necessary. We are attached to the 29th Division which comprises 20,000 men, so there are a certain number of sick to treat even when the troops aren't fighting. We shall probably be very busy later on. I have been made a Section Commander, which doesn't mean much, only a little drill to do as well as whatever medical duties I might be detailed for. At present I am on the Medical side of the Hospital. Till fighting occurs the medical cases are in the ascendant, but when wounded begin to pour in, I expect the larger number of us will be transferred to the Surgical Division.

A large number of us have had gastrointestinal upsets - chief symptoms being vomiting, colic and diarrhoea. I have had the latter 2 symptoms the last 4 or 5 days, but have not been bad, have done my jobs just the same. The cause of it is obscure, probably due to the large amount of sand in our diet, which acts as an irritant to the gastric and intestinal mucosa. However, we have most of us recovered, and probably have become tolerant to the causation factor whatever it is.

I sent some Egyptian stamps home last mail to Billy, but shortly after I posted them learnt from Mona that he was en route. So you had better take charge of them, Mum, they are rather pretty and interesting to have. I learn that our letters are post free now, which is a great boon, so you won't have the Egyptian stamps on your letters.

The photographs I have taken so far are not a success, altho' the exposures were all correct, owing to the fact that a spring on the back of camera is loose and lets light in. However, I think I shall be able to fix it up, and shall send you some, which will be interesting in a way. I have written to Cousin Bessie as I think she will like to hear from me every now and then.

The casualties that have been occurring in Flanders and France have been appalling lately, especially at the Battle of Neuve Chapelle. It is blood curdling almost when one thinks of it, and realizes how many more 100's of thousands are yet to be killed before peace is declared. Steve and I are very lucky being in Egypt instead of France. However, we may be transferred there later on, if it is considered necessary.

We get very scanty news here. Only the telegrams. Papers are 10 days to a fortnight old, so we are rather in the dark as to what is going on exactly.

I have asked Mona to send me a weekly paper which will be very nice to have. Our letters are rather slow in coming and going, as they are often held back, whether censored or not. We only got our first mail last week, leastways all the other fellows did, i.e. 3 weeks after posting. Normally in peace time letters take from 7 to 8 days, I believe; I was more fortunate as I got a letter from Mona a week before the other chaps, she having chanced a letter addressed here direct, instead of C/o Secretary, War Office. It was a great score and I was much envied.

I think, Mum, if you address your letters Lieut. N. Boulton, R.A.M.C., No.15 General Hospital, Special Expeditionary Force, Egypt, they should find me, as if they go to England first, it means another 2 or 3 weeks before I get them, that is they take 2 months or so - a terrible long time.

How are you all? Is the Child still plugging away at Dulwich Hill?[50] What has happened to Cleon? Best love to all at home. Mona will write to you and tell you how things are from time to time in addition to me.

Trust I shall manage to see something of Billy. We have not been to Cairo yet. Fondest love, Mum. Don't worry. It's going to be a very happy home coming.

Yours ever, NIGE

It was originally intended to send the ANZAC troops to England, for training prior to joining the deadly fray on the Western Front, but training conditions in England were considered unsuitable and the troops were diverted to Egypt, where the first convoy arrived safely in December 1914, thanks to *HMAS Sydney*. A training camp was set up at Mena, near Cairo, in sight of the great Pyramids.

Stephen arrived at Mena in late March or early April, 1915, by which time the looming campaign in the Dardanelles was afoot. The two brothers, Nigel in the British Expeditionary Force and Stephen in the Australian Imperial Force, were now both in Egypt, without realising it.

MENA CAMP, MENA, CAIRO, 4 APR 1915

My dear Matee

Here I am at last. Camped right at the foot of the Pyramids. We disembarked at Suez and unloaded the horses and trucked them. Came up to Cairo by train and marched out to Abbassia camp where we stayed for a day. We then came over to Mena Camps where all the artillery are stationed. We are properly under active service conditions and don't get such good food as on the boat. But it is plain and good.

Are encamped right in the desert with sand everywhere. The flies are pretty bad too. Pretty hot in the day time with a glare off the sand. At night it gets pretty cold after the

Mena Camp, Cairo
Source AWM J03262

---

50   Thea was teaching music at Trinity Grammar School, close to Dulwich Hill in Sydney.

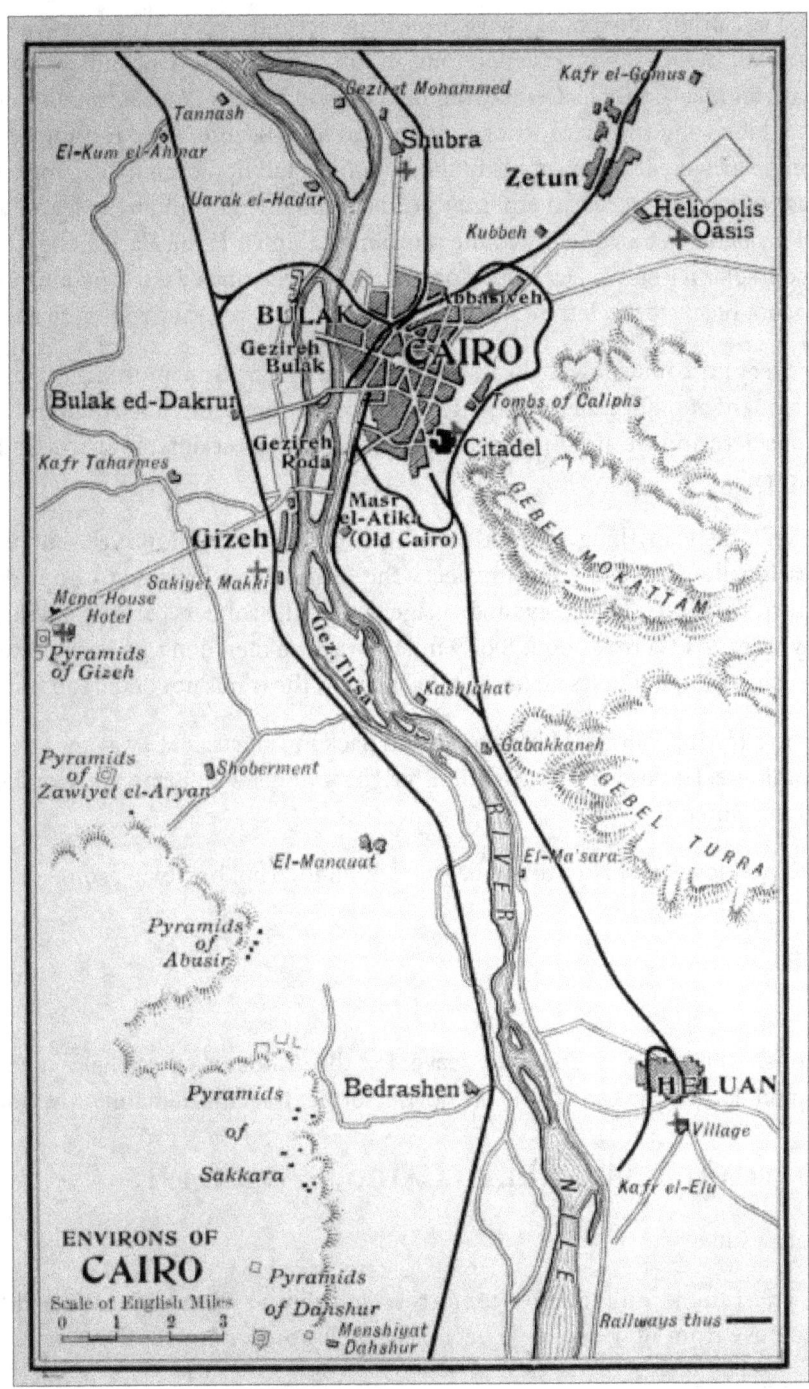

Map 4: Cairo and Environs, c 1915

Source: Barrett and Deane, *The Australian Army Medical Corps in Egypt, 1918*, Project Gutenberg ebook 41911, Ref i093-t.

sun. I am alright though, as I have three blankets and a good overcoat. Was on guard last night - 2 hours on and four off for 24 hours. Have been here about 3 days and have only had ½ day off, being Good Friday. Went into Cairo and had a look round with a sort of a guide who took us into some mosques etc. Would have liked to have gone up the Pyramids, but don't think I can manage it, as we have just received orders to be in readiness at any minute to leave. We will probably get away early in the morning. I think it is the Dardanelles, but of course don't know. Have been on the move ever since we left Sydney and have not received any letters at all and I don't know when they will catch us up.

I get very little time now to do anything as we are going from morning till night with guard at night times some nights. There are thousands and thousands of troops here and we are divided up into several camps at different parts of the country.

Haven't seen anything of Jack Herring[51] or anyone I know yet, but will occasionally meet someone I expect. The camps have their own shops and picture shows etc, in fact a young village, where the soldiers can buy anything they want. As Cairo is about 8 or 9 miles away the men don't go in too often. The trip in and out takes an hour and a quarter, the trams not being too fast.

Am in a terrible hurry as I have to go and pack my kit straight away to leave at any minute. Hope everything is going alright at home with Ermo and Concord and the Hutch.[52]

With best love and kisses to Matee Boo left 'hind, from her loving son,

TOOTIE

Stephen thinks he is about to leave for the Dardanelles, to help unload ammunition, but he and his unit did not get further than the train station at Cairo.

Postcard postmarked Cairo, 5 April 1915

Dearest Mum

We are, I think, on the move tomorrow morning to Alexandria. We will be very busy from now on. Have been very well up till now. Hardly ever rains

---

51   Jack was the nickname for Private Edward Edgar Herring, a 23-yr-old bank clerk of Gladesville when he enlisted on 27 August 1914. He died of wounds on 9 August 1915, at sea, after involvement in the Gallipoli campaign.
52   'The Hutch' was the name of the house on the farm at Ermington.

in Cairo. We are back on the old stews & bread & jam again but the Egyptian Government allows each soldier 6˜ a day to be spent on foodstuffs at the dry canteen. Prices are high here: ever since the soldiers came the natives have asked three times as much for things. The men who came first got things very cheap for a time. English money is no good here but the merchants generally change it & give less value. Much love from TOOTS.

Mena Camp, Egypt, 9 Apr 1915

Dear Mother

Hurrah! at last have received a letter from home. One of the Child's. Was very glad to get it and hear all the home news. There must be several that have got stuck up somewhere, which I may eventually get, at least I hope so. I didn't get away from here after all, but went very close to it. We (eleven of us) were transferred to the Brigade Amm. Column and were to leave last Monday.

We were all marched down to the train with all our kits and blankets drawn and packed and were just off when the eleven of us were detailed off to return, owing to being overstrengthed. It was not so disappointing to me as to the other chaps, as I had just arrived and they had been here for months. I missed a good trip over to the Dardanelles to assist in unloading and return for more. I will now be able to visit the Pyramids which I intend to do tomorrow if I can possibly get off.

In my last letter I said my address was Brigade Amm. Col. instead of D.A.C. I was transferred to the B.A.C. but, as I didn't get away with them, am back again with the D.A.C. Don't forget to put on the above address which may expedite the receiving of any letters.

The camp life here is not so bad as far as it goes, only everyone thinks we're getting trained. As far as the artillery are concerned we are all looking after the horses all day long and take them out in the wagons six in a team. Don't seem to have any gun drill yet. There is plenty of work all day long, but we don't seem to make much headway which creates a great deal of discontent. The men here call this little unit the "circus".

Today was very hot in the sun which is always practically overhead. It is a great relief when the sun goes down and the glare goes off and the flies disappear on to the top of the tent. They are here in millions and worry like the deuce. There are about 15 of us in a tent but about 8 sleep outside which makes things quite comfortable. I am sleeping inside as long as possible, and in fact, not until there are no tents to sleep in, as the flaps can be easily rolled up, and the dews in the night are very heavy. I have been very well up till now and am feeling alright. I have quite got used to sleeping on the ground, and could sleep anywhere some nights. The sand makes a good bed as it is easy to make a hip hole. Have got three blankets and a good overcoat. Pyjamas have long since been done away with as when one is on guard or picquet we have to wear all our clothes ready to jump up when called by the man on sentry go[53]. I now sleep in my trousers, singlet & socks etc. One soon gets used to it, and probably if I had sheets and a good soft bed I wouldn't sleep so well as on the ground in clothes.

I was again vaccinated today. All the new men arrived had to parade before the doctor and show their arms. Those who could not show recent signs of previous vaccination had to be done again. My arm shows nothing and I couldn't bluff him out of it, so I was done again; but as soon as I got out of the tent where he was doing it I rubbed it out as much as possible so as to try and dodge the effects. He only did 2 places, so I don't think it will have much effect.

Major Purdie is the Med. Officer. He was chief medical officer for N.S.W. a little while ago. I won't write any more now as I was on picquet last night and I am feeling tired and sleepy so will turn in.

Was very glad to hear of all the family and am looking forward to another letter. Things will get very monotonous if they keep us here for any length of time. Give my best love to Gran, Aunt Mog and thank the Child for her letter. I have sent her one or two post cards of some of the places I have been to. Is Dicky Dumps[54] still at Coolah? I hope the financial position of the family is still good and they are not reduced to the bone.

Much love and kisses to Mums left 'hind, from TOOTIE

"The escapee" from the oven.

Send some of the Monday's newspapers along when available as all the Sydney news is interesting to me.

---

53 'Sentry go' was an alternative phrase for sentry duty.
54 A nickname for a family friend, visiting from England

No 15 General Hospital, Abbassia School, Alexandria, 11 Apr 1915

Dearest Mother

Am still waiting for your letters, which Mona is forwarding on. They will be pretty old by the time I receive them I expect, still they will be all about Steve's coming over, which I am anxious to hear about. I should think he must be on his way over ere this.

I had a letter from Mrs. Lee[55] written on the 17th January, 2 or 3 days ago. It has just taken 3 months to reach me. It was addressed Dover Castle, and has been forwarded on from Aldershot. Things seem to be going swimmingly with them at Wollongong, and Dr. Harry, from her account is raking in the spondoolicks, which must be very gratifying, especially at a time like this. She enclosed 2 snaps of Tim and the daughter. They are both very like her, especially the daughter, who promises to be a veritable sollicker. She says she has 10 first cousins at the War and can't hear about any of them. Also her brother, Alan Barton, who was practising at Coonabarabran. So her family is well represented.

Mrs. Lee (Nora Barton) & Dr Harry Lee
(Picture Courtesy Julia Woodhouse)

I met a Sydney University chap this week, called Wassall[56], a Queenslander, he was 2 years junior to me. He has just gone across with an Australian field

---

55 Mrs Nora Margaret Darvall Lee née Barton was married to Dr Henry (Harry) Lee, with whom Nigel had practised medicine at Wollongong for 18 months from the middle of 1912. Mrs Lee had two young children at this point – Tim, born 1910, and Virginia, born 1914. One of her first cousins was Nigel's friend Max Barton. Another first cousin was 'Banjo' Paterson. Her brother was Alan Sinclair Darvall Barton, described on the 'Beyond 1914' website of the University of Sydney.
56 This was Charles Edward Wassell, a 25-yr-old medical practitioner when he signed up with the AAMC as a Captain on 20 Aug 1914. The 'Beyond 1914' website of the University of Sydney outlines his wartime career. He married in Sydney in June 1918 but his wife died of influenza a year later. In 1921 he remarried and in 1927 he moved to Brisbane and set up as an ear nose and throat specialist. He served in the Middle East in World War II. Charlie Wassell was a troubled man, perhaps a victim of Post Traumatic Stress Disorder. In 1930 he drove his car into a tram and assaulted the ambulance man attending at the scene of the accident. In 1944 he died of a gunshot wound to his stomach. At the inquest, witnesses disagreed as to whether the wound was self-inflicted, but he'd previously shot himself with a revolver, in Sydney in 1920, after his first wife died.

ambulance with the Expeditionary Force just despatched to the Dardanelles. He told me of a large number of chaps I knew who were at Mena, with base hospitals. A lot of fellows in my year, who were very sick at being left behind. I dare say they may go over later.

This Dardanelles affair is going to be a very tough proposition and I am afraid before it is finished will be attended with a large number of casualties. The Turks have a larger army in the field than they have ever had before, tho' they are short of munitions and equipment. Their leadership and organisation is bad, but with the Germans at the helm of operations they will fight as well as ever they have fought. I think once we effect a landing things will improve. We have sent a large number of pontoons over, and I understand we are going to make a landing at Boulair (marked on most maps of Turkey) on the Gallipoli Peninsula under cover of the fire of our ships in the G. of Saros. Our ships have been getting knocked about a bit in the bombardment, perhaps more than we are informed in the press. I think, however, with the military organization as well as the naval we shall make some headway. Altho' it will probably be a long job, 2 or 3 months at least I should think.

I expect Steve will be stationed at Mena with those Australian forces who are still there, and must be prepared to settle down here for at least 3 months. The weather will be pretty trying soon here as the summer is coming on, however, the heat won't be here at its greatest for another month yet. I wonder if I shall see anything of him. Only if I go to Cairo, which does not seem very likely at present. It is some 90 miles away. We shall probably have some wounded here in 2 or 3 weeks' time and from then on will be tremendously busy; as far as I can see at present we are destined to be here for good altho' it's a long way from the firing line. Still till we make considerable progress up the Straits, there is no other place suitable or feasible for a base.

I am enclosing 2 or 3 snaps I bought from a chap called Collier, which are interesting. I shall send some more when I get a chance. I have not taken any more yet myself, but if I find my camera works well I shall let you have some of its productions.

We are gradually opening this place up, have got about 200 patients at present, but will soon fill up. We are putting beds in every nook and corner.

The harbour here is packed with transports; it contains more ships than it has ever had before. Our boat the *Minnewaska* was the largest boat to ever visit here. She has taken over 14 generals and the other members of the Staff to the Dardanelles.

Well, Mum, I will stop now. I trust you get all my letters safely. I should think if you addressed your letters No.15 General Hospital, Abbassia Schools, Alexandria, they will find me, and would be forwarded on if necessary. It would save their going home to England and coming half way back again.

Best love to all at home. There are only 4 of you now - 'shemale' house!

Trusting you are all well. Don't worry, Mum, things are quite all right with Billy and me for a long time.

Yours ever,

NIGE

I expect Mona writes to you and gives you what news she has. I am afraid she feels very lonely, so far away. However, if she gets my letters fairly frequently she will not feel it quite so much.

Stephen is lucky again – this time he gets as far as Alexandria, but no further, so he just misses being present at the disastrous landing by ANZAC forces on the Gallipoli Peninsula, on 25 April 1915.

Undated Postcard from Cairo, 13 Apr 1915

Dear Child

Many thanks for your letter which was the first news of home that I received. Am very busy now so will not be able to write a long letter. Tell Mum I received two letters from her yesterday dated the end of February & which were greatly appreciated. We are off tomorrow for an unknown destination. It is either Alexandria or the Dardanelles. We may not go further than Alexandria for a while but of course will eventually go on to [blank] at 6am tomorrow morning. Tell Mum I will write whenever a chance occurs but we are now only carrying only that which is ordered under active service conditions. Give my love to Gran, Aunt Mog & heaps & heaps to Matee-Boo & yourself. Don't forget my address No 3872 Gunner S P Boulton, No 1 Section, Divisional Ammunition Column, Aust & New Zealand Army Corps. From Tootie.

Undated Postcard, Mena Camp, 13 Apr 1915

Dear Matee Boo

This is me and how I look now. Cost me 30 piastres to have this done (about 6/-). Am leaving Mena Camp at 6am tomorrow morning, will write as often as possible. Probably won't get beyond Alexandria but we can't tell. Am well and happy. Heaps of love to all from Tootie.

Gunner Stephen Boulton in Egypt, April 1915
(Picture Courtesy Julia Woodhouse)

Postcard, postmarked Alexandria, 18 April 1915, 3.30pm

Dear Gran

Have got as far as Alexandria. It is much better than Mena Camp at Cairo. No sand and we are encamped right along the sea shore. Expect to go any minute and are under 5 hours' notice to move when ordered. However don't suppose we will go for a week or so. We are all enjoying Alexandria after Cairo. Get a swim nearly every day which is very enjoyable. Much love to all at Coolah from Steve.

Postcard, postmarked Alexandria, 18 April 1915, 8.30pm

Dear Matee-Boo

Are now having a good time here and like it much better than Cairo. Are under active service conditions and are only allowed to carry a change of under clothing and what we can manage to smuggle into a rolled overcoat. Our kit bags have been taken from us & sent to the base. We very nearly left but were called back after getting on the boat.⁵⁷ Will write at more length when occasion occurs. Much love from TOOTS. Send some papers over here sometime.

No 15 General Hospital, Abbassia Schools, Alexandria, 19 Apr 1915

Alexandria, Postcard sent as Steve leaves for Gallipoli, 1915.
(The mark shows censorship at work. Picture Courtesy Julia Woodhouse)

Dearest Mother

Bang has gone another week! It has been a pretty busy one too. We are beginning to have something to do, and before long expect to be up to our eyes in work. I have 24 beds at present, nearly all full and practically every one of them bad cases. Nearly all Australians, who have been brought from Lemnos, where they have been waiting for orders. Several pneumonias, 2 abscesses on the lung, a rheumatic fever, a tuberculous pleurisy, a sunstroke, a Bright's disease, a chap with phthisis, who I am afraid is sent for.

They were very battered after 3 days travelling being transhipped from place to place, when they arrived. The next morning, however, they were transformed men. It was a positive treat to behold them. They are all going to pull thro' I think except the phthisis. I am much pleased with my cases. As I have complete charge of them, it is great experience. There will be some wounded in before long, and then we shall have a pretty busy time of it.

We are very comfortable here in tents, very fine and roomy marquees. There are 5 of us in ours, and there's tons of room. They are: Dancy⁵⁸, Campion (the

---

57 This was the *Minnewaska*, the ship which had brought Nigel from England. The ship sailed from Alexandria on 18 April on its first trip to the Dardanelles, transporting the command and some troops of the 1ˢᵗ Australian Division. The ship stood off Gallipoli after landing the troops for the assault on 25 April. The ship eventually hit a mine on 29 Nov 1916 and was beached on Crete.

58 J H Dancy, Captain in the R.A.M.C. in 1916, was a graduate of the University of London in 1911. See pics on page 94, 95 & 129.

Australian), Collier, and a little Welsh weakling called Evans[59] and myself. All decent lads. Collier is a very delicate chap, and wouldn't be much good on service I should think. Dancy altho' a big chap about 6ft. 1 is not at all strong. Not many of our crowd here would do as infantry officers, I'm afraid. However, they will be all right down here at the base, where we shall remain as far as I can see for good.

Capt J H Dancy & Lieut Nigel Boulton at Mustafa Pacha Camp, April 1915
(Picture Courtesy Julia Woodhouse)

Our last mail we heard yesterday has been carried on to Lemnos, so we shall have to wait till the transport carrying them returns. It's very disappointing and aggravating. The Government doesn't care, I suppose, much about whether letters, etc. reach their various destinations or when the troops receive them, altho' the poor wretches are doing their darnedest for their country. My letters to you will be censored from now on, so I shall not be able to give you any information that is of interest of how we are progressing in this part of the world. I haven't had a letter from you since I left England, that is over 6 weeks ago. It's a long time, Mum. I do hope later on the letters will come more regularly. I think if you address all your letters from now on here, they will eventually find me and it will save a lot of time, as it means an additional month if they have to be forwarded on by the Commonwealth offices.

I still manage to get down to Stanley Bay, a nice little sandy bay where we have been bathing since our arrival in Alexandria, pretty often. It is about an hour from here, but it is worth it and when the day is hot it is very refreshing.

I have had a rotten time with the dysentery, as the Tommies call it, and had to go on very low diet for a week, but I managed to do my job just the same. It is rather weakening and pulled me down a bit. However, I have now got completely over it and am eating like a horse and feeling very fit.

We should get a mail again this week, I am greatly looking forward to a letter from Mona as I haven't heard from her for over a fortnight, and am also hoping that some of your letters that she is forwarding will come too.

---

59 Identity unknown: many doctors named Evans served in R.A.M.C.

I haven't heard a word about Billy and am most anxious to hear when he is likely to arrive, what his regiment is and his battalion and company. I have not managed to get to Cairo yet, and am afraid my chances as time goes on will become more remote. However, if I can learn exactly where he is and where to look for him, it is something tangible to work upon.

Well, Mum, my news from now on won't be very exciting, I fear, as when we get busy our life will become pretty much the same thing day after day. Still I shall write each mail.

R.A.M.C. Doctors, Stanley Beach, Alexandria, March 1915
(Dr Rowland Campion (centre, at rear) & Dr Nigel Boulton (far right). Others possibly Dr W T Collier, a Dr Evans & Dr J H Dancy. Picture Courtesy Julia Woodhouse)

Best love to all at home, trusting you are all quite well, and are not worrying your soul cases out about Steve. Bestest love, dearest Mother,

Always yours, NIGE

The two brothers remain unaware that they have both been based in Alexandria for the past week.

Postcard dated 23 April 1915, postmarked Alexandria 24 April and Port Said 25 April

Dear Matee

Am very busy, up all last night, going hard all the time. Am well excepting for a bit of a cold which I don't think will be much. Are on board now and will be off today or tomorrow. We are doing all the loading & storing etc. I think our easy times are over now for a bit. My address does not alter, as all the letters are forwarded by the military headquarters to each unit. Give my best love to Gran, Aunt Mog and The Child hoping that everyone is well & making the best of things. I wouldn't mind being there now myself for a bit of a spell. Your watch is still going and proving very useful. Have not had any letters for a long time. Will write again if I get a chance. It is going to be colder now where we are going. Egypt wasn't so very hot except in the middle of the day. With best love to Matee-Boo hoping the Concord & Ermo are still keeping their end up. "TOOTS"

No 15 General Hospital, Abbassia Schools, Alexandria, 25 Apr 1915

Dearest Mother

I am still awaiting a letter from you. I had a letter from Mona last night in which she stated that she had posted your letters on, so they are apparently en route, and let us trust only temporarily gone astray. The mail in yesterday only contained 1 or 2 letters and a P.C. so that your letters are no doubt with the bulk of the letters wherever they have got to.

Mona tells me that Steve ought to be about here by this time. He is almost certain to have gone to Cairo some 90 miles off. If you can tell me his division, regt, Cr and Regimental number if in the ranks, I can get into communication with him, which I am most anxious to do, so that I may manage to see him if it is within the range of possibility.

The weather here is getting much hotter, and will continue to do so, now the summer is at hand. I see that a landing has been effected at Enos[60] on the Gallipoli Peninsula, and that the Australians took part, so we shall probably have a convoy of wounded in before long, from there on we ought to be pretty busy.

I lost one of my patients last night, an Australian who had contracted broncho-pneumonia, and was invalided back from Lemnos. He was here 9 days before he died and got progressively bad. He was very patient, and did not realize he was going to die, as I assured him he was going to pull thro', so altho' his illness was a painful one I think he escaped the dread of approaching death. A large number of the Australians and New Zealand forces have contracted pneumonia, which is rather a strange thing, as they are in the majority of cases superior physically to the English soldiers. It seems to be quite a severe type of the disease too. It has been suggested that it is largely due to the unsuitability of the camping site at Mena. This, however, has been abandoned I learn, and has been situated elsewhere.

---

60 Enos (now Enez) is Turkey's most westerly port in the Aegean Sea. The landing was not here but on the Gallipoli Peninsula.

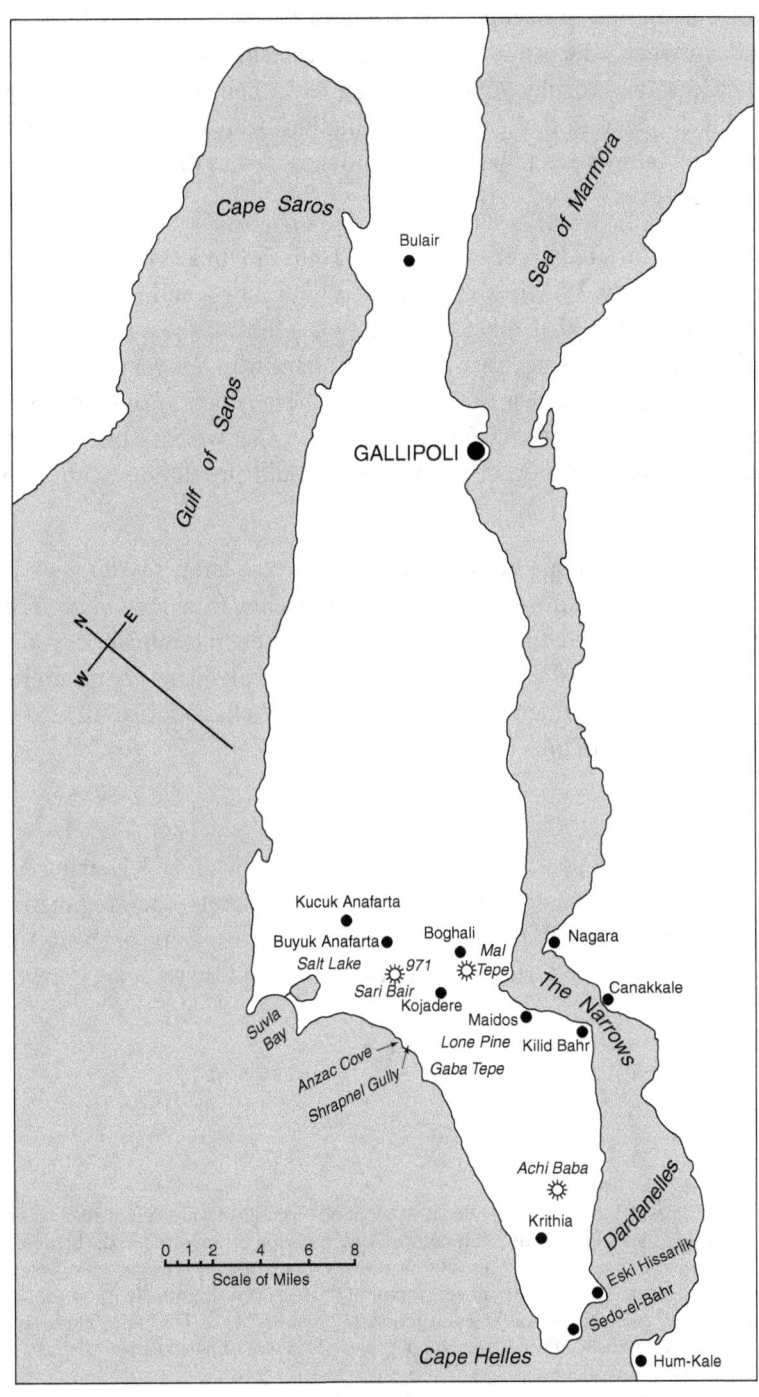

Map 5: Gallipoli Peninsula, 1915

Map © John Newland, 2015

One of our marquees occupied by some of the orderlies was burnt to the ground last week. The origin of the fire is uncertain, probably a cigarette end. All their kits and worldly goods they had with them were burnt to cinders. Since this conflagration, cigarette smoking has been absolutely forbidden in camp, so the fellows are all becoming pipe smokers, as this is countenanced as an alternative.

I am very comfortable here, eat and sleep well, tho' unless one is pretty busy, time palls horribly. We are so ill-supplied with news, and our letters are so irregular in arriving, that one feels rather cut off from the outside world. We so far have managed to secure a swim most days which is very refreshing and provides us with some degree of exercise. There is talk of our starting some tennis, but it has not got very far yet. I also hear that we have been challenged at cricket by an Alexandrian team which would provide us with a certain amount of fun.

How are you all at home? I do hope I shall have a letter by the next mail. 7 weeks is a long, long time to have been without a line from you, Mum. Trusting you are all well and that now the household has been diminished, you won't have quite as much to do. Is Aunt Mog's cottage bringing in a constant rent? It looks a sweet little cottage in the photograph.[61] Well, goodbye till next week, dearest Mum. Best of love to all,

Yours ever, NIGE

What has happened to Max Barton[62], Stirling Macansh[63], Jack Herring & Co? I wonder if you can tell me if I am liable to run across them, their regiments, and where they are stationed. It would be nice to run across some of them. You will write to me direct now, and then your letters won't be such ages en route, I trust. N.

---

61 The photograph does not survive.
62 Francis Maxwell Barton, a 21-yr-old law student of 'Nyrangie', Gladesville, signed up on 9 Oct 1914 as a 2nd Lieut with 25th Infantry. Captain Barton disappeared in the battle at Mouquet Farm in August 1916 and afterwards was sometimes reported either as wounded in hospital, or missing and presumed a captor of the Germans. Eventually it was confirmed on 21 March 1917 that he was killed in action on 11 August 1916. For more details, see the 'Beyond 1914' website of the University of Sydney. Max was a first cousin of Mrs Lee (née Nora Barton) in Wollongong.
63 Walter Stirling Macansh, a 23-yr-old stockman of Hunters Hill, was one of the earliest volunteers for service (No 147). He joined up on 2 Sep 1914 with the 2nd Light Horse Brigade, 6th Light Horse Regt. Sergeant Macansh was awarded the Distinguished Conduct Medal (London Gazette, 26 April 1917) and Mentioned in Despatches (London Gazette, 6 Jul 1917).

Max Barton & friends, Egypt, March 1916

13th Battalion officers play a game of donkey polo with hockey sticks at a camp between Cairo and the Suez Canal. Identified left to right: Captain Francis Maxwell Barton (later killed in action on 11 August 1916); Captain William James Ellery Phillips RMO; Major Edward Twynam; Lieutenant Colonel Leslie Edward Tilney DSO, VD
Source AWM C00550

Like his brother, Steve had blue eyes, but Steve's dark hair and dark complexion contrasted with Nigel's light brown hair and fair complexion. And Steve was a much smaller man. At 5 ft 9¼ ins tall, he was more than 2 inches shorter than Nigel and also very slightly-built: he weighed only 130 lbs (9 st 4 lbs, or just under 59 kg). In a word, he was skinny. His doctor brother worried how Steve would cope with the heavy physical work of an artillery gunner.

No 15 General Hospital, Abbassia School, Alexandria, 2 May 1915

Dearest Mother

Your letters of the early part of Feby came to hand 2 or 3 days ago, and altho' they were nearly 3 months old, by George they were appreciated, I can tell you.

Thank Aunt Mog very much for hers, I must write her one in answer to it when an opportunity offers. I shan't have to wait so long for my letters from you when they are addressed here direct, but that will be some time yet.

I was immensely interested to hear of Steve and his joining. So he has chosen the Artillery. I wonder how he will get on, and whether he will like it. A gunner has a lot of bullocky work to do. He wants to be pretty active at the same time, as it takes a bit of doing hoisting a 100 lb. shell into the breech of a gun, 4 times every minute. Ammunition of any character is pretty solid to lift. However, I daresay when Steve gets used to it, it will do him a wonderful deal of good as Menzies[64] says. Steve's officers will probably spot the possibilities of each man, and will detail him for a driver or range finder, etc. It is a most interesting branch of the service, and one that requires a devil of a lot of training so as you

---

64 The reference is unclear.

say I don't expect Steve will be wanted for a long time as we are very well off for artillery in this Dardanelles business.

This letter won't be a very long one, Mum, not as long as I should like it to be, as we are all up to our eyes in work at present.

The first convoy of wounded arrived 3 days ago, and the wounded have been pouring in pretty consistently ever since. Nearly all the casualties that have arrived so far have been Australians. Our fellows have done splendidly, and are doing all that is required of them. Our casualties, however, have been heavy I'm afraid; we have little idea yet what they are, and won't know for some weeks. Some appalling cases have come in. We have got pretty well all the worst cases here. You can have no idea how shockingly mutilated some of our poor fellows are. The modern weapons of destruction make awful wounds. Our chaps have behaved magnificently and are so cheerful and brave. The English chaps are positively amazed at the Australians. They are the most magnificent men they have ever seen, I heard a chap say the other day. All of them are terribly upset at being put out of action so soon, and are asking most anxiously every day for news of "the boys". Those fellows who are only slightly wounded, bullet wounds of thighs, legs, arms, etc. are only after 3 days chafing to get back again.

The English regiments have been losing very heavily too I hear. A large number of casualties occurred at the landing which was a perilous undertaking really, and probably would not have been effected if the Germans were opposed to us instead of Turks. A large number of casualties occurred as a result of Turkish snipers, who hid in bushes and undergrowth and let our fellows run over them. They potted our chaps as they ran by. A good number of these were caught and bayonetted, but still they wrought a lot of havoc. A good number of them were dressed in Indian uniforms and Australian uniforms and it was very difficult to be certain what was happening.

The Lancashire and Dublin Fusiliers got it very hot, I hear. I heard one report this morning that the Lancashire have only 200 men left out of a battalion of 1000 men. In the Dublins 26 out of 29 officers were killed or wounded. However, now landings have been successfully made in several points, matters will improve and it should not be more than a few weeks before Constantinople is at our feet.

Arthur Champion[65] is in the hospital here. He has a bullet in his left knee joint, and a bullet graze along the top of his scalp, a narrow squeak. I spotted him as

---

65   Lieut Arthur Champion, an old boy of The King's School and a 29-yr-old clerk of Sydney when he enlisted in 1914, was wounded at the Gallipoli landing, wounded in France, and sent back to Australia in September 1916.

soon as I saw him, but he had forgotten me, but remembered me quite well afterwards. He is the only one of the family who has come. Dave and the other brother are working a farm which is just beginning to realize something after 4 years hard work, and they didn't feel it incumbent on them to give up their livelihood at present.[66]

I heard of Max Barton and Syd Herring[67] from 2 or 3 men in the hospital. Max was very popular with them as "he smoked very good cigarettes. They were both quite safe and sound when these chaps last saw them and both got safely ashore. You might tell Mrs. Barton in case she has not heard that all is well with Max.

I hear today that we are making wonderfully good progress, and that the warships are right up the narrows. News here is terribly scarce, we hear less than in England. We depend on French communiqués, and scraps we learn from the wounded.

Well, dearest Mum, must stop now. I am having wonderful experience tho' very gruesome work.

Love to all at home. Thank Aunt Mog for her letter, I will try and answer it soon, we may not be quite so busy in a few days, when the rush expends itself.

Yours ever, NIGE

I am looking after the officers at present; am assisting chap. We have 30 cases, all pretty bad ones. I have 24 other beds besides, so I am pretty busy. The wounds, when they are severe, take such a lot of time to dress, ¼ hour each, it mounts up.

After a voyage taking about a week, Stephen is anchored off Gallipoli, about 720 miles or 1150 km from Alexandria, aboard a ship loaded with ammunition. The

---

66 Arthur's two younger brothers enlisted in the AIF and both were killed on the Western Front, in 1916 and 1918.
67 Sydney Charles Edgar Herring was an older brother of Jack Herring, and belonged to the Australian militia from 1904. He was a 33-yr-old estate agent of Gladesville when war broke out, and he enlisted as a Captain with 21st Infantry on 9 October 1914. Mentioned in Despatches (London Gazette, 28 Jan 1916), As Lieut Col, awarded DSO (London Gazette, 1 Jan 1917) and Mentioned in Despatches (London Gazette, 4 Jan 1917 and 28 Dec 1917); as Temp Brigadier General, for outstanding leadership, he was awarded French Croix de Guerre (London Gazette, 7 Jan 1919) and awarded Order of St Michael and St George (London Gazette, 3 Jun 1919) Mentioned in Despatches (London Gazette, 31 Dec 1918 and 11 Jul 1919). He died in 1951, aged about 70.

Australian troops have landed ashore by this time so, although his letter is dated 4 iv 1915, he must have meant 4 v 1915. The horses he talks about landing are those used to haul the artillery guns.

'Minneapolis', 4 May 1915

My dear Matee

Am in another continent now. I don't know whether you will ever get this letter as no mails seem to be coming or going. Also if censored they may take exception to some of the things I have said and not forward it on. For that reason I don't think I will tell you where we are.

HMT *Minneapolis*, Alexandria, 1915
Source: NLA 15784 78 nla.obj-140978839, PIC 1578478

We are still on board ship the *Minneapolis*, one of the Atlantic Transport Line trading between Liverpool and America in times of peace. We are not treated nearly so well as regards food as on the Australian Transports, but the English Tommies on board say it is quite up to standard and what they generally get. We pulled up and anchored close to the shore with the warships all round us bombarding and pounding away at the batteries ashore.

We had a wonderful view for 2 days. The big naval guns roar and roar all day but especially at night for all they know. Great bursts of flame burst out of the muzzles and then a few seconds after comes a deafening roar like a clap of thunder. From where we were we could see the shells bursting on the hills, and sending up huge clouds of dust 15 to 20 miles away.

A German aeroplane came over the top of us in the bay and drooped 3 bombs, but all fell harmlessly into the sea. It made a bolt away then, with a few shots after it from our guns on the destroyers. The enemy must be getting a terrible doing just here on shore as our gun fire is pretty continuous and the only reply we get back is a few shells which have, since we have been here, done no damage, but fallen into the sea. They send up a huge column of spray and water. When they hit, it is an awe-inspiring sight and one stands looking at it all and never thinks about a shell falling near yourself. All the men crowded up and gaped over the rail to see things and when a shell landed from the shore near us great cheering takes place. As we have rather a precious and important cargo we were ordered to anchorage 5 miles away out of the fire zone. Here it is deadly with the dull booming going on but nothing to see.

We never hear any news of how things are going ashore. The sailors off the boats are not allowed to tell anything. Of course we hear a few things, but they are not always to be believed. The Australians have landed a few miles up the coast and are doing and fighting well which is always the first questions asked by us here.

Sir Ian Hamilton has a great opinion of the Aust. soldiers. Our turn to land will come soon I expect. You all in Australia are getting more news than we do here and probably know how things are going. You will I think in future only get a Field Service P.C. to say I am well etc. as letters are barred, anyway they tell us so, and whenever a mail is to go they issue these post cards out to us to send. I am feeling well now and have quite got rid of my cold which only lasted about 3 days.

Am not getting any fatter now, in fact the men seem to be looking thinner in the face since they left Egypt, due probably to the cutting down of the food. I could do a good feed now myself. This stinginess on the part of the English Transports makes the men very loyal to Australia and Australian foodstuffs. No wonder they say there is no other country like it.

How is everyone at home? It is now 4 months since I enlisted. I received 2 letters about a week ago just as we were coming away, from you and the Child, dated March 20th and 24th. Everything seems to be going on much as usual. Don't forget to send some *Sunday Times* or other newspapers as we never hear any news of the war or outside world.

I will have to give this letter to somebody to post and hope they will do so the first port of call they come to as there is no chance of our sending anything but the service p.c. and then at rare intervals.

Give my best love to Gran and Aunt Mog. I hope Gran is still well and Aunt Mog still goes into town by the 8 boat. Is the Child still going to her School? How is Pugee and Stinky Tom and Whiskers[68]; expect there are one or two more by this time to look after. It is winter I suppose by now or getting close to it with fires going in the oven. It is a nice fine warm and calm morning here

---

68   Family pets

just like Sydney mornings without any north-easters. We can see the shells and hear the roar of the guns bursting over the hills where the batteries are in action, otherwise you would not know there was a war going on.

There is a rumour that we will be landing the horses and all the gear etc, tomorrow or the next day so will close this letter up and give it to somebody to post when they go back for more troops. I hope you will get it safely. Good-bye to Matee Boo with heaps and heaps of love, hoping that you and the Child are still keeping your end up and don't get left 'hind next time. I am very well and in good spurrits and will be back soon for something to eat from

TOOTS.

P.S. Find out if the Defence Department are paying into my account at the Bank fortnightly 3/- a day, the allotment of my pay I left behind. It ought to be about £2.2.0. The £10 I had sent over from Sydney to the Anglo Egyptian Bank at Cairo is still there as far as I know, as I didn't require it while I was there and wasn't able to get in there during banking hours to find out if it was available for me to draw. I wrote to the Manager and asked him just as we were coming away, but didn't get any reply so far. I will leave it there for a while in case I should want it. I have an idea that when we have fixed up Turkey we shall be left here to garrison the place; but of course I don't know. Love from

TOOTS.

No 15 General Hospital, Alexandria, 9 May 1915

My dearest Mother

Your last letter came to hand 2 days ago, sent on by Mona. Also Steve's photograph, which I shall treasure. He looks well in his uniform, which gives him quite an appearance of physical fitness. I am sure he will pick up wonderfully on the voyage, and it is an excellent thing to have got his vaccn. and inoculn. over before embarking, so that he won't have it to pull him down on the way over. I am sorry to hear his quarters are so stuffy and crowded, but I expect the troops will spend most of their time on deck and will sleep there in the tropics. What an experience for Billy; he won't like settling down to bank work again when things are over.

I am sure you must feel his loss very keenly, Mum, and miss him terribly at home, altho' he was only there for his dinner, bed and breakfast as a rule. He will be back much sooner, however, than he otherwise would if he had enlisted earlier. Perhaps I shall follow him soon afterwards, so you will have both your sons back again once more from the other end of the world. The British forces here are very well represented as far as artillery goes, infantry troops are what are needed more than anything so the drafts of Australian artillery will not be urgently needed for a bit as far as I can see. When Steve is ready for service, if the war still continues, things will be so much in our favour by that time that the risk will be at a minimum of anything happening to him.

Gunner S P Boulton, 28 Feb 1915
(Picture Courtesy Julia Woodhouse)

The fighting in the Dardanelles which commenced a fortnight ago today has been of an appalling character. The casualties have been awful. This I believe was to be expected. So far I believe the semi-official figures are 12,000. The Turks probably have lost more than this number, altho' they still infest the country over there like rabbits. Several battalions comprising over 1,000 men have only now 3 or 4 hundred left. One N.Z. battalion only numbered 300 men when the roll was called after some terrific fighting. The Dublin Fusiliers lost 26 out of 29 officers. The carnage has been truly awful. Now that we have secured a firm foothold and are landing additional forces daily things will improve immensely.

The country is very wild and rough and affords exceedingly good cover, and consequently mounted troops will not be of much service. A very large number of our losses have accrued from the prevalence of Turkish snipers. These are very well concealed and exhibit great boldness and daring. They allow our troops to advance right over them and as they are disguised in various Indian and Australian uniforms they are difficult to distinguish and extinguish. These snipers collect the identification discs of the fellows they shoot like so many scalps. It is believed that there is a bonus given for each one. A Turkish sniper was discovered in a little shelter with 2 boxes of ammunition, and enough food to last 3 weeks with 14 of these discs. He was bayonetted without scruple. 2 German officers were caught and shot at sight, one crying "mercy!" Under

German leadership and organization every conceivable and diabolical trick is indulged in by the Turks.

Our troops have received orders to take no prisoners, a drastic but necessary measure, which probably is modified on occasions. I have been terribly busy for the last fortnight since the wounded began to pour in. We have dealt with some 1500 cases, which is good going considering how fearfully understaffed we are. On the 2nd day we had 1070 cases in hospital, that is 30 above our complement. We accommodated the surplus in marquees, and drafted thither the more slightly wounded.

The fortitude, pluck and philosophical bearing of our men is positively astounding. We have nearly all Australians and New Zealand wounded. It is in hospital, away from the glamour and excitement of action that one gets a true estimate of the spirit of our men and one marvels again and again at them. I don't think Australia need worry about racial decadence as far as physical courage and stamina go. The English fellows here - the Medl. officers, I mean - are literally amazed and dumbfounded at the calm philosophy of the colonials. How they submit with unflinching cheeriness and calm philosophy to the enucleation of one or two eyes, to the amputation of a limb, or other operations involving a lifelong mutilation, is truly magnificent. The inherent sporting spirit is revealed in its true nakedness. The work is very gruesome, Mum, and depressing, but one will get to a certain degree hardened to it, I suppose, in time. It brings the tears to your eyes at times tho', when one realizes for a minute that these men one is called upon to treat and patch up are your own flesh and blood, your own country-men; but the tears are caused by the wonderful pride one feels in being a Britisher. It is not difficult to understand in moments like these that the British Empire is what it is, and why it is.

Well, Mum, I must go and see a case, one of a depressed comminuted fracture of the frontal region of the skull. The brain is exposed and macerated. The chap won't live, I'm afraid, perhaps it is for the best. I will finish this off later on tonight.

Well, Mum, to resume - I have just seen Arthur Champion, he has been operated upon today, and a shrapnel bullet removed from the region of the knee joint. I saw the X-ray photograph of it, and from what I could make out, the bullet was lying just outside. He may have a bit of a stiff knee, but should have a perfectly useful joint for all practical purposes.

Sir Ian Hamilton is in charge of the Dardanelles operations and says he will require 250,000 men to complete the job. Up to the present he has only 70,000 or thereabouts. All the mounted Australians and N.Z. forces here are being sent over as infantry. Their horses left this side of the water. They will do quite well as infantry, altho' they are rather disappointed at having to abandon their nags after all the care and attention and training they have given them. Still the country is out of the question for mounted troops at present, and Aunt Mog will be comforted to know that her poor dumb creatures will escape a lot of misery, suffering and decimation. Cavalry, now aerial reconnaissance is so efficient, have lost their greatest value, viz, reconnoitering the enemy's positions and dispositions of forces, and will soon, as far as I can see, become an ornamental rather than a useful branch of the Service.

If England had entered on her military operations in Feby, instead of waiting till the latter part of April against the Dardanelles, the landing of our forces would have been comparatively easy and many 1000's of valuable lives saved. However, owing to this dilatoriness in commencing a land attack, the Turks have been able to mobilize their men on the Peninsula and prepare strong defensive positions, which has been responsible for our extensive losses. England as far as I can gather was reckoning on Greece coming in, as Venizelos the Prime Minister assured her she would, and had mobilized an Army Corps and had arranged various bases for our forces.

Constantine and his German Queen and her Germanophile officers, however, hummed and haa'd all the time, settled in their minds that Greece was not coming in, giving the Turks the necessary time to strengthen her positions before they declared their hand. Venizelos has, of course, resigned, and we are faced with what 2 months ago would not have been a very formidable undertaking, but now is a gigantic task. So much for German intrigue and English slowness.

Well, Mum, I will stop now, I hope this long letter will reach you safely, and cheer you up a bit. Best love to all. Trust Gran is better.

Ever yours, NIGE

Postcard dated 11 May 1915

Dearest Matee

Am quite well & comfortable. Have no opportunity of writing letters. Just been told to send a postcard. Haven't had any letters for a long while. Expect to get a lot together some time. Have just seen *London Daily Mail*. War seems to be about the same in France. Would like to hear from Billy. Not a bad climate here, but cold at nights. Am still on board ship. Food is not very good. Not nearly as good as Australian Transport. Best love to Gran & Aunt Mog the Child & all the animals. Thank the Child for her last letter which came along with one of yours dated 24th March. Am not at Aden. This is the only p.c. I good [STET] raise. Love from TOOTS.

In this letter, Stephen mentions the Indian regiments involved in the war, which was the world's first truly global conflict, due to the web of interlocking alliances and colonial connections between countries. Without it being an exhaustive list, the Boulton brothers' letters mention the names of various countries caught up in the fighting: England, Scotland, Wales, Ireland, Australia, New Zealand, South Africa, Canada, Belgium, France, Germany, Austria, Italy, Portugal, Malta, Russia, Romania, Bulgaria, Serbia, Salonika, Greece, Turkey, Palestine, Egypt, Syria, Saudi Arabia, Mesopotamia, Crete, Cyprus, Libya, Morocco, German East Africa, India, Japan, China, USA.

S.S. 'Minneapolis', 15 May 1915

Dear Matee Boo

Am now on our way back to Alexandria once again. We didn't land on the other side after all after being there 3 weeks, dodging about from one place to another. The country was too rough for the horses and wagons and no landing facilities to speak of. I don't know what they are going to do with us now, after we have taken our horses back, as they will have to have a rest for a bit.

There are rumours that we will be turned into a mule corps of some sort to transport ammunition or stores. Mules are of great use in the rough country and can go where horses can't. They are used a lot chiefly by the Indian regiments.

All the men are fairly fed up with all the humbugging about we get, and our corps is nick-named a "circus" instead of a "column" by them. It will be good to get back to a town and off this ship. The food is not the best by any means and only a few things can be bought at the canteen on board.

We have been away from Alexandria about 3 weeks now. This cruising about the water from one island to another and back again is quite exciting as there are enemy submarines about and there has always to be guards round the decks of the ship on the lookout all the time, day and night. At night-time we run with all lights out. We have collision drill frequently and the boats are always swung out and in readiness.

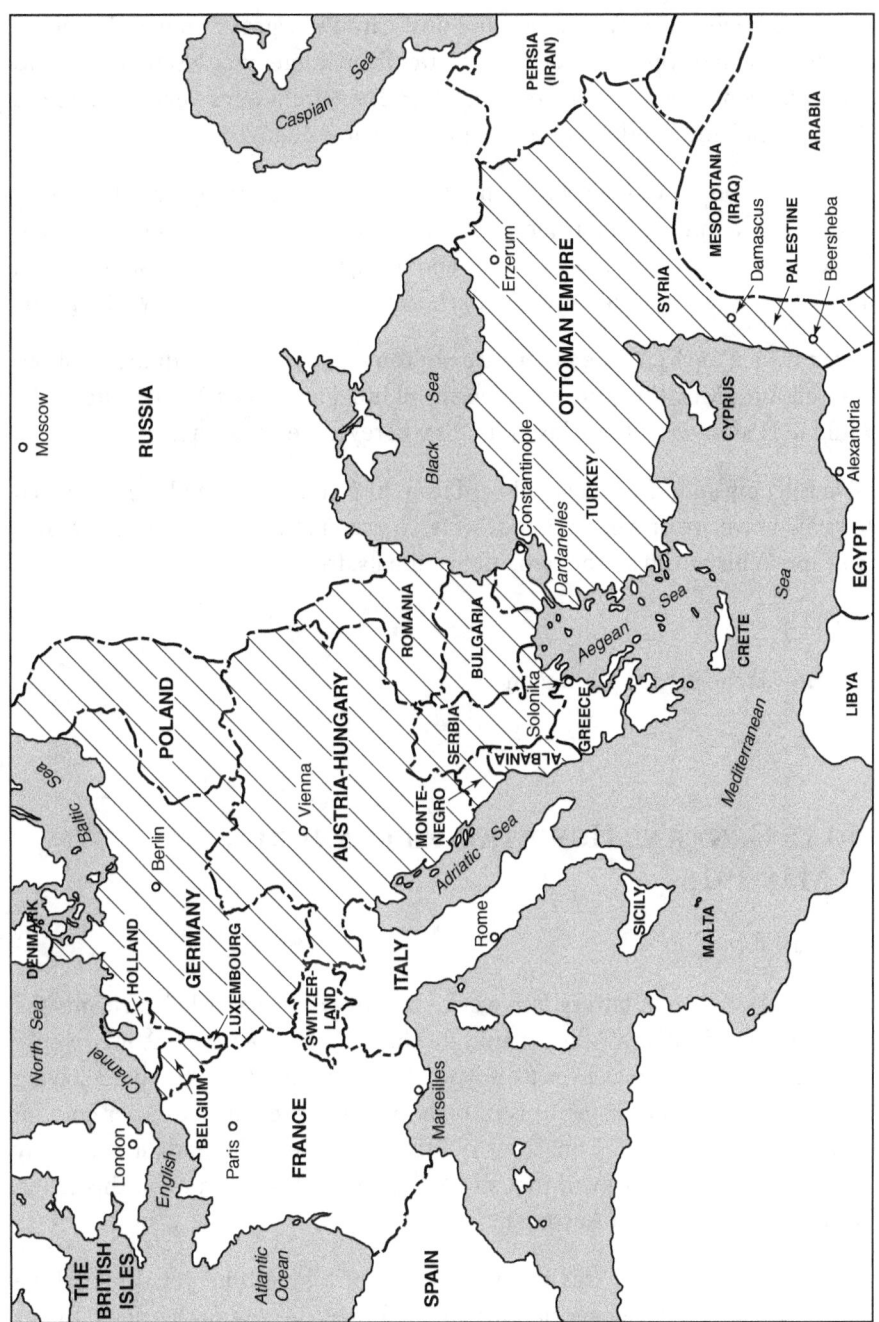

Map 6: The Great War in Europe & Middle East
Map © John Newland, 2015

Have you been getting my letters and post cards all right? Some of the letters may have been stopped. Haven't had a letter from home since last we left Egypt. Have you sent any newspapers along yet? They are always very welcome as they are read and handed on to someone else or exchanged.

I hope everyone at Coolah is well and that winter is not turning out a too trying one. It is beautiful weather here, not hot & not cold and nice mild evenings. Concord and Ermo are still let I hope and bringing in a few bob. I suppose you and Aunt Mog are still talking about the beautiful farms with the cows & pigs etc.

Give my love to Gran, hope there are not too many dangerous draughts about and tell Aunt Mog there are some beautiful fungi in Turkey. I will write to the Child next after we get to Alexandria or wherever we are going.

Give Billy my address, I haven't heard from him yet. We are no longer allowed to say who we are or what our address is, so I can't tell him. Best love to Matee Boo and Whisky and all the remaining animals, from

TOOTS.

P.S. How is the garden getting on?

No 15 General Hospital, Alexandria, 17 May 1915

My dearest Mother

I received 2 of your letters last week, which were forwarded on from the Commonwealth offices. Many thanks for them. Altho' they were 9 or 10 weeks old still it is very nice to hear from you. Am sorry that Gran has been having such trouble with her chest, it is to be hoped that she will shake her cold off before the winter comes on. Poor old thing, I expect she finds it extremely trying. Let's trust, however, that she will be herself when you get this letter. How is the recruiting in Australia?

I am afraid, Mum, that this war will go on for a long time yet. We shall be very fortunate if peace negotiations are on foot at the end of this year. Things are more or less stationary at the Dardanelles as far as I can gather and the fighting there is developing into trench warfare as in France. This means a slow business. The Turks are bringing up big guns and there is every prospect of our progress being slow and tedious. We want a large number of men still, and until there are considerable reinforcements nothing in the shape of a general advance can be made.

It has been a very costly business so far, and the papers at home, at least some of them, are very severe on Churchill for having precipitated naval operations without any support at all by land. It has enabled the Turks to make every conceivable preparation for defence. Altho' the policy up till now re the Dardanelles has been a very short-sighted one not to say somewhat of a big blunder, I hardly think Churchill is responsible for the whole thing. I think Fisher at least backed him up.[69]

The Germans if one looks at things from an absolutely unbiased viewpoint aren't doing so badly, considering they're fighting practically the world. We hear all sorts of things about their being starved, etc. etc. but as a matter of fact they aren't doing so badly I believe and can hang out for a long time yet. The war in France has practically come to a standstill and altho' we make progress from time to time it is only a matter of some 500 yards, and at this rate it will take a long time to drive the Germans back on to their frontier. If Italy comes in it will probably bring the end a good deal closer. However, altho' the populace generally there seem to be markedly in favour of war, if this Dardanelles business looks as if it is going to be a long job, Italy probably will wait a while before throwing in her chances with our side. She wants to make sure she is supporting the winning side before she sinks her all.

The last 2 or 3 days have not been so fearfully busy. We have despatched as many wounded as can travel to hospital ships to England. This will give us more room to take more from the firing line. Only those cases are being sent to England who will not be able to fight again for 2 or 3 months and are in a fit condition to travel. A good number of Australians are among these, and they are very fortunate to be going as they will be treated very well at home and be made much of. It will be a delightful time of year to visit England.

I have had one or two sad cases during the last week. I had 6 deaths in 48 hours. One chap died ½ hour after admission, 30 died on the hospital ship coming here. It is very depressing work, Mum, and one does not want to think too much of what one sees at times. I had one fellow a Scotchman in the 5th Royal Scots who had been recommended for the Distinguished Service Medal for gallant conduct before he was hit. He was wounded by a bullet in the thigh, and the wound became infected with a very virulent organism, and he developed what is termed malignant oedema. We told him we were afraid we would have

---

69 Churchill's disastrous plan for the Gallipoli campaign cost him his job with the government as First Lord of the Admiralty and he returned to active army service on the Western Front.

to amputate at the thigh, otherwise he would lose his life. His condition at the time was so critical that an operation was deemed unwise straightaway, but he was to be bucked up as far as possible with stimulants and subcutaneous salines so that the operation could be performed the same night.

He willingly consented as he said he knew we were deciding for the best. He confided to me that he wasn't sorry he had come out and was to lose his leg as he had done something for his country. I could see the poor chap was doomed as his condition was rapidly getting worse, but I cheered him up all I knew and told him how proud his people would be of him when he got home. He didn't know he was going to die, so I didn't see any point about telling him, he seemed quite happy. He died quite suddenly shortly afterwards, from secondary internal haemorrhage, a large blood vessel had been eaten into by the spreading gangrene and he remarked a few seconds before that he felt a little bit thirsty! He was a rare plucky 'un, Mum, and no mistake. There are lots of cases like this and it makes you very sad and you realize more and more what a hellish business war is.

Mona sent me a small parcel 2 or 3 days ago containing socks, cocoa, boot laces and handkerchiefs. They were all most acceptable and will be most useful. I am very well provided for here and have nothing at all to grumble at. Wonder what has happened to Steve? You seem to think he will be going to England straight, in which case we shall not meet. Does he know my address, as I would like to write him a letter now and then? Will stop now, dearest Mum, Love to all at home. Hope you aren't very depressed and worried. Hope these letters of mine cheer you up a bit. Who knows, the War may crumple up as suddenly as it began.

Best love, Mum, Always yours, NIGE

No 15 General Hospital, Alexandria, 26 May 1915

Dearest Mother

I am not sure when the mail goes this week, but I trust this letter will not have long to wait after it is posted.

I got a letter from you last week and was very pleased to hear that you have really got a good tenant for Ermington. I do hope, Mum, he will prove as satisfactory as you expect. It is very trying and annoying to a degree about

Concord. What bad luck you seem to have had with tenants. How harassing and worrying it must be for anyone who has a number of houses to let, when the tenants prove to be brutes. I wonder if you are still thinking of making a trip to England, or whether the idea has proved impracticable.

I had a post card from Steve last week; it was addressed to Dover, and was forwarded on to me by Mona. It was written 5 weeks before I received it. He didn't tell me where he was, except that he was one of the Divisional Ammunition Column. A fairly safe job, as so little progress has been made on the Peninsula as yet, nearly all the ammunition I understand from various sources is being shipped by boat to the Peninsula, and then being carried up by hand to the trenches, and earth works in the firing line. Steve will be on a boat going backwards and forwards with the ammunition, etc. The column has not landed so far; in fact it is too risky yet to chance a landing till we push the Turks back a bit as every precaution has to be taken to prevent it falling into the enemy's hands. I heard from a patient I have at present in one of my wards, who is suffering from pneumonia and is one of the Column, he belongs to No.2 Section, that he wouldn't be surprised if Steve isn't at Mex Camp at present, that is 4 or 5 miles out of Alexandria, waiting to be sent across again when the next supply of ammunition is required. I wrote to Billy immediately after I got his P.C. and gave him my address, and if he is close handy he should have got it by now. However, I haven't heard from him yet. So you see, Mum, there is nothing to worry you at present re Steve's safety. As long as he remains with the Column he is pretty right. There is not much chance of his being detailed for gun work, as he has had so little training.

The heat is getting pretty considerable. Today is a swelterer. It will be pretty trying here in the summer. Next month I believe is one of the hottest. We have all got helmets. I wonder if Steve has. Those felt hats are nice and shady, but they are not as good as the helmet. I see a lot of the colonial troops have had the topees issued to them. I expect Steve will be provided with one too.

What a tremendous boon it is Italy coming in when she did. She could not have declared war at a more inopportune time as far as Germany and Austria are concerned. The Austro-German army have driven the Russians back a 100 miles on their eastern front, and are doing well; the Germans were holding their own in the western theatre of war, and the Turks are putting up an obstinate resistance in Gallipoli Peninsula. Italy coming in at this moment will relieve the pressure on the Russians a great deal and probably mean shortening the war by several months. However, it won't affect the Germans very much for one or two months at least, as it will take the Italian army all this time to mobilize on her frontier. Austria will feel things pretty acutely soon, as she will be attacked below by Serbia, on the west by Italy and on the east by Russia. I think we shall be very fortunate if this war is over by the end of the year, as the Germans are doing very well and are far from even considering that they are being beaten yet.

I am having excellent experience at this hospital, and have some very good cases indeed. I think I have some of the best medical cases in the hospital. Medical cases in the army are very good practice, as they are practically all acute. All the men are in excellent health and thus you don't get the good old chronics that largely fill civil hospitals, viz. chr. rheumatisms, asthmatics, chr. bronchitis, sciaticas, lumbagos, various nervous diseases, etc.

I have also good chances of doing surgical operations every now and then, as the surgical cases are largely in excess of medl. cases when a rush of wounded come in. I did a skull case the night before last, a bullet entered the top of the skull, passed thro' the back part of the brain and came out thro' the occipital bone at the top of the neck. The wound of exit in the skull consisted of shattered bone with loose pieces of bone lying under the scalp, and a portion of the occipital lobe of the brain protruding! I cut down over both wounds, enlarging the incisions, removed the fragments of loose bone, took away the piece of protruding brain, inserted a gauze drain in the top wound and a rubber tube in the lower. The man is quite conscious and only complains of bad headaches. He is suffering from meningitis as track of the bullet is septic. He may recover and has been given an improved chance by the operation. He thanked me after he came round and said his headache, which was excruciating before, was ever so much better since operation. There have been some truly remarkable cases in this hospital since we started here.

Weil Mum, I must stop now. I shall write again next week, when I may have some more news of Steve. Love to all at home, trusting Gran is keeping well. Best of love, Mum,

Ever yours, NIGE

Cleopatra Camp, Alexandria, 27 May 1915

Dearest Matee Boos

You will see I am back again in Alexandria once more safe and sound. We left Alexandria on the 24th April for the Dardanelles with horses and ammunition for our batteries. The whole column complete. We anchored at Lemnos Island (about 3 hours sail from the entrance to the Dardanelles) used as a sort of base.

We stayed there for 3 days and then went on to the entrance right alongside the shore where the bombardment was going on.

Some enemy shells lobbed in the water pretty close but didn't hit. It was a great sight for all of us and no one took any heed of the shells which might of got us at any minute. We lay there all day and the night, and the following day unloaded some of our ammunition into a tender. That afternoon we were ordered to move away to a safer anchorage owing to our dangerous cargo, should it get in the way of a Turkish shell, so we proceeded to Tenedos Island about 10 miles away and out of range. Here we lay anchored for 8 days doing nothing which became very monotonous. Then went back to the entrance again for orders which soon came aboard and sent us back to Lemnos.

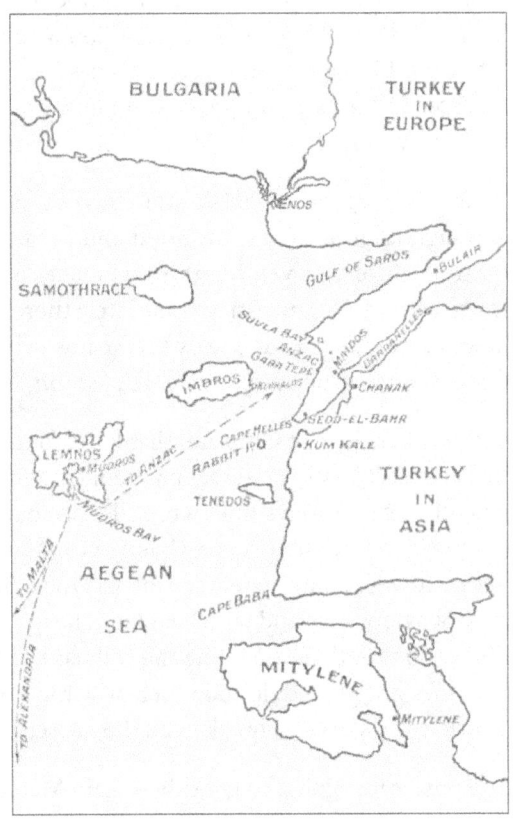

Map 7: Aegean Sea, 1915

Adapted from New Zealand Electronic Text Collection, WaiNewZ069a

A submarine attack was expected hourly so we got right inside the harbour with all lights out. The lights were put out very suddenly and frightened the horses a bit. The noise was deafening, comprised of their stamping, neighing and jumping about in their stalls. Nothing occurred throughout the night. Next day we went back to the Gallipoli Peninsula this time to where the Australian and New Zealand Army Corps had landed. Our men were doing very well indeed, but lost pretty heavily during the landing. We unloaded some more ammn here and then left once more for Lemnos. Another boat came alongside the next day and took off the remaining ammn and we brought on 44 mules. There was no likelihood of our column landing with the horses as the country was too rough and mountainous and not fit for them and wagons. The men were pretty fed up and disappointed.

Am sorry to hear of all the trouble Concord has given. I should think it quite the best to use the furniture you want in Ermo and store the rest in my room. It ought to let better unfurnished, although you won't get so much of course, but then you will have less worry as you won't have the tenants smashing it up bit by bit. Living at Ermo will be pretty deadly all on your own I should think. You couldn't get somebody to go along and stay with you and help potter in the garden. Wonder how the old man will turn out?

I wish the war would finish tomorrow so as we all could come home again, although I haven't done any good and as far as I can see will not be required for some little time yet. It is this that makes it seem so monotonous and such a waste of time. Our turn may come later; there is no hope of an ending for a very long time as far as I can see by the headway being made. However, I think the Germans must soon begin to feel the strain, but will die hard.

Give my best love to Gran and thank her for the letters, and Aunt Mog, hoping there are still plenty of Ramalinas being found. I didn't see any on the Pyramids when I went up. The stones were all worn bare and shiny with the climbing of so many tourists and people. Give the Child my love and tell her I will write to her next week, and remember me to Doos, Tom and Pug[70], hoping that they are not a noosance and with heaps and heaps of love and kisses on the cheek to Matee Boos left 'hind, hoping she still has her masses of hair still under control and does not go and do too much at Ermo on the formation of the farm until Tootie comes back to break in all the horses.

The post is just going so good-bye again Matee, from

Your loving son, TOOTS.

No 15 General Hospital, Alexandria, 31 May 1915

Dearest Mother

I haven't got a letter from you this week yet, but hope to in the next few days. I am also expecting a letter from Mona, so perhaps both letters will come by the same mail. Letters are tremendously acceptable and I look forward to your letters each week, Mum, just as much as you look forward to mine.

---

70 The family's pet dogs

I was walking along one of the streets of the town with Dancy, a chap I have made great friends with since I have been with this hospital, two or three afternoons ago, when a voice croaked in my ear 'Hullo Billy!' It was Steve. He arrived here at the end of March, and then went on to Cairo. From there he went with the Divisional Ammunition Column to the Dardanelles. He called at Lemnos and visited Tenedos and cruised about the Aegean Sea and then returned here, it being considered impracticable to land their horses which they had taken over to horse the artillery. He was very disappointed, I believe. However, he has been stationed here now and is encamped at a place called Cleopatra, 2 or 3 miles out of town and on the coast, quite a nice spot as they always get more or less of a sea breeze, and it is accordingly much cooler than where I am, as we are right in the heart of the native quarters and about a mile from the sea. He gets two bathes a day which is a great boon. He looked well-tanned, tho' a bit frail. However, he appears quite well and in spite of the heat and occasional attacks of diarrhoea I think he must have improved wonderfully in health since he left Australia. He is not fat and I don't think ever will be, as he is one of the lean kind. I think the life is doing him a great deal of good and you will be very pleased with his appearance when he returns to sunny N.S.W. He was delighted to meet me, I think, altho' it is difficult to be sure Steve is delighted at anything.

We went and had some omelettes, tea and bread and butter, and ice cream at a café, and filled in time for a couple of hours till it was time for Billy to return to camp at 9.30. It was very nice meeting one another and if Steve is to be here some time we shall probably be able to spend a good deal of time together. He came up to the hospital yesterday, Sunday, and as I had the afternoon pretty free, we went off to the Nouzha Gardens, some 3 miles out and spent an enjoyable couple of hours there. They are beautiful gardens, full of tropical plants, shrubs and palms. Some of the blooms are positively gorgeous. It is a wonderful sight to see the wealth of foliage studded with flowers, intersected by brown paths and walks which are picked out by the weirdly blended colouring of the native dresses, chiefly Arabic and Egyptian. It looks like a piece of stage scenery, which has vastly exaggerated its subject.

Steve enjoyed himself as it is a change for him to have someone to talk to about things generally and to exchange thoughts about home! He has been getting very few letters; it is very disappointing for him. He doesn't quite know what has happened to them. He has not had any for several weeks. I wrote him a letter before I knew he was here, addressing him as he asked to be addressed on a post card he wrote to Mona and it never arrived. So I expect his other letters are with my letter wherever that has got to. It is rather a shame the Commonwealth military authorities being so slack about forwarding letters on. He is going to write to Mex where he believes they may be to make enquiries.

I heard from a girl called Bessie Wallace, who is an army nurse now and who hails from Wollongong, last week. She is a friend of Mona's. I met her twice while I was at Wollongong and so know her slightly. She has been in Alexandria a month now and is doing ambulance train work running from Alexandria to Cairo. Mona told me she had joined the Military forces in Australia and probably was somewhere in Egypt. I shall have to make myself pleasant to her and promised to take her to the Nouzha Gardens yesterday, but owing to Steve turning up unexpectedly I put her off till another opportunity offers itself. I suggested Steve come with us, but he didn't seem enthusiastic so the lady was asked to forgive my inability to make good the suggested outing.

I am pretty busy here and am very fortunate in having some wonderfully good and interesting cases. They are really excellent experience and should prove valuable later on. I am also getting some operating. Did I tell you I removed some pieces of a man's skull and cut off a piece of his brain which was protruding from a bullet wound in his occiput the other day? I inserted a rubber drainage tube, another gauze drain into his cranial cavity and stitched him up. He had been having excruciating headaches prior to the operation, but was vastly relieved afterwards and thanked me! He has all his faculties and is doing pretty well all things considered. It will be a jolly good case if he recovers, won't it, Mum? Fancy, Pigee having the audacity to do a thing like that!

Must stop now. Love to all at home. Trusting all is well with you. Till next week. Ever yours, NIGE

Cleopatra Camp, Alexandria, 7 Jun 1915

My dear Matee

Received two letters from you by yesterday's mail which comprised eight letters in all. We hadn't had any mails for a fortnight and so an extra big one was expected. 2 from Gran and one from Phil[71] completed the family's efforts. I hope everyone will keep going more especially when I go away as the letters are the best thing about this whole business. Haven't got any of the papers yet that Gran said she had sent. Got one from Harry Lloyd[72] a few days ago which was very welcome.

---

71   His cousin, the artist Phyllis Flockton Clarke, daughter of Aunt Phoebe.
72   Harry Lloyd was possibly a fellow student at The King's School.

News came today asking for 150 gunners wanted for the Dardanelles to relieve the men who have been there from the start. Our O.C. (Lt. Colonel Tonbridge C.M.G.) has been asked to supply some of them. Some of us therefore may be going, including Tootie, but the Colonel is doing his best to stop them going from our Column as he does not want his Column broken up. Anyway there is no definite news of anyone to go yet. It would be good to go back there again, especially without the horses to look after and do some useful work over there. We hear great yarns from the fellows who have been and come back.

Last night I met Billy in town and we went together to see a game of Pelota Basque. A game somewhat like fives and racquets, played a lot in Spain. We had quite a good evening. I left Billy there as I had to come away at 11.30 p.m. These little outings in Alexandria are just the thing, as there is absolutely nothing to do if you stay in camp.

The money here is all in piastres and it seems to go much quicker and not so far as the English shillings. Four and a half piastres go to the shilling. We are paid 2/- a day once a week and it nearly all goes by the time pay day comes round. Most of it goes in buying eatables at the Canteen and fruit when obtainable. Oranges we used to be able to get, but now they are over. Tomatoes and a few grapes are about all there are to buy now and the latter are very expensive. We had a salad tonight for tea of tomatoes, cucumber and onions, all chopped up together. Bread and jam followed with tea.

On May 16th we left Lemnos again this time for Alexandria where we immediately landed our horses who had the trip for nothing, and we're just about done up. We lost about 15 all told. They chiefly died of pneumonia following colds. Over there it is much colder than here and the men too nearly all had colds including myself. Nothing of much note though and has quite gone now.

We are camped now at Cleopatra, the fashionable seaside resort of Alexandria. It is a great spot. We are almost on the beach and get about 3 or 4 swims a day. It has been terribly hot the last few days, but today the wind changed and it became quite cool. Are employed looking after our nags now and getting them back into condition once again. Take them daily for a bathe which they like very much. Generally go into Alexandria of an evening when possible and who should I meet the day before yesterday but Billy. He was standing talking to another A.M.C. Officer. He is just the same as ever and has not changed a bit and does not look a day older since we last saw him. We had a yarn and some tea and refreshments together after the other chap had gone. I had to be back at camp by 9.30 so had to leave sooner than was desired. However, I shall see him again now I know he is here. He has been here since March without me knowing. It was a very pleasant surprise, I can tell you.

Haven't had any letters from home or anywhere else since before I left for the Dardanelles. They must be somewhere. Put on the same address as the others.

Give my best love to Gran and Aunt Mog and the Child hoping that everyone is going strong at Coolah and with much love to Matee Boodles, who still gets going on the tea with the big cups, from

TOOTS.

Don't know where we are going. We may go back to the Dardanelles with pack mules or on to France where the column can work.

Cleopatra Camp, Alexandria, 9 Jun 1915

My dear Matee Boo

Hooray! Hooray! Have at last got your letters including two from the Child and Aunt Mog one from Gran, Harry Lloyd, Jack Jones in all amounting to 14 altogether received in 3 days. They are a great boon and a tremendous comfort. Have not received any socks from the Miss Jones that you and he mentions. I quite expect if they were not sent registered post that someone else has helped himself as they pass through a lot of hands before they get to me.

Now that we are back here and the Military Authorities have found us out I expect we shall be getting our letters fairly regularly. We are still at Cleopatra and as a camp for soldiers it would be hard to beat. We generally do most of the work that is to be done in the mornings, which usually takes the form of exercising the horses and getting the day's forage from the A.S.C. Each man has two horses to look after. He rides one and leads the other. We get a good ride in the mornings sometimes along the beach and in the water and others along the roads.

Afterwards the horses are groomed, watered and fed. Swimming parade comes off at 2 p.m., after dinner, and stables goes at 4 p.m. to water and feed again which lasts (the feed) till 8 o'clock when they get another feed. I can tell you they come first in all things and are properly looked after. All terribly fat and glistening coats just now, having picked up from their trip over to the Straits.

No news yet of when and where we are next going. If the Gallipoli Peninsula falls soon and Turkey still fights on we shall probably go back.

I am writing this letter in our tent with a miserable kerosene lamp for a light. Another chap is sitting as close up as he can get to get the benefits of it too. He is asking me continually how to spell this that and the other word about every two seconds. There are about 14 all told belonging to the tent of all trades and professions. The chap who is writing was a lorry driver in Sydney. Two are ex-sailors and were doing navvying, another a fireman, a clerk in Dalgety & Co, a saw mender and sharpener. They are all fairly decent and good hearted. Only about 4 of them sleep inside, the rest outside round the tent, including myself.

Have not seen Billy for some days as I haven't been into town and I hear that a big convoy of wounded has come in, so I expect he will be busy for a little time. Had a couple of postcards from Mona, also a *Daily Mirror* which was most welcome.

Please thank Gran and Aunt Mog for their respective letters which were received with much gusto, also the two from the Child. I wrote to her last and told her to impress on the family the importance of putting the right address on the envelope. There is no need to put 3rd reinforcements as I am no longer reinforcements but attached to the Column. Copy this address at the top of this letter and put in on the wall where it won't be lost.

I am sending Aunt Mog another card of the Pyramids and Sphynx and which is I think a little different from the others. Gran also gets a card of a new sort. I hope you have been getting all my letters regularly. We are constantly being told not to mention any military matters etc. and that the letters will be censored. Post cards are much the safer and quicker, but less satisfying. Letters from Australia to me are all right and are not opened. It is ours to you that are held up.

Well Good bye Matee boos, was very glad to hear of your little jaunt up to the Mountains. Send along some of the Sydney newspapers when you get time as they would be interesting.

Best love to everyone at Coolah from

TOOTS.

Remember me to Uncle Frank when next he comes out. Good night _ ..orl !!![73]

---

73   His way of emphasising the word 'All'

No 15 General Hospital, Alexandria, 13 June 1915

My dearest Mother

Your nice long letters of April 17th and 18th to hand 2 days ago, together with the cutting from the *Herald*. So pleased to hear you enjoyed your jaunt to Lawson and that you met someone nice and interesting. It makes a great change coming across new people and exchanging ideas with them. I wonder whether you will pursue the friendship further or whether the promised visit to Ashfield will remain unfulfilled indefinitely. Of course, it is rather an awkward place to get at from Gladesville, and now the domestic difficulty has become acute again, well-nigh impossible. Perhaps the two flappers might make friends of the Child? What is the new master like? No one arrived on the horizon to take the wind out of Cleon's sails, I suppose?

I sent your 2 letters on to Mona, as I thought she would like to have them as they were interesting, and she would be pleased to read them. I also had a long letter from Dr. Harry.[74] Things seem to be going swimmingly at Wollongong and he has just launched out in the purchase of one of the latest Fiat cars and a new horse, who has succeeded in sacking both him and his assistant. He has recently made 100 guineas out of some operations at the private hospital there. That was a great windfall. He is beginning to realize the fruits of his well-earned labours. I expect, however, Mrs. Lee has told you of their increasing prosperity. The X-ray apparatus apparently has more than justified the outlay expended, and profiting by his experience it behoves me to bear in mind that when I settle down in practice it would be highly desirable to emulate his example as soon as practicable.

Who was responsible for the cutting in the *Herald*? My name has appeared 2 or 3 times in the *British Australasian*, a paper published in London, price 6d. weekly. I presume the Commonwealth Offices keep them informed of the movements of Australians over here, but that would not apply to the *Herald*.

I have been over here nearly 2 months now and from all appearances things won't have advanced much in Gallipoli, in another 3. Altho' my year is up on Sept 9th I don't suppose I shall be able to give up my appointment if the war is no nearer completion then. I shall, however, agitate for an increased screw, but don't suppose anything will come of it.

---

74   Dr Harry Lee, of Wollongong, Nigel's former employer.

The number of cases of typhoid is increasing in the hospital, and now numbers 40. A good number of the cases are so-called paratyphoid infections, clinically similar to typhoid, but they as a rule run a much milder course and are seldom attended by serious complications in the way of perforation or haemorrhage for example. Dancy, whom I have spoken of to you in my previous letters and my chief friend amongst this crowd, has charge of them. As he has not been efficiently inoculated and is rather a delicate chap and continually subject to gastro-intestinal disorders, it is not altogether a good arrangement his being put in charge. It is possible I shall take over the typhoids from him and let him have my wards, which I am loth to relinquish as they contain some of the most interesting medical cases in the hospital. If the typhoids, however, go on increasing in numbers as they have been doing rather rapidly lately, we may both be required to look after them. The experience gained from a large number of typhoid cases will be valuable all the same.

My case of compound fracture of the skull whom I operated on and told you of in one of my former letters has done splendidly, and in spite of his having had a pus infection of his sterno-clavicular joint (a direct blood infection from the septic cranial focus) is getting up and to use his own words "feels as strong as a horse". Altho' he has had part of the occipital lobe of his brain removed he retains all his faculties and can now read the smallest type and has normal vision. A wonderful case, really.

I haven't seen anything of Steve lately. I don't think he has left Alexandria as he would almost certainly have let me know. Also we have been getting several of his regiment in the hospital for various minor maladies. He probably will turn up in a day or two again. I shall drop him a P.C. but it is not at all certain that he will get it; I will try it, however.

The summer is now here and altho' it is pretty hot the heat is not unbearable. It is not as trying as Australia is sometimes and there usually is some sort of a sea breeze going. Well, Mum, I will stop. Am afraid there is not so very much in this letter; I may have something more of interest to tell you next week. Best love to all at home. Trusting you are flourishing. Bestest love, dearest Mum,

Yours ever, NIGE

Cleopatra Camp, 20 Jun 1915

My dear Matee Boo, Child and Family

I am sending you some snapshots taken by some of the fellows at Lemnos and Dardanelles. They are very interesting and hope that they will be kept and not given away as I shall be pleased to have them when I get back. You will find a short description of what they are on the back.[75]

We are still at Cleopatra and doing the same old daily routine. It is beginning to get monotonous but someday I suppose our turn will come. We have had 48 mules given to us to try and see how they work and generally break in. I expect when we next go away, if back to the Dardanelles, we will take the mules instead of horses and use them as pack mules. They are very useful in rough country and can climb up gullies and rough places where a team of horses couldn't get. They are also extremely stupid and stubborn and unlike horses don't ever get frightened. They say shells can be lobbing and bursting all round them and they don't seem to mind, but just flop their ears about and stare just as if nothing was happening. They are pretty good at booting, and are always kicking one another.

Haven't seen Billy for a week or so, but had a note from him yesterday. I am going to meet him in town tomorrow night if he can get off.

I am writing this on Sunday afternoon in the tent with the other fellows talking, sleeping and others getting dressed to go on leave. Sundays are just the same as week days except that we don't go on parade at 2 p.m. for a swim, all the morning's work being done just as ever. The R.Cs have a church parade at 8 o'clock in the mornings at the French Hospital next door to the camp which is run by some nuns. The Church of England section never have any services at all. Have only been to Church once since I've been in the army. That was at Newcastle when we marched up to the Cathedral.

All the shops in Alexandria and throughout Egypt remain open on Sundays. We had tinned herrings in tomato sauce for dinner today with potatoes and cabbage. Quite a good feed and a very welcome change from the stews. We have been getting them for breakfast as well as dinner lately. We are all in good condition now, but all the chaps are beginning to get boils and sores which take a long time to heal up. I have had a couple on my left hand for about a month, but am now on the mend. I shall have to get Billy to get me a blood tonic, when I see him.

---

75 The photos do not survive.

I had a letter from Aunt Phoebe last mail and will now have to write a line to her.

Hope everyone at Coolah is well and that the winter is not too trying. Haven't seen any rain since I left Australia, except coming thro' the Red Sea. It never seems to rain here, everything that grows is watered by irrigation, also the dews at night times are almost as good as a shower of rain. I sleep outside the tent on a horse blanket with another blanket on top of that and my overcoat on top of that. Over me comes a blanket and waterproof sheet to keep off the dew. The hard ground is much better than a bed.

Please give my love to Gran, Aunt Mog and the Child hoping they got my postcards posted last night, with heaps of love to Matee Boos from

TOOTIE.

P.S. Did you get any letters of mine written at the Dardanelles? Or were they all censored and stopped?

No 15 General Hospital, Alexandria, 22 June 1915

My dearest Mother

I received two lovely long letters from you last week, and how delighted I was to get them, as they were addressed here and contained comparatively recent news of you all at home. It is a great comfort to know now, Mum, that I shall have a regular letter once a week, instead of having to wait till they were forwarded on from England, which meant their arriving at any old time. Mails from Australia are far more regular than mails from England just now.

So pleased to hear you are all well, but am grieved to learn the domestic question is as unsatisfactory and uncertain as ever. I wonder if the mortality amongst the male section of the population will have any influence on the servant difficulty after the war is over. Am afraid not, as it will drive the excess of girls and women still more to shops, factories, and offices to replace the vacancies caused by the men. Altho' perhaps there won't be so many as the clerks, etc. don't form a large part of the military crowd.

Dancy, I think I have spoken to you about him before, he is my chief friend amongst the R.A.M.C. lot here, has just contracted paratyphoid fever. It is not such a virulent form of typhoid as true typhoid altho' death may eventuate, still as a rule it is a much milder infection. He had charge of the typhoid wards and altho' he is a big chap of 6 ft. 1 is not very strong all the same. I have got a ward full of typhoids now and probably will have a ward or two more before long, as typhoid fever is on the increase now the summer has arrived. Still we have had wonderfully few cases of enteric in the hospital all things considered, there is no doubt inoculation has made a vast difference in reducing the number of cases. A good many of our typhoids are the paratyphoids variety and accordingly not so severe. Still, as some of the cases are seriously wounded as well, it has been responsible for carrying off some of the poor fellows.

Typhoid fever is a very interesting disease to study, and I shall or should know a great deal more about it than I did before this campaign started. I have had some valuable experience since I came to Egypt and have been by no means wasting my time. I did an empyema under a local anaesthetic today, it is the 2nd I've done. It is an operation on the chest, where a rib is resected and a tube inserted for draining an abscess on the lung. The same operation as that performed on the King of Greece. He had a general anaesthetic tho'. I am the only lad among the staff here who has ventured on a local for this operation, altho', of course, it is quite easy and often done. The advantage is that the risk of giving chloroform to chest cases is very considerable, and by using a local anaesthetic one obviates this, it being absolutely safe. The man is conscious all the time, of course.

A very sad event has occurred here at the beginning of the week. One of our medical officers died as a result of blood poisoning contracted while operating on a case of empyema, the same sort of case as I had today. I think I told you he was in hospital a letter or two ago. Well he got progressively worse and died after a month's illness. He was a very decent chap, altho' a good deal older than me. He leaves a wife, but no children. His wife, fortunately, was wired for and managed to get here 2 or 3 days before his death. He had been in France and was a Sergt. in the London Scottish Regt. He was sent to England and given a commission in this corps and came out here. We all went to the funeral which was most impressive and solemn. He was buried with full military honours, his wife being the only woman present. It is the first funeral I've been to and I hope it will be the last as they turn me up a good deal. I suppose one would get used to them, still they make one think, who's turn next?

We have rather a nice tennis court here, and it has been put in order. Racquets, balls, and a net have been got so that we should be able to have some games on it this week. It will be rather a boon as there are so few ways of procuring exercise in a place like this.

Mona talks of coming over here to help with the wounded, but as the staff in all military hospitals are fully trained, she would not be wanted. I am going to dissuade her, altho' she has set her mind on it, as this is really quite an expensive place to live and the summer is very trying. She talks of going down to Devon, which I think is a very good thing to do as it is one of England's most delightful counties and very beautiful in the summer.

Well, Mum I must stop now. I meet Steve tomorrow and will have dinner with him, I expect. I think if you saw us you would think we were both looking extremely well. Love to all at home. I must try and write to Aunt Mog next week. Hoping she and you are quite well.

Ever yours,

NIGE

Hope Mona writes you nice long letters.

Cleopatra Camp, Alexandria, 30 Jun 1915

My dear Matee Boo

I wonder what's been happening with you all today. Nothing startling I expect, except for the hundreds of visitors pouring in. I am sitting in the tent writing this letter with a smelly kerosene lamp for a light. All the other chaps have gone out excepting one who has just returned from the canteen with a tin of apricots. Hope he will ask me to partake, which he will, as he wouldn't eat them all on his own. He had just told me to get my fork!!! We finished the apricots and very nice too. We don't get too much to eat as we have our meals in the tent and the sand gets into everything.

We have had 2 cases of typhoid in the camp. Both have been sent to the No 15 General where Billy is. It was he who told me. Have seen him twice lately in the evenings when we had a little light refreshment and gone to a music hall something like the Tivoli, but not so good.

The flies here are very bad, and are all over everything. The very first thing in the morning they crawl over your face and wake you. I am feeling very fit and excepting for two or three stifling days don't find it bad. The swimming is a great boon and ought to keep us in good nick. I am sending you a snap of me taken whilst on guard in the sun at about 110°. You will see they allow us to take off our tunics. The horses are inside the wall in the picture and the horse you see is one of the Major's. (Major Lucas our O.C.) It has a bit of bagging thrown on to protect it from the sun. It's not a good photograph of me as I seem to have my mouth open gasping.[76]

I have got a new job tomorrow instead of guard. Headquarters Orderly which is much better than guard as I will get my full sleep at night instead of raked out to do my shift. There are also one or two more photos taken at the Dardanelles. I wonder if you got the last lot I sent.[77]

There is nothing new in the way of news to tell you as the same old rigmarole goes on here from day to day. I haven't had any letters for about a fortnight. An Australian mail is to come in tomorrow when I hope I shall get something.

Give my best love to everyone at Coolah, hope Gran is well and coping with the wintry blasts. The walk to and from the wharf is still done by Aunt Mog and the Child, without much change. Give my love to Whisky and Pug[78], hoping they are still flying about, hoping that Matee Boos is well and in good spurrits, just as Tootie is at this moment. Am just going to turn in as the last post is about to blow, with much love, from

TOOTS.

No 15 General Hospital, Alexandria, 6 July 1915

Dearest Mother

Your letter of May 11th to hand 2 or 3 days ago. It was forwarded on from the Commonwealth offices. The letters you addressed to Mustafa Pacha have not reached me. They may be at the Military Base Post Office. I must write and enquire for them. You did not put No.15 General. Hospital on the address so that is probably the reason why they have not found me, as there are a large number of R.A.M.C. officers here attached to different units, e.g. field ambulances, stationary hospitals, general hospitals, regimental medical officers, etc. If in future you always include No 15 General Hospital in the address a letter will always find me, even tho' we may move our quarters, which as a matter of fact is extremely unlikely.

---

76 The photo does not survive.
77 These photos do not survive.
78 Family pets

Sorry to hear old Dickie has been laid up. I do trust his will not be a long and weary illness. Bronchitis in old people is often liable to hang on for weeks sometimes. Poor old chap, it is sad his being such an outcast, I expect he feels it at times; old age has very few compensations!

Enclosed are two small snaps taken with my camera. There is a leak in the bellows or in the back somewhere as the band of light that was present in the other photos is still present I see, and occurs in practically everyone I take. I can't discover what it is exactly, and the Kodak people don't seem to be able to elucidate the mystery so the camera is not much good in consequence. The group comprises the occupants of our marquee. The other one is a snap of my corner of the tent, which looks quite comfortable and ship shape.[79] I have a chair besides the bed and table, so am well off for furniture! I can make myself a cup of tea or cocoa with the apparatus you can see at the side of the bed. The piece of Egyptian embroidery hanging on the side of the tent is rather quaint and will do to go at the back of a washstand.

Dancy, Boulton, Campion etc, Mustafa Pacha Camp, April 1915

(Picture Courtesy Julia Woodhouse)

Met Steve on Saturday last. We had planned to go for a sail, but as there was practically no wind and it was a piping hot day we went to the races - we had quite an enjoyable afternoon and Steve found it quite a change from camp life, which is apt to pall and become monotonous after a bit, unless you are in the fighting.

We had omelettes and tea afterwards and walked about the town till 9.30, when we repaired to the American Kursaal where they have a Spanish game called Pelote Basque sport played. It is one of the finest games I have ever seen and is a sort of racquets, tho' far more difficult. Steve was immensely taken with it and has arranged to go with me again on Wednesday night - that is tomorrow.

---

79 This photo has not survived.

Things are going on here much the same. The operations in the Dardanelles are becoming rather tedious, altho' we are certainly progressing, it is not fast enough. Kitchener, I understand, is getting rather impatient and has intimated to Sir Ian Hamilton that he trusts he will push things along, as it is rather essential they should open the Narrows in 6 weeks' time. If this policy of a rapid advance is made, it will mean the sacrifice of a large number of lives and many, many casualties. Still if it entails a more speedy termination of the war it will be justified.

My time is up in September. Just over 2 months now. I suppose I shall continue, altho I'm getting rather fed up with things, as have seen none of the fighting at all. It is my duty to go on tho' if my country still requires my services. I may get moved up closer later on tho' I think there is small likelihood of it, as I apparently have made myself rather useful here. There will be a tremendous number of fellows whose time expires next month, and I dare say a large number of them will resign. Those fellows with families and practices going to pot have some justification, but those fellows without have next to none. The English people don't seem to realize yet altogether how vital and critical this war is, in a large number of cases, but I suppose they will gradually awaken to its grim realities someday. The middle classes have done their duty royally in the majority of instances, but the upper and especially the lower leave much to be desired I am afraid.

We have 8 of our staff away at present. It is nearly 25%, fortunately things have not been very busy just lately, altho' the hospital is full. The majority of the patients are not really very ill. 4 of the 8 mentioned above are typhoids, one has died of blood poisoning, another is off with bacillary dysentery, another with a throat, and another from neuralgia and over-work. So it is just as well we are fairly slack at present. The typhoids are all doing well. I lost one of mine last night, the first one. In the majority of the cases the disease is comparatively mild, this, I think, can be honestly ascribed to the results of inoculation. It is really a remarkable boon to mankind.

Mona and her mother are at present at Queen's Gate, S. Kensington, but anticipate shortly going down to Devon. Mona talks of joining the Ladies Voluntary Aid Corps, but I have not heard definitely if she has had any success. It will entail nursing chiefly of an elementary kind, but may mean a good deal of work, still it will be good for her if she doesn't overdo it. Her mother, I think, proposes returning to Australia at the end of the year. If I am still on the job, Mona will wait behind.

Well, Mum, I shall stop now. Trust Aunt Mog got my last letter safely. Give my best love to her and all at home. Hoping you are all well. So sorry to hear the man at Ermo has been so disappointing after your sanguine hopes of his being a shining light. What is to become of Concord?

Best love, Mum, I hope I shall get your letters direct from now on.

Always your loving,

NIGE

I am sorry the papers at home have been so full of "blow". The Australians here have a tremendous idea of themselves. It is such a pity as they are such splendid fellows otherwise. I am afraid they have done a lot of harm in Egypt. Have undone work that took England 50 years to accomplish! I trust this is an exaggeration tho! Democracy doesn't do in Egypt.

Stephen returns to Gallipoli for the second time, but this time he will be landing on the beach.

Egypt, 12 July 1915

My dearest Matee

Expect to be going off to the Dardanelles any minute now. The 150 gunners who were sent for are to go and I am one of them. Don't think I will be in any great danger for a while. As far as I can find out we are going to carry ammunition up to the batteries and dig gun pits etc. Probably won't be near the trenches, so you need not worry much. I will be quite all right. Will be living in a dug out at night time to sleep in and will be as snug as a bug in a rug.

Have seen Billy and he is very envious of me going. Am going out with him tomorrow night. My address will be the same, and will be forwarded on by the Military Post Office here. Tell Gran I got her *Sunday Times* today and thank her for it. They will be more welcome than ever over on the Peninsula. I won't be able to write so often now and everything will be read and strictly censored, if we are allowed to write at all. Field Service Post Cards may be served out, and only allowed to be sent. Anyway whenever an opportunity occurs I shall write and let you know what is happening,

Won't be able to write any more now as we have only been given half a day's notice and we sail at 12 o'clock noon 14th July. So good bye Matee Boos, with heaps of love to all the family and the Child, also kisses on their various brows, also heaps and heaps for Matee, hoping to be back again soon.

I've got £15 (about) in the Comptoir National D'Escompte de Paris. (The French Bank in Alexandria.) They have a branch in Sydney. Have kept it there in case of emergency.

Well Matee Boos good-night alllllll[80]

from your loving son, TOOTIE.

They are only waiting for me to get over there to finish the job. Am sending back some photos.[81]

No 15 General Hospital, Abbassia Schools, Alexandria, 14 July 1915

My dearest Mother

Your letters of May 23rd and 29th came to hand last week, very many thanks for them; as with you the mail only appears to come in once a fortnight and is accordingly very eagerly looked forward to. The Australian mail goes out tomorrow so you should get my last week's letter by it as well.

I have seen a good deal of Steve lately. He is looking well and seems to be pretty cheerful. 150 of the gunners of his crowd left for the Dardanelles today. He managed to his delight to be selected as one of them. All the other fellows left behind here are very sore, as they are very bored with being here so long and always expecting to be sent over to Turkey. Steve's crowd don't know what they are going to do exactly, but think they will be required to dig gun pits and make roads and railways. They won't be under fire much, occasional shell fire, certainly not rifle fire. They have had all their rifles taken away from them before they left so it doesn't look as if they will be near the fighting line.

This should comfort you, Mum, as I know how horribly anxious you will be about Tootie. He will be quite all right, and probably be sent back soon if it is found he is not wanted, as he was before. They seem to be sending a tremendous number of men over there now and a large number are always returning. I had the last night with him before he left, and have taken charge of his razor case, provided

---

80   His way of emphasising the word 'All'
81   The photos do not survive.

him with some aperient pills and diarrhoea pills and offered him clothes. He, however, refused the latter as he doesn't want to take any more than he possibly needs. His first trip over there was valuable in that he formed an estimate of what to take and what to leave behind. He promised to write to me as often as he could, so I will let you know how he is getting on whenever I hear from him.

We are going to be very busy here soon I think as a general advance is being anticipated and it will be a costly procedure. However, it is up to us to get through with the business as speedily as possible, as once the Dardanelles are open, it will have a tremendous moral effect as well as a real effect on the termination of the War. After 6 weeks or so the weather conditions become very bad and it will be most difficult to land troops, supplies, etc. Thus it is that it is rather vital to hurry things along.

I have got charge of 117 patients now and I find it pretty hard work. I have 48 typhoids and 59 medical cases chiefly. The latter belong to a chap called Roberts[82] who has had quinsey so I am looking after them till he returns. Altho' it is pretty hard work still I enjoy it as I have a good many good cases and some of them are very interesting, and one feels, in addition, that one is earning one's pay.

My rank is Lieut. The Australian army differs from the British Army in that the lowest rank in the R.A.M.C. (i.e. commissioned rank) is lieutenant, whereas in the Australian Medical Corps it is Captain. So you address me - Lieut. Nigel Boulton, R.A.M.C. etc.

Mona has applied for a job in the Voluntary Aid Corps, which chiefly comprises nursing and work connected therewith, and hopes to hear soon that she is to start work somewhere or other. I hear from a N.Z. nurse who has charge of one of my typhoid wards that the V.A.C. girls have been excellent and have been found a very great help, so Mona will love having something to do and it is a comfort to know that one is really doing something useful, and not misdirecting one's energies, which is very liable to happen in times like this. The trip to Devon is postponed for a bit, I believe, in consequence of the probability of her getting something to do pretty soon in or round London.

Pleased to hear Aunt Mog's cottage is proving such a success. How gratifying for her. Wonder when you get this letter whether you will be wrestling with Ermo? You will enjoy it. I hope you won't go and overdo it, and not be worried by the old man you get to help being an incompetent. Shall be very pleased to hear how you get on. Well, dearest Mum, I must stop now.

---

82   Identity unknown: many doctors named Roberts served in R.A.M.C.

Love to all at home, trusting all is well with you and that you are getting all my letters safely. Don't worry, Mum, please.

Ever your loving, NIGE

The summer here is very trying at times. But I believe the weather is much more agreeable at the Dardanelles, in fact it is quite pleasant, which is comforting for the troops' sake.

No 15 General Hospital, Alexandria, 21 July 1915

Dearest Mother

Your letter of June 12th to hand yesterday, also the cutting from the *Sunday Times*. Thank you for them, Mum. Am sorry you have been so terribly worried over Steve, but hope to hear soon that you have received my letter telling of our having met, and of Steve having returned from the Dardanelles. Still I'm afraid, Mum, you will again be very anxious over him now he has gone back again to the Dardanelles. I haven't heard from him as yet, but hope to have a letter from him in a few days. He has only just got there I expect and there is just barely time for a letter to have arrived from him so far. He will be quite all right, I feel sure. He is ever so much safer than the infantry, who are in the trenches. Steve will probably be in what is called a dug out a long way behind the firing line. He won't even be in a battery, so, Mum, you see you mustn't worry too much, as it is unlikely that he will be hurt as long as he is on his present job. I expect he will write to you pretty soon after his arrival, but I am afraid his letters will be slow in reaching you as the military post office arrangements are lamentable. Still I may get any letter he writes me more promptly and will let you know anything there is from him.

Am very much interested to hear of Ermo and your taking it over. How exciting it all sounds, and what a great little place for you to have all to yourself. I trust things will go well and that the Old Age Pensioner turns out to be really useful. I expect there will be a lot of bullocky work to do, and am afraid Dickie and the pensioner sound rather feeble helpers, but I daresay you will manage by degrees. The mosquitoes in the summer will make the place well-nigh uninhabitable, but at other times of the year it ought to be quietude itself. Perhaps the 'skeets' won't be so bad indoors and with mosquito nets. I am very interested to hear of all your plans of improvement, as I remember the place very well. So you must tell me how you manage about the bathroom difficulty, and the pantry. What about a wash house, and where is the stable to be? At the side near the river, I suppose. Is the long room that has been lined with tin a success, or is it dreadfully cold in winter and hot in summer? Poor old Dickie, I wonder how he will enjoy himself there. It is rather cut off from the pubs!

Things are going along here much the same. We have not had a rush of wounded in for some time now, but are expecting them any day now as a big engagement is impending, I believe. I am still looking after my 48 typhoids and 59 of Roberts' cases. The latter lad makes out now he is peeling and that he has had scarlet fever!! A pretty unlikely tale, but he is going to have 2 or 3 more weeks of convalescence, and as he has just got his wife out here he is doing rather well. He has practically negotiated a month's leave so far, I am getting the strength of his cases now, so don't mind the extra, but rather enjoy it as it is all experience and practice.

Mona and her mother are at Richmond again. They are not as pleased with it as they were before. Mona is still anxiously awaiting for news of her having been definitely appointed to a job in the Voluntary Aid Corps. The Sisters here tell me that the movement has been really most useful and has done a great deal of good work. So Mona will be pleased to feel she is truly doing something during this era of stress, struggle and trial.

I was to have been put in charge of the Medical Division here I heard as a secret the other day, in the event of Capt. Carson[83], who is a regular and he's at present got the job, leaving for the Dardanelles, but owing to the energies of a fellow called Wacher[84] it has been squashed. The Colonel was dead nuts on giving me the job, but Wacher who is a temporary lieut.

Capt Carson, Lieut Dolling & Capt Kennedy-Taylor, Alexandria, 1915
Source AWM P10636.038.001

---

83 Herbert William Carson, Registrar, who died of pneumonia at Damascus on 12 Oct 1918.
84 Harold Wacher was appointed as a Temporary Lieutenant in the R.A.M.C. on 16 December 1914. (Supplt to London Gazette, 31 Dec 1914). Harold Wacher was from a medical family prominent in Canterbury.

same rank as I am, and a man aged about 40 with a practice in Canterbury, and who bosses the old Colonel frightfully, in fact "manages" him, pointed out to him that I was far too young and that the appointment would be unsuitable. The fact is he is after it himself, as it carries with it an extra screw of 10/- a day, which is thundering good. Wacher is at present in charge of the Officers' Block, and very unpopular there too, I hear. He is a would-be gay Lothario and consequently is always running after the petticoats and gadding about generally, and leaving his patients to their own devices. They naturally resent this. As Carson is still here, I am waiting to see what does actually happen. I am certainly much younger than the majority of the men over whom I should be placed, and perhaps it would lead to petty jealousies and unpleasantnesses, so perhaps it is just as well.

I have got a beast of a cold the last 3 or 4 days, chiefly a sore throat and stuffy hay fever sort of feeling. It is very silly as the weather has been a regular corker the last few days and the fellows have been feeling it. I hope to shake it off soon, it's the first I've had for months.

Well, Mum, my pen is running out and so is my news, therefore, I must stop. Love to all at home. Trusting you are all well. It is possible when my time is up here, only a little over a month to go now, I shall get moved up closer to the firing line. But I must wait for a bit and see. Don't worry about Tootie too much. Bestest love,

Always your,

NIGE

Dardanelles, Gallipoli Peninsula, 24 Jul 1915

My dearest Matee

I hope you received my issue p.c. by the last mail. It may however be no earlier than this as I don't know how the mails go. This letter is right from the front. It will be strictly censored and I am to be as brief as possible. Am sitting in my dug out which is proof from shrapnel and rifle fire and therefore run only the minimum amount of danger whilst in it.

The Turks keep sending over shells amongst our fellows, chiefly onto the beach. Most of them go right over the valley in which our column is camped.

We can generally hear the shells coming for about 2 seconds before the burst in which time you must dive straight into the nearest dug out available. There is not much danger as regards rifle fire, except for stray shots, spent bullets etc. and snipers when standing on the sky line. My work starts as a rule at 8 p.m. and I work in the night and rest during the day. But lately we have been going all day and night, as the Turks were expected to be making a move our way.

Life in the dug outs is a great change from camp life. We have to do all our own cooking of course. Our rations consist of bully beef, biscuits, tea and sugar in very small quantities, sometimes onions and others potatoes, a little jam and bacon. This does not make a change of diet very easy, but now we get bread every other day and fresh meat of a sort also. Rice in very small quantities is also issued. I and another chap (Easterling by name[85]) are batching together and unite our rations. He is an ex-navy man so can cook fairly decently. We soak the biscuits overnight and make them into porridge by mashing them in the morning. It is a pity they give us so little sugar, about 1 tablespoonful per man for a day. About enough to put in your tea once. Milk would be an asset also.

However we are at war now and on active service so can't have all these luxuries. I am living for the days after all this when we come home again and live in comfort once more. Stirling Macansh is up here and lots of chaps I know. Haven't seen Jack Herring although his battalion are supposed to be here. Was inoculated for cholera yesterday for the first time. Will be done again in a day or two.

Am quite well Matee Boos except for a slight cold which is going to be nothing much. Give my best love to Gran and Aunt Mog and the Child, hoping everyone is well and in good spurrits from

Your loving son, TOOTS.

Pity you can't see us all for about 5 minutes also hear the booming of the Turks guns. They are pretty rotten gunners. It is altogether different from what people think. Am quite used to it all now and everyone gets about as if nothing was on at all.

---

85 Frederick George Easterling, English by birth, was a 33-yr-old storeman of Rose Bay in Sydney when he enlisted on 2 Nov 1914. Later in the war, on the Western Front, he suffered a serious shrapnel wound to the abdomen and was evacuated to hospital in England, where he was joined by his wife, who came over from Australia.

The ill-fated August Offensive in the Dardanelles is about to begin. Stephen is now living in Shrapnel Gully at Gallipoli. He drops a line to Nigel.

Postcard, Gallipoli, Undated

Dear Billy

Am quite all right. Working very hard night and day. Living in dugouts into which when we emerge we have to dive in. Very exciting at first but getting quite used to it now. It is far different country to what most people think and our fellows have done wonderfully well in getting what they have. Write & tell Mum. I have sent her a F.S.P.C.[86] which she will get sooner than anything. Love from Billy.

No 15 General Hospital, Abbassia Schools, Alexandria, 29 Jul 1915

Dearest Mother

I'm afraid this will be rather a short letter as I have very little of interest to tell you.

I heard from Maude Jacob[87] the other day, she is engaged as you doubtless know to a chap called Alan Garbett[88], who is in the Light Horse. He is over at the Dardanelles now. She asked me to keep a look out for him in case I should come across him. He is a Corporal.

Harry Jacob[89] has left with some more reinforcements and should be here very soon if he has not already arrived. I don't suppose I shall run across him unless by chance. There must be a large number of fellows whom I know who pass thro' Alexandria and I never hear of them.

---

86 Field Service Post Card
87 Maude Eliza Jacob of Homebush in Sydney was the granddaughter of the first Professor of Mathematics at the University of Sydney and a granddaughter of NSW MLC Archibald Hamilton Jacob. Her mother was the published poetess Maude Jacob/Maude Pell.
88 Alan Montague Garbett, a 22-yr-old farmer born in Maryborough, QLD and son of a C of E Minister of Raymond Terrace, NSW, enlisted as a private on 30 Aug 1914 with the 1st Light Horse Regt. Served at Gallipoli, Sinai, Palestine and Syria. His service number was 203. Very short man (5'4"). Departed Suez on 12 July 1918 and married Maude in Sydney later that year. He was a public servant after the war and lived in the Sydney suburb of Artarmon in 1954 and 1967.
89 Maude Jacob's brother, Trooper Harry Alan Jacob, an old boy of The King's School, was a 22-yr-old grazier of Homebush in Sydney when he left Australia in June 1915 as part of the reinforcements for the 1st Light Horse Regiment. He died of his injuries after an accident at the Cadet School in Zietoun, Egypt, on 9 November 1918.

Steve has not written to me yet; he probably has written but the military post office authorities have not managed to send on his letter. It is very annoying, really scandalous in many cases, the way the correspondence of the troops is handled. People are always complaining, but the Government doesn't make the slightest effort to improve things. Don't worry, Mum, I am sure he is perfectly safe, and I expect any day to have a letter from him.

Troops are fairly pouring into Gallipoli now and once a general move is made it is to be hoped this Dardanelles question will be speedily settled and done with. It has been one of the muddles of the War, how it has been bungled and it behoves England to push it thro' after the 1,000's and 100's of lives that have been sacrificed. It will also set free a large number of troops for France, guns, ammunition etc, and should help to decide matters there a little more definitely.

Bob Owen (Col. Owen of Wollongong) is wounded, only slightly, I hear and is in the Deaconess' Hospital: a German hospital here that was commandeered at the beginning of the War. I must go and see him if I can arrange it. I sewed his leg up once if you remember when I was in Wollongong. His wife is in London and Mona has met her. I hope ere this she will be relieved to hear that her husband has not been seriously hurt.

How are you getting on with Ermo? I hope to hear in your next letter of all the things you have been doing there and of how your henchmen, Dickie and the O.A.P. have been acquitting themselves. I may not get another letter from you for a week yet, when I shall probably receive two, a fortnight is a long wait for news, Mum, isn't it?

The weather here is very hot and trying. I think far more trying than an Australian summer as it never rains apparently. There hasn't been a drop since we landed over 4 months ago. It is literally wonderful how plants and trees live at all. Irrigation is the only means of watering the ground and that is how cultivation is carried on. There seems to be a fair number of wells. The Nile and its flood, of course, is the saving of the country as it makes the ground so peculiarly fertile.

Mona has made me two pairs of pyjamas from a pattern she secured at home. She has sent them out to me and they fit very well indeed and are nice and thin and comfortable. She is a very clever little girl, as she had never made a pair before. She is very annoyed and exasperated over the Voluntary Aid Corps as they are still keeping her on the string. She is going to chuck it up and do something else if they don't shortly make a move. It is very trying being kept waiting in uncertainty, as I well know.

Well, Mum, I must stop now. This is a poor letter, but I dare say you are pleased to get any news from Steve and I. Love to all at home. Trusting things are going well with you.

Fondest love,

Yours ever,

NIGE

Anzac, Gallipoli, 30 Jul 1915

Dear Matee Boo

Am still going strong and in good health although a little troubled with dysentery, as is nearly everyone at different times. We get quite decent rations of their kind, but of course miss such items as milk and butter and a general scarcity of vegetables and fresh meat. We can't have everything though, under our present circumstances, and taken on the whole the food is not bad at all. We have had a couple of tots of rum issued since arriving here, also an issue of lime juice, both of which are greatly appreciated. The only thing wrong with them is we don't get enough. We go great guns on the tea, and always have great baths of it with our meals.

I have again been transferred, this time to the D.A.P. with about 2 dozen other fellows. We have shifted our quarters and now have our dug outs on the beach slightly up the hill overlooking the cove. It is a good place as regards seeing everything going on, but comes in for a fair amount of attention from the Turks as it is the centre of operations so to speak, where everything and everybody is landed.

Have had two swims today and feel greatly refreshed. It is the only method of washing ourselves and clothes.

I don't know if I told you I had met Jack Herring here. I went up into the firing line where the 3rd Battalion was and saw him up there. He is just the same as ever, but not looking too well on it. Has had good luck so far as regards not getting hit. Also saw Stirling Macansh who is in the 6th Light Horse. He is supposed to be the thinnest man in his squadron. An awful lot of King's

Beach at Anzac Cove, 1915
Source AWM C01551

School[90] chaps are over here, but I can't get away from my work to see any of them. Most of them are a long way away from the beach. Have tried to write this now for 3 days and each time something has come along and stopped me so will finish it now and post it and write again soon.

Please give my best love to Gran and Aunt Mog. I hope they are both very well and that the cottage is still paying its way. The Child still goes to the School I suppose, give her my love and tell her I haven't had a letter for a long time. I hope Concord is now proving a success also Ermo. Could do with some of the vegetables here now. Well good-bye Matee, hoping the spurrits are being kept up by large quantities of tea, with heaps and heaps of love from

Your son

TOOTS.

---

90 Once she came into possession of the money from her husband's estate, in England in 1901, Dora Boulton wanted her sons to finish their schooling at a local school deemed of suitable status. This was The King's School, at Parramatta.

DIVISIONAL AMMN PARK, ANZAC, GALLIPOLI PENN, 30 JUL 1915

My dear Billy

Am still going strong. Have been transferred from the B.A.C. to the D.A.P. and note the new address. Don't know if it is to be permanent or not. The work is much the same only we don't hump the ammn. The rest of the unit is in England as you know.

All our transports are done by motor but there is nothing of that here. Have now got my dug out right on the beach, a little way up the hill with a good view of everything. Am quite handy to the sea and can run down for a swim when occasion offers. Have made the place as safe from shrapnel as possible as the Turks pay a good deal of attention to the beach where all the loading of stores and men goes on.

Have seen some wonderful and miraculous escapes as well as some stiff luck by our chaps caught before they could get under cover. We can generally hear the shells coming as they make a sort of whistling sound as they rush through the air and get nearer and nearer until you think it is going to get you. After it has burst you find out that it is quite some distance over and therefore harmless. The first shot generally gets a few after which the men take cover until they finish which only goes on for a little while at a time.

We had a tot of rum issued the other day much to everyone's delight. Also an issue of lime juice yesterday. Our rations are not too bad now. Get fresh meat every other day and bread every other day. Had 2 eggs since I have been here. Vegetables such as onions and potatoes every other day. We cook all our own meals of course, and it is mighty hot standing over a fire in the midday sun.

Have seen Jack Herring, Stirling Macansh and a whole lot of chaps I know. Did you know Pop Lloyd[91] had got the D.C.M. or D.S.O.? I don't know which. Jack Herring told me. I met Jack in the firing line of the 3rd Battn and had a look at the Turks through a periscope.

Well Billy, have other letters to write so will not say any more this time, bout time I had a letter I reckon, from BROTHER BILLY

---

91 Apparently referring to the Victorian career soldier Herbert William Lloyd, aged 31 when he signed up in August 1914 as Adjutant of the 1st FAB. His DSO was publicised later that year.

No 15 General Hospital, Alexandria, 4 Aug 1915

My dearest Mother

Two of your letters came to hand 2 or 3 days ago, and very pleased was I to get them. Yes, I expect you have been working terribly hard at Ermo. There will be an enormous deal to do to get it at all comfy and get things in the ground. The initial outlay of money and energy is always very heavy. I hope, Mum, you won't go and knock yourself up and go and overdo it, being carried away by the realisation at last of your fondest dream, viz. the sole possession of a little farm.

It will be most interesting and delightful for you if everything goes well and the crops grow apace. I do trust the little place will turn out trumps and that you will make a greater success of it than the incompetents before you. I shall be keenly interested to hear in every letter from you how things are going. The next 2 months will be a very busy time with you, altho' I daresay you will have got most of your seeds and plants in the ground by the time this letter reaches you. What about tomatoes? I wonder if the soil would suit them, I should think they would do admirably, and they should pay pretty well. Altho', of course, peas are excellent if they turn out well. The picking of them is rather back-aching work, but one forgets that in the excitement of gathering them in.

I haven't heard from Steve yet, altho' I dare say he has written well before this. The postal facilities and arrangements on the Gallipoli Peninsula are deplorable. Damnable! would not be too strong a word under the circumstances. The Australians and N. Zealanders have been terribly sick with their relatives and friends at not writing to them as they naturally think, in spite of their repeated letters and P.C's, whereas the poor unfortunate anxious folk at home have been sending letter after letter and parcels galore which have never reached their destination. It is a gross iniquity how the poor fellows who are doing their darnedest for their country should have their correspondence so treated. An Archdeacon Richards of Tasmania, who is with us and has been over at the Dardanelles with the troops, said it made your blood boil with the authorities as he knew for a fact it was not the fellows' people's fault, their not getting letters, as they kept on writing and it did so depress the poor chaps having no comforting words from their dear ones at home.

I expect Steve has written to both of us ere this, but not a line do we receive. There has been very little fighting going on over there lately, altho' I understand some very big effort is to be made within the next 10 days. Troops have been fairly pouring into the place. It is time a determined offensive was made, as while this Dardanelles affair drags on, the war on the western front is more or less at a standstill for want of munitions. This campaign here is absorbing a tremendous lot. Things are getting very grave now and the Russians, altho' they are making a tremendous effort and putting up a magnificent struggle, are getting it in the neck I'm afraid. Warsaw is getting more and more surely encompassed about. I daresay we shall have the disquieting and depressing news of its downfall before long. Once the Germans are across the Vistula they can strengthen and establish their line and release 2 million troops who will then be hurled at the Western front again. We haven't had any inspiring or cheerful news for weeks and weeks. It is all most depressing. Of course, we shall win out in the end, but it becomes more and more apparent that the war will drag on for another year at the least.

This brings me to the question of when I shall be returning to Australia. My contract expires on Sept 8th, which is the end of my year. I have been asked by the Colonel here whether or not I am willing to renew it. I said I should like to, as I understood medical men were being more and more urgently needed as the war went on and the number of casualties increased, as they are bound to do. But that I should like leave to go home to England for a fortnight, as I hadn't had a day's leave since I started. He said he thought my request was reasonable, but it was quite out of the question my getting any leave at present, but that he thought it might be managed later on. Mona has been eagerly looking forward to September coming, as she thought I should be returning to her. I am afraid now the little girl will be greatly disappointed when she hears that she will have to wait on indefinitely. However, she is quite at one with me in my continuing if my country still urgently requires my services. An order came thro' today stating that all Lieutenants holding temporary commissions in the R.A.M.C. were to be promoted to Captains on the expiration of a year's service should they decide to continue, so you may address me as Capt. now, Mum, on letters. It will not mean any increase in pay, but it is a sort of sop to Cerberus, and is rather nice in a way.

We are all making preparations for a big influx of wounded and have rigged up an additional 300 beds on the roof of the hospital. It is being covered in with rush matting, and altho' it will be pretty hot, be far superior to tents and should be deliciously cool at night. We are also getting rid of as many cases as possible, by sending them to England and elsewhere to render as many beds empty as possible. So I foresee a busy time in the near future.

I have been relegated to the tents on the football ground where there are some 250 lightly wounded cases. So I have lost my typhoid wards, which has rather distressed me as I was getting very interested in them and doing rather well. The reason of this move is that the fellows who have been looking after the football ground marquees up till now wanted a change in the wards, which after all is only fair. One of the fellows who took over my typhoids from me is now in the hospital, having contracted the disease. He was rather a delicate chap and got blood poisoning after vaccn. at the beginning of things out here and has never been allowed to properly recover. 2 new men have just reported themselves for duty here at this hospital - an Australian from Adelaide and 2 Canadians. One of the latter has now charge of some of the typhoids.

The number of cases has been increasing, but fortunately the majority of them are not serious. I may be put back later on again. I hope so, as I was very keen indeed over them. I heard yesterday that one of my Sisters, quite a nice English girl from Staffordshire and whom I got on very well indeed with and who was upset (at least so she politely maintained) when I was taken away from her wards, has also got typhoid. So there are one or two casualties among the staff here. 6 medical officers and one Sister have so far fallen victims, but fortunately none of them have been really bad.

I am afraid I shall be glued to this base hospital till the end of the chapter now. If I had got home to England there might have been a possibility of my being transferred to France to a field ambulance, a field hospital or a casualty clearing station, where I am rather anxious to get. The work would not be so good as here, of course, by a long way, but one would see some of the fighting and I am anxious to do that. I saw one of the fellows who was at Dover with me and got sent to France has now secured a D.S.O.!

Well, dearest Mum, I hope you will like this letter, it's a little longer than usual. Don't worry, Steve is quite safe.

Best love to all at home. Best luck with Ermo.

Ever, NIGE

This is rather a rambling letter, but I trust you will get the gist of it.

Since Nigel's last letter, the August assault on the Dardanelles had begun, attempting to capture the heights of the Sari Bair Range behind Anzac Cove, including Chunuk Bair (New Zealanders), Hill Q (Ghurkas) and the highest point, Koja Chemen Tepe or Hill 971 (Australians). It began on the afternoon and night of 6 & 7 August with a diversionary attack further south at Lone Pine and senseless slaughter of Australian soldiers in the futile assault on the Nek on 7 August. The campaign inspired the ongoing and ever-growing legend of Gallipoli.

No 15 General Hospital, Abbassia Schools, Alexandria, 11 Aug 1915

Dearest Mum

Am not quite sure when the Australian mail goes out, but write to you regularly in the hope that you will get my letters pretty regularly.

Well, Mother, I've heard from Steve. I had a post card from him a couple of days ago, and a letter from him today. He is well and safe and in good spirits. I enclose his letter which you will like to have, I know, altho' I daresay you will have had a letter from him by the time this letter reaches you. He wrote you a service P.C. at first as he says they go thro' much quicker than ordinary communications as they are not subject to censorship. His letter makes me wish more and more to be over there with him, instead of being immovably tied up at a base during the whole war which will inevitably happen to me. However, I suppose Mona is very thankful I am so situated and I suppose now I'm married I should have some regard for my personal safety. Still there are lots of men with children depending on them who are over on the Peninsula whom I could well replace. Still one ought not to grumble with one's lot, but do one's darnedest for the good of one's country wherever one is.

We are very busy here this week as a large number of convoys of sick and wounded have just come in. Egypt has accommodation for 12,000 and it will be tried to its utmost in this direction, I hear. A larger number of them fortunately are only "light" cases, bullet wounds of arms, flesh wounds, etc. so they will be able to be discharged fairly soon and a good many of them return to the firing line. I think I told you we had rigged up 300 beds on the roof of 2 of our 3 blocks, with a rush matting roof, and it is nice and cool, there is nearly always some sort of a breeze blowing. Only cases who can walk will be treated here.

Dysentery is becoming a scourge, we are having more cases of this disease than typhoid and it is a heart-breaking thing to treat. Of course, diet is one of the most essential items in the treatment of the condition and the fellows in the majority of instances have not been able to procure a suitable one and so when they arrive here are in a parlous state in a large number of instances. The convalescence is slow, as even small dietetic indiscretions are attended by a recrudescence of the diarrhoea with the passage of blood. It is very weakening and it takes a patient some time to recover, accordingly it is depleting the fighting line to a considerable degree.

The stench from the unburied dead bodies is appalling at times over on the Peninsula, as the corpses which lie in exposed position remain unburied for days on end, and with a blazing sub-tropical sun beating down on them decompose readily. It is one of the trying features of the campaign. It is pretty trying in France, but not nearly so bad as in Turkey, as the innumerable flies that are swarming everywhere in the latter country facilitate the decomposing process and also tend to spread disease. The Turkish trenches which fall into our hands are positively uninhabitable owing to the stench and filth which assails one on entering them, I hear. The first thing our troops have to do is to set to work to clear them up a bit. We have heard little to no news of how things have been progressing over there. Achi Baba still remains untaken. I do trust we make some decisive advance soon, as it is imperative we should, to counter the set back the Russians have just received.

How is Ermo? The crops ought to be well on by the time you get this letter, and I trust are full of promise. Another of our medical officers has got typhoid, so we are still shorthanded. Shall stop now, as I must write to Steve. Love to all at home, with very best love to yourself, dearest Mum,

Ever your Pige.

Have been married a year in 4 days' time. How strange it seems. I trust Mona and I shall see a little more of one another during the second year. I wonder also whether I shall be able to give you a kiss.

Divisional Ammunition Park, ANZAC, 16 Aug 1915

My dearest Matee

It is a good while since I have written a letter; there are heaps of reasons though, as first have been worked terribly hard lately and 2nd, the only spare time we get is taken up in cooking our wretched meals. Also the letters I have already written from here I don't think have gone on, as Billy doesn't seem to have had one I sent him. 3rd, I have not been too well lately and am not right yet. Just felt like lying down and doing nothing at all.

We have now been issued with the green envelope in which this comes and so this letter ought to reach you safely. I hope it will anyway. It is quite a new idea and is being given a trial. No military matters are mentioned at all and an occasional envelope will be opened and read to see that the privilege is not being abused. If it works all right we may get some more issued.

I got a mail about a week ago with three letters from you, one from Gran and another from the Child, all exceedingly welcome. You had just gone up to Ermo after putting in the Concord furniture. I expect Ermo is altogether different with the furniture in and being properly looked after. I would give anything to be there now with plenty of fruit to eat and tons of vegetables. I hope you will be able to stay up there and get some enjoyment out of the place. My present most happy desire would be to be lying in a hammock under an apple tree with ripe apples to reach down and eat and something good in the drinking line alongside.

There is no mistake I am now, after six weeks good solid going here, heartily sick of the whole business. Ever since about the third day after arriving have had diarrhoea with a good touch of dysentery. There is apparently no chance of ever getting rid of it until we leave here as everything helps you to get it. The water food and sand all are the cause of it all and at least 80 to 90 of the men here are the same. Of course lots get away to a neighbouring island for a spell and come back much better.

The getting away is all a case of luck as far as I can see. Some fellows will go sick and get sent over straightaway whilst others almost on the point of dropping and after parading sick each morning for about a week will be given 2 calomel tablets and a lead and opium one to follow. I went along to see the A.M.C. for two mornings and was presented with every sort of pill. The 3rd morning was told 'I won't give you any medicine today and you must eat milk foods and soups etc.'

As there is as much chance of getting any milk or soup as there is of flying I thought it pretty brainy. Felt like asking if a little roast chicken and a bottle of champagne would hurt me. However, I haven't been down there again and am getting a little better. Will hang on until we get away if possible, but it will be a very long time yet as far as I can see. It will be a happy day for everyone when this job is finished. I wonder what they will do with us then. Home to England I expect, to be reorganized for the French campaign.

Everyone here considers the Australians and New Zealanders will have just about done their share after this, as it is so different from France where the men get a rest after a week in the trenches or whatever they are on. Here they have very little of that sort of thing and can't get away from shell fire although out of the firing line, and no decent food to help pick up. They will want every man I suppose, especially as one Australian or New Zealander is worth about 6 of Kitchener's Army men from what we have seen of them.

You will know by this that Jack Herring is wounded. He stopped one in the late advance. Don't know how he is getting on. I went up to his battalion to hear of him and see him, but his other company men told me he had got wounded and had gone away. He got a bullet in the stomach and out again at the side fairly low down. Hope he pulls through and gets home. It is a good job it was a bullet and not shrapnel. I see lots of gruesome sights here daily from the bursting of shells coming over.

The war in other parts seems to be going on pretty much as ever, although from what news we get Russia doesn't seem to be able to hold her own. This Turkish bit has been a hard nut to crack after all the blunders made, but we will eventually win here and it ought to make a great difference to Russia. There is no mistake the Turks are great fighters behind entrenchments and live on the smell of an oily rag. They could easily fight a war on the stuff we waste. Some of the wise heads here seem to think that the war will be over in another 6 months as Germany hasn't got any money to carry on with. Ian Hamilton is supposed to have told his wife when he came away from home to expect him back for Xmas. We will I think be away from here before then.

Last night we had a drop of rain in the form of a thunderstorm. This is the first we have had here. I hope the last. We are all living in dug outs which are holes and caves cut in the hills and ground, so you can imagine what things will be like if we are still here for the wet weather. The winter here is very bad indeed, with gales, rain and snow, so it is essential to finish the job before the winter arrives and the weather changes which it generally does about September.

Everyone is living for the day they arrive back home again in Australia. The meals they are to consume are also a favorite topic of conversation. I don't think I shall be hard to please for a while anyway, so long as I don't get a stew. If you are at Ermo you ought to be bottling all the fruit you have on the trees. I'm afraid there is only pears though. I shall like brawn and pressed beef and all those sorts of country things with home grown beans and peas and spuds etc. I could go anything in the way of a cooked dinner now, and feel like a large beef steak pudding, but haven't had a meal for nearly a fortnight. Have got so sick of the same daily rations issued to us that it is impossible to try and stomach them. Bully beef is out of the question and is, under our present state of health, disastrous to touch. Boiled rice we keep up our strength on chiefly about once every other day. Even this without milk and with just a bare shake of sugar takes some eating. Had tea this morning with a piece of bread and jam for breakfast. We have some preserved dried vegetables in soaking to make some soup, but a chap gave us some of his last night and we were up pretty well all night, so don't feel like tackling them again.

Have some washing to do today in the way of a shirt and pair of socks. Will take them in to the water when I go for a swim & do them. Have been quite free from these things since being here, although lots of the men are troubled that way.

Tell Gran I was very pleased to get her letter but didn't get the *Sunday Times* she sent. I got about two of them when I was in Egypt. The papers don't come as letters I suppose. Also thank the Child for her letter with all the local news in. She always says it is time she got a letter, but as this is read out to the family I suppose it does for everyone. I expect Aunt Mog stills wanders up and down the Wharf Road to and from town daily to the museum. Have we got any more dogs? Expect Tommy and Pug[92] still have their rows.

Well Matee I shall send this off now and hope you will get it all right. By the time it reaches you I trust we shall all be away from here having a rest somewhere, and that the end of the war will be in sight.

When I get back shall come and stay at Ermo if no one is in it, or it hasn't been sold. Shall want to have a good rest after this little lot.

Give my best love to Gran and Aunt Mog also the Child and let me know what is for Xmas dinner when I come back. I shall have to pay Cashman[93] a visit to help celebrate the occasion.

Good-bye Matee Boos with heaps and heaps of love, hoping to be home again someday soon, remember me to Uncle Frank and Aunt Phoebe and anyone who enquires, from

Your loving son

TOOTS.

P.S. Haven't heard from Billy since I left Alexandria. Has he been moved, I wonder? Had a *Daily Mirror* sent me by Mona which was very interesting.

---

92 Family pets
93 Cashman reference is obscure.

No 15 General Hospital, Abbassia Schools, Alexandria, 22 Aug 1915

Dearest Mother

Another of your very welcome letters came to hand a few days ago. Many thanks for it. I love hearing from you and it is a comfort to know all is going well so far in spite of the increasing difficulties of living, which this war is bringing about.

Don't go and overdo it, Mum, at Ermo, you're not as young and strong as you used to be! Write and tell me all about the crops and how they progress, and all about everything connected with "the farm". What about some pigs, could you arrange for two or three? An old sow with a litter sounds as if it may bring in something to add grist to the mill.

I am getting all your letters now pretty regularly; they usually arrive 2 at a time. I also received a *S. M. Herald* from you last week and found it interesting in many ways - what ages it is since I saw one! It aroused old memories. How we used to tear to the gate to scan it eagerly on many a morning to see if there were any University results! It seems years and years ago somehow.

Re Rust[94] - I should like you to have her immensely, Mum, if you can make use of her. She is down at Dapto at a farm called 'Cleveland' and owned by Chas. Minnett. He is taking care of her for me and I think using her too, which won't hurt her. The difficulty would be in getting her up to Ermington. She would have to have a horse box and come via Sydney. She really ought to have someone to travel with her, as they aren't very careful over horses and cattle on the railways. The other alternative would be to get someone to ride her up. It is about 60 miles or so, and probably would take 2 days for her to do the journey. Dennis would have managed it all right in years gone by. If you did have her, you would have to use her pretty often, as she has a good deal of "blood" in her as they say, and would soon get very fresh and require a good deal of management if not worked. If you have a sulky shed and a sulky you could have her by all means as I should love you to, and I think you and she would become fast friends as she is a sweet tempered little thing, altho' rather full of fun at times.

I haven't heard from Steve again yet. Mona tells me in her last letter she had a letter from him written from his dug-out. He was well and getting used to things. She is going to send him some tobacco and cigarettes and some

---

94 Nigel's horse

chocolate, altho' the latter I'm afraid will be almost a liquid on arrival in this climate. Still she may pack it carefully. It is nice and kind of her and Steve will appreciate it I know. I sent him over some envelopes several days ago as he asked for some. I must write to him again shortly, as there always is the chance of letters miscarrying over there. I hope he gets all the letters we write. He probably won't write again till he gets one of my letters. I hope he is kept on his present job as it is comparatively safe and much to be preferred to the trenches.

The Australians and N. Zealanders have been doing very well and we hear they have made a considerable advance. They are thought highly of by the English troops and the Ghurkas like fighting beside them more than anybody else. They are undisciplined to a degree and are very reckless and more or less run wild when ordered to attack, and they go on advancing and advancing till they are all practically wiped out. This accounts for our casualties being very high. We have lost far more men than we should have done as a result of this failing.

They are the very devil as far as fighting goes and fight till the last man. Still it is a sad thing that such magnificent chaps should be lost and it is a pity they can't be restrained somewhat. As time goes on I expect they will drop to things and fight more concertedly and thus escape the decimation they have suffered so repeatedly. Fire discipline takes years to acquire and so it is not surprising our men are lacking in it to a large extent. They endure their wounds with fortitude and remarkable spirit and contrast more than favourably with the average English Tommy. They are marvellously good patients and I have a large percentage of them among my lot to look after. I also have an Australian Sister and 2 New Zealanders looking after them, so get on pretty well together as we understand their weaknesses and can manage them better than the English R.A.M.C. officers in many cases.

From present accounts and reports this Dardanelles business promises to become a winter campaign. Altho' our troops have done marvels and have been fighting their very darnedest, owing to natural difficulties and obstacles of the Peninsula, progress is apt to be slow. Anything like a lightning-like advance or an overpowering onslaught cannot be achieved. It is becoming a question as Joffre[95] puts it of "nibbling 'em".

This war, the more one looks at it, is a war of attrition and is almost certainly bound to go on for another 12 months, possibly longer. The Germans are doing wonderfully well against the Russians, who to put it bluntly, have been "getting

---

95 General Joffre, Commander-in-Chief of the French forces on the Western Front, used this phrase to describe the process of wearing out the enemy.

it in the neck". Let us hope the enemy has reached the zenith of his power and from now on his star will begin the descendant.

Frank Lee, Doc Lee's brother whom I met at Wollongong, came to see me today. He has joined the Austn. Army Service Corps as a motor driver and mechanic and was to be sent to France, but he was put off here with several other reinforcements in mistake a few weeks ago and is now kicking his heels about here, champing at the bit. Doing guards, picquets, and funeral parties. He is getting rather fed up, as he feels he is wasting his time, and anybody could do his job. He is being paid 8/- a day as he is a skilled workman so keeping him idle seems a waste of money. At any rate he hopes to be moved from here soon. He asked me to lend him 2 or 3 pounds as he was stoney broke and could not draw any money till he got to England, where he has it tied up, and is only drawing a bob a day here. So I had to comply, altho' I'm rather hard up. I shall probably get it back, but will have to wait a long time. However, I did not mind doing it for Doc Lee's sake. Fortunately I had £3.10.0 on me so I proferred £3 which he gratefully accepted.

We have 2 chaps attached to us this week who were rescued from the *Royal Edward*, the transport which was sunk on its way over to the Dardanelles. About 400 were saved, but I hear more than this number were drowned. A large number of R.A.M.C. people were on board. These 2 fellows say it was a ghastly experience, and one could have no conception of what it was like unless one went thro' it. The hospital ship *Sudan* which was loaded with wounded from the Peninsula rescued most of the survivors and had 2 M.O's from this hospital on board. They state it was a most pitiable and gruesome sight to see the floating wreckage strewn for miles over a glassy sea, consisting of helmets, water bottles, tunics, haversacks, and various kit, with several upturned boats and struggling bodies here and there. The vessel sank in 4 minutes. She was torpedoed on the port side, altho' officially it was reported a mine.

Well, Mum, I had better stop now.

Mona sent me an extra-specially nice stethoscope for our marriage anniversary.

Love to all at home, trusting you are all well.

Yours ever,

NIGE

Nigel Renews Contract, 29 Aug 1915

Dear Boulton:

Colonel James has informed me that you have renewed your contract. I am very glad that we shall not lose the services of such a promising young officer and I feel your example will do much good.

Yours sincerely,

(Sgd) M. J. SEXTON[96]

Divisional Ammn Park, ANZAC, 3 Sep 1915

Dearest Matee Boos

Have got a morning's spell today so am writing at once as the opportunities we get during the day are few and at night time it is impossible owing to no light to see by.

Am feeling a little better now although as you may imagine very weak. It is a hard job to get back one's strength on the food we get here. The life here is getting terribly monotonous. We get a good amount of work to do with generally only time to cook the meals in between knocking off and starting again. If you work after tea you generally get the next morning off. My work is pretty well all done in the day time. There are separate gangs to work the night shifts.

The day before yesterday a large number of papers arrived for me. About 8 altogether. Some from Gran and you and Uncle Frank and Harry Lloyd and I think Jack Jones. They were just what I had been waiting for in fact I had given up hope of getting papers as they seemed so terribly slack about delivering them. I see there are a terrible lot of letters written from the soldiers at the front. They are truly awful some of them and require a good deal of imagination to grasp the meanings of them. They cause a good deal of amusement here amongst the chaps. Of course some of them are pretty correct.

The whole place here now is very different from what it was at the beginning, but even now the beach gets shelled for a short time each day and your dug out is the best place to be, if it is a good one, whilst it is going on. The firing line is

---

96   Michael John Sexton

only a short way in from here and you can hear every shot fired and the whiz of stray bullets is fairly constant. Most of them pass over and land in the water. Our two flanks have been pushed out and inland a long way and in this way the Turks cannot get their guns near enough as before, to shell the beach.

My dug out mate has been making some duff and dumplings lately with some flour which we managed to get hold of. We are not issued with flour so it is particularly scarce and now as equally precious. He is an ex-sailor and so can make these things. The duff went down a treat and was a great change. Wouldn't turn up my nose at some of yours now Matee. For fat we boil down our bacon after which we fry the fat out of it. We had what he calls "dough boys" in a stew and a few there were left over we had with treacle, half a tin of which we had given to us by an English Tommy who had it sent out from home in a parcel. Pancakes as well have we been eating so you see we have been living high. It is a pity we can't get things, such as some proper suet to make a few more things. This war will be a great thing to look back upon once it is over, but I would like to do some of the looking back part now. It will be a treat to be able to have a bath and shave every morning and a good breakfast to follow.

How are you all getting on at Coolah? I wonder if you are still at Ermo and how the place is getting on. I expect if you can only remain there for some little time there will be some great improvements made. The mosquitoes used to be one of the great drawbacks down at the bottom of the garden. No doubt with a lot of the rank vegetation and weeds etc. these would in time disappear.

Gran I suppose is still much the same and going as strong as ever. Thank her for the *Sunday Times* she sent with Gran written on it. Aunt Mog still potters round the garden on Sunday mornings I expect. Have you got any vegetables going in the garden now? Did the hose ever eventuate? And how did the front part of the garden get on? And the Child still goes daily to the school and gets a good bit of fun out of it too I expect. How are the Bartons? Max seemed to come in for a good thing what with his trip home to England. Did I tell you that Jack Herring got wounded about 3 weeks ago? I don't know how bad he was, but he got it in the stomach low down and out again, so some of his company chaps told me. They said he would be all right they thought. I hope he does anyway, and I am glad he is away from here.

I have one or two relics here with me now but don't think I will be able to bring them away with me as we are not allowed to keep them. I went up to one of the Turkish trenches the day after an advance by our troops and got hold of a Turk rifle and a couple of bayonets. They would have been interesting could I have only got them home.

Well Matee will not write any more this time. I hope you are keeping well and not doing too much. Will want to see something of you when I get back and there will be some scrambled eggs etc. to cook for me to go with the Ermo tomatoes.

Please remember me kindly to Uncle Frank and thank him for the newspapers he sent and which are being greatly read and enjoyed by lots of Sydney men round about in the neighbouring dugouts.

Give my best and fond love to Gran and Aunt Mog and the Child, hoping that everything is going on as it should at home. With heaps and heaps of love to you from

Your loving son, TOOTS.

No 15 General Hospital, Alexandria, 8 Sep 1915

Dearest Mother

Your letter of July 18th to hand two or three days ago. Many thanks for it. You will be gratified to hear I have taken your advice re remaining on; altho' as a matter of fact I was called upon to make my decision 2 or 3 weeks before your letter arrived. I never really contemplated giving up, it was only in the event of the War seeming near a definite conclusion when my time expired that made me think of it. So I am booked for another 12 months; surely by this time next year peace negotiations will have made some headway. Of course, we cannot conclude peace on Germany's terms, accordingly it will take every bit of another year before Germany is beaten to her knees. There is a very grim and bitter struggle ahead.

There will be a chance, I think, before long of my being able to get over to the Peninsula. Old Colonel James hangs on to his men like a leech, otherwise it would be an easy job to make an exchange. If I can get another man who can efficiently fill my place, I don't think he can very well refuse to let me go, especially now Steve is over there. I should be far happier nearer the fighting and I think it is only fair that we fellows at the base should take our turn up "forrard" and give the fellows who have been working their "guts" out, so to speak, at the front a rest for a bit. I know little Mona won't like it at all, but she will be brave, I know, and understand. I have not said anything to her about it, as it is no use worrying her till there is some certainty of my being transferred.

I am certainly getting very good experience here at this hospital and have had some rattling good cases, but the experience I am getting now is not as good as I had at first, as I am getting next to no operating now, and am purely a physician. I have all the same derived some valuable information as to the treatment of dysentery, both the amoebic and bacillary forms, and the experience I have had in typhoid is superior to that gained at my age by the majority of medical practitioners. I have also posed as a skin specialist (just like my cheek!) on the strength of what I have learnt from Dr. McMurray of Sydney and Graham Little of Shadwell[97], and so get all the fellows here to let me have any skin cases they have of interest. None of them know much about dermatology as far as I can gather so I put up a big bluff and they listen to me with a certain amount of respect. Rather funny, isn't it? The skin cases I have had have been limited, altho' I have come across one or two good ones. I have charge of some 130 cases now, so have a fair deal to do. I don't think many of the other fellows have as many, but I am not really very hard worked.

There may be a chance a little later on of my getting an opportunity of swapping jobs with a fellow nearer the firing line and if I get it I shall take it. Am getting rather tired of Alexandria, but now the worst of the summer is over perhaps it won't be so depressing.

Am greatly interested to hear you have been slogging along pretty satisfactorily at Ermo and do trust you will be able to carry on. Am sure everything must be getting very dear out there, it is everywhere, and am fortunate I haven't got to cope with housekeeping for a bit at any rate.

I trust things may be a little easier after the War; one doesn't quite know what will exactly happen then. So many breadwinners will have vanished and a very large percentage of those left will be more or less crippled and handicapped for earning a livelihood in the labour market. However, I suppose trade and industry will revive and things will come out somehow all right in the end. Women will take a far larger share in the industrial and economical affairs of the nation. It will be an instructive and interesting revolution sociologically.

I am daily expecting a letter from Steve. I ought to have one soon now, as he said he was writing me a letter on his field service post card. I am very anxious to hear whether he has got any of my letters. It will be very disgusting if he hasn't. I shall write to him again very shortly. He may also mention whether he has heard from you since he has been on the Peninsula. Mona has sent him two parcels.

---

97 Dr Little worked at the East London Hospital for Children, Shadwell, and also at St Mary's Hospital at Paddington.

Many thanks for the *Sunday Times* to hand a few days ago. There is quite a lot of interesting matter in it. Thank Uncle Frank for the *S.M.Herald*; I recognized his handwriting on the outside. How is he? Still at Sydney? Have his family migrated to N.S.W. and if so do you see much of them, or has Chatswood monopolized them? I expect he is much taken with Ermo. What I am wondering about is the mosquito peril in the summer. It is a pretty formidable question to deal with, as far as I can remember the skeets are particularly numerous and voracious. Let's hope they won't trouble you much.

How is Harry[98] and what is he up to? Fiji or elsewhere? Hasn't felt it incumbent on him to enlist? A wonderful opportunity of seeing something of the world. A phenomenal chance which won't occur again during our lives, probably. I suppose being the only son there is a good deal to be said against his coming over here. Still I dare say the Sugar Co. would keep his job open for him. It is only fair of them to do so.

Clarke Cousins, Bulli, Christmas 1909
(From Left, Hal Clarke, Nora Barton, Cleon Dennis, Thea Boulton, Phyllis Clarke & Stephen Boulton. Picture Courtesy Julia Woodhouse)

Well, dearest Mum, will stop now. Trusting all is well at Gladesville. Love to the family. What ages it is before I shall see you again. Perhaps the time will soon pass. Bestest love,

Always your loving Son,

NIGE

Still a Gunner, Stephen was transferred on 6 September from the Divisional Ammunition Column (D.A.C.), serving everyone in the 1st Division, to working specifically with the 2nd Aust Field Artillery Brigade's Ammunition Column (B.A.C.). The role was short-lived due to his serious case of dysentery. By 10 September,

---

98 Nigel's first cousin Harry Flockton Clarke (Hal), an industrial chemist with CSR, was Aunt Phoebe's only son, and brother to Phyllis (Phil).

arrangements had been made to send a small proportion of officers and other ranks to Lemnos Rest Camp for a period of 14 days, and Stephen was among this evacuation group. Their ship's destination was Mudros, a deep water anchorage and naval base on the island of Lemnos, but half way to Lemnos, weather conditions forced the ship to drop off the patients at Imbros, an island only 24 km from Gallipoli.

Island of Imbros, 11 Sep 1915

My dearest Matee

You will note my change of address. Have been sent over here to hospital. It is an island quite close and handy where a big hospital has been made. I am not terribly ill so don't worry. Have had diarrhoea and dysentery for so many weeks that I am wasting away a bit and getting terribly thin. The M.O. I saw at Anzac decided to send me away to get alright as I didn't seem to be making any signs of improvement or getting better at Anzac.

I am now sleeping in an E.P. Tent with about 23 others more or less on stretchers. They are much more comfortable than the dug-outs and no doubt I will get right again soon with proper dieting etc. Incidentally I have also got a cold and cough, but I always used to have them at home. It is delightful to get a rest, and not have to do any cooking directly your work is finished. Have had nothing but bread and milk so far, but have only had one tea and breakfast. Am able to walk about so have come round to a large marquee which is run by the Y.M.C.A. for soldiers who want to write letters and read, also they have the gramophone going now and I believe have concerts etc. during the evenings. It is a very good thing for the men and is much appreciated.

The weather here now is rapidly changing and getting much colder. Some of the nights are bitter cold already. Last night blew a gale and it was a bit of a "perisher". Will probably lose the run of all my letters now for a bit as I was supposed to be sent to Mudros which is at Lemnos, but owing to the roughness of the weather and water the mine sweeper left us all at Imbros which is not far away. However, we may be sent down there later. Just before I left I had a couple of letters from Mona with some *Daily Mirrors*. She said she had sent me a parcel of delicacies and socks. However, I got the letters, but the parcel had not arrived by the time I had left. It was very kind of her to think of it wasn't it, and it will be a great pity to lose it for I don't suppose I shall get it now.

This change and rest and absence of gun shell fire will do me a lot of good and I shall be able to get properly well again before I am started again. One's nerves get very nervy whilst over at the front having to be on a continual strain of looking, watching and listening all the time. You will see some chaps walking along when all of a sudden they will duck behind something and get under cover when it is only a steam boat blowing off steam which sometimes sounds similar to a shell coming. Of course everyone laughs at the time but still nearly everyone gets doing it some time.

Hope everyone is well at home and not worrying about me as I will be alright again soon and with good food will soon pick up again.

I cannot write any more now Matee this time, as I got out of bed to write this and they may think there is nothing much wrong if I am away from my tent much longer, so with love to Gran and Aunt Mog and the Child and heaps and heaps for yourself, will write again when I am up and about properly, from

Your loving son,

TOOTS.

P.S. Haven't had any letters from home for some time now. One of our mails was sunk coming over from Mudros on the lighter. 1,000 bags I believe were lost. I expect there were some of yours in that lot.

Hospital, Island of Imbros, 15 Sep 1915

My dear Matee-Boos

You will see that I am still at Imbros in the hospital there. Came here on the 10th. Am going on all right I suppose, but of course, am very weak and ever likely to be on the present diet I am on. However I think I am leaving here today for another hospital either at Mudros which is the capital of Lemnos Island or back to the base at Alexandria. Naturally I hope it is Alexandria, more especially if I could get into No 15 General but I'm afraid there is no hope of that.

I am not feeling ill now except for being run down and unable to do much or move about energetically owing to my general weakness. The hospital here is only a sort of detail place where everyone is left for 3 or 4 days before being sent on. Have been on milk diet ever since arriving here which consists of bread and milk for breakfast, rice and milk for dinner and bread and milk again for tea. This is all right as far as it goes but it does not take long before you begin to feel hungry.

There are a few miserable Greek stalls here run by the Greeks with eggs, biscuits, grapes, chocolate and some tinned fruit and sardines etc. for sale. No patients are allowed any pay. So unless you happen to have some splosh on you, it is likely you will go hungry for some time. Luckily I had about 10/- on me when I arrived, but this is going fast as biscuits are 3 for 1d., butter (tinned) at 2/- the ¼ lb. and eggs 1½ d. each.

I have been having eggs chiefly with what bread is left over from the bread and milk. You can see that this is a good place to get away from if you want to get well again. I don't think I am much better than when I first came. At Mudros I believe we can draw some money and it is a sort of a town with more shops and also a canteen run by the Military Authorities where we could get a change of food and plenty of it. I hope I get on to the Hospital Ship which we are now supposed to be waiting for and get back to Alexandria for a while. I think a few good feeds properly cooked and decent water to drink would put me right as quick as any medicine. We get an issue of grapes here; it generally runs about 10 grapes a man. They are fairly cheap to buy being grown on the island - 3d a lb.

Last night and this morning we had some rain, fairly solid too. It will go hard for the chaps on the Peninsula when the rain starts as probably most of the dugouts will fall in and the trenches and parapets[99] collapse. It is getting pretty cold already at night now, and it certainly looks like being a winter campaign here. The Australian troops I should think will feel it if they are left over there for the winter. Most of them are looking physical wrecks now having had 19 weeks of it at a stretch. They give them a week in France and then a spell in a village or town well away from the fighting line or sometimes leave to go home.

Next day 16th.

The hospital ship came in this evening, but we did not go after all. They collected about 50 of us and marched us out, all thinking we were going aboard the ship. However we were disappointed once more and we finished up in a fatigue camp, or camp where all the men do fatigues and guards etc. There was some mistake somewhere as most us were still on milk diet and we weren't supposed to leave hospital on that diet alone. Next morning we all paraded sick and were told if we were discharged we were fit. That is generally the military style of medico. Give you two pills and write fit for duty against your name for anything at all. I explained to him that I was still on milk diet and couldn't get it any more when I had left hospital so he said to the orderly "Give him a tin of milk" and 2 pills.

---

99   Earth wall (either loose or in bags) protecting the front of a trench

In the afternoon they took us before the Colonel who must have found out some mistake had been made and so now we are re-admitted back into hospital. Since leaving hospital yesterday I have had a good feed of biscuits and eggs (boiled) and feel ever so much better and stronger, so I expect it won't be long before I am back again in the fatigue camp. Once I am a little stronger the fatigue camp won't be so bad as they don't have very much to do and no very heavy work. Before sending us back to the Peninsula we all go to Mudros to go before a medical board who examines us to see if we are fit for service again. The rest is doing me good meanwhile and it won't be long before I am back on the Peninsula.

How is everyone at home? Will be very glad when this war is finished and are once more back with you all. There will be everyone talking about the war and what you saw and did that I am thinking we will not be finished with it for a few months after we do get back. Have seen some of the letters that have appeared in the Sydney papers from chaps who were at the front, and hope you don't believe all of them. Some are slightly exaggerated.

Give my very best to Gran and Aunt Mog and the Child and with lots of kisses on the brow and heaps of love for Matee Boos, hoping everything is going well for her and a few dibs coming in from Concord etc., from

TOOTS.

No 15 General Hospital, Alexandria, 16 Sep 1915

My dearest Mother

Your long and loving letter of August 8th came to hand 2 or 3 days ago. It was written from Ermington and was all about the farm and your labours connected therewith, and accordingly very interesting. I do hope, Mum, you will be able to make things go, as once you get things going a bit it ought to bring in something and make your cost of living less. It is a boon letting Concord at last, I do trust the tenants will pay up and not knock the little place about. Perhaps it being now unfurnished they won't be able to do so much damage.

There is not much to tell you this mail I'm afraid. I was very nearly going to the Peninsula this week, but it proved a "wash out". A chap just out from England was very anxious to become attached to this hospital, as he was a great friend of a fellow called Wilson[100] here, but he was detailed to proceed to the Peninsula 3 days after his arrival in Egypt. He was keen to exchange with any of us here, and I managed to get Wilson to put before him that I was very keen to go over and would be delighted to swap with him. Wilson did so, but when he learnt I was married he wouldn't hear of it in spite of all the pressure I could bring to bear, so another chap called Parmiter[101], a little man of about 30, who is a single man and one of a family of 9, chiefly boys, did. I was rather disappointed as I should have greatly liked to have gone especially now Steve is over there, altho' I don't suppose I should have seen anything of him, as I would be attached to one of the British divisions. It was for a field ambulance, which would have been quite exciting work, and one would gain first hand experience of what modern warfare is like in the field.

I shall feel wretched if I return to Australia having been potted away at the base all the time, but I am afraid that is what will eventually happen. I suppose it is selfish wanting to get up to the front, and very inconsiderate from your and Mona's point of view. One should be content with one's lot and not desire to run any unnecessary risks - still the way I look at it is that I have no children, and by taking a job closer up to the firing line I would be relieving someone else, probably a married man with a family who could be ill spared comparatively speaking. There are lots of them over on the Peninsula, who should be at the base, while we younger men with lesser responsibilities are lurking about in safety right back. Still I don't suppose I shall get another opportunity as it is only occasionally that a chance of exchanging with a man comes along. Where an exchange could be effected there are, of course, many instances, but one doesn't personally hear of them, it is only if one happens to know some chap knowing the man involved. I think I will see old James about it, and represent to him that I am keen to get up if by doing so I can relieve a married man with children. I dare say old Sexton, the A.D.M.S., would come across cases and arrange an exchange if Col. James was agreeable; the latter old boy, however, is much averse to losing any of his staff, and unless he was favourably impressed with the man who was to take my place would not be at all disposed to come at the swap.

I have had my "3 stars" up" a week now, and gave a small dinner to the fellows in my tent last night. They comprised Collier, Campion, Webb[102], a dentist, a chap called Dolling[103], a S. Australian and an interstate cricketer, and myself.

---

100 Identity unknown: many doctors named Wilson served in R.A.M.C.
101 Bernard Rayne Parmiter. The Dover College Register says of him: (12th Dec, 1885) [J. P.]; Prefect; Lond. Matric, 1904; House Fives Representative; left, '04 (b); entered Guy's Hospital; Inter. M.B., Lond. (Honours in Physiology), '09.
102 Identity unknown: many doctors named Webb served in R.A.M.C.
103 Charles Edward Dolling, who came to England in 1915 to further his studies and joined the R.A.M.C. See picture on page 135.

We had quite a pleasant evening and were a very sober party as 3 of us were teetotallers practically speaking.

I had another letter from Steve. He is much happier now and settling down to things, now he has got over the dysentery. All the Australians and New Zealanders seem to suffer greatly from it on their arrival over there, much more than the British troops, altho' this is rather inexplicable as they have been used to roughing it to a far greater extent to the average English Tommy. Steve has an ex-sailor as a "dug-out" mate and he apparently is something of a cook and has looked after Steve and provided him with soups, etc. I sent him over a parcel which I think will cheer his heart some days ago, I think I told you in my last letter, and Mona has despatched no less than 3 she tells me, the last one containing some most acceptable luxuries. I do hope he receives them. I think she registered the last one, which increases its chances of reaching its destination and also hurries it on its route a bit too, I understand.

I haven't heard from Cousin Bessie for a while now, altho' she owes me a letter. I shall write to her again very shortly, as I think she likes hearing from me.

Well, Mum, I will stop now, as there is little to tell you this mail. Give my love to all at home. Best of luck with the farm. Don't worry, Mum, all is well with Steve and I.

Till next mail.

Always your loving Son,

NIGE

25th Casualty Clearing Hospital, Island of Imbros, 19 Sep 1915

My dear Matee Boos

Just another short note to let you know how I am progressing. Am feeling better and am being kept here for a couple of days to be fed up. The last three days have been off the milk diet and had chicken (tinned) for dinner and custard and 2 eggs for tea and breakfast. Naturally, the amount of chicken is not very great, but tasted very nice in spite of it being the tinned stuff. The eggs go well too at tea and breakfast times, so you see things are beginning to look up. I still have a bit of cold and cough which I don't seem to be getting rid of as soon as I usually do. Expect it's because of not getting the usual amount of food.

Today is Sunday and I have now been here 9 days. You will be pleased to hear that I went to Church last Sunday at the Service held in the Y.M.C.A. tent. Shall make a business of again attending this afternoon's service in the hospital. These are the first church parades I have been to since leaving Newcastle last February. Sunday in the army is just the same as any other day. It is a case of "Good Boy Tootie".

Haven't any idea what is going to happen to me after I leave here. Will probably go to some light duty camp for a while before going back to the Peninsula. In any case, will have to go down to Mudros to be examined by a Medical Board before being sent back. Will write and let you know as soon as they shift me anywhere else.

Give my best love to everyone at Coolah, hope Gran is well and Aunt Mog I suppose still journeys to the museum each day up and down the Wharf Road. Don't suppose there will be any very great alteration to Gladesville by the time I see it again. How is the Child? Getting on alright and have they made her Head Mistress of the School yet, or has she married any of the budding masters?

Only a short letter this time Matee, as it is only two days since I wrote last. I wonder if you are still living at Ermo and how is the place and garden progressing. With many kisses on the brow and ear and much love from

Your loving son,

TOOTS.

No 15 General Hospital, Abbassia Schools, Alexandria, 22 Sep 1915

Dearest Mother

There is a mail going out tomorrow morning early for the Far East so I am going to try and get this letter off by it. You will probably get a letter from Steve also by the same mail and will hear that he is in hospital at Imbros. I am less anxious about him now as he will be well looked after and will stand a chance of getting properly right again. He probably will be sent back here to convalesce if he doesn't rapidly improve, as the hospital at Imbros is a so-called Stationary Hospital, and only hangs on to cases that they can return in a comparatively short time fit to the firing line. As Steve is a dysentery and will probably take 2 or 3 weeks before he is well again, I expect he will come back here, and in which case I hope to see him again and tell you all about him.

So, Mum, it ought to be an anxiety off your mind to know he has left the Peninsula and is in comfort and security. Mona is coming out here in the early part of November, that is in about 6 weeks' time, with her mother. It will be nice having her here and I daresay she will be able to make herself useful as there is a branch of the Red Cross here which is doing good work I understand. I shall probably be able to get 48 hours leave off when she arrives as I haven't applied for any leave since I joined the Service and surely am entitled to it, as everyone else has secured it at some time or another. I haven't been to Cairo yet, so hope to see a little of that city, as I shall have to go thro' it on my way to Port Said, where I shall go to meet Mona.

I don't think Mrs. Little will stay here long, as it being a foreign place and she being unable to speak either French or Arabic won't be able to get to know anybody as, excepting the troops and a few Civil Servants, the English colony is a small one. All the hotels and boarding houses are kept by foreigners, and are largely filled with foreigners too. So as she will stay a good deal of her time in boarding houses if Mona is out on her Red Cross job, and I am busy here, she will get rather bored I am afraid, and feel a bit lonely. As this is almost half way to Australia and as she is very anxious to get back to her mother and her business in Wollongong, she probably will go on from here when she has seen all there is to be seen and gets tired of the place. She won't like parting from Mona as she has had her with her all her life, but once the wrench is over, she will settle down to things, I daresay, and once she gets amongst her own people once more won't feel it so much.

She and Mona have had a fortnight at Torquay in glorious Devon. It must have been perfectly delightful. I wonder whether I shall see that beautiful county before I return to Australia after the war is over, as I don't suppose I shall ever get the chance again.

Mona will be coming via Paris and Marseilles, which is quicker and far more interesting and I don't think any more expensive. I dare say they will spend a day or two in Paris, which must be a wonderfully different Paris to the usually gay Paris that tourists know. One will get a much better idea of the tremendous struggle that is going on for a nation's freedom and liberty by visiting France than one gets from England, where "everything as usual" is the boast.

The days are drawing in here now and the weather is getting much cooler to what it was. It gets dark soon after 5 now, whereas 2 months ago it was light at 8. I am very busy and have got a large number of bad cases to look after at present. A convoy of 50 came in on Sunday and they were all medical. More than 50% were dysenteries. Some of the poor fellows looked very played out and exhausted. I lost one last night. If we could only get them a little earlier we could save a lot more. I expect now the weather is getting cooler the dysenteries won't be so numerous, at least I hope so. But I daresay there will be almost as many cases of pneumonia and rheumatism which is very rife in a winter campaign which this Gallipoli affair seems certain to prove. At any rate sufficient unto the day is the evil thereof.

I must stop now, Mum, as I have to give an anaesthetic for a chap. I got a letter from Cousin Bessie the day before yesterday, and must answer it shortly. She asks me to make enquiries for a friend of hers whose son has been reported missing. The Red Cross people here have been laid in by me and are writing to me tomorrow about him. Trust everything is going well at the farm, and that the crops are coming on well. Shall be very interested to hear of the agricultural capabilities of Ermo under your supervision and control.

Am afraid Mona's three parcels and my one won't reach Steve now. Wonder what will happen to them? I only wrote to him last night.

Love to all at home,

Bestest love to yourself, dearest Mum,

Ever yours,

NIGE

25TH CASUALTY CLEARING HOSPITAL, IMBROS ISLAND, 25 SEP 1915

My dear Matee Boos

Still here. Am feeling better, but not too strong yet by a long way. Luckily I have got a very decent doctor in charge of me. He is in no hurry to send me away he says, and wants me to get properly well. Am still having eggs and porridge, chicken and custard as my diet, but unfortunately I can't get enough of it. Bread even is hard to get and none is allowed more than their ration. Yesterday he said I was to have a bottle of stout. It went down alright, but didn't agree with me so I am not getting another today. He tells me that I shall probably get a week or so spell after leaving the hospital before going back to my unit. I asked him if he could send me back to Alexandria and let me have my spell there, but it wasn't within his power to do it, otherwise he said he would have done it. I haven't got rid of my cold yet. It no longer worries me, but still remains. Suppose I want a change of air.

The nights here are pretty cold now and days too when the sun doesn't come out. I am alright here at night as I have three blankets over me and one under, besides my overcoat. After I get out again it will be a case of sleeping in one's clothes again with an oil sheet underneath and 2 blankets on top. Am not looking forward to the winter a bit.

The Tommies here seem to notice the cold already, much more than we do. And they come from the North of England and Scotland. All the Australians are greatly envied by the Tommies on account of their much smarter uniform and felt hats and the 6/- per day. They (the Tommies) are turned out in the sloppiest made khaki with helmets which as a rule are about 2 sizes too big.

Remember me to the family at Coolah. Hope Gran has not found the winter too trying and Aunt Mog has not got too many walks to the wharf in the rain, also the Child who I hope is still a great help to her Ma. Have not had any letters for ages and am not expecting any until I can have them forwarded to a fairly permanent address. I may leave here any day now. Am living for the time when we all come back safely and settle down again with the Mee Maw.[104]

Best love to all and heaps for yourself from

Your loving son,

TOOTS.

No 15 General Hospital, Alexandria, 29 Sep 1915

My dearest Mother

Here goes another letter to you altho' I have very little news to tell you. I haven't heard from Steve again since I wrote, so I don't know whether he is still at Imbros, or whether he has been sent on to Lemnos. I wrote to him 2 or 3 days ago and addressed my letter to Imbros. I hope he gets it, as I know a letter

---

104 This term is sometimes used today to describe a grandmother, but Stephen's mother was not a grandmother in 1915.

would cheer him up, still if his whereabouts is uncertain it is difficult to be sure whether one's letters are likely to reach him. Unless I hear from him again shortly, I shall drop him another letter to the Hospital at Imbros.

The success on the western front is the great excitement of the week.[105] It is time we had some cheerful news, isn't it? Altho' our success is only a local one, it will oblige the Germans to keep a good number of their army in the west and thus relieve the Russians a bit in the East.

We have been having a large number of dysenteries here lately. Dysentery seems to be a far more troublesome disease to deal with than typhoid in this campaign. It has been responsible for depleting the firing line considerably, and seems difficult to cope with. We are not getting very many wounded now, and so our surgical wards are largely being commandeered by dysentery cases. The fellows on the surgical side are rather sick, as they are not getting the experience they expected, the large percentage of the cases being medical. However, when another large engagement occurs I expect we shall be deluged again with wounded.

Mona expects to leave England at the end of next month, October, and should be here in about 5 or 6 weeks' time. Colonel Sewell[106] who is in charge of the surgical division is getting his wife out too, she arrives in a few days I believe. There is a fellow called Roberts who has only married recently I believe, who has had his wife out here several weeks now. I don't know that I altogether approve of fellows having their wives out here, but I don't see all the same why they shouldn't, provided it doesn't interfere with their work. Roberts has rather overdone it, and made fellows a bit disgusted with him, as he is only in the hospital about 3 to 4 hours a day. I did his work for him when his wife first arrived, and when he subsequently developed Scarlet Fever for 5 or 6 weeks, but he didn't even thank me.

However, I shall profit by his example and give the chaps here little ground for objecting to Mona being here. She understands I shan't be able to see very much of her, and will not countenance my running the risk of neglecting my work, I know. It will be very nice having her here as there is very little to do sometimes when we are occasionally slack in the evenings, and it will be very pleasant and enjoyable to be able to spend them with her.

Egypt is one of the resorts for the wealthy and aristocracy of England during the winter, and I expect Alexandria will be well crowded this year, with such

---

105 Presumably he refers to the Third Battle of Artois, around Vimy Ridge, Loos and Lens, which commenced on 25 September, but any success was short-lived.
106 Lieut Col Evelyn Pierce Sewell

numbers of the military here, altho' I daresay a large number of the usual visitors will not make the journey, owing to the difficulties of travel at present.

Gran wrote me a letter which I got with yours last mail, and sent me 2 *Sunday Suns* - I must write and answer it, as I think the poor old thing will appreciate a letter from her grandson. Am sorry to hear she is so troubled with her legs and her breath. I trust she will not become bedridden in the end. She is not quite the sort to stay in bed, altho' I don't suppose she would mind doing the invalid - one feels sorry for her.

No, Mum, I never got the 2 letters you addressed to Mustafa, goodness knows what has happened to them. I received some letters while at Mustafa and some have been forwarded on to me, but those 2 never turned up. So I did not hear the full strength of the Phillips affair. Have you heard the end result? I should like to know further details. Anything in the papers about it, or was it hushed up?[107]

Well, Mum, this is a very uninteresting letter, I'm afraid, but there is little fresh to tell you. My chances of being moved from here to the Peninsula are practically nil now as far as I can see, so have given up trying. Trust everything is well with the farm, that the peas and the potatoes were a success. Poor old Dicky, he seems to be at a loose end. Love to all at home. Bestest love,

Ever yours,

NIGE

Stephen was transferred from Imbros to a hospital ship on 1 October 1915.

At Sea, Hospital Ship 'Grantully Castle', 4 Oct 1915

My dear Matee

This address will come as a pleasant surprise to you as it did me, as you can imagine. Was almost alright in hospital at Imbros Island when orders came for the hospital to be moved. All the patients who were not well enough to be discharged were to be sent to Mudros by hospital ship. My doctor (Dr. Sunderland) was very good to me and could have discharged me easily, but he

---

107   One hundred years later, the reference to the Phillips affair is unexplained but may have related to Thea's music teacher, the Russian society pianist and teacher Laurance Phillip, who died of the Spanish flu in San Francisco early in 1919.

sent me down to Mudros. So at 2 p.m. we all proceeded on board the *Grantully Castle* which came into the bay during lunch time.

We stayed on board in harbour all night and didn't sail till next morning. The Captain's orders were for Malta via Mudros. I bustled about and make myself useful on board as the patients were lying on mattresses all over the decks. The ship had all her beds full and fully 250 more patients than was her full complement. Naturally there was not a great deal the matter with lots of them, but being mostly Tommies are very helpless and dense. There are only eight Australians on board and of these, when volunteers were asked for to assist in handing out the food etc., 4 volunteered. So I have the job of feeding the dysentery patients.

Hospital Ship *Grantully Castle* off Salonika, 1915
Picture Courtesy Peter Biles

The Tommies almost require it put into their mouths. When we arrived at Mudros 150 of the patients on deck were to be put off. By being generally useful I was told to stay on board and assist. So after dropping the 150 we sailed for Malta and are now about half way there. It is great getting into civilisation again. The nurses on board are all Australians except 2 and it was like getting home. They naturally were pleased to see us amongst so many Tommies, and we are made much of. Some of them have been to Sydney and know some of the Doctors there. They are excellent types as nurses, being so very cheerful and gay. They have had a great time since leaving Australia having been home first and backwards and forwards from the Dardanelles and England, Alexandria, Malta ever since, sometimes with no patients and not much work.

This is a nice and comfortable boat and am getting plenty to eat. We will all get off at Malta I expect where there are numerous hospitals and convalescent camps. I was indeed lucky to drop into this trip aboard a hospital ship. These ships are fitted up at great expense, having operating rooms and numerous wards with rows and rows of swinging cots. Am sending the Child a post card of the ship printed on board. Will write after we get to Malta and tell what and where I am.

The orderlies on board these boats have a great time and live well. Seems to be a good idea to join the Army Med. Corps and get one of these jobs at 6/- a day.

Yesterday was Sunday and it was again a case of "Good Boy Tootie". I suppose you still go to Ryde occasionally or have you gone back to "Hoppy"?

Give my very best love to Gran and Aunt Mog and the Child, hoping they are all keeping well and in good spurrits and with heaps and heaps of love and kisses to Matee Boos from her loving son,

TOOTS.

The island of Malta (south of the Italian island of Sicily) was known as the 'Nurse of the Mediterranean' during the Great War. Tens of thousands of patients from the Gallipoli campaign and the Salonika campaign passed through the 27 hospitals and convalescent camps on Malta. St. John's Military Hospital functioned in today's St Clare College in Blanche Huber Street, Sliema from 1 September 1915 to 9 October 1917.

ST. JOHNS MILITARY HOSPITAL, SLIEMA, MALTA, 7 OCT 1915

My dear Matee Boos

Here I am at last, for a little while I expect. Had a good trip over in the *Grantully Castle* and arrived at Valletta Harbour at 5 o'clock on 5th. We remained on board all night and next morning motor cars came down to the wharf alongside our ship with stretchers and seats in. Walking cases went off first and the cars took 8 in each to the various hospitals. The Australians were pretty well kept together and came off nearly last.

We were sent to St. Johns Hospital at Sliema and it is a suburb of Valletta; quite close being only ½d. ride in the ferry boat. Walking off the gangway we were handed a packet of cigarettes and box of matches and offered a drink of milk by some of the English people on the island. On arriving at the hospital we each were told off to a ward. There are 52 wards in all containing about 400 beds. I am in No 47 with 6 other patients in. It is a big roomy place, all stone with huge windows and 3 doors to it. The building itself was formerly a school, I suppose something like No 15 General. It is run by English R.A.M.C. with English nurses. They seem very kind and all that sort of thing, but not the stamina or build of the good Australian "strapper". They also are of the La de da type which greatly amuses a lot of the chaps, me included, who often feel like bursting out with a mighty guffaw.

The doctor seems a very decent sort of a cove standing no buck and has me back in bed on milk diet with bread and butter. The milk here is very funny stuff being very sweet, indeed almost sickening, but with soda water in it makes a fair drink. But am getting tired of milk now. Expect he will try me on some other diet soon. Am only suffering from debility now with still a little diarrhoea, which according to the doc. will always return if we go back as the whole lining of the stomach has been worn away with the grit and sand etc. But of course whether we go back or not is not for him to say. There are convalescent camps here after we leave hospital where we shall go to start with.

St Clare College, used as St John's Military Hospital, Malta, in WWI

I have not seen much of Malta so can't tell you anything about it except that it is like no other place I have yet seen. The water of the Mediterranean runs right up to high stone cliffs which in places have been reclaimed. The streets and houses then run along in terraces up from the water. There are also sorts of tunnels and subterranean passages all over the place. At night the gondolas get about with their red green and white lights showing, which makes the harbour look very pretty. Somewhat like Venice I expect. The streets are very narrow, there being only room for one carriage to pass another and no footpaths.

The doctor will be round at any minute now and he takes the letters, so will not write more this time in case there is a mail going out today. I think you could send my letters in future to the hospital and they will send them on to wherever I have gone. It will save a good deal of time not going to the various units I have been to in Egypt and the Peninsula.

Give my best love to Gran and Aunt Mog and the Child, hoping everything is going on all right at home. It is a treat getting back into a nice spring bed with sheets again. Will write again soon and let you know how things are progressing. Haven't had a letter or paper from anyone for months owing to my moving about, but expect they will come along some time. Have written to the Base Post Office at Alexandria telling them to send my letters here. I ought to hear from Billy fairly soon as I have written and told him I am here and to send me some news as soon as possible.

Good-bye Matee Boos, will soon pick up now and put on some flesh. With heaps and heaps of love from

Your loving son, TOOTIE.

St. Johns Military Hospital, Sliema, Malta, 16 Oct 1915

Dearest Matee-Boos

Just a line to let you know what is happening. About 4 days ago my temp. went up suddenly to 100.2 with a bad head. Was sent back to bed and the next morning when the doc. came round temp. was up to 102 still with the same bad head. He had a look at me and found a scarlet fever rash on my body and back. Didn't have any of the other symptoms of scarlet fever, so the doc got the whole medical staff up round the bed for a conference. There were about 8 in all and each one said that it wasn't scarlet fever.

However, the whole ward in which I am in had to be isolated and await the plainer appearance of the rash. It had not shown up on my limbs at all which is what was bamboozling them. Next day my temp. was about the same with the splitting headache. Had one of the big bugs up to see me in the morning, a Lieut. Colonel and professor somebody. He however didn't diagnose it or commit himself in any way, but said "how very interesting". The rash had got a little fainter by this time. Next morning it had nearly gone, but my temp. and head were still the same. The ward are still isolated, the rash has almost quite gone but the temp doesn't go down much, it is 100.4 this morning and my head is still busting.

I don't think I have got scarlet fever. Was feeling well just before this attack and had my phiz.[108] taken with some other patients which I am sending. The weather here in Malta is very trying and unhealthy. I may have perhaps got a touch of Mediterranean fever. Lots of docs seemed to think the rash was brought out

---

108 Abbreviation of physiognomy, a slang term for photo

by some of the medicine I had been having. Am on a beef tea diet with a pudding at dinner time.

This letter will get to you about the time of your "birthenday" so will wish Matee Boos many happy returns of the day and may she have plenty of

Patients, St. Johns Military Hospital, Malta, Oct 1915
(Stephen Boulton seated on ground, at left. Picture Courtesy Julia Woodhouse)

them. Haven't got anything to send out except what's already in the envelope. Hope you will all drink my health in some of Tooth's best and that you have a proper birthenday.

Give my best love to Gran and Aunt Mog and the Child. Hope everything is going on all right at Coolah or Ermo and that you have got some vegetables on the go. And heaps and heaps of love from Tootie to his Ma. Will I expect be alright again when my temp. goes down and head stops aching.

Love from TOOTS.

No 15 General Hospital, Alexandria, 18 Oct 1915

Dearest Mum

This day next month is your birthday, I expect when this reaches you it will have passed by.

I wonder what sort of a year is ahead of us all, and whether we shall be able to celebrate your birthday next year at closer quarters. I wonder whether if we could see into the future the vista would please us or otherwise. Oh, I do hope, Mum, happy days are ahead and that when this awful war terminates things will run on smoothly for us all.

How I wish I could be with you again in dear old N.S.W. It seems a lifetime since we said goodbye, altho' it is only just about 2 years. But 2 years at this time of one's life seems to be such a large slice of time, such radical events have happened and are happening, in my life at any rate. I am still your Pige in spite of it all tho', Mum. Blood is thicker than water, and I often long to see you again and often wonder when that time is to be.

I heard from Steve today, a fairly long letter. He wrote me a short note 2 days ago to tell me he had got to Malta and was very comfortable. He is picking up a good deal and is on the full diet, tho' his innards aren't quite in working order yet. The convalescence of dysentery is tedious and such a thing as a rapid recovery is unfortunately not the rule. It is such a depressing disease, but Steve is getting quite perky again by the tone of his letter and this is a very true index of improvement and is very cheering. I won't send his letter on to you, as I expect he has written to you also and will tell you all he has to tell. Malta seems to be a wonderful place, and quite unlike any other place he has ever seen. I do hope I shall be able to see something of it before I return as it certainly is one of the places in Europe to visit. It is filled with hospitals and convalescent camps, and I should think a far better place for recovering from an illness in than Egypt, which tho' a pleasant enough country to live in when one is fit, is apt to be very depressing when one is ill.

I am still seriously thinking of the Assistant M. O. of Health job here, which I wrote to you of in my last letter. I should love to know what you thought of it. I am to interview the head of the Municipality in a few days – he is at present away at Cairo – and learn what the requirements necessary are, and whether I would be qualified to fill the billet efficiently. I should require to have a working knowledge of French, and a little Arabic would be extremely useful I dare say. So if there is a probability of my taking hold of the appointment it is up to me to try and get hold of some French straightaway. Arabic is an appalling language, but a smattering would be sufficient as far as this goes. I should have to work very hard for the first 18 months or two years till I got the hang of things, but then things would become easier.

After the war is over and Egypt becomes a fixed British Colony, it is bound to go ahead by bounds, and Alexandria would be the port of the Levant. There may be side issues that one cannot see at present, but which would arise in the future that if I were on the spot and in the know I could grasp. I am still quite young, on the right side of 30, and this opening might mean a great deal. The Principal Medl. Officer of Health retires in 3 or 4 years, so if I had fulfilled my billet well there is scarcely a shadow of doubt I should fall in for this. I wonder what Mona will have to say about it? She will be quite willing to fall in with things I know, if she thinks I am bent on taking the job and if it means success ahead. The billet is at present being kept open, it only being filled temporarily as the Govt. are most anxious to get an Englishman. They want all the civil appointments as far as possible filled by whites, which is quite a comprehensible policy.

Mona comes out at the latter end of next month. I have spoken to the Colonel here about it, and he was very decent, and expressed himself quite agreeable, and said he thought I quite deserved to have her out as I had worked conscientiously and had done my duty, and had foregone the leave others had got. He is a decent old bird, tho' supposedly a misogynist! One of the fellows who went home some weeks ago at the expiration of his 12 months service, has returned after having secured 5 weeks holiday at home from the War Office. I dare say I could have done much the same if I had stuck out for it, but I considered I was badly wanted here at the time, so I hung on and went without. I may be able to get a week off when Mona comes out. It would be glorious if I could. Things aren't quite so busy here at present, there not having been any wounded on a large scale for several weeks. We still get a large quota of dysenteries and some typhoids, but we are hoping these epidemics will subside as the winter draws on.

From information from different sources our chances of getting thro' to Constantinople via the Gallipoli Peninsula are considered small now, and another large attack is not to be made. We missed our chance at Suvla Bay, owing to faulty organization and leadership, and after sacrificing 1,000s and 1,000s of lives, the whole show is a state muddle. All we hope to do now is to keep the Turks occupied, and to prevent them from doing damage elsewhere. Cheerful, isn't it? Such sacrifices and such a cost for what? Our efforts and energies are now being directed towards relieving Serbia and joining up with Russia and thus cutting off Turkey from Bulgaria. There is to be another carnage in the Balkans. What a shambles Europe is becoming. It is a little encouraging tho' to hear we are having some success on the Western front, and the Russians are certainly doing very much better of late, and seem to be the deciding factor at present.

Well, Mum, I fear there is a good 12 months of war ahead yet and the end will be - what? Such lots of things may happen. Germany will bleed us terribly before she is beaten.

Shall stop now. Hope Ermo is going along well and that you are getting to love the place and are not fearing that it is going to be a bad spec., but that it will justify all the money and labour you have expended upon it.

Love to all at Gladesville. Best love to your dear old self,

Always your affectionate, NIGE

St. Johns Military Hospital, Sliema, Malta, 23 Oct 1915

My dearest Matee

Am up and about once again. The rash turned out to be nothing and finally disappeared and my temp. came down with a run after a dose of ol. rec.[109] So am allowed up once more and have escaped the scarlet fever. The doc. is of opinion that the rash was caused by some medicine I had given me. Am feeling well again now and enjoying my meals. The ward were very pleased to be released from isolation, but only escaped for a couple of days. Yesterday the whole side of the hospital was again isolated, this time for diptheria.

They got two cases in adjoining wards, but neither case in mine. So we are all isolated again, today were inoculated. Double dose in the back below the shoulder blade. This makes me partially immune from smallpox, typhoid, cholera, dysentery and diptheria, all of which I have been inoculated for. Not a bad effort. It is a wonder to me that they haven't got a special isolation block belonging to the hospital as this business seems to be recurring pretty frequently now. We are only in for 4 days.

When the time is up I am going to put in for a pass to get out on some afternoon to stretch my legs and see something of Valletta. It is best to get out once or twice whilst in hospital and close to Valletta as I might get sent to a convalescent camp about 16 miles out of the town. I shall probably be kept at one of these camps for a month or so, as far as I can gather from chaps here, and then will go back to Alexandria and be detailed off to my unit on the Peninsula or wherever they happen to be. There are lots of fellows who seem to manage to get a trip home to England from here, but they have to be pretty unfit.

Yesterday I had a very welcome letter from Billy in answer to one of mine from here. In it he enclosed two from you and one from Gran. It was a treat getting a letter and getting news from home, after such a long time without getting anything at all. He and Mona have been sending off parcels to me, none of which I have ever received. Don't suppose I ever shall now, although I have

---

109 Most likely he's referring to castor oil, oleum ricini.

written to the Base Post Office at Alexandria asking them to send all my letters etc. on here. It is a great pity my not getting them, to say nothing of the waste of brass.

Billy seems to have been pretty busy. It was a pity I didn't get back to Alexandria and into No 15 as he says he could easily have engineered a trip to England for me. However, I shouldn't have liked it much if there was nothing wrong with me, although there are hundreds who do work their way with what is called "swinging the lead" which means shamming.

He tells me that Mona and Mrs. Little are going out to Alexandria about the end of November. Should think Mrs. Little will go on to Australia from there and it would be best for Mona to go too after they have had a month or so together. No doubt Billy doesn't think so though.

Am very glad to hear that you are still at Ermo and that you seem to like it. I hope the young man will turn out a success and that you will grow a lot of vegetables and generally improve the farm.

So Dickie is to go back to England. What a terrible mistake it was his coming out. Seems pretty stiff luck on the family having to part up for his fare back. Don't forget that you have power to operate on my account at the C'wealth Bank should you want any money to help things along. I have never found out yet whether the Defence Dept. are paying in my allotment money that I left behind. Next time you are in town you might call in and ask the Accountant and incidentally tell him I am quite alright. He is a very decent chap and will only take a minute to find out. I don't want Uncle Frank writing to them and asking because they might object to telling him as he has no authority or p/a from me. Well good-bye Matee Boos, am feeling A.I. again, with heaps and heaps of love to you and all the family, hoping Gran and Aunt Mog and the Child are all well with a kiss on the brow from

Your loving son, TOOTS.

No 15 General Hospital, Alexandria, 25 Oct 1915

Dearest Mum

Well, in 4 days' time I shall be 27 years old. How time flies. It won't be long before I am 30 and from then on it is only a short while till I am classified as middle-aged. Altho' I still like to think I am a boy, I have left boyhood behind, and am really getting on. However, I shall endeavour to stick to my youth as long as possible, as it passes by before you know where you are. You must feel yourself to be getting an old woman, with such an elderly son. Now you have the farm and feel you are running it I dare say, though, you feel quite young again, especially if things are going well, which I trust is so.

How is the partner turning out? I wonder if the arrangement of share and share alike will be a success. If he is a decent chap, there is no reason why the scheme shouldn't work out well. Shall be very pleased to hear of any new improvements you have put in, the size and character of the crops and the yields. Wonder whether the piggery suggestion will be considered practicable?

I received a *S.M.Herald* and an *Evening News* from you yesterday, Mum, with an account of the Sari Bair attack by Ashmead-Bartlett[110] in it. It was very interesting reading, but if one reads between the lines, one cannot help coming to the conclusion that there was some incredible bungling and dilatoriness in sending up supports. Ian Hamilton has been recalled to give a report, and perhaps, tho' it is hardly likely, we shall hear an explanation of why the assault and plan of campaign so signally failed after such heroism and reckless bravery on the part of the Colonial troops, viz. N. Zealanders, Australians and Gurkhas.

Most of the troops coming from the Peninsula are terribly depressed, and seem to think our chance of making any headway as far as an advance is concerned very small indeed. It is all very gloomy. I believe, at least it has been stated on good authority, that at the beginning of the War the Turks could have been bought over for £100,000,000 as easily as winking. Instead of that, our policy was war, and with Churchill and Fisher at the helm we were going to blast our way thro' the Dardanelles. The British bull dog, nothing can resist him. The Balkan business altho', of course, we don't know the ins and outs of it, seems to have been extremely poor diplomacy. Surely we have enough to cope with, without adding on an additional campaign to deal with.

I wrote to Steve and sent a letter from Mona to him, as she had not his address, but I have not heard from him since. I wonder what will happen to him when he is fit to leave Malta. I expect he has been moved to a Convalescent Camp there 'ere this.

I had a long letter from Aunt Mog this last mail which I must answer. Perhaps I may manage it by this next one.

---

110 Ellis Ashmead-Bartlett was a noted British war correspondent, particularly famous for his coverage of the Gallipoli campaign. The various headlines for this article eulogised the Australian troops who 'fought like lions', with 'reckless courage'.

There is practically nothing new to tell you. The weather is very delightful now, and the heat is much less. The days are really lovely, and one wants a blanket at night. I heard from Dancy 2 or 3 days ago. He is practically right again now, but is not being sent abroad again. He had a rotten time after he left here, he says, and was not able to walk for a month afterwards. The so-called post-typhoidal weakness.

Well, Mum, I must stop. This is a very scrappy letter. Best of love to all at home,

Ever yours,

NIGE

One of the fellows here, a doctor, lives at Pangbourne, and is practising there. I told him you were born there. He was very interested indeed. He told me to ask you if you remembered the Coxes, the blacksmith people, as they have been there for ages. His name is Birch.[111]

St. Johns Military Hospital, Sliema, Malta, 30 Oct 1915

My dearest Matee

Am still in the "horspital", more by good luck than anything else. The doc. came round Thursday and said I was to go out on the Saturday to the convalescent camp. On Friday another case of diptheria turned up, also one of the hospital doctors have got it. The whole hospital is now isolated for 5 days so I have got a little extra spell which will no doubt do me no harm. Will most likely be going on Wednesday next, as Wednesdays and Saturdays are the two days of the week which we go out to the camps. They have traced the infection to carriers in the Maltese workman and barber employed by the hospital. These have now all been sacked. Of course we are not allowed out anywhere, but we have always got the roof to go on to, which are all the same here being flat and of stone.

On Wednesday last I got a pass from 2.30 p.m. to 5.30 to go into Valletta. Had a great afternoon. You cross over from Sliema to Valletta by a ferry costing ½d. which lands you at the foot of a tunnel and up into the town. It is a most

---

111 Dr Charles Birch, born in 1876 at Eccles, Lancashire, was a member of the Parish Council at Whitchurch, close to Pangbourne, in 1915.

unique place and very old. The houses and streets seem to run along in terraces with steps from one to another street. The streets are very narrow indeed, but there are quite decent shops in the main thoroughfare, the "Strada Reale". We walked up this and looked about most of the afternoon. Saw the Governor's Palace from the outside and the opera house, the two chief buildings. Had some cakes and tea at a small shop and bought some chocolates etc. The time allowed us was extremely short and after having a good feed of sausages and coffee at the flash restaurant it was time to get back.

The feed was rather expensive but we went to the only and most aristocratic shop. 4 sausages, one egg, coffee and bread and butter and some cakes came to about 1/10. Anyway I enjoyed it, being the first good feed for some months. The place is spoilt by the goats that run about all over the streets. There are no cows apparently on the island and the populace depend upon the milk of the goat. A chap drives them along the road and anyone who wants milk comes out of their house with a jug which the milkman takes and milks the goat into the jug. It certainly does away with the milk cart business, but if you go to buy a milk and soda in one of the shops you see your milk put into the glass underneath the goat. It put me right off milk.

I have not had any more letters since the one from Billy, but hope there will be another along soon. The mails here seem to come at very irregular intervals, especially from Alexandria. Should be getting a letter from Mona soon now. I hear from Billy that she had been sending off one or two parcels to me whilst on the Peninsula, but have not yet received any of them, don't know whether I ever will now. Have written to the Base Post Office at Alexandria telling them where I am and to send my letters here.

Will be quite sorry to leave the hospital, as I have had a good spell here except for the times when I had to go to bed and the nurses are quite good and we get quite a lot of fun out of them.

This letter will get out to you too late for your birthenday and I haven't got any present of any sort, except some Turkish bullets and belt buckle. Don't know whether it is any good my hanging on to them, and they would be awkward things to send home, being rather weighty and also of not much value as relics. I left a Turkish rifle and two bayonets also some fuses off some of the Turk shells in my dugout when I came away, being unable to bring them with me. They should have been of some value if I could have got them home, as I went into a newly-captured trench during the advance in August to get them. But we were told we were to hand them up to the armoury at the beach and wouldn't be allowed to keep them. I kept mine as did a lot of chaps who had them, with the hope of smuggling them through, and it was an everyday sight to see the Officers getting away from the Peninsula with Turk rifles tied on to their kit.

Best love to Gran and Aunt Mog and the Child, hoping they are all keeping well and with heaps and heaps for Matee Boos with some kisses on her brow and cheek, from her loving son,

TOOTS.

P.S. In case I haven't wished you many happy returns in my previous letter I will do so now, hoping you will have a happy birthenday and drink the health of all the family both absent and present in some of the good old X.X.X. Tooths.

Union Club, Alexandria, Egypt, 4 Nov 1915

Dearest Mother

I hope you weren't very disappointed at not getting a letter by the last mail. I wrote to Aunt Mog as I owed her a letter and found I had left the writing of one to you too late. However, I daresay she will show you hers.

I am writing this week in good time to make sure of getting this letter off by the next mail. As you will see by the address above I am writing from the Club, where I have just had afternoon tea. It makes a change from the hospital to get away now and then. All officers of H.M. Forces are honorary members as I told Aunt Mog in my letter to her, and have all the privileges of full membership - all for the tune of 2 bob a week, a great boon I can tell you. As a result the rooms swarm with all men military and one or two navalites besides. It is their meeting place and haven of retreat during their stay at Alexandria.

I had a letter from Steve today. He is getting along very well now he says, and feeling almost himself again. He has got one of my letters, so I hope he will get the other one I have addressed to him at Malta, and the parcel from Mona which I despatched this week. He expects to be pushed off to a convalescent camp on the island in a few days, where he will probably remain a month and then be drafted to Alexandria to the base details camp before resuming duty. So if he does come here I shall see him, which will be a great thing and Mona should be here by that time, and will be able to look after him a bit, when I can't get away. I was under the impression, however, that the Australian base was at Cairo, but perhaps he is correct. The A.F.A. (D.A.C) is still at Cleopatra and that is probably where he will go.

I went and interviewed the Director General of the Municipality 2 days ago, re the Assistant M.O. of Health appointment. His name is Dr. Granville[112], and a very fat and prosperous looking gentleman he is, but a very decent chap indeed apparently. He explained to me the whole thing, which I will give you a brief outline of below.

The Public Health Department here is run by the Principal Inspector of Health (screw £900 - £1000 per annum) under him come 2 sub or assistant inspectors (screw £600 per annum) and below these again other officials which don't concern us. The 2 assistants' duties differ - one has the practical job and the other the bacteriological work to do. Before the war the Chief Inspector's job was filled by a German. He has been booted. The Assistant Inspector by a native, who has 28 years' service and is incidentally a very decent chap, and the bacteriological post by a Greek. Granville's scheme is to have all these places filled with Englishmen. The native has been moved up to the Chief Inspector's billet, and his position is the one now vacant and which he wants me to fill.

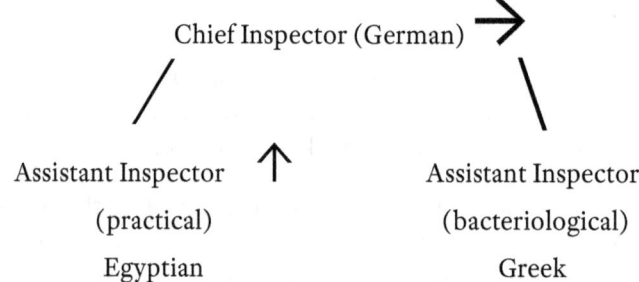

My duties would be largely official - I should be concerned in handling epidemics, chief of which are smallpox, typhus, typhoid, cholera, plague, relapsing fever, etc. The sanitation of dwellings from shops to factories. The carrying out of vaccns., job of seeing all births and deaths be duly registered, etc. etc. I should have to be at home with both French and Arabic.

1st year on probation.

No pension – 2½% of salary put aside each month towards Provident Fund - and 2½% added by the Government. In the event of dismissal for disciplinary measures - lose it all. In the event of sickness being cause of your departure, you get both. If you voluntarily leave service, you get what you have yourself paid in refunded. If I am agreed on accepting the job, would have to start soon. He would represent to the Government at home that he required my services here urgently and I should be forthwith switched out of the R.A.M.C.

---

112 Dr. Alexander Granville, Director of the Municipality of Alexandria

I asked for time to think it over. The post of Chief Inspectorship now occupied by the native would fall vacant, he thought, in about 5 to 6 years, in which case I should almost certainly get it, if I showed myself efficient. He was an old man, had 28 years' service and was rather delicate. 5 - 6 years he thought would finish him.

Mona asked me to promise not to definitely decide till she came out. So I am thinking it over. It has its advantages and disadvantages. One becomes an official as far as I can see and loses one's profession, which, after all, is what keeps one going - I mean the practice of medicine itself. It's a job that requires great tact and patience in dealing with the native. Attributes which I doubt if I possess. I have talked it over with 2 of the fellows confidentially and they agreed with me. It's a question of whether one has a bent that way. I wish I knew what you thought. At any rate at present, Mum, I am inclined to give up the idea of accepting it, but will deliberate over it a bit longer before giving a definite answer.

Well, Mum, I am pretty busy again now and have got some rather interesting cases to look after. Another of our M.O.s has contracted paratyphoid - the eye specialist, a very decent lad, so he will be going home. I have 136 beds to attend to now. One's work is all that keeps one alive here.

Love to all at home. Wonder what you think of this offer I have had?

Till next week, dearest Mum,

Ever yours,

NIGE

St. John's Military Hospital, Sliema, Malta, 6 Nov 1915

My dearest Matee

Am expecting to be leaving here on Monday next if nothing unforeseen occurs between now and then in the way of more diptheria cases. This infection which broke out gave me an extra week here which I have enjoyed and benefited by to the full.

Of course, we have not been allowed to go outside the hospital and so haven't had much in the way of exercise, but there is a huge flat roof on top of this building on to which we can get and so get a little up there. Am feeling quite well again and will probably get another 3 weeks in the convalescent camp before going back to my unit. On the whole I was very lucky getting so long away from the Peninsula as I thought I should have been going back from Mudros whereas I managed to get the trip to Malta and an extra month in hospital including of course my scarlet fever attack or rather medicine rash and this infection isolation. There will be a big clearance when the quarantine is lifted and ¾s of the hospital will go.

Lots of chaps chiefly the serious cases of rheumatics etc. go on from here to England, but that is not for me. Billy no doubt could have worked it if I had gone to No 15. It has been great in hospital here with a beautiful spring bed with sheets to sleep in and nothing to do except lie and read and smoke in between meals intermingled with plenty of chaff for the nurses who are a good lot. I shall miss it all when I leave, as it has been as much like home as anything since I left Coolah.

It is a great pity I haven't had any letters from anyone at home, not for the want of your writing but I suppose they are held up somewhere. This trouble always seems to occur to the wounded or sick who leave the Peninsula, as no one seems to know what hospital you will arrive at until you arrive at the port the boat is ordered to sail for and the patients are taken off. I have written to the Base Post Office and all the various units I have been attached to, so I suppose and hope they will turn up someday. Billy and Mona have also sent me two or three parcels which I cannot expect to see as they are invariably opened at the front if the men are not there to receive them.

When over at a convalescent camp we will have a certain amount of leisure, being allowed out of camp every afternoon after 2 p.m. so I shall be able to get into Valletta a little and look round, provided of course I don't go out to one of the camps that are 13 miles out from there, as it will take too long to get in. There is not a great deal to see but it greatly relieves the monotony of the camp life, especially as there is nothing to do in them, and also I shall be able to get some good food apart from the Army rations. Once I leave the convalescent camp I think all the Australians get sent back to Alexandria, their base, and then get in touch with your own unit wherever it happens to be. But am not thinking about that until it gets closer. Don't want to get on to the Peninsula for the heart of the winter, although at present no one knows where we will go, now that Bulgaria has come in against us.

I hope Greece and Rumania come in now on our side and so help to finish the war quickly as I am looking forward to coming home again and being "looked after". Am afraid it is too much to hope for, for a long while yet. Every Tommy in the place has only one idea here and that is to get on a boat sailing for England so as he can get back home for a while, if not Christmas.

I ought soon to get another letter from Billy as it is now nearly 3 weeks since the last and only letter arrived and I am anxious to get some news of you all again as this seems my quickest way. Hope everyone is well and keeping up their spirits, not worriting too much about Tootie who will look after himself to the best of his ability. Hope Gran is still going strong, the spring weather coming on will no doubt suit her better than the winter, also Aunt Mog and her trips to town. Please give them my best love and not forgetting the Child, who I hope is still looking after her Ma in a proper manner. With heaps and heaps of love and kisses to Mee Maw from

Her ever loving son,

TOOTS.

St. Johns Military Hospital, Sliema, Malta, 14 Nov 1915

My dearest Matee Boo & Family

Still in hospital as you see and am quite content. More cases of "dip" turned up at the eleventh hour last Sunday night and we convalescents were all detained again. This time it is for an indefinite period. Seems as if they are going to wait until they can get most of the patients well, and then move the whole lot of us off and close the hospital down for a proper disinfection. So am now in full enjoyment of this extra time in hospital and am very lucky in falling into it. Am in no hurry at all to part from my nice comfortable spring bed with two sheets on it to get between. They have started some physical exercise classes for us now to help get us fit and keep us in good health. We only have an hour in the mornings and it is quite optional for anyone to turn up or not. So if anyone doesn't feel fit they needn't go.

Last Wednesday I received a parcel from Mona who had sent it to Billy to send to me, as she didn't know quite what my address was. It had in it a big box of chocolates and some plain cakes, chocolate also, two tins of OXO cubes and tin of potted ham and tongue, some cafe-au-lait made by adding hot water and two tins of cocoa tablets, also made by the addition of boiling water. The whole thing must have cost a good tidy sum including the postage 1/-. It was very kind indeed of her especially as she had already sent off one or two others which must have gone to the Peninsula and which I don't think I shall get now. The general idea of parcels getting to the front is that if the men are not there to receive them, having been wounded or sent away, they are to be opened there and divided amongst the men there, as the men in the firing line are more deserving to have the stuff. This is heartily agreed to by all the men as far as I have heard and it seems only right. Consequently my other parcels have possibly been consumed ere this. The only thing wrong with this idea is that generally the same men open all the parcels and scoop everything.

I received a mail from Australia this week and got 8 letters from different sources, but none from Coolah. I think perhaps you must have had a different address on than these and it would be a good plan I think if you sent my letters to Billy as long as he is at No 15 Alexandria and he can send them on to me, as he is so much closer and is aware of any change in my address a long time before you, and after I leave the convalescent camp at Malta I shall most likely go back to Alexandria our headquarters before going back to the Peninsula.

Everyone here is in good spirits who is well and there is lots of fun with the nurses and sisters who are out for a bit of sport at any time, as the life here apart from their hospital work is pretty dull for them. They all live in quarters in an hotel but, being in the army, are kept strictly to certain rules the same as ordinary soldiers. They have for instance to be in by 9 p.m. and are not allowed to stop and talk to any soldier in the street who is not an officer. They as well as us are pretty sore about such a ridiculous idea as they call it and generally don't mind running the risk of being caught by their Matron in Chief. Everything here is for the officers and there are hundreds of them in the place having the times of their lives and thinking of anything but getting back to the front. It would do good if Kitchener called here and shook them up a bit.

Am glad to hear that you are still at Ermo and no doubt the little spot is looking a great deal improved since you went to live there. The child and Aunt Mog I suppose go up to spend their weekends there occasionally which no doubt relieves the dullness and monotony a bit.

Will write again soon and tell you of any likely movements as soon as there is anything doing. Give my very best love to Aunt Mog and Gran, and hope the Child is having a good time with the various admirers, with heaps of love and kisses on the brow for Matee Boos, from

Your loving son, TOOTS.

No 15 General Hospital, Alexandria, Egypt, 15 Nov 1915

Dearest Mother

I haven't had a letter from you for nearly a fortnight, but I expect I shall hear from you any day now. Two of your letters usually come together, altho' they are generally posted at a week's interval.

I haven't very much to tell you this time. The weather is becoming much cooler now, in fact it is delightful here at present and the nights are quite fresh and invigorating. The climate here till March at any rate ought to be perfectly beautiful.

We are getting an increasing number of enterics in daily now. The dysentery epidemic is waning, and enteric is the prevailing disease. The cases that have been arriving recently are much worse than our previous cases - the reason for this is probably that the effects of inoculation are working off, as most of the troops have not been done for over 12 months now. Also the autumn months, it has been found, usually mark a great increase in the occurrence of typhoid and predispose especially towards its spread. All my medical beds have been invaded by typhoid cases, and I am doing nothing but typhoid again - it is very interesting work, and I guess I should know a few things about enteric by the time this war is over. A large number of the surgical beds have also been commandeered by typhoids, so the surgery of this hospital is at a minimum. The casualties at the Dardanelles are very paltry at present, and we have had practically no convoys of wounded for many weeks.

Things as far as any fighting goes have come to a stalemate or an "impasse" as the French have it. All eyes are turned to the Balkans just now.

It will interest you to hear that I read a paper before the Medical Staffs of the various military hospitals here in Alexandria last Sunday week. It was on the subject of Epidemic Jaundice, which has been very prevalent amongst the troops. The greater number of the cases have come from the local camps. There are 4 other military hospitals here besides ourselves, each with over a 1000 beds. I was detailed by Col. James to represent No.15. We had had 138 cases here so I was able to give a fairly satisfactory account of the condition. At any rate old James was pleased, and I think I acquitted myself pretty well, altho' my views were strongly antagonized by 2 medicos from No.19 whose findings on 70 cases were very different in some respects. As they had written a paper to the Lancet, it must have been galling for them to have their views challenged and contradicted. However, I think the bulk of the audience were in my favour.

I heard from Steve yesterday. He is well and expecting to be transferred to a Convalescent Camp almost immediately for 2 or 3 weeks which he is looking forward to, as the open air after hospital will be refreshing. He will then be returning here before he rejoins his Unit, so I shall, if all goes well, see him again. He has got 2 of my letters, but has not received the parcel yet, but would have got it ere this.

Mona is not leaving Marseilles till the 20th. as she could not get a berth on the boat which sailed on the 13th. After much bargaining I have secured rooms in the Grand Hotel at £14 per month full pension, which is very reasonable as the tariff goes here, prices being very high and accommodation at a premium. This is for both of us - I shall be able to spend the night with her occasionally which will be very nice and I may be able to arrange to have a day or two at Xmas with her. I am greatly looking forward to her arrival. It is less than a fortnight now. I trust nothing unpleasant happens during her trip down the Mediterranean, as two Italian passenger ships have just been torpedoed, and nothing is exempt from attack apparently. I will say, however, that no hospital ship has been sunk so far, which is something in the German's small book of favour.

She is coming by P. & O. from Marseilles. She will spend a day or two in Paris, which will be very nice, altho' rather a short stay. Still, Paris will be quite a different Paris now, and far less given up to gaieties than London is. Mona is very loth to leave her work at the Anzac buffet. I wonder if she has told you about it. It is a sort of Club for the wounded and convalescent Australians during their stay in London. They are provided with luncheon and tea and have 2 concerts a day sometimes. Also have a reading room and lounge and music room. It has proved such a success that they have been obliged to move into larger rooms.

Mona started as an assistant waitress and now has become assistant secretary. They have 700 there some days - so she has proved herself very capable apparently. She knows a great number of the "boys" as she calls them, and being an Australian they are delighted to see one of their women folk again. They have been taking her to the theatre and for taxi rides and dinners and she has been having some of them out at Richmond at weekends. She has met several chaps she has danced with, several King's School boys among them. They have been very good to her, tho' chagrined at her being married! She will miss it all when she comes out here I am afraid, but I daresay a job will be found for her. The hospitals have Red Cross kitchens attached to them now in Alexandria, where jellies and blancmanges and various little delicacies for invalids are made, and I think it quite likely she could prove herself capable in this direction.

Anzac Buffet, London, c Nov 1915
(The "'Self' on the photo is Mrs Rattigan, a co-founder of the Club. Mona is most likely in this photo. Source AWM RC06143)

All the fellows here have been to Cairo, some of them twice, they have 48 hours leave granted them, which is the maximum period one can obtain out here. I am the only one who has had no leave since I joined. I could have secured 48 hours easy enough, I daresay, if I had applied to go to Cairo, but in the first place it's rather an expense, and in the second, I thought now Mona is coming out I might be able to go with her later on.

Some of the fellows here are returning to England in a week or so's time as their year is up. They have practices to attend to, which have gone to pot under the tender care of locums - they want to give other fellows who have not been able to get away the chance of enlisting. Owing to the tremendous number of medicos required by the Army, the unfortunate general practitioner at home has been having a very trying time of it.

Well, Mum, I must stop now. I have a letter to write to Steve yet.

There is a chance of conscription coming into operation in England shortly. I wonder if a similar state of affairs will prevail in Australia as well.

Love to all at home. I hope you will be able to keep Ermo going and that your energies in the farming direction will be rewarded. Dicky's fare was a big drain.

Bestest love, Mum,

Yours ever, NIGE

St. Johns Military Hospital, Sliema, Malta, 19 Nov 1915

My dearest Mother

Am still in clover and still enjoying it. Am expecting to go out next Monday 23rd Nov, provided of course no more "dip" cases show up between now and then. Am writing this to you now sitting on my bed whilst a gramophone is going strong on the table in the ward. Naturally we are all cheerful and well excepting one or two exceptions who are not quite convalescent.

Yesterday I received my first letter from you since August last. It is dated 20th Sept. and written from Ermo where I hope you still are. Am delighted to hear such good news about the farm and that all the fruit trees are putting on all their spring leaves and showing promise of providing some good fruit. Also the vegetables. The new man Brazier seems to be going on well and I trust he sticks to it and gets in some good work before he thinks of clearing out. I don't suppose you will make a great deal out of their sale at first, but expect you will make as good a deal as anyone, as well as providing all the neighbours. It is a pity the place is so far from town as regards the getting in and out. I hope that Gran has been able to find someone in Mrs. Williams place as it would be a great pity if you had to leave Ermo without anyone to keep an eye on Brazier.

About that lump of chocolate you mention in your letter. I didn't get it, and it must have arrived after I had left the Peninsula and so I expect was opened at the front and consumed by some of the fellows. It would make a great change for them as cocoa was unprocurable over there and would be just the thing these cold nights and mornings, also it wouldn't have the same effect as tea on the stomach if anyone was at all inclined to dysentery or diarrhoea. It was a pity though me not getting it, especially after the expense incurred including the postage which was pretty solid.

You ask what work I was doing on the Peninsula. For the first fortnight or 3 weeks I was attached to the Brigade Amm. Column and had my dugout amongst the rest of the Column in Shrapnel Gully and generally started work at 8 o'clock at night, just about dark. Then proceeded down to the Ammunition Park on the beach from where we carried shell to the different batteries round Anzac. Each shell with cartridge case etc. for the 18 pounder field gun weighs about 25 lbs each, so we only carry two at a time, one on each shoulder. This is not a great weight but having to climb gullies and steep hills covered with big boulders and rocks it fairly pumps the wind out of you and numerous rests are taken. All this is done during the night, some nights we would only get one or two trips, but others, where a lot of firing and heavy bombardment had taken place, we would be kept going till the small hours in getting the required number of rounds up. This sort of work is always done at night when possible as there is a good deal of risk attached to it and the Turk snipers are always on the look out to stop ammunition from getting up, and the brass cartridge cases of shells make an easy target to pick up. Of course we use all the saps communications trenches and firing line for cover and you are always told to keep off the sky line even at night time.

For the first week my shoulders got terribly sore with carrying the shell. Other shell of course was carried heavier than these, but we only took one at a time then. The 4.7 gun, one that was used at Ladysmith in the Boer war, went nearly 100 lbs weight and meant a walk of nearly 2 miles from the beach. Then there was the 6 inch howitzer which shells went over 100 lbs. without their charge. This work of course was rather uninteresting, but being fairly out in the open all the time, there was a fair amount of risk attached to it and the infantry chaps in the trenches used to tell us when we rested alongside them in the firing line they would sooner have their job. Some nights we wouldn't get any shell to carry at all, but about a dozen of us would be told off with pick and shovel to dig a gun pit for a new gun to be in a new position and be concealed. This was always done at night so as to keep its position utterly unknown to the enemy.

After leaving the B.A.C. to be lent to the D.A. Park I moved, as you know, my dug out down to the hill rising off the beach and quite close to my work which was done on the beach alone, amongst all the Ammunition. In this case we generally worked throughout the day, stacking ammunition unloaded off the punts and barges on the beach. Also loading ammunition of all kinds on to mules to go to the trenches and batteries where they could get to. These mules with their Indian drivers are wonderful animals and adored by the Indian Johnnies as they are called. A mule could carry as much shell on specially made saddles as 4 or 6 men, so you can imagine how valuable and useful they were. They indeed saved the situation for us and did wonderful work with their transport of stores, munitions etc. The Indians take the greatest care of them and after getting his cart loaded, should anything in the way of a case of jam or bag of sugar fall off, the Indian will never stop to pick it up as the load is made all the lighter for his mule who is all he thinks about. They suffered fairly heavily from shrapnel fire, but the Indians used to say "plenty mule get killed" but "plenty more mule."

Loading the Mules, Beach at Anzac Cove, 1915
Source AWM H16550

This work on the beach came pretty heavy as the lifting of the big shells and boxes of 18 pounders and .303 small arms am sure affected my insides and never gave me a chance of getting well over there, as if I had a rest for a day I would be better, but as soon as I returned to the lifting the whole recurrence would occur as bad as ever.

Am sending a small offering to the various members of the family as a Xmas gift, but hope its humbleness will be overlooked as we find all our available cash comes in handy in the way of getting little comforts in the way of eatables and making the best of a sort of holiday away from the front. One of the hospital sisters has been kind enough to make the purchases as we are unable to get out of the hospital. It is all genuine Maltese lace made on the island, and one article for each member wishing you all a very Happy Xmas and good luck for 1916, hoping to get back to you all someday in that year safe and sound. With heaps and heaps of love to Gran, Aunt Mog and the Child and a big hug and kiss for the Mee Maw from

Your ever loving son, TOOTS.

St. Johns Military Hospital, Sliema, Malta, 26 Nov 1915

Dearest Mother & Child

We are now out of quarantine but am pleased to say have not yet left for the convalescent camp. We all expected to be sent out as soon as the isolation was over, but it appears that the convalescent camps had no bed accommodation and we are remaining here a little while extra, until they have room. Of course, it is all in our favour as we are ever so much better housed here and each day advances the winter, which I have no wish to be out in on the field without any shelter to speak of. It is already getting pretty chilly here now with cold winds and it is great in having a good comfortable bed to sleep in of a night.

On Thursday last I and another chap by the name of Brown out of the Royal Scots obtained a pass for the afternoon to go into Valletta. We didn't go in by the ferry but thought we would walk. It is a good long walk by the way but quite interesting and enables one to get an intelligent view of the island. It took us close on 2 hours to get into the town and we were feeling a bit tired by the time we got there and greatly enjoyed a rest and a meal of eggs and bacon with some tea.

This place is absolutely under the thumb of the Military authorities and the ordinary Tommies are only allowed into certain shops to get meals and no one is allowed to sell a soldier under the rank of Sergeant Major a drink at all. So you can imagine what sort of a place it is. Should think it greatly resembles German Militarism. The Maltese are absolutely cowed by the police.

Last Saturday we arranged a sort of impromptu sports in the courtyard. The Australians won almost everything and at the finish in the tug of war pulled and beat the staff of the R.A.M.C. belonging to the hospital. Wasn't a bad effort on the part of the patients and invalids pipping the staff. They, the Austrns, seem to provide all the fun here with the nurses and sisters, and appear to be very popular.

I hope you are still at Ermo with the vegetable and fruit in abundance and enjoying yourself to the full amongst them. You must excuse a short letter this time as there is no news being still shut up in the hospital. Give my best love to Gran and Aunt Mog and heaps for yourself and the Child, hoping you are all well and in good spirits, from

Your loving son, TOOTS.

Ghain-Tuffieha Convalescent Camp, Malta, 3 Dec 1915

My dearest Matee and Child

Have arrived at the convalescent camp[113] and already am glad I didn't get here sooner. The camp is 13 miles drive out of Valletta in perfectly barren and rocky country with no sign of life anywhere. It is a deadly hole without any amusement or anything to do except walk about and very occasionally go into Valletta. The trip into town takes pretty well half the day, as you have either to drive in all the way by cab or drive to Cittia Vecchia which is the terminus of a railway running into Valletta. We are only allowed 10/- a week pay and the trip into town costs generally 2/- by cab or 1/- to 1/6 by tram and cab according to the number who go together. By four going which fills one of the native cabs it comes cheaper as each man pays his share and so comes lighter for everyone. By the time you have done the trip in and out your brass is about finished.

Ghain-Tuffieha Camp Hospital, Malta
Source A. G. McKinnon, *Malta, the Nurse of the Mediterranean*

The grub here is a great come down after hospital fare and it seems very few chaps improve much in health in camp here. Seems to be that if you spend all your cash on buying food and other little articles necessary, it is your only chance of getting any strength back after leaving the hospitals. We have a good bed but no sheets, and of course after so many different men coming in one

---

113 Ghain-Tuffieha had 4 convalescent camps, holding 4,000 men.

after another the tents and blankets are not too clean. There doesn't seem to be any of "de louse" but there are bags of fleas and they are extremely busy and have night attacks at great strength.

Haven't seen any doctor since coming here but will be doing so shortly I expect. There seems to be a sort of parade of the men about once a week when they are classified for active service, or if not well enough for that, they are given a job belonging to the garrison at a base or anywhere excepting active service, and if not well enough for that they are invalided home. At these parades the doctors appear to be guided chiefly by one's face, so if you are looking well, you stand a good chance of getting back to the front after a bit of a spell with drill of a light nature. The colonials have been stopped going home to England quite recently. They don't seem to know quite what to do with them as they are such a long way from Australia to send home to convalesce, and they have stopped sending them to England. Expect it will be Egypt after being here for a while.

There is a very bad feeling here amongst all the Colonials, in fact all the Tommies as well, at the way they are all treated after coming off the Peninsula. After being over there for some months and get either sick and wounded and come back, they naturally expect to have a little leisure and enjoyment. In France after coming out of the trenches and away from the front, the Tommies' soldiers have the best of times with theatres and outings, entertainments of all descriptions. Here it is exactly like being isolated. No N.C.O. and men are allowed to go to the opera and are debarred from most of the decent restaurants. Also the pay of 10/- a week is considered an insult to lots of the wealthy lads from the Colonies. Most of these restrictions are made by the present Governor, Lord Methuen, who is extremely unpopular. He calls the Australians and New Zealanders the "Beastly Irregulars" and so I suppose he treats them accordingly. He came out here to speak to the men in Camp yesterday and at the finish the Colonel in charge called for three cheers for his Excellency Lord Methuen. There was hardly a murmur and was a great failure which must have been very noticeable.

Have been for a walk out to St. Paul's Bay where St. Paul landed. It was a good 6 miles there and back and wasn't a bad effort for the first time out. Had some tea at the Soldiers Home and a feed of a sort comprising 2 boiled eggs and bread and butter and tea for 1/- at an hotel. By the time we got back to camp was feeling nice and tired, but didn't get such a good night's sleep owing to the fleas. Have got my blankets out in the sun today. It made a bit of an improvement by putting them out yesterday. Expect I will be going into town early next week after we are paid, to pay a sort of duty visit to the hospital.

St Paul's Hospital Camp, Malta
Source A. G. McKinnon, *Malta, the Nurse of the Mediterranean*

Am afraid I have written a rambling sort of letter, but it is not an easy job in the tent with chaps all round talking hard. Please give my best love to Gran and Aunt Mog. I hope they are both well and in good spurrits. Expect you are still at Ermo watching over the fruit trees and vegetables coming or going. Things will be looking dry I suppose, now that it is midsummer over where you are. With heaps and heaps of love to you both and several kisses on the various brows from

Your loving son, TOOTS.

GHAIN-TUFFIEHA CONVALESCENT CAMP, MALTA, 9 DEC 1915

My dearest Matee and Child

Am still jogging along all right and making the most of things. Am beginning to settle down in camp and have not the slightest idea how long I will be here. There is supposed to be a shortage of transports just now owing to the movement of troops to Salonika, and convalescent patients are not being worried about much. So I may be here for Xmas and yet should a boat come in going to Alexandria it might take a great load of Australians including myself along with it.

Everything is gloriously uncertain as you can easily understand. Once your mind is made up to this sort of life here in camp without much to do, it doesn't seem so bad. So far I don't have to do any drill and just please myself what happens. Later on I shall have to do a bit of drill I expect, both in the mornings and afternoons. Generally will try and manage a trip into Valletta about once a week. Went in on Monday last and paid a visit to all the nurses at St. Johns at Sliema. Had a very enjoyable outing and stayed the night at the Soldiers Sailors Institute where we got a good dinner much cheaper than at a shop and bed and breakfast.

Had to get up at 5.30 am. the next morning to catch the train to get us out to Cittia Vecchia from where we drive the remaining 6 miles by cab. We arrived back just about 8 o'clock feeling all the better for the trip and no one any the wiser for our absence. We are only allowed a pass out of camp from 2 p.m. to 6 as a rule, so we took the trip on our own account and risk.

This is done a good deal as it is the only way, as it takes nearly half a day to get into Valletta. There is not much risk if you don't appear in the streets before 2 p.m. and are out of them by 9 p.m. The Soldier's Home is quite close to the station and it is very bad luck if you meet the picquet in the early morning on your way home. The whole trip makes a very pleasant outing but uses up a lot of the week's pay which is only 10/-.

Saw a lot of cases of frost-bitten feet and hands whilst over at St. John's. The troops over there now seem to be having a terrible time of it and I am indeed thankful I am not over on the Peninsula, in fact am lucky to be alive at all. Most probably the men who are not fit for active service soon will not go out again till next spring. The Aust. Light Horse or what is left of them have gone over to Salonika. They are rather pleased as they will be on their horses once again and will not get so much of that trench warfare.

I hope you are getting some of my letters. Generally write weekly but don't know whether they all go on. Expect you are doing pretty much the same, but they are taking ages to get to me and I am only getting about one a month at present. Haven't had a letter from Billy for a long while now, it seems that the mails from Alexandria to Malta are very irregular.

Was today warned to appear before a Medical Board. Don't quite know what the outcome of it all will be and also don't know that anything much is the matter with me. However, it might mean a job somewhere at one of the bases or anywhere else away from the front, what is known as "Lines of Communication work". Am expecting to go before them in a day or so, when they will tell me what is to happen. Some other chaps who are also warned are hoping to get a trip to Australia out of it. I will not argue with them if they give me a job on the "lines of communication". Was examined by one of the doctors here yesterday on one of the weekly parades amongst a big batch of newly arrived patients, and he sounded and tested me all over the chest and back. At the time I have got a bit of a cold and cough which doesn't seem to go away properly but doesn't worry me much. This thickness of phlegm in the tubes may have bamboozled him a bit, but he didn't say anything at all, and away I went. The next thing I knew was my summoning to the Med. Board to be held soon. They can do what they like with me, but I don't want to be sent back medically unfit. It may be just to be sent over to Egypt, this seems the most likely thing to happen.

Give my best love to Gran and Aunt Mog, hoping everyone is well and happy and in good spirits. With heaps of love and kisses to you both, from

Your loving son, TOOTS.

Mona and her mother have arrived in Egypt but the letter with that news has not survived. In this letter Nigel refers to trouble brewing in Egypt. He seems unaware that on 21 November Egypt had been invaded from the west by the Senussi sect of Bedouins living in Libya. It was an attempt to distract the British, so that Turks could make another attempt at seizing the Suez Canal, after failing in February 1915.

No 15 General Hospital, Alexandria, 12 Dec 1915

Dearest Mother

Your letter of Nov 11th to hand yesterday, enclosing a letter to Steve and also snaps taken at Ermo. The latter were very interesting and as you say 'tricks'. I sent Steve's letter on as soon as I got it and I think it ought to reach him quite safely. I heard from him today, and he tells me he was then leaving for the Convalescent Camp, where he would probably remain for 2 or 3 weeks before being returned to duty.

Dora Boulton at
'Ermo', 1915

(Picture Courtesy Julia Woodhouse)

He had not received any of the billies[114], which is a d ---d shame. I don't think they will arrive somehow, but there is just a slim chance they may be forwarded on. Mona has sent him 3 parcels and I sent him one, none of which he received, excepting one that I posted from here to Malta.

It is enraging after spending money on nice parcels and things he would appreciate to learn that someone else has profited by them. Steve was wanting some money to buy some luxuries, as he had spent all his ready cash at the Canteen, and did not have a chance of drawing any more while he was in hospital, so I sent him along £2 which I trust will reach him safely. You say in one of your letters that I am getting £10 a week. Not quite as good as this, Mum, I am receiving £8.8. One has a certain number of expenses as there are several subscriptions to the Sporting Club, Union Club, Bathing Club, Tennis Club, Mess guests, and other little odds and ends that run away with about £1 to 30/- a week, usually the latter figure. I have managed to save £150 during my first year and hope to save a similar amount at the end of my second year, which won't be so bad. I shall have to buy new uniforms, etc.

I am sorry, Mum, I did not manage to write you a letter by the last mail. I wrote to Aunt Mog and Aunt Phoebe, and also one to Steve, and did not manage to get one to you finished. I am writing this time early to make a bird of your getting a letter by this mail. I daresay Aunt Mog will show you hers which will be almost as good.

Thea and Dora at 'Ermo', 1915
(Picture Courtesy Julia Woodhouse)

Thea & Dora at 'Ermo', 1915
(Picture Courtesy Julia Woodhouse)

---

114 These were metal billy cans with lids, often used in Australia to boil water over an open fire and make tea, or as a receptacle for home deliveries of milk. In the Great War, billy cans were a practical form of packaging for supplies and gifts sent to soldiers overseas.

I have got rid of all my cases of enteric now, and my wards are being given up to ordinary medical cases, such as pneumonias, rheumatic fevers, etc. We are receiving some very nasty cases of frost bite and trench foot from the Peninsula and the Balkans. They are experiencing great privations over there at present, poor fellows. The cold is bad enough, but wet and cold combined is what works such havoc. Some of the cases have been so severe that amputation has been necessary. War is a gruesome thing.

An order has just been issued here that no civilians are to be allowed to embark for Egypt till further notice and that after the 20th of this month, no-one is to be allowed to land in Egypt without the permission of the War Office. I don't know what this means exactly. There are rumours that are becoming more persistent that there is to be some trouble before the war is out.

I have practically decided to give up the Public Health job. I have spoken to Waddy[115], who is one of the N.S.W. Waddys and incidentally a Rhodes Scholar, about it. He has specialized in eyes and has been practising out here prior to the war under the Egyptian Government, and can give me first hand information about the country and the advantages of living here. He advises me not to take the job, as one gives up such a lot in many ways. That living here is pretty expensive, that the English colony is quite a small one (of course, it may be greater after the War) and that one has to live up to a certain standard. That £600 a year would not be as much as it sounds - that the summer is exceptionally trying and that one's women folk usually clear out for the worst 3 months, which is an expense. He is a married man with a small infant. He thinks that a man worth his salt should make quite as much in Australia and that it is infi-

Captain Waddy with Some Eye Patients
Source AWM P10636.012.004

---

115 Richard Granville Waddy, an old boy of The King's School, a Rhodes Scholar in 1908, and based in Egypt in 1913-1914. See the 'Beyond 1914' website of the University of Sydney for more details of him.

nitely a more pleasant country to live in. So weighing these things over I have decided to give up the idea. Wonder whether you would have advised me to take it or not. It is a vital decision to have to make - still I think I ought to make a livelihood in Australia.

Bessie Wallace, a Wollongong girl, who came over here as a Nurse and has been working at No.19 General Hospital, has become engaged to one of the Medl. Officers, and is to be married in about 3 weeks' time. As she is a great friend of Mona's I shall have to fork out a wedding present which is a bit of a blow. Also have to be present at the wedding ceremony. I have met the chap, a N.Zealander who has travelled a great deal and qualified at Edinburgh. He is a very decent fellow, and I think she has done well for herself.

Sorry to hear, Mum, that you have been having such dry weather, and are having such an expense with the water. The potatoes look a likely crop from the snapshot. I trust the roots are as fruitful as the top hamper.

Will stop now, Mum. Mona and her mother are well. Mrs. L. is probably returning to Australia in January, but it is not definite yet. Mona is going on the war path this week and hopes to find something interesting to do.

Best love, Mum, to you and all at home,

Ever yours, NIGE

Ghain-Tuffeiha Convalescent Camp, Malta, 17 Dec 1915

My dearest Matee

There is nothing much to tell you this week. Have been in camp the whole week and nothing happens here outside the usual camp routine. Have been marked down by the medical board here as I.H.[116] which means a trip away somewhere before going back to the Peninsula. There is a rumour of a boat going back to Australia fairly soon, but this rumour is always about the camp and nothing much ever comes of it. Anyway my luck has stuck to me ever since joining the Army and I am in great hopes of getting back to see you some time for a month or so.

---

116 I. H. Invalided Home

There are a lot of other Austns and New Z'landers also down to go home and as soon as they have got a ship load and can find a ship to carry us we may yet get away from here. There is of course Alexandria to get past and it is quite on the cards some of us might get put off there to make room for some worse cases to go home in our place. You see everything is a matter of luck and you don't know what is to happen from one day to the next. However, it would be a treat if I could get the trip out and be able to see you all again for a while and then come back again. The second time of coming away would be worse than the first though, as in the first time you didn't know what was ahead of you and what to expect.

Nothing happens here in camp and, after seeing the Medical Board, I haven't felt like taking the risk of a trip into Valletta as I might be away when the fellows left for the boat and miss it. This has been done a good bit by the Tommies who were off to England. A big batch of them get away from here every week.

I have just received your letter dated 4th Oct. You say you are going to send me a sheep-skin coat. I may get it if it arrives soon after your letter, but it is doubtful and I hope you haven't paid a large sum for it. The old under pants would be good to have too, but as I now am off the Peninsula these may be kept and opened over there. I hope they are, as the fellows over there are in great need of them this weather. It must be truly awful now in the rain and cold. It was bad enough when I was there but it is a lot worse now. I have seen some fellows in the hospital with frost-bitten feet which don't look at all pleasant to have. Of course they don't have any pain with them yet as their limbs are numb, but as soon as the circulation comes back and they begin to get well again the pain will come too.

Nothing more to tell you now and hope to see you sooner than we both expected. Am feeling pretty well and am only coming back to get properly fit and strong again, my complaint being general debility following dysentery, and Malta and Egypt are no good owing to the climate of the former and sand of the latter for dysentery patients to recuperate properly. Naturally it was a huge surprise to me when the doctors told me and I didn't argue with them about it. The board didn't ask me any questions but seemed to take the M.O.'s statement of the case and merely looked at me generally and appeared to be quite satisfied. All the same I wouldn't be much good if I went back there in the cold weather.

With much love to Gran and Aunt Mog, hoping everything is going on as usual at Coolah and that the vegetables at Ermo are turning out a success and not being burnt up to nothing by the hot weather.

With heaps of kisses and love to Matee Boos and the Child, hoping my good luck sticks to me and gets me this little spell, from

Your loving son, TOOTS.

Ghain-Tuffieha Convalescent Camp, Malta, 18 Dec 1915

My dear Gran and Aunt Mog

Just a short note to tell you that I may be coming back to see you all again somewhat sooner than was expected. Have been marked down I.H. here which stands for "Invalided Home" for a spell to recover after wounds or sickness. The dysentery has pulled me down a bit, but it came as a very great surprise to me when the medical officer recommended me for a trip. Needless to remark I didn't argue with him or the board of M.O.s I had later to pass. Only hope it will come off and not be cancelled, as at previous times they have been, much to the disappointment of the men who were going.

The life in this camp is pretty dull and monotonous. It is 13 miles out of Valletta and 6 miles from the railway which takes us in. There is almost nothing to do in the way of amusing the troops and it is too far from Valletta to be of any use getting into town and also absorbs most of the money they get.

Am writing this letter in the soldier's home at St. Paul's Bay. This is the spot where St. Paul landed as mentioned in the New Testament and is one of the sights of the place and visited by everyone who comes to the island. It is about 4 miles from the camp and makes a nice walk after tea. Generally go into the soldier's home there, a sort of club for the troops to go and get a cup of tea etc. and sit down and read and play the piano. Quite a number of chaps come over in the evenings.

Am hoping and looking forward to seeing you all again someday now and trust you are both keeping fit and well this summer, with much love, from

TOOTS.

P.S. Hope the lace arrived safely and turned out useful in the way of patterns and designs etc.

The decision being taken on 7 December that the Gallipoli campaign was hopeless, all Allied troops remaining at the Gallipoli Peninsula were progressively withdrawn. Over two nights on 18/19 and 19/20 December a well-planned strategy for evacuation, including self-firing rifles invented by an Australian soldier, allowed thousands of ANZAC troops to deceive the Turks, sneak down to the beach at Anzac Cove and safely escape.

NO 15 GENERAL HOSPITAL, ALEXANDRIA, 31 DEC 1915

Dearest Mum

This is the last day of the old year and I am on duty here all day at the hospital, and so shall not see Mona till tomorrow afternoon. She is rather disappointed as she was looking forward to our being together when the New Year came in, as we were last year - however, it can't be helped.

I wonder what 1916 will have in store for us all? Will it see the end of this appalling war, or will it still be dragging on? How tired everyone is getting of it, but I hope the Allies will pursue it to the bitter end, and not pursue a "peace at any price" policy, which would be disastrous. The Germans must be getting just as tired too, let us hope.

I got your letter of Nov 29th this afternoon, also one addressed to Steve to forward on. I don't know quite what to do regarding it, as Steve in his last letter was expecting to be moved from Malta any day, en route for Australia. He is very excited about it. I do trust nothing will happen to hinder him from going. He has been passed by a Board as a case for invaliding home so unless something very unprecedented occurs he should be a "dead snip" to go. If I forward your letter on, he will probably not get it. There is just a chance of his calling in at Alexandria on his way, in which case I could give it him, but don't suppose there will be such luck as that. Port Said is the more likely place. It is only 15 miles from here, and there is really no point in his calling in here. I think I will send it on, on the off chance, you won't mind his not receiving it so much, if you know he is on his way to you! How delightful for you and him to see one another again, Mum! What a day of rejoicing. You will sort of feel he has come back from the dead!! I wonder how long it will be before I can give you a hug and a kiss, Mum, a good year yet at any rate, I am afraid.

I have given up the idea of the Public Health job. I thought it all over most carefully, and I think Dr. Granville thought I was wise unless I had a special bent or liking for public health work. Egypt is not a country for women really, and I am getting rather tired of it. It would be no good my taking on the job temporarily unless I meant to stick to it for good, as the first 3 or 4 years would be all the bullocky work, and I should miss any subsequent reward. Waddy has been here 3 years now and is beginning to long to get away. Mona wrote to you by this mail, as I was afraid I should miss it. I don't know when it is supposed to leave Suez. The sailings are not so regular now, as the submarines have been very active in the Mediterranean lately and have secured 2 French mail boats and a Japanese one too.

There is some trouble expected in Egypt soon, now the troops have withdrawn from the Peninsula, and the Govt. are trying to get all the women they can out of the country. They have stopped anyone else arriving or landing both in India and Egypt now. So Mona has got out here just in time.

I have applied for a week's leave to go to Cairo, and have been granted it. Col. James could not give it, but warmly recommended my having it, as I hadn't had any except 48 hours for 15 months, to the Genl. Officer Commanding the troops here, and his recommendation was successful in my obtaining it. Mona and I ought to have an enjoyable time in Cairo, and it will be the treat of our lives. Mrs. L. will feel being left, I expect, but I dare say she will get a chance of seeing Cairo before she returns to Australia. She talks of getting back in February, but it is not definite. I am going to get her and Mona into a flat in January as they hate the Grand Hotel and cannot stomach the food. It certainly is a bit of a contrast after English stuff. I can eat anything now. The meat is very poor, there seems to be next to no nourishment in it. The troops get Australian frozen meat, but the hotels and places, of course, don't.

I am leaving for Cairo on the 6th of Jany and return on the 13th. We are sharing the flat as I daresay Mona told you in her letter, so we should do things pretty reasonably I am hoping.

I sent Aunt Julia and Cousin Bessie Xmas cards and a Xmas letter. I haven't heard from them for weeks and weeks, and am rather worried. It is quite possible they have written and the letter has gone astray, as they frequently do. It is very unsatisfactory all the same. I shall write again later on if I don't hear.

Am grieved to hear you have been having such a disastrous time with droughts. The papers report the much longed for rain having at last arrived. I do hope it will make things easier. Am pleased you liked the small present. I do trust you will receive it safely.

Do hope the Child will pick up a bit, am sorry to hear she has been so peaky. Give my love to her and Gran and Aunt Mog. With best of love to yourself,

Mum, I do hope and trust you will be having better times at Ermo when this reaches you, and that Steve will be well on his way out.

Goodbye for the present,

Ever yours,

NIGE

Ghain-Tuffieha Convalescent Camp, Malta, 31 Dec 1915

My dearest Matee Boos & Child

Have just received your letter of Oct 16th, also one from the Child. Am sorry to say I haven't yet received any of the Xmas Billys, but suppose they are still on the way, and owing to the unusual amount of parcels now arriving for the troops are being delayed a little. The sheep skin waistcoat has not turned up yet either, and I will not have much use for it if I don't go back to the Peninsula.

Am still expecting to leave here any day, but rumour has it that January 4th will be about the time. There are a good crowd coming back from here and the number is being added to daily. Suppose the time will arrive eventually and as long as we get away in the end it doesn't matter much. Shouldn't be surprised if we don't get past Alexandria though, as there seems to be some trouble brewing over there. I hope to be able to see something of Billy and Mona if we do go there on our way out. I had a letter from them both this week. They seem very happy and pleased with things in general except that Billy is expecting a trying time when the Colonel comes to call. Expect he will feel like "booting" the brute out. Mona seems to like Egypt with the exception of the natives, but misses the work of the Anzac Club and finds the time drags a bit. She is trying to get something to do in the motoring line, having learnt to drive whilst in England. Don't quite know what there is in that line for her to do, except driving convalescent patients about, but then the owner of the car generally does the driving himself in those cases.

I got a great Xmas parcel from Mona and Billy yesterday, containing a Xmas pudding, one of Crosse & Blackwells and a tin of cream, 2 tins of sardines and some chocolate. The Xmas pudding was consumed yesterday with the able help of all the other chaps in the tent. It was just the thing. Am keeping the cream to put on some tinned fruit I will get from the dry canteen. It was very kind of them to send it along. Luckily I sent Mona and Mrs. Little a small offering in the way of some Maltese lace a few weeks ago.

Our Xmas in camp here went off as well as the circumstances would allow. All the troops received a small gift from the Red Cross Society. The Australian Red Cross sent quite a good turn-out to the Australians and was envied and admired by all the Tommies and N.Z'landers. It was a tin box holding a pack of cards, 50 cigarettes, some chocolate and tobacco and some pieces of writing paper and envelopes. The Tommies only got some sweets and a pair of socks. We had some Xmas puddings dished out at dinner time and some firm in Malta gave a lot of oranges to be distributed amongst the hospitals and camps on the island.

I went into Valletta on Wednesday last and paid a visit to the hospital at Sliema. The whole place was decorated and the nurses and staff seemed to have given the patients a great time of it. All the wards were looking very gay with festoons etc. and on Xmas afternoon a band off one of the French warships went over and helped enliven things up a bit. As there were hardly any cases of dysentery in the hospital almost everyone was able to have a good time and tuck in without suffering from any after effects. Most of the cases seem to be frost bite.

Now that Anzac and Suvla Bay have been evacuated there cannot be much doing for the Austns now until next spring. Should I ever have the luck to get home in the meantime, I shall probably come back for the "box on" that will come off then. Probably be Salonika the next time. That will be better than the Peninsula anyway. Billy tells me there is a rising supposed to be brewing in Egypt. Our chaps will like that if they are only able to use their horses.

Am glad to hear that Ermo is turning out such a snug little place. It is a pity about the water, but perhaps the Board will wake up some day and make a start. No washing or baths sounds much like the Peninsula conditions.

Matee Boos I will say au revoir now, am greatly looking forward to the time when I get back, but don't know quite whether it will ever happen as things are so terribly uncertain. Give my best love to Gran and Aunt Mog, hoping to be back to see them all again someday. With heaps and heaps of love and kisses to both the Child and yourself, hoping there will be some "vegengubbles" left by the time I arrive, from

Your ever loving son, TOOTIE

Hospital Ship, *Essequibo*
Source www.peoplescollection.wales, Items, 45027

Unloading a hospital train
Source AWM PS1174

Luna Park, Heliopolis
Source AWM C04052

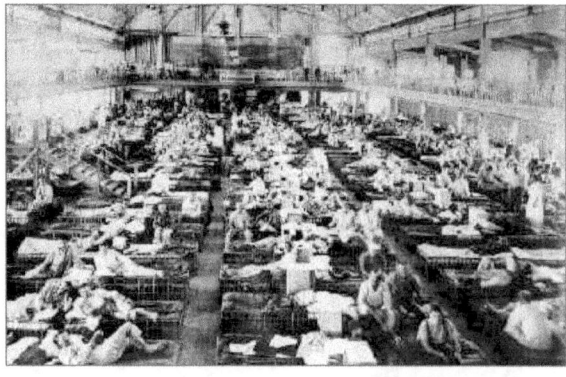

Patients, Luna Park
Source AWM H18510

1916

On 15 January 1916 Steve's mother was advised by authorities in Australia that he'd left Malta on 7 January bound for Egypt, thence to Australia.

It was not to be. He got as far as Heliopolis in Cairo. Here, before the war, a large pleasure resort known as Luna Park operated close to the Palace Hotel. In 1915, Luna Park's large wooden skating rink, with balconies all round, was converted by the Australian Army Medical Corps into an overflow hospital, the No 1 Auxiliary Hospital, taking the lighter cases from the main hospital operating out of the Palace Hotel. And, it seems, it took the convalescent cases from Malta. For medical and nursing staff, the work at Luna Park was quite boring, but in its sixteen months of operations it treated thousands of sick and wounded, with an infinitesimal death rate.

Luna Park, Heliopolis, 13 Jan 1916

Dearest Matee Boos

Have at last got out of Malta. Last Tuesday morning we had 10 minutes warning to get ready to go aboard the Hosp. Ship *Essequibo* for Alexandria. Naturally we were all very pleased and although we thought we were started for Australia we had a good trip over and arrived at Alex. yesterday about 9 a.m.

We got off the boat and straight into a hospital train. Most of the boys thought they were bound for Suez overland to pick up another boat there. They were all disappointed at not going all the way by the hospital ship. The train only brought us as far as Cairo and we afterwards came out here to a big convalescent camp. The camp itself in most things is a huge improvement on the Malta Camp as here we get good food and plenty of it, and all the patients are Australians and Aust. Sisters and Doctors. Goodness knows how long I will remain here or whether I shall ever get any farther.

It seems that these doctors in some cases don't recognise the decisions of the Malta Board. Also in Egypt now the climate is great at this time of year and only Enteric and Typhoid fever cases are sent back excepting, of course incurable cases and bad wounds. Dysentery men are being kept here as it is now cold and people are inclined to become the exactly opposite. This does not look too good for me.

It seems very doubtful if I ever get beyond Egypt if the M.O.s do not take the Malta Board's View. Should I have to go before another board of doctors here I'm afraid I would have no hope of getting through as I am looking well and, having been in the sun a good bit lately on the way over on the hospital ship, have a healthy and tanned appearance. Our full histories etc. will be gone into as soon as our papers arrive from Malta, so it is no good worrying as everything rests with the Gods. I'm not depending on getting back though.

Yesterday I went out in the afternoon to my old unit the D.A.C. who are encamped about 3 miles from here. I knew a good number who were still with them, but lots of reinforcement have joined them since I left. They have got a good camp now at the New Oases on the Suez Road and are expecting to go on to the canal soon. If I don't get away from here and there is going to be all the business over again I shall ask to go back to the old crowd and be amongst the boys again. Meanwhile I shall remain here until something definite happens.

Am expecting the doctor (Dr Pilcher of S. Aust.) around at any minute now so will not say more now. By the way Billy was introduced to him at Alexandria, he seems a decent sort of chap.

If I am remaining here I will let you know what is going to happen as soon as I get a chance. Very best love to Gran, Aunt Mog and the Child from

Your loving son TOOTS.

Partial Postcard to Thea, Egypt, Jan 1916

Write me a line shortly & tell me what everyone is doing & who is getting married & who isn't. Lots of the young bloods are getting their wives over here but I think it has been stopped now. No more women of any nation are allowed in Egypt now I believe.

I haven't had any of the 'Billys' yet and it is rather doubtful if I ever will now. Most likely they have been opened by this time & consumed by someone else. Remember me to the Bartons next time you see any of them & by the way, where is Biddy now? I often see some Sydney chaps over here whom I know. Well goodbye Child & good luck from Brother Toots.[117]

Postcard to Grandmother, Heliopolis, 22 Jan 1916

Am very pleased to be back once again in Egypt. Am about 5 miles out of Cairo and at present have got a good job, plenty to eat & a warm bed so don't want much more. Best love from Steve.[118]

No 1 Auxiliary Con. Depot, Luna Park, Heliopolis, 27 Jan 1916

Dearest Matee & Child

Just a hurried note that is being taken for me by one of the chaps going back to Australia for a change. He is coming by the *Kanowna*, the boat I should be on too. However it is no use grumbling and so far I am quite comfortable here. Am lucky to be alive at all I suppose.

There are a whole host of fellows coming back for a change who have been suffering from debility following dysentery. I had the bad luck to be looking well when I saw the Board here. I don't know how long I will remain here as I am only on a temporary job and it may not last longer than tomorrow. I am hoping to stay here for the winter until the cold weather is over.

It has been bitter lately with some showers of rain. All the rest of the boys are down at Tel-el-kebir[119], getting ready for the next scrap against a big force of Turks coming along towards the canal. All the Australians are down there and working like niggers. I couldn't tell you this and post it here as all letters

---

117 The first of two postcards written by Steve to his sister is missing but the context suggest they were written around January 1916.
118 Addressed to his grandmother, Mrs I M Flockton, at 'Coolah', Gladesville.
119 Famous as the location of a famous British victory in 1882, it was now vital for the strategically-critical defence of the Suez Canal. Situated 110 km nor-nor-east of Cairo and isolated from established transport links and amenities, it was the site of a large training camp and hospital for Australian forces, and a large prisoner-of-war camp. A Commonwealth War Graves Commission cemetery is located there.

are terribly censored from Egypt, and no news whatever gets out. Only four languages are allowable, English, French, Arabic and Italian. So you see things are pretty strict, but I suppose it is necessary as there are or was a terrible lot of news about the Dardanelles that got out through Egypt.

Well Matee the lads are just off. Best love to Gran and Aunt Mog and the Child. Keep up your spurrits. I expect I will be home before the end of this year.

With heaps and heaps of love and kisses from

Your ever loving son

TOOTS.

P.S. Hope you get this letter all serene and that it is not left in the chap's pocket or he loses it on the way.

The following card indicates that Nigel & Mona did make their sightseeing trip to Cairo and met up with Steve.

Postcard, No 1 Auxiliary Conv Depot, Luna Park, Heliopolis, 30 Jan 1916

Dearest Matee

Hope you got the letter I sent by one of the chaps returning to Australia by Hospital Ship. Am still at Luna Park & so far there is no word of my going. Do you remember the watch you gave me? It stopped whilst over at Malta & I am now getting it mended. It had some pretty hard knocking about all the time I had it & the balance was broken. To get it fixed & a new wrist case is costing me 30 piastres (6/-). Have lost the run of all my letters once again. Expect a lot of them found their way over to Malta. No doubt they will catch up again someday. Haven't heard from Billy or Mona since they left Cairo. Went out to Shezireh yesterday to the races. Had quite a good afternoon & came home with some piastres to the good. Met a lot of 'the boys' out of the old mob I was in before leaving Alexandria. Heaps & heaps of love from your loving son

TOOTS.

Postcard from No 1 Aust Conv Depot, Luna Park, Heliopolis, 30 Jan 1916

My dear Gran

Here are 2 postcards which no doubt will be interesting to you. Where I am now is right on the opposite side of Cairo away from the Pyramids. It is much handier here as a fast electric train gets us into town in about 15 minutes whereas from Mena it usually took over an hour. Am having a pretty good time here, as I have a sort of temporary job in the ... [120]

No 1 Auxiliary Hospital, Luna Park, Heliopolis, 7 Feb 1916

My dearest Matee[121]

Am still making the most of my time here. Am feeling very fit now and quite well again; also putting on weight, owing to the amount of good food which one gets here. I was in Cairo on Friday last and weighed myself and with all my uniform on consisting of tunic, breeches, boots, leggings etc. went 10 st 11 lbs which is a good weight for me and deducting about 6 lbs for clothes is more than I have ever been before to my knowledge. So you can see that there are what you would call great heaps of fat all over me. I should lose some of this I dare say when I get back to good hard work again and not the best of food. Meanwhile I shall continue to make the most of my opportunities here, the latest being to take the good old cod liver oil and malt after meals which I get from the sisters without the knowledge of the M.O. It did me good once before and am now at it again at the expense of the Government this time. There is nothing like it.

I received a letter from you dated Nov 29th under cover from Billy and which had gone over to Malta and come back again. The parcels you mention from Mrs. Barton I have never received, this being the first intimation of them. Expect they were lost in the Xmas rush and devoured by someone else. You are a nut with your orderly in the army service. There are no orderlies in that

---

120 Steve's second card to his grandmother is missing.
121 The date is written as 7.11.1915 but is likely to be 7 Feb 1916 as he wrote an earlier letter in Nov 1915 using the Roman numeral xi for the 11th month. The context definitely places the year as 1916. There were other occasions when he put the wrong year on letters when they were written early in the new year.

crowd. I suppose you mean Army Medical. I wouldn't take the job on at any price, even if you were allowed to pick and choose. Even in the A.M.C the job of stretcher bearer is as bad as any other and the S.Bs on the Peninsula did excellent work and were complimented by everyone. You haven't been sending me any letters addressed to the Div. Ammn. Pack lately. The chaps often used to think they were a pack of hounds or fools. It ought to be PARK. The old original address is the correct one again now and I have put it on the top of this letter.

Old Doos[122] still stands on the paper when you want to write. Remember me to Cleon if he has arrived back in Sydney and tell me all the latest news of the *Sydney*. Am going to turn in now, "lights out" has gone and I have some sewing to do to my breeches before I can put them on in the morning.

When you next write to me, you had better ask me some questions as to what you want to know as it is pretty hard to make up a decent letter every week with the same little things going on every day. Give my best love to Gran and Aunt Mog, hoping they got the parcel safely and with heaps and heaps of love and kisses to the Child and yourself, from

Your loving son, TOOTS.

I have only had one letter since coming over here from Malta. This Army Postal Service doesn't apparently exert itself too much.

No 1 Auxiliary Hospital, Luna Park, Heliopolis, 17 Feb 1916

My dearest Matee

Have just received a letter from you through Billy's hand dated 2nd January. This is fairly prompt, but is a good job you sent it by Billy as I haven't had any other letters of any sort for a long time now. They must be storing them up somewhere or other. Perhaps out at my old unit the D.A.C. I am thinking seriously of going back to them again now, they are camped only a short way from here, at Zietoun, and now that I have had a good spell and am quite fit again it is just as well for me to be back there getting ready for the next box on.

---

122 One of the family pets

Also I don't know many of the chaps belonging to the hospital here, excepting those I work with during the day, whereas I know a lot of the old chaps in the D.A.C. and excepting for being as comfortable as I am now it would not be so very different, and I think it is better for me to go back and get into nick again.

There are rumours going round of some of us going away some time in the near future, and I don't know, France seems to be considered the most likely, but of course no one knows. It is not certain whether I will be able to get back to my old crowd as since leaving them they have had hundreds of reinforcements from Australia and are now greatly over strength. Being an old hand the Major or Colonel may take me back again. I am going over to the Column on Friday next to see some of the heads and try to get the transfer made. Failing all this I shall endeavour to hang on to the hospital job as long as I can which I don't think will last much longer, or get sent to the Details Camp or Base Camp from where all reinforcements are sent up to their various units.

It is a rotten camp to go to, and every chance of staying there some time before getting away. So my idea is to get straight from here to the D.A.C. I shall miss all the good food and nice comfortable bed etc. but will soon settle down to camp life again, once I get back. I think I told you in my last letter that I nearly go 11 stone in my uniform which is not such a bad effort. Camp life will bring this down and at the same time harden me up a bit. It is a fair time since I did any strenuous work now.

I see by your letter that you are back at Gladesville awaiting the arrival of a new maid.[123] I hope you did not have to wait long and that she turned out to be of some use for a good term.

It is bad luck that Ermo gets such a set back every summer during the dry weather. If you are going to sell it at all it would be better to wait till the winter when it is looking its best, and would perhaps fetch more. Am very glad to hear that the handkerchiefs arrived safely and that you all liked them. I sent one each to Mona and Mrs. Little at Xmas. They had sent a lot of parcels and food etc. over to me on the Peninsula, most of which I didn't ever receive, so I thought I would have to spring to something or other. I still haven't heard from Billy or Mona since their leaving Cairo. Billy sends your letters on (two altogether now) but hasn't put in any note of any sort yet. Suppose everything is going on as usual with him and there is nothing to write about.

There is very little to do during any spare time we get, and most evenings that I am off I go to a picture show or read. There are no theatres and our leave is

---

123 Needed to help look after his grandmother.

up at 10 p.m. So there are not many opportunities of enjoyment. They have got Charlie Chaplin the Comedian on now at the Cinematograph which I occasionally go and have a look at.

Give my very best love to Gran and Aunt Mog and the Child, also remember me to Cleon if he still is in Sydney, hoping that an end will soon come to the family worryings one way or the other, with heaps and heaps of love and kisses to Matee Boos from her loving son TOOTS.

Stephen returned to his old unit on 21 Feb 1916, as a Gunner with 2nd FAB, No 1 Sect, 1st D.A.C. On the same day, in France, the Germans launched the Battle of Verdun, tying up the French Army and forcing the British Army to make plans for the horrendous Battle of the Somme later that year.

1st Divisional Ammunition Column, Egypt, 27 Feb 1916

My dearest Matee

Am back again with the old D.A.C. Managed to work it successfully and certainly had a bit of luck in getting back straight from hospital. I left Luna Park on Monday last and came out here in the afternoon. Was taken on the strength straight away and am now back again with some of my old and former tent mates. There are only 4 of us of the first lot here now, the rest being late reinforcements who have only been over 3 or 4 weeks. It didn't take me any time to settle down to the life again, and although I miss some of the luxuries from the hospital, I think I would sooner be back here with all the other chaps.

We are in camp at Zietoun, about 10 miles out of Cairo only this time in the opposite direction to that of the Pyramids at Mena. The sand here is not quite so bad as the Mena desert, being firmer and more gravel in it. It is much harder to sleep on, almost like a pavement and lots of the chaps get a sore and stiff hip when sleeping.

About two nights of this and I was used to it and have got a corn bag and 3 waterproofs under me which makes it slightly softer. The work here is just the same as before, exercising horses and carting fodder and stores for the column. Today and last night I was on picquet, it being my first since coming back here. A picquet is better to do than a guard, although you do your 4 hours on and 2 off just the same through the night, only you don't have to keep on one post with a rifle up all the time whilst on picquet. It means looking after one of the horse lines and seeing that no horses get loose and that their rags are not kicked off etc.

We have been warned to go away at any time now, down to Tel-el-kebir, most likely next Tuesday. All the old hands and a few of the older reinforcements. We are going down into the batteries a good number of which have been formed lately. Well we are all pleased at getting into the guns, but don't like the idea of getting down to Tel-el-kebir which is miles away from anywhere. I suppose soon we shall be making another move out of Egypt now that the winter is over.

I ought to get my letters again regularly now that I am here again, so don't make any mistake about the address which I have put on the top of the letter. I found out that all my letters have been going home to England where the military authorities in Malta advised the Aust. Base P.O. I had gone to.

I have just received a letter from you dated August 1915 which has been going 6 months, also one each from the Trugannir Bartons[124] wishing me a happy Xmas. These had gone to England and come back. So I expect I shall lose a good deal of my mail which has gone on there and not been sent back. I have written to the Aust. Base P.O., and told them where I am and have got an acknowledgment so things ought to go smoothly for a bit.

Another of your letters came to hand saying that you had called at the C'wealth Bank and seen Mr. Armitage.[125] Am very sorry to hear that no money has been paid into my account there. Before I left I made an allotment of 6/- a day to be paid into my account and filled in the necessary allotment form. This I understood was to be paid into my account weekly by the Defence Dept. or Military Dept. I hope that I have not been done for all the money and interest for all this time. In your next letter I hope to hear that it has been paid into the Savings Bank Dept.

I am writing this in the tent on Sunday afternoon, very hot outside with a dust storm blowing and everyone's eyes feeling sore and generally fed up. There are 9 others in the tent, 3 or 4 writing and the others talking and sleeping and resting.

---

124 The Bartons who lived at Trugannir – the name of a rural property? Or Truganina, a parish just west of Melbourne?
125 Hugh Trail Armitage, Chief Accountant at the Commonwealth Bank in Sydney. Later Governor of the Bank.

Please give my best love to Gran, am sorry to hear she hasn't been so well lately, and hope she picks up again quickly. Also Aunt Mog and Child, hoping you are all keeping well, with heaps and heaps of love and kisses from

Your loving son

TOOTS.

No 15 General Hospital, Alexandria, 29 Feb 1916

Dearest Mother

Your letter and a long one from Mrs. Lee forwarded on by you came to hand a few days ago, two to be correct I think. Many thanks for them. The photographs have not arrived yet. I think I shall wait a few days to give them a chance of turning up before I reply.

I had a letter from Steve two or three days ago too. He has returned to his Unit. His address now is
3872 G^r S.P. Boulton, A.F.A.
No. 1 Section,
1st Divisional Ammunition Column,
Australian Forces - Egypt.

He says he feels pretty fit now and is glad to be back again, as hospital is very monotonous after a bit. Also he thinks there is a good chance of his getting attached to a battery, which he seems very anxious to happen - it certainly would be much more interesting helping in the working of a gun than just supplying it with ammunition. He is camped just near Cairo, and as the weather is delightful now, he should not be having such a bad time of it.

Mona and I are very anxious for him to try and get 48 hours leave and come and visit us. He could easily be put up in the flat and if he came on a Friday he could be taken to the "Pops" to see Mona in their performance.

I am afraid, however, such a thing is quite out of the question at present, as no N.C.O. man is to be allowed to travel by train unless on duty. The only chance would be if he was transferred to Alexandria again. Mona is taking part in a sketch in the Pops next week and she is rather excited about it, as up till now she has only been one of the chorus supporters. I hope she will be a success. I am pretty sure she will, as the audiences here are not at all exacting.

I have finished my job as Officer in charge of the Medl. Division, as Carson has returned. I performed the duties satisfactorily as far as I know and everything went quite harmoniously. We had a case of smallpox during my period of duty which created a mild stir, as the man came from a camp right in the middle of the city. No further cases have cropped up as yet and a good number of contacts and others are being vaccinated. I shall probably be done again as I handled the case.

I have not yet answered A. Phoebe's and Phyll's letters[126], and I have one to write to Cousin Bessie again too. She is very anxious for me to join some Laymen's Crusade for stimulating further spiritual thought and prayer during the present crisis. I suppose I had better join to please her. I hope, however, they won't start dunning me for subscriptions, which is the usual sequel of any such step. Everyone is a free subject and has his own destiny to look to, and I don't altogether hold with would be well-intentioned people going about worrying their neighbours to look to their spiritual welfare and profit by the terrible example of God's righteous indignation for our wickedness as evidenced by the present war. It's a parson's duty and not a layman's. I admit at the same time that laymen can do a great deal by means of influence and personality. Well, Mum, it is a vexed question.

I dare say I must stop now. Trusting you are all well at home. Looking forward to your next letter! With very best love to all at home,

Ever yours, NIGE

Two Australian divisions are being moved to France in a few weeks' time now. There are also a large number of the British Forces to go too. I don't know whether Steve's lot will be included or not. There is also a probability of our going thither, as now the Gallipoli campaign is finished and the Canal business is petering out there is not much need for such a lot of large expensive hospitals being kept up. However, it is not settled yet what is to happen to us. There seems to be an increasing feeling that a move will take place in a month or so.

---

126 Phyll (or Phil) was Nigel's artist cousin Phyllis Flockton Clarke, living with her mother Phoebe at Chatswood in Sydney.

1st Section, 1st D.A.C., Zietoun, 1 Mar 1916

My dearest Matee

Am still out at Zietoun with the D.A.C. I think I told you in my last letter that I was expecting to go down to Tel-el-kebir to join up with some battery. We haven't gone yet but are 'standing by' ready to leave at any minute and have packed up everything in readiness. Of course we may still stay here for a while under these orders, and I hope we do. I would much rather be up here close to Cairo and Heliopolis where there is some sort of amusement to go to and also where we can get something to eat when inclined.

Down at Tel-el-kebir from most accounts seems to be pretty deadly. About once a month 12 hours leave is granted to the men to come up to Cairo. Some big move ought to be coming off soon now that the winter is over and so it won't be surprising if most of the Australians are moved off somewhere or other. It is a good job it is not back to the Peninsula. There are frequent rumours of France and Mesopotamia also Salonika. By the time you get this letter no doubt everyone will know which it is to be.

Am getting pretty fed up with the war by this time, especially as now a terrible lot of late reinforcements are just arriving from Australia and amongst whom I could easily have been. Anyway it is no good worrying over this part of it; am afraid that the end will not be till next year sometime, as Germany has still got a huge army in the field.

I got a letter from Billy tonight asking if there is any chance of me getting off for a trip up to see them all at Alexandria. Am afraid not as all leave is supposed to be stopped now, including officers leave, since the fear of local risings in Egypt. Also being on the point of being shifted somewhere from here, it is I think out of the-question. Billy writes from Camp de Caesar where he has got the flat and seems to be very comfortable. Cleopatra camp where we were camped last May and June is quite close. It would be good if I could get back to Cleopatra again. I don't suppose we will have the luck to go there again.

I have been getting the letters you have sent me through Billy but now this will be my address and I can rely on getting them again regularly.

Went in to Cairo with Holland[127] the other afternoon. He used to stay with the Knibbs and who I enlisted with. We had quite an enjoyable afternoon, doing it

---

127 Captain Austin George Selwyn Holland (1889-1965), a 25-yr-old insurance broker of Sydney with long-standing service in the militia, embarked on 16 June 1915. He was a son of Colonel George Henry Holland.

in style. Went to the Egyptian Museum first and saw all the old antiques such as the Mummies of Rameses!!! etc. etc., also the old writings on the tablets of stone. Got kicked out of here at 4 p.m. and drove in a Garri or cab to Groppi's which is the place where all the elite take afternoon tea. We did the heavy here for a while amongst all the Generals and "crowned heads". Then had dinner and finished up at a picture show. The latter doesn't sound much, but there is nothing else to see here but these shows. Anyway it made a very pleasant change from camp life and brought back old memories of tea at the stores in Sydney.

Holland has got his pater over here now who is a bloated "Colonel" and so is having a pretty good time. He is on transport duty and has the job of bringing over the troops from Australia. He is going to touch him for a £5 or tenner so he says, so we may be having another afternoon out in the near future before we go away.

Am sending Gran a post card in this letter, hoping she is keeping well and in good spirits. Give my best love to Aunt Mog, hoping to come back soon to do the trip into town in the *Gannet*[128] again someday. Also remember me to Cleon if he is still in Sydney, expect they will shortly be finding some work for him again on his ship and with heaps of love and kisses to Matee Boos and the Child from

Your loving son TOOTS.

No 15 General Hospital, Alexandria, 10 Mar 1916

Dearest Mum

The mail goes out today so I am just hurriedly scrawling you a note, so that you will have a line from me.

I wrote to Aunt Mog earlier in the week, and I dare say she will give you any news there is from me, which I am afraid is not very much just now.

I had a letter from Steve two or three days ago, he has rejoined his unit as you will have heard when this reaches you, but he tells me he is now being transferred to Tel-el-kebir on the Canal for a bit. Two Australian divisions are

---

128 The Sydney Harbour ferry which he used to catch to the city each day, with Aunt Mog

leaving there almost immediately for France, but it is not definite whether he is going with them or not.

Things are rather unsettled at this Hospital just now, opinion seems to be growing daily in favour of our being moved shortly, probably next month. Destination unknown, but most likely France. Whether we shall preserve our identity as a General Hospital or be split up into field ambulances, casualty clearing stations, stationary hospitals, etc. remains to be seen.

Mona is rather disturbed at the news of a move and doesn't like the idea of it at all. She has just made friends with Egypt and is not looking forward to leaving it yet awhile, and she doesn't take kindly to our being separated again, as we have been so extremely happy.

However, she will have to do so, as I don't think women are allowed to land in France. She wonders whether she will stay here or return to Australia with Mrs. Little, and then come back to Europe later on - her mother has offered to pay her passage back if she will do so. Mona tho' doesn't want to return to Australia just yet. The two journeys make a very tedious and trying trip as well as an expensive one - at any rate we are at present waiting to see what is going to happen first in the way of a move for me.

Well, Mum, I must stop now. Trusting all is well with you. With bestest love to you and Thea. I will write you a longer letter next week,

Yours ever, NIGE

A lack of suitable gun positions on steep terrain full of fissures and gullies meant that the Artillery played a minor role in the ANZAC's Gallipoli campaign. The farmland of the Western Front would be the opposite.

Before the AIF moved to France, the Artillery was re-organised to suit the anticipated conditions and Field Artillery Brigades (FABs) now contained a fourth Battery. Each Battery contained four 18 pounder field guns, making 16 guns per FAB. The field guns fired low trajectory, high velocity shells with a range of about 7,500 yards (about 4¼ miles or almost 7 km). Each Division also had a Brigade with twelve 4.5 inch Howitzers firing 35 pound shells.

Both types of guns could fire high-explosive, shrapnel and gas shells, but Howitzers were better suited to trench warfare in flat country, as they could fire at a higher elevation, lower velocity and shorter range. This steeper angle of descent delivered larger amounts of explosives more reliably into a trench, with less wear and tear on the gun barrels.

18 pounder gun near Ypres, Oct 1917
Source AWM E01209

On 8 March 1916, Stephen and hundreds of other men were sent to Tel-el-kebir and placed in various brigades to bring them up to full complement. Stephen was assigned to the 22nd Battery, 1st Field Artillery Brigade (1st FAB), destined to work with the 18 pounder field guns. In the general promotions and transfers dated 12 March, he was promoted from Gunner to Bombardier (Temp), that date unknown to him at time of writing.

Tel-el-kebir, 14 Mar 1916

Dear Matee & family

You see where I have got to now. Have left the D.A.C at Zietoun and with about 200 or so other gunners have joined up with batteries. My new address will be No 3872 Gr S.P. Boulton, 1st Field Artillery Brigade, A.I.E.F., C/- Intermediate Base, Egypt. This will be permanent for me now. I am in one of the batteries forming the 1st Brigade. There are four to each brigade. Am not allowed to tell you the no. but will do so as soon as we move off.

Am afraid I missed a mail but they are very irregular now and sometimes they go before we know anything about a boat leaving. There are rumours that there will be no more outward mail from here for about 6 weeks, owing to the lack of vessels whilst the big movement of troops is on and because they don't want any of the enemy subjects to know when we will be going across.

Have been down at Tel-el-kebir nearly a week now. It is away in the desert between Cairo and the Canal. All or most of the Australians are encamped here which makes the camp an immense size. It is not the most pleasant of camps being as near to active service conditions as possible, being some 60 odd miles away from Cairo, and one has to practically exist on army rations. No doubt it is the best for training purposes and will help to make the men fitter. Nevertheless a few meals and luxuries would have been very nice and useful to me. We can occasionally get the day off and get up to Cairo for the day leaving here at 7.15am and getting back to camp at 9.30pm. Only a few men are allowed up at a time though and it is hardly worth while going up unless you have something to do.

You all by now will be wondering what they are going to do with all the Australasian troops and by the time you get this we shall, or I shall, expect to be in England or France. We are expecting to move off from here in a week or so, that is all the 1st Division. I don't know about the 2nd or later Divisions. We are supposed to be going to England or France. I think it will be to the former for a little while & then over. My battery is only a new one, just formed, and is attached to the 1st Brigade, so I am lucky to be going.

I am at present in a new job being in the Battery Orderly Room. In some ways it is a good thing to have as I don't attend any parades and have the office tent to sleep in on my own. Also I may be getting a stripe which will make me a Bombardier and pay of 8/6 a day. I won't get the training that the other fellows will get and so I may not stick to it for ever. My O.C is Mjr McLaughlin, & he's a very decent chap.[129] Am very busy with the forming of this new unit and will continue to be right up to the time we go away. If we get to England I will dread going to see Aunt Julia & Cousin Bess and all my other relations. But I suppose if I get the time I shall have to do it.

I don't know when you will get this letter as we hear several reports about no more letters going to Australia for some time. Anyway I am sending it on the off chance it will get away in time to catch some boat. Am sending it in one of the active service envelopes; the censoring of all letters is very strict here & we are only supposed to write one page & as you know mention no military matters. I don't think any of my information herein would be very valuable.

So good bye Matee boos & the best of luck & love to you and all the family, hoping they are all well. Am feeling quite well again now and ready to start the 2nd spasm of this turn-out, hoping I have the same luck as before up till now.

From your ever loving son TOOTS

---

129   Major Geoffrey McLaughlin died of wounds in Belgium on 4 Nov 1917, aged 30.

On 19 March the 1st FAB was ordered to move the following night.

Postcard, Postmarked 21 Mar 1916

3872 Bdr S P Boulton
22nd Battery
First F.A. Brigade

This is my address. Am leaving Egypt tomorrow. I don't know where to but think it is to the western front. Am well & will let you know where I am as soon as I can. Sorry I haven't time to write a letter but we are on the move. Best love to all from TOOTS.

The ANZACs had not yet left Egypt for the Western Front when Erzerum, the city in Eastern Turkey now famous for the Armenian genocide by the Turks in 1915, was captured by the Russians in February 1916. This article from *The Age* in Melbourne[130] indicates that the Germans had no idea that the ANZACs were coming their way and would eventually astonish Europe with their fighting prowess. The racist attitudes expressed herald the subsequent rise of the Nazis.

The ANZAC Heroes

VIEWED THROUGH GERMAN SPECTACLES.

A VITRIOLIC OUTBURST.

It is not surprising to find that Germany, bereft of her colonies, should view with feeling or uncontrollable anger the support Britannia has received from her dominions oversea. Australia in particular has lately been the subject of vitriolic outbursts of Hun word-frightfulness, of which the following extract from the 'Vossische Zeitung' is a typical example:

> The indescribable joy with which the fall of the fortress of Erzerum was welcomed in the English press has no doubt evaporated sufficiently for the Britons to see clearly that their cause in the Near East is in a very shaky condition. Because, of what elements do the forces they have available in Mesopotamia and in the adjacent regions consist?
>
> Of Australians and Canadians mainly, the very riff-raff of humanity, descendants of murderers and thieves, drunken hordes, who despise the very thought of discipline and decency. This applies particularly to the

---

130   The Age, Melbourne, Sat 22 April 1916, p 18

Australians, the worthy posterity of men who for their crimes were once deported from their own country to found a colony at the extreme ends of the earth.

These are the white allies of the black culture bearers who have set notoriously civilised England against us; these constitute the unspeakable human refuse against whom our heroic sons and brothers are doomed to fight. And yet there are sentimentalists who would urge us to be dainty in the choice of our weapons when facing such bestial creatures as these!

At sea, H.M.T. 'Knight Templar', 25 Mar 1916

My dearest Matee Boos

All outward mail has been stopped I hear for 4 weeks so I don't know when you will get my letters. Anyway it is best to keep on writing I suppose and you will probably get them all in a bunch.

You will notice by the address that I am at sea once again, but on a different and new route. Just at this minute we are slowing down and wending our way along the north African coast and will I think soon make a dart across the Mediterranean for Toulon, which port we are bound.

It is good to get out of Egypt with its hot sun and sand. We came up from Tel-el-kebir on the 20th and travelled all night in the train up to Alexandria. Got alongside the transport about 5 in the morning and had a sort of a breakfast. Was kept busy most of the morning getting horses on board, and so wasn't able to get away to see Billy till about 1 o'clock. The O.C. allowed me two hours off, and I hurried out to the hospital only to find that he had gone home to lunch. I didn't have time to go out to Camp de Caesar and get back to the docks again, so I missed seeing him.

We left Alexandria about 5 o'clock accompanied by an escort comprising a destroyer or submarine guard. This little boat remained with us for a couple of days and then left us. All ranks now have to wear their life belts at all times, and guards and lookouts are posted for the length of the voyage. We have also a useful gun mounted on the stern, a 4.7 Q.F., so you can imagine we are continually on the lookout for any subs.

In spite of all these precautions they seem to do a good deal of damage. Yesterday we received the S.O.S. signal from the *Minneapolis*, another transport just

190 miles away, but on our course. She had been torpedoed. We didn't get any farther call so we think she must have gone down.[131] Indian troops were supposed to have been on board. This makes the second boat that I had been on previously to go down. The *Marere* [132] went down some time ago with all hands, and now the *Minneapolis* gets it, both of these boats I had been on for several weeks.

I can't tell you whereabouts we are going to when we get to France, but we are expecting to land at Toulon, a big French naval base north east of Marseilles about 40 miles. The general idea seems to be for us to do a little more training a few miles behind the firing line, to get used to the conditions etc.

I expect censoring of all letters will be very strict in France and it may be a hard job to let you know something of where I am and what is happening. It will be something new getting into a different country. Am glad to be out of Egypt for lots of things, but after a few weeks rain in France I think I will soon wish to be back there. I don't think I saw more than a week's rain the whole time we were there. They got us out in a good time though just as the summer was coming on.

Did I tell you that I have got a stripe up? You will address me in future as Bombardier which is abbreviated Bdr.[133] There is a difference of 2/6 a day in my pay which is better than nothing at all. In camp I shall probably have the office tent to myself to sleep in, and shall be able to get it fixed up fairly comfortably, that is if we are remaining in any one place any length of time. Another privilege is getting a mustang or horse of your own to ride which is much better than sitting on a gun timber or wagon.

When you write you had better send me Cousin Mary's address in England, also anyone else who should get a letter. I don't say I will write to them as it will be a bit of an ordeal and no easy matter. Anyway I might spring to a field service card or something in that line. Send me a list of relations with their addresses and who they are, like this "Mrs. John Charles - Aunt Julia" so that I don't make any mistakes, because I don't know any of them or I have forgotten them and their address. I don't suppose they will be very interested in me in

---

131 *HMT Minneapolis* was torpedoed on 23 March 1916 by U-35, 195 miles NE of Malta, and sank on 25 March with the loss of 12 lives.
132 The *Marere* was shelled and sunk in the Mediterranean Sea on 18 January 1916, 236 miles east of Malta by the same submarine. U-35 was the most successful German submarine of the War, sinking 224 ships. Stephen's belief that all hands were lost was incorrect - her crew survived.
133 Stephen's rank as a Bombardier was officially confirmed on 22 April.

any case. I suppose John and Ken Dixon belong to something and have got commissions.

Give my very best love to Gran and Aunt Mog, hoping they continue to keep fit and well. Tell Gran I will send her some post cards of the places I go to in France, after I have settled down somewhere.

I suppose the Child is still going to the School at Dulwich Hill and gets a certain amount of fun out of it. Has Cleon joined his ship I wonder? Remember me to him if he is still in Sydney. When you write to me my address will be

No 3872 Bdr. S P Boulton
22nd Battery
1st Field Arty Brigade
A. I. F.

This will find me, but be sure to put this and nothing else and don't confuse the number of battery with brigade. Better cut this address out and post it on the wall where it won't get lost.

Well good bye Matee Boos, with heaps and heaps of love and kisses from

Your loving son TOOTS.

P.S. It is my birthday next Friday. Spent in France this time. The last one was in Egypt.

The 1st FAB reached La Valentine Camp, Marseilles on 28 Mar 1916 but two days later was quarantined.

Somewhere in France, Sunday night, 2 Apr 1916

Dearest Matee

Here we are in France. In my last letter I think I told you we had left Alexandria on the 21/3/16. We got orders from Malta to make for Toulon where we eventually arrived without being torpedoed. We spent a day and night in Toulon harbour and then came on to Marseilles. After unloading all the horses etc, we started away from the wharf to march out to a little village called La Valentine about 10 miles out of Marseilles. It is a good walk especially at the end of a day's work. We left Marseilles about 6.30pm and arrived out here about 9pm after tramping through mud & slush all the way.

We are now billeted in an old disused mill which if nothing else is nice and dry. The billeting is quite a new idea for all of us, and as there is tons of rain here it is about the only way of housing us. It is a great improvement on Egypt and everyone is very pleased at getting out of that country. The country round here is very pretty, there being big hills at the back covered with fir trees and everything is looking very fresh & green and is much admired after the sameness of the desert.

It is very nippy here still and all our extra clothes are brought into use. The water we wash in in the mornings which is drawn from a creek at the back of the billet is just like ice. Most of us are now feeling the effects of the change in climate and several of the lads are getting influenza & colds. I have got a bit of a cold still but have managed to dodge the 'flue' I think. Was feeling a bit off yesterday but am better now and expect to be rid of my cold in a day or so.

Coming over on the transport the *Knight Templar* we had a case of smallpox and are now supposed to be undergoing isolation & quarantine. Actually it is a very difficult thing to quarantine troops properly. The first two days we were here we could do & go almost anywhere and after that the quarantine started. I managed to get into Marseilles and have a look round. It is not a bad city at all and very up to date. Of course the 'Orstralians' caused the populace to be not a little interested and we got some cheers marching through the streets on our way to camp. Now that we are being quarantined all leave has been stopped for us and we are not allowed into Marseilles or out of the billet. There is one or two little farm houses adjoining the billet where we get some bonzer coffee for two sous. It is just the thing early in the mornings. Omelettes too are very much gone in for but eggs are very dear being 2^s each, but are the biggest eggs I have seen anywhere.

We will not be here very long now, as soon as our time of isolation is up I think we will move off up north. No-one knows where to, some think England to get guns and equipment, but all the big ordnance depots are over here & so we may put the finishing touches on here. If it hadn't been for the case of smallpox we would have gone straight on from here some days ago. My new address is now, in case you don't know

Bdr S P Boulton No 3872
22nd Battery
1st A.F.A. Brigade
AIEF France

So far there are no postal arangements working yet. It is considered unsafe to post letters in the French Post Offices as more often than not they don't go. I am giving this to a Tommy who I hope will post it in an English P.O. It is in one of the green envelopes so you should get it all safe & sound.

With very best love to Gran, Aunt Mog, The Child & heaps of love & kisses to the mee maw from her loving son

TOOTS

On 10 April the men embarked on the 800km train journey to the Channel port of Le Havre in the north of France.

Somewhere in France, 10 Apr 1916

My dearest Matee

Am on the move still and am now writing this letter whilst waiting to move off. We have been here now nearly a fortnight having been delayed by the outbreak of a smallpox case coming over on the boat. We were supposed to be quarantined and have all been vaccinated. So far I haven't felt any effects of the vaccination and am hoping it won't affect me at all.

Have quite lost my cold and am feeling A.I. in spite of the incessant rain which seems to be the usual thing here at this time of year. After about three or four days rain you can imagine what the country is like with black soil. Everywhere it is like a quagmire with mud and slush up to the ankles. It is a good job we are not under canvas. The billets keep our sleeping things dry and a change of clothes, but the chaps' boots come in for a hard time. Luckily I have got a pretty new pair and have applied dubbin pretty frequently. This keeps them in good nick and helps to make them watertight.

Today is beautifully fine and quite hot and everything is looking very fresh and spring like. The surrounding country is very pretty and is looking great. I wonder what sort of a place it will be where we stop at next. We are going up north and I think to Le Havre where the big base camps are. I may of course be wrong as no one ever knows what is going to happen or where we are bound for. I expect it will be much colder up there anyway and the sheepskin coat you sent would have come in a treat if I had only got it. There are several of them being worn by the men.

Yesterday afternoon I had the afternoon off on leave and went into Marseilles. Had a great hot bath at the Hotel Regina which was very good and I thought I mightn't get another opportunity for some little time. It cost me 2 francs and was well worth the money. Put in the rest of the afternoon having afternoon tea and a good feed for dinner and a general stroll about.

Now that I have taken this job of battery orderly on I have a much better time. Have no guards or picquets and generally get my full night's rest, at least until we go into action when my work will increase a hundredfold. Am practically my own boss, excepting of course for the officers. In camp have my own tent in which is the orderly room.

Will have to stop now, but will write again soon after we get anywhere settled down. Am getting pretty fed up of this moving about, as it always means no sleep and on the go all the time until we arrive at our destination.

This time we have got to do two days and nights in the train with 3 hours halt each day. Terribly slow work having horses to look after - makes it worse.

With heaps and heaps of love to all the family from

Your loving son TOOTS.

P.S. Still haven't had any letters for an age. Hope you are getting mine regularly.

No 15 General Hospital, Alexandria, 18 Apr 1916

Dearest Mother

A letter of yours came to hand 3 or 4 days ago, also one for Steve which I have forwarded on to him in France. His address seems very indefinite, but most military addresses do, I do trust he receives it safely. Mona and I have also written him letters, but as we have not heard from him yet we do not know whether he has received them or not. We ought to have a word from him any day now.

Rumours are becoming very persistent now about our leaving. A census of all the patients is being taken today and a large amount of packing up has been done, so it looks as if our departure from Alexandria is really going to take place soon.

Opinion has it that we are not going to either Mesopotamia, Salonika, or France, but are destined to go to German East Africa! Mombassa is the port, just opposite Madagascar. You can see it marked on the map. It is very near the equator so should be pretty sultry. They say it is a very mountainous and beautiful country, rich in vegetation and tropical herbage, also abounds in game of all sorts. However, it is not at all certain whether we are going there, but it is considered likely. I daresay I shall be able to tell you in my next letter if there is anything in it.

Enclosed is a letter I received from Harold Boulton[134] yesterday, containing news of various members of his family, and also news of himself. I am sure you will be much interested, and may feel inclined to write to him. He is probably going to write to you as I have given him your address. The address at the top of his letter will always find him, as it is the home of his fiancée, who will always know his whereabouts.

Harold Boulton & wife Nan, 1928
(Picture Courtesy Julia Woodhouse)

Also enclosed are some photographs which you will like to have I daresay.[135] The one taken of Mona and I is rather good, especially of Mona, but I am afraid I look rather a sawny, still I appear to be very happy, which is true. The photographs of Mona are taken of her in the Gaby de Lys costume which she wore on the stage with great success, and the other one is of her riding rig. She is rather disappointed in this one and hope you won't think she always looks like this!

I am sorry to hear, Mum, you are feeling very lonely at times and are thinking of giving up Ermo. It makes me feel like returning to you as soon as possible. I have been considering resigning at the end of my second year, which comes to an end in September, as I am wanting to get back to Australia more and more. However, I don't suppose I should be very popular if I returned before the war is over. I should very much like to see it to a finish, having gone so far.

Nigel Boulton, Egypt, 1916
(Picture Courtesy Julia Woodhouse)

---

134 Thomas Harold Boulton was Nigel's first cousin, resident in New Zealand at this time.
135 See picture above, 1916, but the other photos mentioned in this paragraph have not survived.

Conscription is being mooted in Australia, and there is a chance of my being seized as soon as I return. I must wait a bit and see how things are going in 2 or 3 months' time. Doctor Lee's offer was tempting, and I still wonder whether I could have made it pay at £400 a year. £1,000 p.a. is pretty hefty in the way of expenses before one begins to make anything, isn't it? Housekeeping and upkeep of practice would run into £600 and this with the £400 I should have to disburse to him makes this sum to pay off. I think I was right in refusing on his terms.

The lease on the flat expires very shortly, in 9 days to be exact. I am wondering whether it is a wise thing to have taken another on. I am going to try and get them to let us have it for 2 months instead of 3, with the option of taking it on monthly. If I am leaving so shortly, Mona will be very lonely, I am afraid. Her mother is very anxious to return to Australia, but Mona won't hear of it and wants to go back to England before doing this. It is difficult to know what to do for the satisfaction of all parties concerned.

Well, Mum, I shall close now. I hope your worries will not be so trying as time goes on. Remember me very kindly to all at home. Love to Aunt Mog, Gran, the Child and your precious self,

Ever yours, NIGEL

On 16 April the men of the 1st FAB arrived at their billets after picking up their 18 pounder guns and vehicles from a British depot at Le Havre. The billets, at Caëstre, lay north-east of Hazebrouck and south-west of Ypres, in what was supposed to be a relatively quiet part of the battlefront. Here in the 'nursery sector' the newly-arrived troops had a chance to reorient themselves to the new conditions.

SOMEWHERE IN FRANCE, 30 APR 1916

Dearest Matee Boo

Am quite well and comfortable. Forget when I last wrote but have been very busy. We left Le Havre and went up near the front. Only the 3rd line of defence[136] though so we haven't seen any of the fun yet. We stayed up there a week and then had orders to come down to Calais with our guns etc.

---

136 Bgdr Genl J J Hobbs' unit war diary says 'In rear of Petillon and Fleurbeau'. In his war diaries, Sapper Edward L Moore refers to it as Fleur Beaux. Today it is spelled as Fleurbaix. It is adjacent to Fromelles.

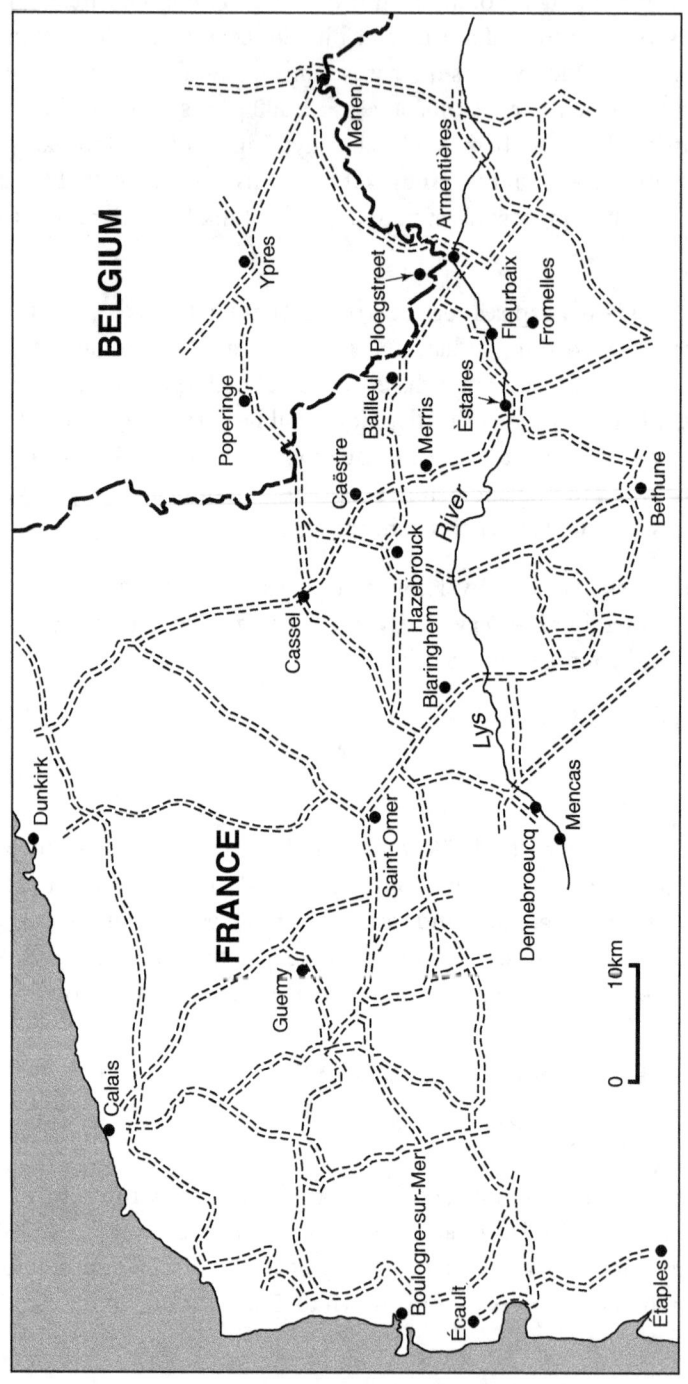

Map 8: North East France, 1916-1918

Map © John Newland, 2015

We had one good fine day coming down and after that it rained in torrents for the rest of the trip. The whole trip only took 2½ days thank goodness, and we were all very glad to get in to our billet and get our wet things off and get into our blankets. Fortunately the next day was fine and sunny and we were able to get all our clothes dry once more.

It is bad luck when it rains when on active service as we only carry a change of underclothing. All our boots and trousers generally have to go on the next morning just as we take them off. It is all in the game though. We have been down here for about 10 days now trying our new guns and are off again up the line this time to take up our own position and join in the scrap. This frontier or "line" is nothing like the Peninsula as here we get good food and rations and after a time in the gun pits we will be relieved and have our regular spells. Also when we spell we will come right away from the firing line.

There is very little sickness amongst the troops which is again very different from Anzac. Everyone seems very confident about the war here, and Frenchmen and Belgians don't think it will see another winter through. There doesn't seem to be much progress being made yet though. No doubt in about another month's time there will be a big advance on all fronts simultaneously. There is no doubt we have a big advantage over them in the way of artillery. All our explosives and shells are of the best whereas some of their stuff is becoming inferior and their shells don't always explode.

The Australians are very popular here with the Frenchies, much more than the Tommies are. We are billeted a little way out of Calais quite close to the sea and on a fine day with glasses can see England. The billet is quite comfortable though and dry with plenty of straw on the floors of the barns which make great beds. We have reveille at 5 am every morning and are out till 5 at night on the range, so you see we are not having much of a holiday. Most of us generally turn in early.

The weather since coming here has been grand and some days are quite like an Australian spring day. But it won't last long, even now there is a change in the wind, and I suppose the rain will be starting again soon. This is the only drawback, when it rains it generally keeps going for weeks at a time.

Now that I am in the battery it is ever so much better than the D.A.C. as it is a much smaller unit and rations etc. are slightly better. Also an occasional lot of gift stuffs come along for the 1st Brigade of Artly., which we being in the 1st Brigade get a share of. We haven't had any since coming over to France but I suppose later some will come along. Mr. Budden of Hunter's Hill is Secretary I believe.

Haven't had my letters for ages, none since coming over here. When you write, don't forget to put on the number of the battery and also the Brigade and don't mix them. Am quite used to not getting anything now.

Give my best love to all at home, hoping everyone is well and happy with heaps of love and kisses to the mee maw from

Her loving son TOOTS.

P.S. All leave for the 1st Aust. Division has been stopped at present, so there is no hope of getting over to England.

To allow for the greater mobility and easier exchange of artillery units among the Allied forces, so dependent on the artillery in the Great War, the Australian artillery was further reorganized in France. To create 6-unit Artillery Brigades, the separate Howitzer batteries were broken up, aiming to spread their shorter-range higher-angle guns around the existing 18 pounder batteries as far as possible.[137] As part of this process, on 6 May the 22nd Battery (Stephen's Battery) ended up as part of a new 21st Field Artillery Brigade, which remained reliant only on four 18 pounder longer-range guns, there being insufficient Howitzers to equip each Brigade.

In his next letter, written from the billets at Caëstre, Stephen makes his first mention of gas attacks. Wikipedia explains that

> *Chemical weapons in World War I were primarily used to demoralize, injure, and kill entrenched defenders, against whom the indiscriminate and generally slow-moving or static nature of gas clouds would be most effective. The types of weapons employed ranged from disabling chemicals, such as tear gas and the severe mustard gas, to lethal agents like phosgene and chlorine. This chemical warfare was a major component of the first global war and first total war of the 20th century ... The use of poison gas performed by all major belligerents throughout World War I constituted war crimes as its use violated the 1899 Hague Declaration Concerning Asphyxiating Gases and the 1907 Hague Convention on Land Warfare, which prohibited the use of "poison or poisoned weapons" in warfare.*

---

137 Four Howitzer guns were moved into each 18 pounder Battery wherever possible, replacing four of the 18 pounders. On 6 May the 22nd Battery from 1st FAB (Stephen's Battery), 23rd Battery from 2nd FAB and 24th Battery from 3rd FAB were reassigned to form a new 21st FAB. The Batteries retained their old names and personnel and were still part of Australia's 1st Division.

Somewhere in France [Caëstre], 8 May 1916

My dearest Matee

Am still going strong and feeling O.K. Am sorry I cannot tell you where we are or what we are doing, but it is against the rules. Am fairly comfortable in billets and the weather is keeping good, fairly fresh in the mornings, but afterwards quite pleasant.

Am not in action yet, but within range of the German's big stuff. Another week now and our turn comes to go up. It is tremendously different from the Gallipoli business as here it is ever so much more comfortable and quite easy to get any little requirements. Also the food is good and no want of water. We will be up on the front line for a month and then come out again for a spell. So you see it is a wonderful improvement on Anzac.

There is very little sickness now that the weather is still a little cold and I should think it would always be the same. It is almost like living in a house the same as at home, only no bed to sleep in and one or two other trifles which make it a bit rougher.

There may be a chance of me getting 5 or 8 days leave to England in the very distant future which will be a bit of a change from this life. The 1st Division of Australians are getting leave. About 1 man per unit every 5th day. It will take some time for my turn to come round, especially as so many chaps have their parents over there and they are generally the first to go.

I think I told you that I had been to Calais for a fortnight with the battery to do some shooting. We left there a week ago and trekked back up here. It wasn't a bad trip and a good way of seeing the country.

I haven't heard from Billy for ages or from anyone for that matter. I don't know where my letters are getting to at all. It is rather a disappointment in never getting any letters. Hope mine are reaching you safely. I sent you an Anzac book from the publishers in London. I wonder if it has arrived yet. We haven't seen them, but arrangements were made for the publishers to send them on our written order.

We all now have to take the greatest precautions against enemy gas attacks and have to frequently drill at getting on our gas helmets. We are carrying them at all times ready to slip on immediately the alarm is given. A few seconds is long enough to put you out if you take a breath or two, so they are getting us pretty slippy at it. The infantry in the front line carry them already rolled on the top of their heads to fall down directly they get any smell of it. Seems to be a pretty rotten thing, but once you have your helmet on you are safe.

I still fire off tons of letters but never get any replies and so will not say more this time, as there are one or two more I have to do. How is my money now? Is the 3/- a day I allotted to leave behind being paid in to the Bank? I hope so, for if not it will be a hard job getting it afterwards and besides which I am losing all the interest. You said some months ago that Mr. Armitage was to find out. I haven't heard since whether he did or not.

Please give my best love to Gran, Aunt Mog and the Child, hoping everyone is well and strong, with heaps of love and kisses to Mee maw from

Her loving son,

TOOTS.

Gas Masks, Ypres, Sep 1917
Source AWM E00825

No 15 General Hospital, Alexandria, 21 May 1916

Dearest Mother

Only a short letter this time, Mum – I haven't heard from you for over a fortnight and I am rather worried. Perhaps your letter missed the mail, as the Australian mail has come in. I trust everything is well with you, and that I shall hear from you in a day or two. Mona and I had a Field Service P.C. from Steve, and he said he was writing, and that he was quite well, so we ought to have a letter from him before long too.

I also had a letter from Harold Boulton, and he is shortly to have his commission. He expects he will go to France shortly then. He tells me that Jack Doherty[138] is a doctor and is practising in Harley Street. What ho! He evidently gave up the dentistry. If you remember he always wanted to go in for medicine, but old Doherty thought dentistry more lucrative. I wonder what sort of practice he has. I must try and look him up when I return to England. The Doughpunchers are at Putney where Uncle Willie is still managing. What I pity I didn't know this, as I was informed he was managing at Basingstoke by the Manager at Wimbledon, which was too far off. I could easily have run down to Putney.

We are moving from the new little flat which we have taken now there is every possibility of my remaining in here for some time to come, and have taken a larger one right on the sea at a place called Cleopatra, where Steve was camped. In fact the house is right opposite his old camp. We are sharing it with a young chap called Courtenay[139], a great friend of Mona's, who is a regular and in the Army Service Corps. He was very anxious for us to share a flat with him as he has been practically living at the house where we are at present. He was invalided home from France with gastritis and nervous breakdown and has been sent out here since. The gastric trouble has recurred, so we are dieting him and endeavouring to put him straight again. He is in charge of the mechanical transport at the A.S.C. depot, and so has the run of all the Government cars. He takes us for rides when it is dark occasionally, as civilians aren't allowed in Government cars. I, of course, being in uniform am not affected by this rule, but Mona is. I have had some good spins in a 40-60 H.P. Rolls Royce, one of the armoured cars, and they are glorious machines. Can cut out 70 miles per hour 45 seconds after starting, which no other car is supposed to be able to do. I think we shall all get on well together, as a man is much more reasonable to deal with than a young married couple.

Well, Mum, excuse this very hurried letter. I will write you a longer one next time, I hope. Best love to all at home. I do trust everything is well with you all,

A big hug from NIGE

I am writing to Cousin Bessie.

---

138 Jack Doherty was another first cousin, of both Nigel Boulton and Harold Boulton. Nigel spent some of his holidays with the Dohertys (nicknamed the Doughpunchers) when at school in England. Jack's father William Pemble Doherty (Uncle Willie) was a bank manager. Jack's mother Connie, née Constance Bishop, was a half-sister of Philip Boulton and thus the paternal aunt of the Boulton boys Nigel and Stephen.
139 A R Courtenay, Temp Lieut, ASC, 1916 (British Army)

On 15 May the 22nd Battery took its turn 'in the line' at Fleurbaix, a few miles south west of Armentières. Supposedly a quiet position, Fleurbaix is better known today as the location of the soon-to-be-fought Battle of Fromelles. From his unit's war diaries, here's an example of Steve's 'baptism by fire' for the period 19-25 May 1916:

> Our batteries have been active during the period, the work being similar to that previously carried out, i.e. Battalion on front line and communication trenches, fire on hostile guns, buildings and roads. "Mobile" guns have been successfully employed. The positions of the latter have been changed to perplex the enemy as to the number of guns on this front, and to obtain distribution and concentration of fire from new and unexpected directions. These tactics have been very successful, good control and quick fire effect being readily obtained. Mobile guns have also occupied positions from which our batteries have been withdrawn on account of hostile fire.
>
> On 22nd inst, in conjunction with Loring's Group Heavy Artillery, an effective bombardment was carried out. The batteries employed were two 4.5 Howitzer Batteries and two 18pdr Batteries. The howitzers were employed against the houses and in demolition work, while the 18pdrs searched and swept the adjacent areas, particularly the roads and approaches. The bombardment was carried out in three rapid series, and it is believed good effect was obtained. The clouds of smoke rising for two hours after the bombardment indicate excellent material results. The enemy artillery replied vigorously after the first series but was silent after each of the two last.

Steve's next letter was written on the day of this bombardment.

IN THE LINE, SOMEWHERE IN FRANCE [FLEURBAIX], 22 MAY 1916

My dearest Matee Boo

I have just received your letter of 4th March sent on by Billy and very pleased I was to get it. I think now that you know my new address, so you are pretty safe in sending them straight to me, and I then get them quicker.

We are in a new brigade now so put on the number of battery and underneath put 21st F.A. Brigade. I ought to get your letters pretty regularly now I think without much delay.

You see I am up 'in the line' as it is called here, and we are all doing our little bit again. It is a wonderful improvement on the Gallipoli stunt, as we are not in dug outs and don't get all the discomforts attached to them. Neither do we do our own cooking as we are in an old farm house and have a cook who cooks for the whole battery. I am quite comfortable, having a small room to myself in the farm which is the orderly room. I have got a shakedown[140] to sleep in, also a table and chair and have fixed up everything as comfy as possible. Of course the great idea is to keep the position we are in as much concealed as possible, as it wouldn't stand long if we were spotted and they got on to us.

We have action every day and occasionally at night and are doing well. We remain in the line a month and then get a spell for 10 days or a fortnight some little way back. So you can see it is a picnic compared to Anzac. Goodness knows how long it is all going to last, but am afraid it will go a very long while yet as the process of tiring and starving out the enemy is a long and tedious one. Meanwhile there appear no signs of any sort of the Bosches turning it in. We have now got the ascendancy in artillery and appear to do what we like with our aeroplanes. It is only occasionally that the German machines come over, when they get a pretty warm reception.

All around us are the effects and results of their shell fire on houses, billets, churches etc. but they don't seem to waste so much now on bombarding for the sake of destroying empty houses. Also we have got shelters close at hand when anything is expected along. The gas attacks are the most dreaded and sometimes prove the worst form of causing casualties. Things have on both sides been brought to the most scientific end, and we always have our gas helmets with us at all hours ready to slip on at a moment's warning.

Was very glad to hear of the rain coming at Ermo just after you had finished ploughing and getting in the oats and barley. I hope the crops and vegetables turn out well and wish I could be there to help partake of them. I wish you could get some of the rain we have been getting here, although for the last week it has been delightful, just like Australian spring days.

Am sorry to hear Gran has not been so well lately, please give her my best love and tell her to keep her end up, also Aunt Mog, and the Child whom I hope is becoming more sociable and of some comfort to her Mee maw until I come home again.

With heaps and heaps of love and kisses to everyone and a big hug into the bargain for Matee Boos from her loving son TOOTS.

---

140 A makeshift bed, presumably a portable fold-up, stretcher-type bed

Meanwhile, back in Sydney, sister Thea married Cleon, the papers not quite getting her name right:

> DENNIS— BOULTON.— On June 3, at St. James' Church, the wedding took place of Engineer-Lieutenant Cleon Dennis, R.A.N., son of Mr. James Dennis, of 'St. Levan,' Bondi, and Miss Dorothy Boulton, only daughter of Mrs. Boulton, of Gladesville. The bride, who was given away by Mr. Frank Bryant, wore a cream coat and skirt, and white hat. Mr. R. Holloway[141] acted as best man. The Rev. Edward Owen, rector of All Saints', Hunter's Hill, performed the ceremony. The reception was held at a city café, and later Engineer Lieutenant and Mrs. Dennis left for Cairns, Queensland. (Sunday Times, Sydney, 2 July 1916, p 27)

> A war wedding, held at St. James's Church, King-street, was that of Dorothy, only daughter of Mrs. Boulton, of Gladesville and the late Philip Boulton, manager of the Union Bank at Clunes, Victoria, and Engineer Lieutenant Dennis, of H.M.A.S. Brisbane, who was on the Sydney during her encounter with the enemy. The young bride wore a cream Gabardine coat and skirt, and cream panne velvet hat, with a white seagull. The bridegroom was in uniform. The bride was given away by Mr. Frank Bryant, Sydney. Only relatives of the bride and bridegroom were present, and no reception was held, as the bride's two brothers are on active service, one in France, the other in Egypt. The couple left for Cairns immediately after the ceremony. (SMH, 8 July 1916, p 10)

Cleon had such a serious nose bleed that the marriage ceremony was almost postponed. One guest wrote 'after Cleon's attack I thought that it could not possibly take place on that day'; another mentioned how 'dreadfully ill' he looked.

In later correspondence Steve refers to Cleon's 'little trouble' on his wedding day, no doubt how he viewed it when men were dying all around him. Four days before Thea's wedding, Steve's unit was close to Cordonnerie Farm where a German mortar shell killed 40 Australians and wounded another 60. On the same day three men in his battery were wounded by shellfire and next day one was killed. Five weeks later Steve himself was buried and just escaped death from an incoming shell which killed three men in his unit.

Where women's health is concerned, when he next writes home Steve is unaware that Mona has 'not been feeling too well' because she is pregnant.

---

141 Rupert Arthur Holloway was an engineering friend of Cleon's. He enlisted in 1916 with the 1st Pioneer Battalion. The 'Beyond 1914' website of the University of Sydney provides further details of him.

In a Farm, Somewhere in France [Fleurbaix], 13 Jun 1916

My dearest Mateeboo

Your letter of the 26th March just to hand sent on by Billy. I was very pleased to get it as I haven't been getting many letters lately. Do you know my address, if so I think you could send my letters direct to me now as I would get them much quicker.

Am still feeling very well and we are still in the line. We have got a nice sheltered and comfortable position and so are remaining instead of going for a short spell. We are all content with this arrangement as it is not much of a spell if we do go out and after coming in again we mightn't get such a good position, and be so comfortable. Also moving about is a bit of a nuisance with the horses & all our gear.

The last three days here have been pretty miserable with rain & wind. It is pretty cold even now and this is nearly midsummer, so goodness knows what it is like in winter. I wonder if it all will be over by that time. It seems years since I left home now.

We don't have such a bad time here. We get our regular rations of bread & fresh meat with jam & cheese & butter. The butter is Canadian & is tinned. Nevertheless it is very good & quite like the real thing. There are also a few miles back military canteens, to which we occasionally send a man to procure any extras. We spend a fair amount of our money on these things, which prevents it from accumulating like it did while over on the Peninsula. But still I would rather be here a hundred times than at Anzac.

I had a line from Billy about a week ago. He seems to be doomed to remain in Egypt for some months yet and must be getting pretty fed up with the place. Mona, he said, had not been feeling too well. No doubt the work entailed in the Pops combined with the heat was beginning to tell on her.

Our leave to England has been reduced to nearly half, both in number of men going & the length of time over there. So it will be a few months before I get over there if ever at all. All the chaps who have been & returned seem to have had a glorious time & are made a tremendous lot of by the English people. The people at home are just beginning to learn that there is such a place and after the war it ought to increase trade tremendously as well as in other ways.

Everyone is very pleased at the big Russian offensive & things are beginning to look up all round. I don't think there will be much done in the advancing line just here for a long while, as we are in the wrong place for a push but must wait for both our flanks to be straightened on either side. Meanwhile the Australians are putting in good work all the time, making successful raids & generally annoying the Bosches.

I suppose that everybody is much the same at home. What is the garden at Coolah like and the front lawn? It ought to be pretty well covered by this. I hope that some of the 14 packets of flower seeds come up at Ermo and that Ruby & Jim didn't cook them all by sleeping on them. I don't know either of these dogs, by name anyway. What of Pug & Doos?[142]

M y very best love to Gran who I hope is feeling well again, & Aunt Mog & Child, with a big hug for the Meemaw from her

TOOTS

Largely ignoring the brutalities of his own life, in his next letter Stephen shows his usual concern for the welfare of those at home. He's now been in France long enough to realise that his location is known as Flanders, the boggy flatlands area in the north-east area of France and south-west area of Belgium.

IN A FARM, SOMEWHERE IN FLANDERS, 21 JUN 1916

My dearest Matee Boos

Your two letters of April 16th and 24th just to hand. Am beginning to get your letters fairly regularly now. And so the Child and Cleon are married by this time. Naturally I wasn't very surprised to hear the news, and hope they will be very happy.

The preceding weeks must have been very busy ones for you and I can quite believe your feelings about the wedding, that it is an awful proceeding to contemplate. Now that it is all over, I am sure it was a success and went off all right.

About that overdraft, if you like you can pay it off straightaway by drawing on my account at the Commonwealth Bank, the power of attorney of which you hold. That is the General Bank and not the Savings Bank. It would save you

---

142   Ruby, Jim, Pug & Doos were all pet dogs of the family.

paying 6½ or 7% on the overdraft and you could pay me off at any time. The money is only lying there and not doing anything, and may as well be used.

Will you also draw £10 to go as my wedding gift to the Child and Cleon (£5 each)? I cannot get anything here and it will be better for them to get something they want themselves.

No doubt the furnished cottage is at present the best idea and you will be able to see more of the Child I suppose when Cleon is away. Am anxiously awaiting further news of the wedding and honeymoon.

Was very sorry to hear of you having to give up little "Ermo" just at the time of the rain and good seasons coming on, but if Gran picks up a bit you may be able to run over there again. Was very glad to hear from the Child that Coolah is being taken again on a year's lease and perhaps longer. Don't forget to keep him[143] up to the scratch with money in advance, as if they once get behind it is very hard to get it out of them afterwards.

Am going to write to the Child and Cleon now, so give my best love to Aunt Mog and Gran and with heaps of love and big hugs for the Mee Maw from

Her loving son, TOOTS.

In early July the 21st FAB was moved to billets at Trou Bayard and Éstaires but within days was assigned to an area just north of Armentières, across the Belgian border at Ploegsteert, where they actively engaged with the enemy on the front line for a few more days.

After six weeks of active duty on the supposed nursery sector of the Western Front, the 21st FAB came out of the line on the night of 8 & 9 July, prior to redeployment southwards to the horrendous battlefields of the Somme.

They were replaced by fresh troops newly-arrived in France and about to be decimated in the first major battle fought by Australians on the Western Front. The catastrophe at Fromelles on 19 & 20 July 1916 produced 5,533 Australian casualties in 24 hours, the worst by far in Australia's entire history. Designed by the British as a feint to distract the Germans from the real offensive on the Somme, the Battle of Fromelles ordered for this sector was a complete failure. The ruse did not fool the Germans and no strategic advantage was gained by the extreme loss of life.

---

143   i.e. the tenant

Stephen's next letter is written just before he leaves Ploegsteert.

IN A FARM, SOMEWHERE IN BELGIUM [PLOEGSTEERT], 8 JUL 1916

Dearest Matee boos

Just a hurried note to say I am still alright and going strong. We are very busy shifting round up and down the country. The last farm we were in[144] we only made a very short stay and now we are off again. It makes things very busy and unsettled for us.

About 3 or 4 days ago I received a large mail of very old letters dated August to November of last year. They had been touring the world and finally came home to roost. I was very pleased to get them despite their age. There were 26 in all. Please thank the Child for her share of them.

We have not had any sort of a spell yet, and don't suppose we will get one for a long while now that some sort of advance is being made. I cannot tell you where we are off to this time as I am not too sure about it, but it is somewhere down south in France. I hope it won't be too uncomfortable and unhealthy.

I won't be sorry when this business is all over as I am feeling terribly fed up with the life. Someday I suppose it will come to an end, but not for a very long while yet. Things are not so bad for me now as they were at first. In my present job I generally get a small space to myself in which is, up to the present, a bed and table and chair. I have yet to learn what happens when we become mobile and move about all day.

There is no chance of getting over to England now as all our leave has been stopped. Perhaps in another year's time my turn will come round.

Please give my best love to Gran and Aunt Mog hoping Gran is keeping fairly fit and that the Gardens still find something for Aunt Mog to do. Am anxiously awaiting news about the wedding and how the married couple are getting along in their new abode. With heaps and heaps of love and kisses to Matee Boos, hoping that Ermo and Concord are running along smoothly again and bringing in a little bit of dough. Will write again soon, from

Your ever loving son, TOOTS.

---

144 Billets at Trou Bayard and Éstaires

After coming out of the line, the 21st FAB was billeted at St Jans Cappel while packing up and preparing to move south. Two wagon loads of their surplus kits were sent to be stored with Mme Nuyts at 7 Rue Douchal, Hazebrouck on 9 July. The men of the 21st FAB were able to take a longed-for wash when they attended the Divisional Baths at Bailleul (north west of Armentières) on the morning of 10 July.

The 21st FAB entrained on the morning of 12 July, headed for the Somme and their own equally hellish field of slaughter, around 50 miles to the south at Pozières. The Somme bombardment had begun on 22 June 1916, with the first wave of infantry men sent over the top at the end of June. Along a front of just over 20 miles, the next five months symbolized the pointless carnage of this appalling war.

After leaving the train the 21st FAB marched to new billets at Havernas, about 12 miles north of Amiens. Havernas was one of the villages surrounding Vignacourt, a centuries-old town used as an army base and as a rest & recovery camp for Allied troops fighting on the Somme battlefields. It was far enough back from the front line to escape artillery fire but close enough to be convenient as a base.

Stephen's next letter was written during his journey to this place.

Vignacourt
Source AWM E05280

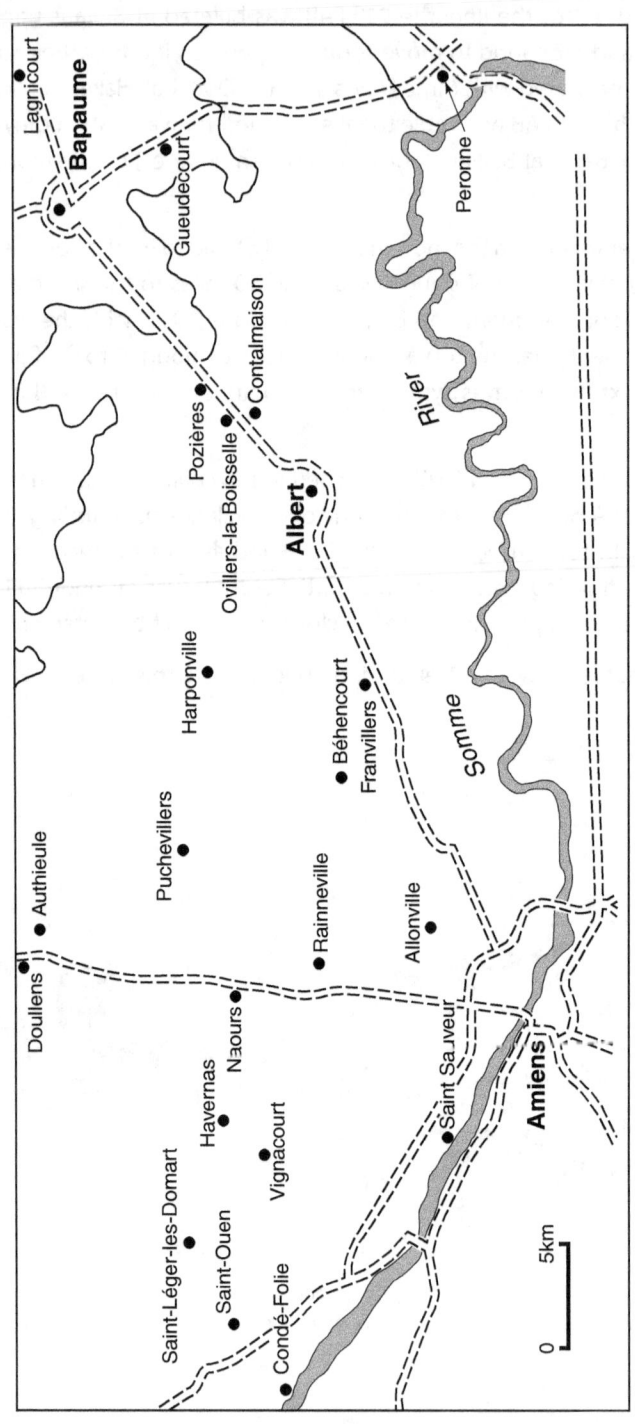

Map 9: The Somme, 1916-1918

Map © John Newland, 2015

Somewhere in France [Somme], 14 Jul 1916

My dear Matee

Just a short and hurried note to let you know all is going well with me still. Am writing this on the road as we move along. This moving about keeps up and we get pretty busy as we are on the go all day and pull up at the end of the day to find suitable billets for the men, also water and feed the horses for the night.

It keeps us fully occupied, but at the same time makes a sort of a spell, as we are not under the strain that exists when in the line. It has been showery for the last two days which hasn't improved matters. It seems to be nearly always raining here. The country is looking grand with every inch under cultivation and excellent crops of wheat and oats are everywhere. The cherries are ripe and in some places we have been able to have a feed of them.

Yesterday I got a letter addressed by you to me but written to Billy. No doubt you put mine in his envelope. I am sending his on to him and I expect he will do the same.

Am glad to hear that Cleon and the Child are so happy. I am looking forward to news of how the wedding went off. I expect it was a success and not the awful trial you imagined it would be.

I hope you have been getting my letters safely, not that there is much in them except to know that I am well etc. It is very hard to write not being able to mention any Military matters at all. Everything is Military and when they cut that out it doesn't leave much to be said. We hear lots of letters don't get past the censor who is very strict over here. I hope none of mine have been pulled up and that you are getting them regularly.

I heard from Harry Lloyd yesterday telling me all the latest local news. Things seem to be going on just the same and it seems to be as if there was no war on. It will end someday I suppose, people over here seem to think fairly soon now, but I don't see how it can unless the Bosches throw it in very suddenly, which I don't think they will do as long as they have millions of men in the field. We certainly have a great superiority in guns, but it will take a very long time to shove them back.

Please give my best love to Aunt Mog. I suppose Coolah is much the same as ever and the daily trips to town are still made by her. I hope Gran is picking up a bit and not getting in any dangerous draughts. Am sending her an autographed photo of King Ned[145] which will be able to go in the scrap book.

Please give my best love to the Child when next you see her, hoping that she and Cleon are still in the 7th heaven, with heaps and heaps of love to the Matee boos with a big hug and kiss from

Your ever loving son, TOOTS.

At their Havernas base, for the next 3 days, the 21st FAB carried out training exercises – route marches, signaling practice and driving drill. On the morning of 16 July the 21st FAB marched to new billets at Puchevillers, and engaged in more training.

On the afternoon of 18 July they marched to Harponville and next afternoon took up position 'in the line' near La Boisselle, ready for the attack on the village of Pozières, where the Germans held a strong tactical advantage of highly-fortified trenches and control of all the high ground.

Then from 10pm on 20 July to 6pm on 21 July they maintained a bombardment on an enemy trench, starting again four hours later, the 22nd Battery being ordered to fire 1 round every 3 minutes on a 2-hourly rotation with other batteries, until midday on 22 July.

The barrage continued from just after midnight on 23 July to 4pm that day, when they were ordered to cease fire. The Australian infantry of the 1st Division captured the village of Pozières that day and held on in the face of almost continual artillery fire from the enemy. A participant in Australia's 11th Battalion later wrote:

> There were many complimentary messages sent to the 1st Division after the capture of the village, and the following from the 1st British Division may be taken as typical: The 1st (British) Division desire to express to the 1st Australian Division, alongside of whom they have been fighting for the last few days, their profound admiration of the magnificent feat of arms which culminated in the capture of Pozières.[146]

Steve gives his mother a hint of the hell he's managed to survive by writing his next letter to her from a captured German trench.

---

145 King Edward VII, who'd died in 1910.
146 Belford, *Legs Eleven*, Ch 10

In a German Trench, Somewhere in France [Pozières], 23 Jul 1916

My dearest Matee boos

Have just received your letter of June 6th telling of the Child's marriage. I hope that both young parties will always be very happy and contented. No doubt you are feeling rather down in the dumps now that the Child has gone, but I suppose it had to be sooner or later.

We are extremely busy just now and are in the big push doing good work and going night and day. Am feeling pretty tired owing to not getting any sleep last night and not much the night before. Also the terrible roar and din of all the guns is terrific. We are all feeling the effects a bit and becoming slightly deaf; we have to shout as a rule when talking. This will all wear off in time. Am feeling very fit and well nevertheless and have got a fairly weather proof shelter just at this time. Luckily it has been fine lately. There are millions of souvenirs round about, such as German helmets, water bottles, rifles and all sorts of things. I wish I could have sent you home some interesting relics, but am afraid it is impossible.

I am getting your letters regularly now which is very pleasant and satisfactory, also without much delay, so don't lose the address and you can give it to anyone who wants to know where I am. I would like to tell you whereabouts I am but cannot. You must follow the movements of the 1st Aust. Division which will have, I think, been mentioned in the papers by this time.

In one of the gift shirts I got hold of at Tel-el-kebir in Egypt there was a little card pinned on with the maker's name and wishing good luck to the wearer. I dropped her (for it was in female writing) (M. Wren) a card saying I had got it, and last week a parcel containing 2 packets of cigarettes, pair of socks, *Bulletin* and writing paper came along from her. She lives at Bega at 'Tarraganda', evidently a station and from the post card just received saying she had sent along a parcel she said she went to Normanhurst. The chaps here say I should cultivate her and are highly amused at the thing. Will drop her a short note.

Well Matey will write again soon, this is not much of a letter, but we don't have much time to ourselves just at this juncture and even this is better than a field service post card. With best love to Gran, Aunt Mog, the Child and Cleon hoping he is quite recovered from his little trouble by now with heaps of love, kisses and hugs for my mee maw from her loving son TOOTS.

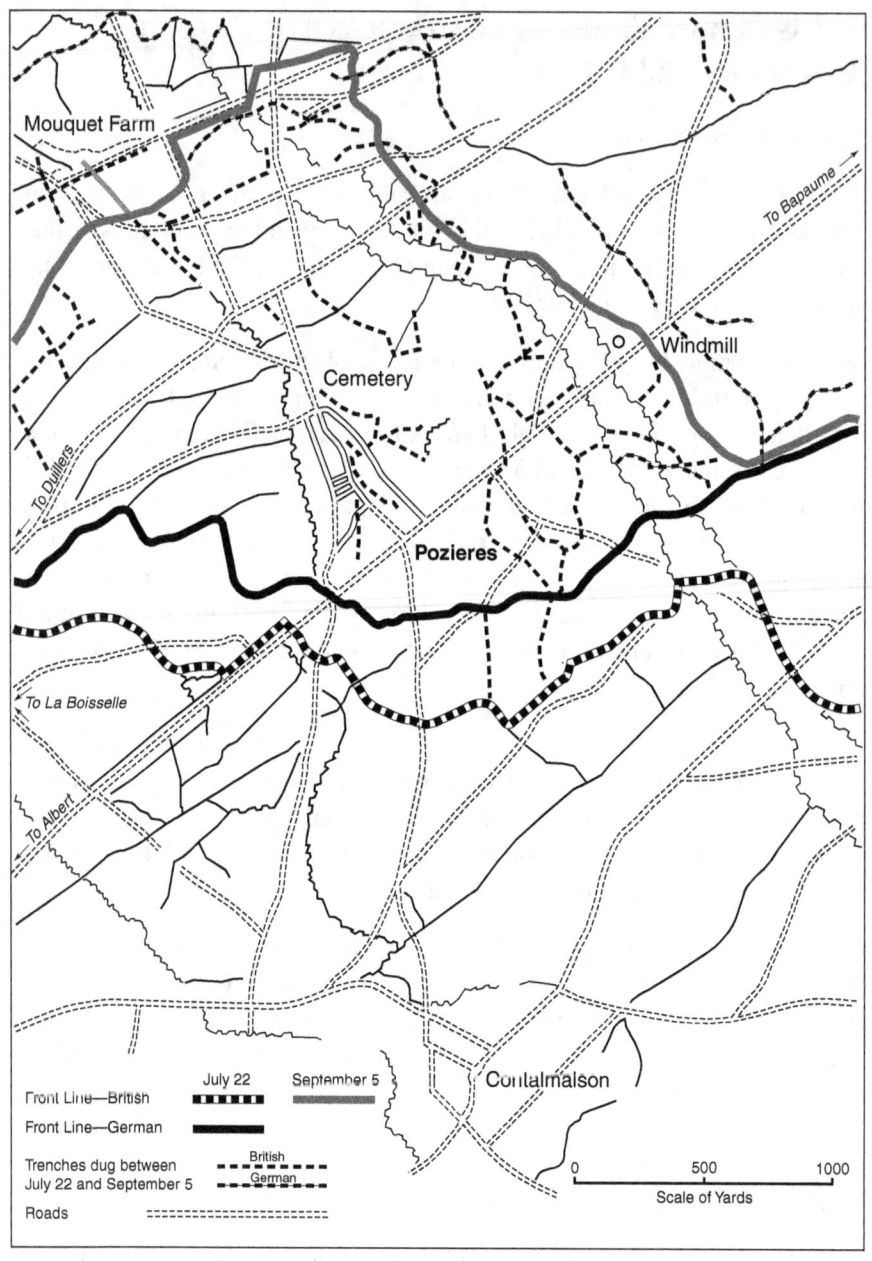

Map 10: Pozières, 1916

Map © John Newland, 2015

The Battle of Pozières continued. From 3.30am to 10.15am on 24 July and from 1.58am to nearly midday on 25 July, Stephen's unit fired their guns at different enemy targets, backing up the occupation by the infantry of the 1st Division of the whole of Pozières as far north as the Cemetery. The infantry of the 1st Division suffered horrendous losses (5,285 casualties) before it was relieved on 27 July.

The Australians had overcome a German bombardment equal to anything yet seen on the Western Front and far beyond their battle experience to date. Communication lines were maintained primarily by runners as the telephone lines were continually cut. The artillery had great difficulty in keeping the guns in action, caused by excessive strain during prolonged bombardments, and requested a greater supply of springs for the future. Sleep-deprived Steve writes his next letter as if he hasn't quite processed the horrors he's just survived. 'Very busy' was an understatement. He'd just endured the heaviest bombardment the Australian artillery had ever known, the 18 pounders firing 46,660 shrapnel and 17,181 high explosive shells in seven days, with nearly 8,000 more shells fired by the Howitzers.[147]

IN A BOSCH TRENCH, SOMEWHERE IN FRANCE [POZIÈRES], 28 JUL 1916

My dearest Matee boos

A mail is going tomorrow morning we hear by Frisco so I am scribbling off this note to catch it. We are very busy, going night and day, and getting sleep whenever an opportunity occurs. By this you will no doubt guess where I am and you will have read in the papers of our doings.

I am keeping very well and am able to get fairly decent tucker, not like the Peninsula. There are Army Canteens a few miles back where we are able to procure tinned fruit, biscuits, coffee and cocoa by sending a man down occasionally. This makes things ever so much better.

Heard from Billy a few days ago in which he tells me of Mrs. Little's illness and the likelihood of it turning out to be typhoid. I hope it won't be so serious as Egypt is not an altogether desirable place to be ill in, especially with typhoid. Mona seems to be rather anxious about her.

I was glad to hear of the wedding and that the Child looked well. Cleon I hope by now is feeling better and has no further trouble with it. I saw the announcement of their engagement in the *British Australasian*.

---

147 Lyall, *Letters from an Anzac Gunner*, p 56

Pozières Village, before and after the battle.
Source AWM G01534I and AWM A05776

Captured German trench at Pozières
Source AWM-e00007

We haven't had a spell for a long time and in fact no spell yet at all. We will all be glad when it comes along but so far there is no word of it.

I wonder what you are doing with yourself now; whether you went to the farming college. Well Matee I will have to stop now, this short letter is better than a field service post card anyway. I am getting your letters regularly now and hope you get mine too. Please give my love to Gran and Aunt Mog, and the Child when next you see her, hoping everyone is keeping well. With best of love to Matee Boos with heaps of kisses and hugs from

Her loving son, TOOTS.

And so the slaughter continued. Pozières being critical to their defensive line along the Somme, the Germans were determined to win back the ground they'd lost. Their unrelenting bombardment continued for the rest of July and through the first week of August, when the 21st FAB came out of the line for a rest, along with the decimated 2nd Division which had just captured the Pozières Heights (the windmill), also at great cost (6,848 casualties).

The 4th Division took over, with more massive losses as fighting around Pozières and the adjoining Mouquet Farm continued into September, the Allies managing to hang on to their hard-won position.

Australia suffered as many casualties in six weeks at Pozières as in the entire Gallipoli campaign. Immediately preceding this slaughter had been the losses up north at Fromelles. The news shocked Australians at home. They blamed these horrendous outcomes, following on from the disastrous Gallipoli campaign, on ill-judged leadership and this had a big influence on the failure of the first attempt to introduce conscription in Australia, in October 1916.[148]

Conscription Posters, 1916
Source AWM RC00305 and AWM check

---

148 Australia & South Africa were the only countries at war without conscription. Australia's conscription campaign split the country, with 51.6 % voting No including most men in the AIF.

A year later, on 8 July 1917, an impressive parade assembled at Pozières to hear an address by General Birdwood and pay respects at the unveiling of a memorial for all the troops of the 1st Australian Division killed near Pozières during the offensives in July and August 1916.[149]

Unveiling the Pozières Memorial, 8 July 1917

Stephen's presence in England meant that he missed this ceremony. Source IWM Q2598

Years later, a plain memorial stone was laid on the site of Pozières Windmill, now an official Australian War Memorial site. The stone is inscribed:

> The ruin of Pozières windmill which lies here was the centre of the struggle in this part of the Somme battlefield in July and August 1916. It was captured on August 4th by Australian troops who fell more thickly on this ridge than on any other battlefield of the war.

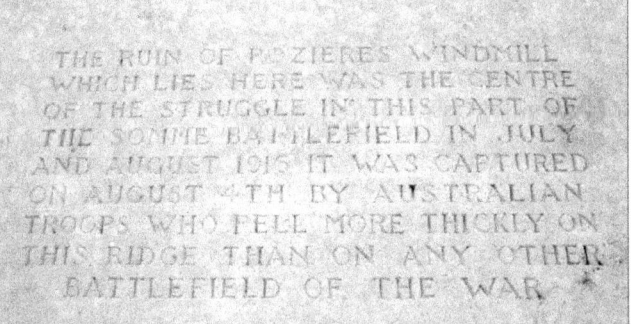

Memorial Stone at Pozières

Picture courtesy Curry and Marchment, Research Family War Diaries

The 2nd Division's permanent memorial was eventually built at Mont St Quentin, a 1918 battle site.

---

149 Belford, *Legs Eleven*, p 465

Steve's unit having escaped the carnage on 7 August, the men moved to their wagon line and bivouaced. For the next two days they were on the road, trekking to billets in a rest area at St Léger les Domart, one of the villages surrounding the Vignacourt centre for Allied troops. In his next letter home, Stephen makes light of his descent into hell at Pozières, although he does mention the incident on 2 August, when three Other Ranks (like Stephen) were killed and two wounded by hostile shell fire on his battery between 3 and 4 am, near Pozières Cemetery.

SOMEWHERE IN FRANCE [ST LÉGER], 13 AUG 1916

Dearest Matee boos

Your letter of 11th June just to hand. We are now having a glorious spell which although only a few days is very acceptable right away from the line out of sound of the guns. We are camped alongside a big wheat crop on some grass. Most of the men have made small bivouacs to keep out the rain, but I have a tent shared with the Sergeant Major, de Lepervanche by name.[150] He is of French birth but from Narrabri NSW. We are quite close to a small village where we can purchase fruit and other little things.

The last fortnight up in the line was pretty hot and we were all very glad to come away for a spell. We were living in the old German trenches where they had been pushed back and made use of their dugouts some of them being 30 ft and 40 ft down and fitted up with beds and other conveniences.

Some of the officers' quarters are most elaborate having chests of drawers, wash stands, electric light and almost like living in a hotel. It must have hurt them to have to leave them. It was a good thing we had these deep pits to get into as we were occasionally and towards the end pretty continually shelled.

The Australians have done very well again and I don't think got the credit of doing all they did. In the *Daily Mail* it had two mornings after the taking of Pozières by the 1st Div. Australians 'Pozières taken by the British Tommy'. It made our chaps pretty wild especially as the Tommies had had previously 4 tries at it. Coming out I passed Max Shelley[151] going in with the 4th Battn. Infantry with a star up. Also passed one of the Kirkwood lads[152] who is in the 19th Battalion. Wasn't able to say anything to them as they were going one way and I the other.

---

150 Steve's tent mate was commissioned as a Lieut on 6 Sep 1916 and transferred to the 2nd F.A.B.
151 Mac Robert Shelley, a 20-yr-old clerk from Gladesville, who sailed off with his older brother Eric Ralph Shelley in 1915. Both survived the war.
152 Lieut William Russell Barton Kirkwood, formerly a farm student of Wharf Road, Gladesville, survived Pozières but was killed in action on 3 May 1917 at Villers-Bretonneux, aged 24.

I am keeping very fit and well in myself except that my nerves are anyhow, especially just before coming out, but everyone was the same then. We had a pretty fair dose and stayed in three weeks longer than the rest of our division.

We had some casualties and I had rather a narrow squeak. There were about 9 of us sitting in the trench and drinking coffee when a shell comes over right into the middle of us and bursts. It killed 3 outright and wounded 2 others and buried the lot of us. Excepting for those above mentioned none of us were hurt excepting to be shaken up a bit. But this quiet life soon picks us up again.

Was glad to hear that Cleon and the Child are enjoying themselves so much and hope they will continue to do so for a long time to come. I wonder if they have found a cottage yet.

Have you started at the Women's Farm yet and does it come up to your expectations? It is a pity you had to unfurnish Ermo, but no doubt it will let much easier. Please give my best love to all the family, hoping Gran, Aunt Mog, the Child and Cleon are all well, with heaps of love and kisses to Matee boos from

Her loving son TOOTS.

Haven't heard from Billy lately.

After a few days' rest, Steve's unit trekked back to re-enter the line near Albert at 1pm on 16 August. Here on 19 August he was again promoted, 'in the field' this time, to the rank of Corporal (Temp) in the 21st FAB, an honour he failed to mention in his usual modest way. This form of promotion became a key reason for the success of Australian soldiers. Australia did not rely on the old school tie and family influence for promotions, as in the British Army. Instead, Australia chose men with demonstrated competence as decision-makers and leaders, with rapid replacement 'in the field' when existing officers fell, a system encouraging the other men to follow their leaders out of respect.

Once again, troubles up north forced change. The 21st FAB was moved out of the line on 23 August. Next day the men travelled overland and billeted themselves at Authieule near Doullens, where they spent a few days grazing the horses and cleaning their vehicles and harnesses, preparatory to moving away from the Somme back to Flanders. Steve writes this letter from Authieule.

Somewhere in France, 26 Aug 1916

My dearest Matee boos

Received the newspaper report of the wedding two days ago. Am glad to hear you have had some news of the happy couple and that they are both in the seventh heaven. Am anxiously awaiting to hear where abouts they have decided to live. Expect it will be Hunter's Hill, as you say there is a very nice and suitable cottage there.

We are now having a good time again if only for 2 or 3 days. Have been away from the line resting for the last 2 days and very nice and peaceful it is. It is a pity we could not have a few weeks of it.

We are about to leave this part of the line for another spot, I suppose to do some more work that the Tommies can't do. They are making great use of the Australians now and they are reckoned absolutely the best and not greatly over-exaggerated after the Anzac turn-out. The next Divisions after the 2nd however are not much chop, but perhaps in a year's time will be as good as any. What is Hal[153] in? I suppose he has gone to England to do some training.

Had a letter from Billy telling me he was on his way to Salonika. He seemed very pleased to have at last got away from No 15 General, but wants to get back to London and then over here. I tried to persuade him not to take on a regimental M O. as they don't as far as I can see get all the experience, only doing the very first dressings of the wounded before sending them down to the Casualty Clearing Station.[154] I told him the C.C.S job ought to be good, as there the docs do a tremendous amount of operations of all the men who are too bad to move back to the base and require immediate attention.

I suppose Mona will return to London and Mrs. Little probably go back to Australia as soon as she is well enough.

Well Matee I won't write anymore just now as reveille is at 4 a.m. tomorrow morning with a big day in front of us. Please give my best love to Aunt Mog and Gran hoping that she is still keeping well, also Aunt Phoebe and Phil, if you see

---

153 Hal was first cousin Harry Flockton Clarke.
154 Casualty Clearing Stations (CCSs) were generally located on or near railway lines, to facilitate movement of casualties from the battlefield and on to the hospitals. Although quite large, they moved quite frequently, especially in the wake of the great German attacks in the spring of 1918 and the victorious Allied advance in the summer and autumn of that year. Many CCSs moved into Belgium and Germany with the army of occupation in 1919 too. The locations of wartime CCSs can often be identified today from the cluster of military cemeteries that surrounded them.

them. I wonder if you are at the Women's Farm yet and how do you like it. Am afraid you won't get any more "layouts".

With heaps of love and kisses to the Child and Matee boos from

Her loving son, TOOTS.

On 27 August Steve's unit moved back to Belgian Flanders. Using the terminology in the unit's war diaries, the men 'entrained' from Doullens, 'detrained' at Nopoutre and Proven, near Poperinge, then marched to billets in the vicinity of Ouderdom. The diaries refer only to being 'in the field' without specifying exact locations, but the unit appeared to be based in or near Halifax Camp, which was close to Vlamertinghe, just west of Ypres. They remained 'in the field' until 17 September.

Somewhere in Flanders, 2 Sep 1916

Dearest Matee boos

Am scribbling this off to catch the mail we hear is going tomorrow. I received your letters dated June 22nd and July 6th. I am getting yours regularly now and expect will always do so if I remain with the same address the whole time. It is being transferred from one unit to another that makes them go astray.

By your letter you are once more back at Ermo and not at the Dural Farm. Aunt Phoebe has started looking after Gran and I wonder how they will get on. I don't suppose she will like it overmuch. I think I would hang on to Ermo and live there as long as you can while you are not going to be away at the Farm.

Flockton Sisters & 'The Moles', c 1916
(Front row, from left, Dora (Dolly), Aunt Mog, Aunt Phoebe. At rear Cleon & Thea Dennis. Picture Courtesy Julia Woodhouse)

I had a letter from Billy a few days ago from Salonika. He says that the heat is pretty bad and even worse than Egypt and that he is getting plenty of dysentery and malaria cases. I should think he will get pretty fed up with the hospital over there getting all the same old complaints to fix up.

He told me he had written to Harold Boulton, a cousin of ours. I don't think I have ever seen him in my life. I certainly don't remember him. Billy wrote to him and gave him my address, so I may be hearing from him. Billy must have met him in his Dopuncher[155] days. About the same time I had a letter from a Miss D. Newcomb[156] who appears to have become engaged to H.B. since his arrival from New Zealand from where he arrived on January 1st 16 to enlist with the Tommies.

Miss Newcomb says that she knew Billy, having met him in his knickerbocker youth and that he has stayed with them. She sent me Harold's address and hopes we will be able to arrange a meeting over in France. He came over in January last and went to an Officers School and now is 2nd Lieut. in the R.F.A. Evidently took him a long time to find out a war was on. I think I was a mug to come away when I did. I should have stayed and started thinking about it now and come over as a Captain with the aid of Officers Schools etc.

I wonder at him not joining the New Zealanders as the pay is much more in their little turnout.

You will see that my address is different now. We are busy fixing up new quarters and now that it has stopped pouring in torrents we are trying to make ourselves comfortable and watertight in the wet weather and winter which will not be very long in coming. The days are getting shorter already. Needless to say no one is looking forward to the winter.

I am sending this letter to Ermo where you will no doubt be or in any case it will be sent on. I haven't heard from the Child [since] she got married. I suppose things are going on very smoothly for them both. Please give my best love to them and Gran and Aunt Mog and Aunt Phoebe and Phil. Am glad the Anzac book arrived safely.

And now good-bye Matee, I hope you are settled in little Ermo for a bit in amongst your flowers and vegetables and that they are coming on satisfactorily with heaps and heaps of love and kisses from your ever loving son

TOOTS.

P.S. Am glad my money is being paid in to the Savings Bank and is O.K.

---

155 Dopuncher or Doughpuncher was the family nickname for their Doherty cousins.
156 It's not clear that Harold Boulton ever married Miss D Newcomb. In 1927 he married Annie Alberta (Nan) Crum in Auckland, New Zealand.

Somewhere in Flanders, 9 Sep 1916

My dearest Matee boos

Have just received your letter of 16th July, addressed to 21st Brigade. I have been getting all the others quite regularly, being sent on from my old Brigade, so now everything in the garden is looking lovely. Was very interested at getting the little newspaper cuttings. Poor old George came to a sad end after all. It will be a blow to the old man I'm sure.

Am sorry to hear of the temporary parting with little Ermo and am sure you would rather be out there than living in town. You will however be able to have a good deal of leisure & have a bit of a fly round occasionally, not being so tied down in a rather far & out of the way place. I think you will miss the pottering about in the garden with the vegetables etc. Is the man Champion or Campion going to work it at all? I wonder whereabouts in town you will be and how you will like the boarding house. It will greatly remind you [of] Mrs Branston's in Woburn Place I should think. For a time at least you will have more interesting surroundings.

Am afraid it is too early to think of my homecoming although there are lots of rumours of the Germans crumpling up in October. I don't think so though, they will probably keep their soldiers going right to the death. Everything in the way of news of the outside world is kept strictly secret from their men, who all think they must & are still winning the war. They are getting a terrible doing down where we came from, the Somme, and are coming in every day in bunches.

I am still keeping very fit & well. It has not started to get cold yet although we are getting our full share of rain which makes things very muddy & slushy. However once the rain stops & the sun gets out the days are generally glorious. We are all rather dreading the winter, most of us are somewhat interested to see what it is like having heard so much about it. It cannot be too pleasant I'm sure. We are all getting busy making improvements & getting ready for the wet season.

See by the papers that Billy Hughes[157] is working the people at home up to conscription & talking about having a referendum. If he only gives the troops over here a vote, I know what will win.

Please give my love to Gran when next you see her. I don't suppose she enjoys the daily 'tub' too much. And best love to Aunts Mog and Phoebus, hoping

---

157 Australia's Prime Minister

they are both well & get good news from Harry. I hear that Phil is doing her bit in town still. Tell the Child to drop me a line occasionally, haven't heard from them since before the wedding day. And with heaps of love, hugs & kisses to the mee maw till I come back home again

From her ever loving son TOOTS.

Around August 1916 Nigel served briefly with the 28th General Hospital near Salonika (today Thessaloniki in northern Greece), before he too was 'en route' to the Western Front.

All Saints Camp, Malta, 11 Sep 1916

Dearest Mother

Am writing you another letter before I leave here. I expect to go tomorrow if nothing crops up to prevent it. Am going to Mudros first and there tranship to the *Aquitania* and so to England. It seems a very roundabout way and so it is. But there are only two harbours in the Mediterranean that the *Aquitania* can get into, and those are Naples and Mudros. The *Aquitania*, which has been converted into a Hospital Ship, is fed from Salonika and Malta with patients for England - I'm not a patient but, being R.A.M.C., am allowed to travel on hospital ships. I suppose I shall reach England about the 19th or 20th of this month, having left Salonika on the 28th August, that is to say over 3 weeks to do a journey which should take 9 days.

I am very tired of Malta and shall be very pleased to get away. Unless you know people here there is absolutely nothing to do to amuse oneself, except swimming. There is a cricket match on this afternoon between the crew of *H.M.S. Agamemnon,* a battleship, and this camp. I am playing, so this will be a slight diversion. I am very anxious to get back to work again. I hope they won't keep me in England for more than 2 or 3 days, as I don't want to be kicking my heels about there for long. Mona leaves Egypt on the 20th so if I'm not sent to France immediately it is possible I may see something of her. This would be very nice if it so comes about. I haven't heard from Mona for nearly a month now, as she expected me to go straight to England after leaving Salonika. I daresay there are one or two letters waiting for me at Holt's where I told her to send my letters to. You had better address yours there too, Mum, for the present. I think I told you in my last letter or the one before it. To repeat: C/o Messrs. Holt & Co., 3 Whitehall Place, London, S.W. They will always know my whereabouts.

I am quite fit again and was very lucky to get over my malaria so well. I put it down to my recognizing what was the matter with me at once and dosing myself with large doses of quinine straightaway. I have a marked tolerance to quinine which is very fortunate, as I can take huge doses without it upsetting me, which is not very usual as a rule. I am still taking 10 grains a day and must do so for 3 months, otherwise one is likely to get a relapse, and if one has several relapses, the condition is apt to become chronic, and then you have a yellowy white complexion (the so-called malarial cachexia) for years afterwards. I am not anxious to acquire this, and I don't think it's very likely.

How are you getting along, Mum? I am much interested to hear of your doings at Dural. How is Gran and is Aunt Phoebe still looking after her? Also I should like to hear of Thea, she might write to me quite easily if she finds she has not much to do.

Well, dearest Mum, I shall stop now as I have to change for cricket, I shall write again when I get to England. Best love to all at home. Try and not feel too lonely. Bestest love and a hug and kisses,

Yours ever, NIGE

Somewhere in Flanders, 16 Sep 1916

My dearest Matee

Have just received your letter of 29th July direct. I see you are now installed at Riviera, Neutral Bay.[158] I hope you will enjoy the little rest there with no house work etc. to do for a bit. It is good being so handy to the Child whom no doubt you will see more of than you have been doing since she was at home.

It will certainly be a bit of a wrench parting with Ermo, but if you can get the £350 in cash from the tenant, I think it is a good deal and it will have turned out a tip top spec. I have forgotten what you gave for it in the first place, and what the improvements cost, but you will be making something considerable on the whole deal.

I hope you will like Pitt Town and should think you will have plenty to interest you and much to learn in the way of farming from all the stock and cattle on the place. It is no good however, working too hard and trying to do too much

---

158 A boarding house.

as it will spoil the whole turnout. The first week will be the worst as you say, but after that it will be plain sailing and you will be easily able to hold your own with any of the others.

How long will the training take, and can you stay on there as long as you like, provided you pay the board. Should you find it just the thing you wanted and are enjoying the life and surroundings, I should think it would almost be better to stay there as long as you could, as it might be better than being at a boarding house in town.

Am very sorry to hear of the Lloyd family's sad losses.[159] They seem to get more than their share of troubles. I wonder if Mary will stay on at Glen Innes and run the station on her own. What was wrong with Jeoff Taylor I wonder?

I am still going strong and feeling quite fit. We were down at P, which you mention in your letter and did excellent work. Am sorry I cannot give you details about the show, but it was pretty hot and they very nearly got "Tootie". He however, with another of his mates was very lucky being only buried and shaken up. There were about 8 of us in a trench having just finished making some coffee on a stove (German). A 29 came over and lobbed right on the trench on the top of the parapet and burst. It killed three outright and wounded two others at the same time, burying the lot of us. It was pretty close.[160]

However after a quiet spell away from the place one's nerves are able to recover. We were all more or less deaf in that position as all the time the 'riot' did not cease. It is however only temporary and most of us are fairly right again. We are busily getting prepared for the winter now, and the weather is getting noticeably colder, especially the mornings. It rains a good deal and even when not raining the sun doesn't get much of a chance. Things remain pretty wet, cold and clammy for a long time.

Have heard from Billy at Malta. You will have heard too no doubt. He expects to get over to France soon. I've advised him not to rush the Regimental M.O. job as the winter is coming on, he will probably only get all the discomforts of the trenches and wet and wintry weather of Northern France, and there will be

---

159 Probably refers to the death of Harry Lloyd's father-in-law James Stoops in March 1916 and brother-in-law William Stoops the previous year. William had an older sister named Mary, who was in legal trouble in May 1916 for registering the birth of a child in 1915 and claiming she'd married James Mitchell in 1914. (She married him in 1916.)
160 The Australian War Memorial records the date as 1 August but the unit's war diary reports heavy action between 3 and 4 a.m. on the morning of 2 August 1916, near Pozières Cemetery. Gunner John Andrews, Sgt Douglas Allan Elliott and Gunner Cyril Charles Kimber are buried 2 kms north-east of Albert, at Gordon Dump Cemetery, Ovillers la Boisselle, Picardie. In a separate incident, Lieut Lachlan George Paterson died of his wounds on 6 August.

very few cases of wounded. Trench feet or frostbite etc. will be very frequent. However he knows best I suppose.

Also had a note from Harold Boulton a cousin of mine apparently who has just arrived over here. After coming from New Zealand he went to school for Officers and got his commission in the R.F.A. His fiancée "Diddie" (reminds me of your ducks) Newcomb wrote to me and asked me to go down to see them when I get my leave. Goodness knows when that will be though!

Will not write more this time, am glad to hear that Gran is better, please give her my best love, also Aunts Mog and Phoebus hoping they are both keeping fit and getting some joy out of life. Will try and write to the Child by this mail too. With heaps and heaps of love and kisses to the Mee maw from

Her loving son, TOOTS.

The 21st FAB went back in the line on 17 Sep, launching retaliatory fire at the enemy at the request of the infantry. Enemy artillery on this front was very quiet and unit war diaries state 'we undoubtedly have the upper hand.'

They stayed in this position until mid-October, engaged in shelling the enemy positions on most days but without suffering any significant casualties.

Somewhere in Flanders, In the field, 23 Sep 1916

My dear Child

Your letter of 23rd July to hand after a rather lengthy interval. I see by your address that you are installed at Neutral Bay and I expect you rather enjoy being there without any housework to worry about, also being so close to town is very handy. Mum is I hear just round the corner from you, just for a while until the Pitt Town farm scheme is ready for her. I hope she will like the farm life and that it will come up to all her expectations. Meanwhile she will enjoy her little spell at "Nootral Bay" close to you.

Things do seem to have been happening over there at a pace. The Lloyd family seem to have been getting their full share of all the bad luck.[161] I wonder how Mick Taylor and his bride manage to do it. I suppose after being broken in

---

161 Referred to in an earlier letter from Nigel.

on the one meal a day racket it is going to remain for all time. What is Mick supposed to be doing - making munitions?

We are still jogging along in pretty much the same old way. It is beginning to get on the chilly side now, and we are beginning to get our winter clothes which so far consists of a cardigan. We have been getting tons of rain in fact, there are quite as many wet days here as there are fine, and the roads are feet thick in mud and slush. We are naturally not looking forward to the winter much, and at present are busy making ourselves as comfortable and dry as possible pending the wet season. We are however very fortunate at present at being on a much quieter part of the line than what we recently came from.

I heard from Billy some days ago and he was then in Malta waiting for a boat to take him on to England. He had had a slight touch of malaria on the way over, but had quite recovered when he wrote to me. Mona is following him to England, but he didn't say whether Mrs. Little is going on to Australia or remaining with Mona. He says he expects to get out here soon.

Please remember me to Cleon hoping he is keeping fit and getting the *Brisbane* into good working order.[162] She ought soon to be finished surely.

Won't write any more this time, so if you see mum you will be able to show her the letter and give my best love to Gran and Aunts Mog and Phoebus, hoping that everyone is keeping well and not being roasted yet in the oven and with heaps of love and kisses to the Mee maw and Child, hoping soon to get another letter when you have time and which you may address as "Corporal" now.

from your affect. brother, TOOTS.

The 21st FAB continued to be 'rested' away from the Battle of the Somme, defending the same quieter section of the front line, where Stephen was promoted permanently to the rank of Corporal on 27 Sep 1916.

Somewhere in Flanders, In the field, 27 Sep 1916

My dearest Matee

I have written to the Child only a day or so ago saying that everything over here is still going on much the same. You will no doubt get the letter from her.

---

162 Cleon Dennis, Engr Lieut, was installing the engines on the new *HMAS Brisbane* in Sydney.

You may address me now as Corporal, having arrived at that exalted rank. I have given up my last job of looking after the archives of this little turnout. I was very comfortable but thought it advisable to give it up and get on a bit in case of something better turning up in the future. Naturally I have much more to do now which will keep me going most of the day. The pay is a slight improvement now being 10/- a day with 2/- a day deferred which we don't get until we get back, if ever we do then. So I suppose it is a step in the right direction.

Leave to England for our Division has commenced again but at a very slow rate and it will be about 3 months before my turn comes round if it is not quickened up a bit. It extends at present over 10 days which is not bad. All the fellows who have been come back having had a glorious time and spent tons of money generally seeing about 2 or 3 theatres a day. I don't feel like going over there and calling on all the relations and spending my time playing at mams in their drawing rooms. However we shall see when the time comes.

Billy must have arrived in England by this time. I haven't heard from him since he was at Malta waiting for a boat. Mona will also be on her way across having left Alexandria on the 20th or thereabouts of this month.

I saw in one of the English papers that Max Barton was missing. His battalion were down in the "scraping" where we came from. It is always a bad sign where there is heavy fighting. I expect Mrs. Barton has had later news which I hope is of the best.

I wonder if you are at Pitt Town now and how you are liking it. It ought to suit you alright if you don't go and be too strenuous and take on too much ploughing etc. The Child seems to be very happy in her swagger boarding house at Neutral Bay and no doubt Cleon and she are often going over to the theatres and concerts being so handy to the city. She will be glad not to have any of the house work to do.

For the last week we have been having gloriously fine weather which is a great and most acceptable change. It has been quite warm, I hope not the last before the arrival of the winter. Now nearly October, so I don't think we will get much more sunshine for a bit. The nights are much longer already and are inky black.

Am afraid this is only a short letter, but you will have seen the Child's and nothing much out of the ordinary is happening at present with us outside military affairs. Am sending this as usual to Coolah as I don't yet know of your new permanent address.

Please give my best love to Gran and hope she is still feeling well and fit. Also Aunt Mog hoping the museum is treating her well still, also the rent of the cottage at Tennyson still comes along regularly. And best love to Aunt Phoebus and hoping they get good news of Harry if he has left by this, with heaps of love to Matee boos and the Child trusting everything is going well, from

Your loving son

TOOTS.

Nigel's prayers were answered when he joined the No 17 Field Ambulance, one of three Field Ambulances attached to the British Army's 6th Division throughout the war.[163] It was a mobile front line medical unit, with a number of officers and hundreds of men establishing and operating the system for transporting and treating men leaving the Regimental Aid Posts and passing through the Advanced Dressing Station, Main Dressing Station and Walking Wounded Collecting Station to the Casualty Clearing Stations further back, where a different group of doctors and medical staff took over. (See the diagram on page 59.)

In this letter, written from the Somme area, Nigel refers to his new transport duties. The Field Ambulance relied heavily on horses for transport of the officers, and hauling the baggage wagons, water carts, forage carts, ambulance wagons and cook's wagon. Several motorised ambulances and a bicycle were also used.

No 17 Field Ambulance, B.E.F. France, Oct 1916

Dearest Mother

Well here I am, in France at last and attached to a field ambulance, the job I have been striving for for some time. I was attached to this unit about 5 days ago after a 30 hours train journey from Boulogne, one of the slowest and most tedious that I've ever experienced. The division was in the line when I came up, so I walked right into things. There was "Somme" fight going on I can assure you. I was sent up to the advanced bearers' dressing station about a mile behind the line, and was able to experience firsthand what modern artillery fire really is like. The Bosches were very kind to us this time, and didn't shell us, altho' they put a few shells round about. We fortunately didn't have any casualties this last stunt, altho' prior to this we have lost several bearers and one or two M.O's.

---

163 The 'Beyond 1914' website of the University of Sydney incorrectly lists his unit as No 14 Field Ambulance.

You can have no idea of the state of the ground, what with the large shell holes and mud and slush. I was plastered with it from head to foot. The bearers have an appalling time carrying back the wounded, but not half so awful as the poor unfortunate fellows who are hit. Those wounded in No Man's Land laid out for 48 hours and more before they could be collected, owing to the German artillery fire, in the mud and cold. The last 2 days have been bitterly cold, hard frosts, but it is a comfort to get a chance to dry one's things. We are in billets now for a day or two, and altho' the rooms are bare and cheerless, it is luxury to dugouts and icy tents. We are going back 40 miles for a rest, as this division has been "in" 3 times recently and are considerably below strength. We are then going into the line again further north between Bethune and Arras.

I have been made officer-in-charge of transport, and have to see to the moving of our goods and chattels. We have 4 or 5 wagons and 2 horse ambulances, 1 or 2 carts and 4 motor ambulances with several riding horses. Being transport officer I have the pick of the horses, and have chosen a buck-jumper who periodically gets rid of everyone who rides him at unexpected times. But as she is quite a good mare, I don't mind getting pitched off. No one else will ride her, so it is a pity to see her going to waste. We have 15 miles to do tomorrow and 25 the day after. It is very tedious travelling as we can't go more than 3 miles an hour. I walk some of the way to get warm, as it gets pretty chilly riding at a walk.

I haven't heard from Steve yet, as to his whereabouts, I have written to him tho'. I hope to hear from him soon. I haven't had any letters from Mona yet, as I have been so much on the move, and I didn't know my address. However, I should have a letter now in a day or two.

I have given Holt's my address, so they will forward your letters on. It is the best way, as it is indefinite how long I shall be with this unit.

How are you, Mum? I dare say I shall have a letter from you before long. I hope you are not wearing yourself out on the farm, & will give it up if you find it too strenuous.

I am quite pleased with this job, and will become as fit as a flea after a bit. The open air life is excellent in spite of the cold when one gets used to it. I shall have some interesting first hand information to give you when I return.

Will stop now, best love to all at home, hoping everything is well with you. A big hug, and a kiss, dearest Mum,

Ever yours, NIGE

Will write you again, when I get a chance; would love to know what Steve is up to. There doesn't seem much chance of our meeting just at present.

Somewhere in France, Oct 1916

Dearest Mother

We have been moved a bit further up the line since I last wrote and are now about 5 or 6 miles behind the front line.[164] We have taken over a school, which makes quite a good hospital. We, of course, only detain patients here for 3 or 4 days, to see whether they will require sending further down the lines of communication. A field ambulance is really a clearing station, it is nearly all evacuation work, there is very little medical or surgical treatment involved. I have a very comfortable bed and nice large room in the Schoolmaster's house, with the Colonel. The rest of the men are billeted about the town and are quite comfortable.

We have not had very much to do since we arrived; things seem to be very quiet in this area. There is practically no fighting, with the exception of half-hearted artillery duels. I rode up towards the front with the Colonel and another fellow yesterday afternoon and we got a good idea of things. The Colonel and I climbed the tower over a ruined mine pit shaft, which was about 70 feet high, and we had a splendid view of the surrounding country and the German lines, altho' it was a big hazy. We subsequently learnt that it was very unsafe as we could be easily seen by the Germans and there were one or two German snipers not far off. What struck me particularly yesterday was the almost uncanny stillness, only broken now and then by the sharp report of one of our guns and the more distant boom of one of the enemy's. It was a scene of desolation. The houses were tremendously knocked about, not a single one intact. No birds, no animals, no cries, just an oppressive silence, like a city of the dead. I am going up to the front line trenches probably tomorrow, which is Sunday. As I shall most likely sooner or later be detailed as a Medl. Officer to a regiment, it behoves me to familiarize myself to a small extent at any rate with trench life.

I had a letter from Steve a day or two ago. He has only had one letter from me since I left Malta. Can't quite understand it, as I have written him 3 as well as a Field Service P.C., also forwarded 2 of Mona's letters on. But I daresay

---

164 This letter is dated 11 October but the content suggests it was written after the last letter dated 22 October. There is a transcription error somewhere.

they will turn up eventually. It took his letter to me 12 days to come, while I can write a letter home to England and get an answer in the same time. It is rather sickening there being such a delay. He doesn't tell me where abouts he is, doesn't give me the slightest clue, so it will be rather difficult for us to run against one another. Still I give him a good idea in my letters where I am so he probably will look out for me if he happens to be in the same neighbourhood. He is getting pretty fed up with things I think, the weather has certainly been pretty awful, and he has had a bigger dose of France than I've had. Also an officer has a much sweeter time than the men in the ranks. He should be getting his leave very shortly now, he must be due for it. Perhaps he may get it at Xmas time. If he doesn't, Mona is going to send him a very nice Xmas parcel of foodstuffs and delicacies. Poor old Steve, he has been promoted to the rank of Corporal, the next step is Sergeant, when he will get many more comforts, and have a mess of his own, as well as more pay.

I wonder he doesn't apply for a commission; there must be plenty of vacancies, with these new troops and reinforcements. Lots of fellows who joined in the ranks with the first lot have since got commissions. Mona knows several of them. I have suggested to Steve he makes inquiries and considers the question.

I also had a letter from Hal about 2 days ago. He wrote from a camp in Dorset, about 15 miles from Bournemouth, so quite comfortable.

I must try and write to one or two of them, if I can. A. Mog and the Child at any rate. Bestest love, dearest Mother, do take care of yourself. I wonder whether we shall be together next Xmas at all, I think it sounds hopeful.

A big hug and a kiss,

Yours ever,

NIGE

The 22nd Battery was relieved 'in the line' on the night of 14/15 October and by 18 October they and the rest of the 21st FAB had moved by road to billets at Guémy, about 50 miles west of Ypres and about 23 miles north east of Boulogne. After a few days rest they endured another train journey and route march to their bivouac position just south of the Amiens-Albert Road, and quite close to Albert. This was their third posting to the horrors of the Somme battlefield.

They moved back into 'the line' near Gueudecourt (south of Bapaume - see 'Map 9: The Somme, 1916-1918' on page 250) on the night of 25/26 October, relieving

New Zealand artillery units. The weather having been showery for days, roads were bad and ammunition and rations had to be taken from the wagon lines to the batteries by pack horse. Accommodation for personnel was poor, but efforts were being made to improve their conditions. As usual, Steve minimized his hardships.

Somewhere in France [Gueudecourt], 7 Nov 1916

Dearest Matee boos

Just a very hasty note to let you know that everything is still alright with me. We are still existing under the most unfavourable conditions with little prospect of things improving.

It still rains incessantly and the mud and slush is as bad as ever. After a good innings of this life under our present conditions it ought to be easy for us to enjoy the ordinary every day routine life after it all.

We haven't had any mail lately owing to the transport difficulties etc. and our letters have not left too regularly, I'm afraid. I hope this one gets away and catches the mail so you will know that everything is alright. We get an issue of rum every night to help keep out the cold and wet which everyone turns up for and apparently appreciates.

Am now sitting on the ground where my bed is spread out under our little tin humpy with the rain coming down on the top. We are indeed lucky to have a bed to sleep in out of the wet. The infantry must have a pretty rough time. They are not kept in more than a few days though.

I hope everything is still going well with you and that you are enjoying your farm life at Pitt Town. You had better hang on to it as long as you can if you find you like it so much. Haven't heard from Billy lately. I suppose he is still at Boulogne.

Good-night now Matee Boos and please give my best love to everyone at home from

Your loving son

TOOTS.

From 12 November the 21st FAB had a six day respite from the line, resting in the wagon lines. The Battle of the Somme was also being wound down. It had succeeded in relieving pressure on the French army at Verdun but the series of small assaults had pushed the German Army back by only 6 miles and failed to reach overall territorial objectives. Casualties damaged the Allies far more than the Germans and the period from 1 July to 18 November 1916 was one of the bloodiest in human history, with more than one million people killed or wounded.

After the 21st FAB returned to duty on 18 November, relieving a British unit, extremely foggy conditions set in for the next 12 days, making observation practically impossible for the artillery men. Nevertheless, barrages were ordered for the night of 22/23 November. The rates of fire were to be 4 rounds per gun per minute for the first 5 minutes, then 2 rounds per gun per minute until further orders were received. The idea was to disrupt any attempts by the enemy to move men, equipment and supplies overnight.

In late November 1916 Steve's Battery was still based in the Gueudecourt area just south of Bapaume. On 29 November a minor operation involving the infantry was ordered, to clear up & consolidate the line but German defences around Bapaume were strong. The opposing armies settled in to wait out and endure the harshest winter on the Somme for 40 years. The Australians had to hold their positions at Gueudecourt in appalling conditions. Constant rain filled the trenches with water & mud, with drainage impossible. Nothing could dry out.[165]

Biscuit Trench,
Gueudecourt, Dec 1916
Source AWM E00103

Mud on the Western Front
Source AWM E01235

---

165 The Gueudecourt site of suffering is not well-known to today's tourists to the Great War battlefields.

Somewhere in France, In the field, 1 Dec 1916

Dearest Matee boos

Your letter of Sept 2nd arrived quite safe and sound last night, and you are addressing my letters quite correctly and they are arriving regularly. I have already told you that the waist coat arrived and will be of great use and comfort. I have not taken it in use yet as we have all been issued with a sheepskin which I am at present wearing in the wind and which is getting some rough usage. Yours will come in very handy later on, when my present one wears out a bit.

It is already very cold with frosts in the morning and it continues to freeze, right through the day at times. We have had one light fall of snow, which gives us an idea what it is going to be like in winter proper. When not freezing or snowing it is generally raining, with an occasional dry day now and again.

And so we are scratching along, keeping well wrapped up. I have got a hole or dug out cut in the ground about 7 ft. x 3 ft. and sleep when not on the gun. Just now I am sitting on my bed with a fire going in an impromptu fire bucket made out of an old oil drum, punched into holes. It greatly helps to cheer things and keeps us warm. There is a quiet spell just now

I am glad to hear that you are still enjoying your farm life and getting a lot of good experience. It is not much good you going on though, too far into the heat of the summer, when the work will no longer be any pleasure.

Yesterday I had a letter from Hal who is still in camp in England. He had been to stay with Aunt Julia at Harrow and seems to have enjoyed himself seeing London with Cousin Bess in her car. I suppose if I ever get over there I shall have to go through that ordeal. Goodness knows how I shall get on, coming right out from 2 years of this into their drawing room. Shall probably grab a loaf of bread in one hand and stick my knife into the butter with the other before I know what has happened. It will be a case of "Aren't the schools awfully rough".

Cousin Bess wrote to me a day or so ago asking for news of me. She wrote in her usual kind way and wants me to go and stay when I get my leave. She said Hal had been staying with them, which they had much enjoyed. She also wanted to know if I wanted anything sent out. I have written to her, but didn't ask her to send anything along as I thought it was making it too hot. By the way Miss Wren of Bega, NSW sent me another parcel with some chocolates, cigarettes and tobacco in it. 'Trés bon' as they say here.

Am very glad to hear Gran is so much better and hope that everything at Coolah is going on O.K. Please give my best love to the Child and wish her a successful and prosperous New Year. Also Aunt Mog and Phoebus and Gran if you will be seeing them. Am sending this to Coolah as you say you don't quite know where you will be after Xmas. With heaps and heaps of love and kisses from your ever loving son

TOOTS.

Somewhere in France, In the field, 4 Dec 1916

Dearest Gran

Just a hurried line to wish you all happiness and prosperity in the New Year. This is another Xmas for me away from home, and let us hope it will be the last. It would be good if we are all back again by this time next year to have a sort of reunion. We would perhaps have to send up to Cashman's to celebrate.

It is now pretty cold here, very different to the weather you are getting. We always have to break the ice in the mornings now, owing to the heavy frosts. We have so far only had one fall of snow and light, only about 2 inches.

I have had a letter from England where Hal is in camp. He says he expects to be sent out soon. It would have been better if he could have stayed over there until the winter was over. Bill has been down this way where I am now, but has gone out some weeks ago and is now I believe having a bit of a spell. I suppose the Division he is in will come back again before very long. He seems to like his change of work.

Our leave to England has commenced again. I should, with luck, get over there in about 6 weeks or 2 months' time for 7 days which won't be so bad.

Please give my best wishes for a happy New Year to Aunt Mog, hoping it will be a very successful one for her, also Aunt Phoebus and Phil. I shall try and write to them later. With best love to you all at Coolah from

Your loving grandson

STEVE.

Back in England, Nigel and Mona's son was born on 21 November 1916. Mona, her mother and the baby lived at Seafield, Parkstone, near Bournemouth. Nigel had not yet seen his son, named Philip in honour of Nigel's long-dead father, when Steve wrote his next letter, from the Gueudecourt area on the Somme.

Somewhere in France, In the field, 14 Dec 1916

My dearest Matee boos

I hope you have received my last letter which was put in Mona's envelope by mistake and which she said she had forwarded on to you. You have heard long before this of your being made a grandmother. Billy and Mona are apparently both delighted with the son and heir; although up to the present he is a very tiny lad. The image of Billy, Mona says, but it must be a bit soon to see. I am expecting to get over there on leave sometime in January if all goes well from now till then and the leave is not stopped, so I may see my nephew before his proud papa. I am to be a godfather by the way. Now you have become a grandmother, that feeling only 21 will disappear I suppose.

We are still sticking it out and hope to get a bit of a spell soon now. We haven't been having quite so much rain lately, although still too much. Yesterday morning we had another light fall of snow, which didn't improve things.

I haven't received the Child's parcel yet which you mentioned in your last but I expect it to arrive by the next mail as the letters generally get here first. Am greatly looking forward to it. We haven't been able to get much in the way of luxuries or extras in this position, excepting Quaker Oats and milk, which we generally make once a day and it greatly helps to fill up. Mona tells me Cousin Bess is going to come to light with another of some dimensions including a turkey etc. Hope it reaches me alright.

There is very little that I am allowed to tell you so won't say any more now. Please give my best love to the Child, Aunt Mog, Gran and Aunt Phoebus and Phil, hoping everyone is keeping well and in good spirits, with heaps of love and kisses to my mee maw from

Your loving son, TOOTS.

Enemy shelling on and around Gueudecourt was constant, so the 21st FAB was very happy to be relieved in the line on 22 December and billeted overnight at

Franvillers, en route to their familiar rest area at Havernas, one of the villages around Vignacourt. Instructions were issued that the exhausted men were to be marched in their columns and were not to take any advantage of riding on the vehicles or wagons.

When they arrived, arrangements made to send 48 men per day to the military baths at Naours, another of the villages surrounding Vignacourt. The men of the 21st FAB were instructed not to repeat the bad behavior of Allied troops while on leave in nearby Amiens but the warnings were ignored by unnamed men over Christmas and all leave to Amiens was then cancelled until further notice. Steve does not complain because he had his own leave to look forward to.

Somewhere in France [Havernas], 31 Dec 1916

My dearest Mateeboo

You will be very pleased to hear that we are now enjoying a bit of a change out of the line. It is supposed to be a spell, but there is always plenty to do and to make things less pleasant it is always wet and raining and the wind, mud and slush don't improve things. It is however good to get away from the line and all its worries.

I am expecting to leave for England in about 3 days' time if nothing happens in the meantime to stop me, and by the time I get back the unit will be back in the line again, where I shall rejoin them. It is not a very pleasant feeling I believe, the coming back to the mud after a bit of a spell in England with all of its comforts and luxuries. I shall probably go out to Harrow and also try and find Cousin Mary at Kew. That will be 2 days at least taken up, valuable days too. I shall also have to see my nephew and godson and I want to try and get some teeth fixed up. Goodness knows if I will have time to get it all done.

We had a very tame Xmas, shut up in a tiny little French village with a blacksmith's shop and store. It wouldn't be so bad if the weather was at all decent. I have written to the Child by this mail thanking her for the parcel which arrived quite O.K. and was a beauty. It is not finished yet and will last me till I go away on leave. I get 10 days in England which is not so bad. And now good-bye Matee. Please give my best love to Gran, Aunt Mog and Phoebus, Phil and everyone at home, hoping you all have a successful and happy 1917, with heaps of love and kisses from

Your ever loving son, TOOTS.

1917

Somewhere in France, 6 Jan 1917

Dearest Mother

1917 is well started and here I am at another job! I have taken on Sanitary Officer for a month in relief of a chap who has got leave for this period, lucky beggar. My duties comprise laundry, baths and sanitation of the division. It is some job, I can tell you, but scarcely a M.O's job. The fellow who has been running this outfit was a sanitary engineer, so I feel rather in deep water, as I know practically nothing of sanitary engineering.

We have about 14,000 troops to look after. Each man gets a bath every 10 days, perhaps more often, and after he has his bath, he is provided with a clean change of underclothing, shirt and socks. We have a large laundry with about 60 women working in it, and outside workers as well. The laundry is fitted with machinery and turns out about 1,000 shirts and a 1,000 drawers each day, with socks and towels in a smaller amount. A lot of the socks are washed outside.

We have 5 different bath houses, some of them are provided with tubs and some with sprays. The sprays are quicker and the water is always nice and hot. We can bathe about 50 to 60 men an hour in some, and a 100 in others – it is a great godsend to the troops as you may imagine.

Then in addition to this, each man in the trenches has a dry clean pair of socks every 24 hours, to combat the trench foot evil, and there is some sock washing to be done. I have to pay the laundry hands this afternoon. I have 2,500 francs to dole out, so it will take me about 2½ hours to get thro' with it. The sanitation comprises supervising the disposal of refuse, etc. from the 3 brigades, the control of the water supplies, inspection of cookhouses, billets, horse lines, etc. etc. So you will gather from this that at present I am rather a busy man.

Steve got a sweater from Aunt Julia for Xmas, but his parcel from Cousin Bessie had not turned up when he wrote about a fortnight ago. It may have arrived since. She sent it from the Army & Navy Stores. My parcel has not arrived either, but I am living in hope. As it was posted in the latter part of November it should have turned up by this. Mona's parcel should be here too, but hers wasn't posted till Boxing Day. I received a leather waistcoat, lined with wool, the day before yesterday from her, which will be a great boon; also a nice thick pair of Jaeger wool socks, which are keeping my toes warm now. I am quite fit again now, except for a small cold. The weather has been very raw and cold the last day or two, it looks as if it would like to snow.

The paper is crammed full of New Year's honours the last couple of days, Military Crosses and D.S.O's. 100's of them are deserved and 100's undeserved, but this is always the way. It is largely a matter of luck. One man is recognized for the good work of several.

Steve should be getting leave very shortly now. Cousin Bessie has very kindly told him to make Harrow his headquarters. I don't know if he is going to do this. One of our fellows goes on leave tonight, so my turn should come now early in February.

The young son is getting a regular fatty. He weighs 8½ lbs now, which is very satisfactory to practically double his weight in a month. Am very keen to see him. Mona has lost her nurse now, and is managing him on her own - she feels the responsibility. I hope she won't worry herself too much and interfere with her milk.

No more just now, Mum. Best love to all. Trust everything is well at Gladesville. Wonder if you are still at Scheyville.[166] Very best love, dearest Mum, a kiss and a big hug,

Your loving NIGE

Imperial Hotel, Russell Square, 9 Jan 1917

Dearest Mateeboos

You will see by the address that I am now on leave at last and am enjoying every bit of it. I came over on the 5th and go back on the 15th, so I have had half of it by now and the thought of going back is not a pleasant one at all.

I have just returned from spending 2 days with Mona and the boy and Mrs. Little at Parkstone. They were very kind. The boy Philip Hugh is grand and a splendid looking chap. Quite the best I have seen. They are generally ugly looking things, but this lad is something out of the box. I don't know who he is like, his face isn't

---

166 The location of a Women's Farm, near Pitt Town, in the Hawkesbury district about 50 miles north west of Sydney.

long enough to be like Billy's and his hair is not dark like Mona's. He is looking very well and doesn't squawk much; chiefly at night times I believe. He was very good when I was down and I had the great honour of nursing him.

I have now come back to London preparatory to going out to Harrow tomorrow and Cousin Mary the next day. It will be a bit of an ordeal, but has to be gone through. The time seems so short and seems to fly and is gone before you know where you are.

I will not get any of your letters until I get back to my unit. I wonder where the Child will be going when Cleon sails. England is just the same as I remembered it, with the same awful weather. I have been to one or two theatres and shall be going to another tonight whilst in town.

I don't know how long I shall be out at Harrow, but I hope not more than one day. The christening of P.H. Boulton comes off on the same day as I go back. Someone is standing for me and I have given the lad a silver mug. It is a pity Nige cannot get over for it, he is to get his leave in February I believe. Cousin Bess has been invited down to stay with Mona during the event. She is a godmother as you know.

And now good bye Matee boos, I wish the war was over and we were all back again home and living in comfort. It is a great treat to get into a decent house after the Somme turnout.

Bestest love to all from TOOTS.

KENNET HOUSE, HARROW, 11 JAN 1917

Dearest Matee boos

Am now at Harrow. Cousin Bess and Aunt Julia are very kind indeed. Came here yesterday morning and spent the night. Am going out to see Cousin Mary Dixon this afternoon. Am just waiting now for Cousin Bess to come to town and she is very keen on getting my photograph taken. Am sure you will like to have one, and it is a good opportunity to have it done. I was going to

Cpl S P Boulton, Jan 1917
(Picture Courtesy Julia Woodhouse)

get one done whilst over here and she says there is quite a good man at Harrow. Everything seems the same as when I was here last. Cousin Bess asks is there any chance of you coming over here again.[167] She wishes you would. You and she were great pals she says.

They are ready now Matee so good-bye, this will catch the mail I think. I hope you get my other letter too, written the day before yesterday from London. With bestest love to all at home from

Your ever loving son, TOOTS.

Somewhere in France, In the field, 19 Jan 1917

Dearest Matee boos

Have just arrived back from England and my leave is all over and a thing of the past. I have left only the very happy memories of it all to recall. I had a great time and enjoyed every bit of it, but of course it was all too short and the time went like lightning.

I hope you got my two previous letters, one written from London and the other from Harrow whilst staying at Kennet House. After leaving Harrow I had a day in London and then went on down to Parkstone again, where I finished up by spending my last 2 days. I enjoyed being down there very much. Both Mrs. Little and Mona were kindness itself. A friend of Mona's and Nige's, a Mrs. Manser, arranged a little party to go over to see a variety show at a neighboring theatre and it was jolly good. We first of all, that is Mona and I, went round and had dinner with the Mansers and then a taxi took us all over to Boscombe where the theatre was. Came back after the show in the taxi and had a little supper again at the Manser's house, before getting home and to bed.

The next day was Sunday and I had my breakfast brought to me in bed which made a great contrast to getting up at Reveille. After that Mona and I took out Phil in the pram for a short walk before dinner. We had afternoon tea at the Manser's and then went to Church in the evening, the church where the boy

---

167 Dora (Dolly) had left England in 1882 and had returned to England with her daughter Thea aboard the *Runic* in June 1902. Anxious to rejoin the boys (at school in England), she'd enjoyed a lengthy stay in England as guests of various family members. Dolly, Nigel and Thea arrived back in Sydney on 28 February 1904 on the *Medic*. Stephen had not yet completed his schooling in England. Aged 15, he returned alone to Sydney on 22 September 1905, also aboard the *Medic*.

was to be christened next day. The next day was my last in England and I left Parkstone about 11 o'clock in the morning to catch the train from Waterloo back to France. On Sunday Mona took one or two snaps of Phil being nursed by his Uncle, which he didn't seem to like at first, but soon became used to and didn't mind. They were taken in the drawing room, with Billy's camera, and I am rather doubtful about how they will come out if they ever do.[168]

Phil is as I have said before a fine looking chap and is getting quite fat. I had the pleasure of seeing him in his bath one morning and he is a fine round and plump little chap. He doesn't like being prepared for his bathing operations but once in it enjoys the whole thing immensely. He of course rules the whole household at present and occasionally doesn't go to sleep at night, keeping the whole female part of the household up till the small hours of the morning. I have given him a silver mug as his christening offering with the inscription "Phil from Uncle Steve 15.1.1917" written on it, the date being when he was christened. I was returning to France on the day he was christened, so somebody stood proxy for me. Cousin Bess couldn't get down either as she had a wedding on in the house the next day. Mrs. Manser had the arrangement of the whole thing and lent Mona a christening robe for the boy which is considered a very lucky thing I believe. Mrs. Manser was the other godmother.

When in London I saw a few theatres which I greatly enjoyed. Whilst in town I stayed at the Imperial Hotel in Russell Square, quite close to Woburn Place as you will remember. I generally had my breakfast brought up to me in bed and as you can easily imagine I enjoyed the comfort and luxury to the fullest. I went out to Richmond and saw Cousin Mary Dixon who was very pleased to see me. She was at home all by herself so I didn't see Ken or John. Ken is at work at Darracq, the motor people, and has been turned down for the Army on account of bad eyesight. He wears specs. John was at Woolwich where he is training to become an officer in the Artillery. You knew he was married. I don't know who the girl was, but saw her photo. I went round on my way back to London and called on Mrs. Bertie Dixon. I don't think you met her. And next day called on Bob Dixon at his office in town. So I had a bit of a fly round.

And now I am back again and it is by no means pleasant. We are still enjoying a bit of a spell, but it is not going to last much longer I'm afraid.

I think I told you I had my photo taken at Harrow as Cousin Bess was very keen on having me done. I have asked her to send you one when they are finished. I hope they are good. They are cabinet size.

---

168 These photos have not survived.

And now Matee boos I will not write any more just now, please give my love to everyone at home. I hope they are all well. I have just received two letters from you dated Oct 28th and Nov 8th. You are just on the point of going back to Coolah to look after Gran And many thanks for the 'bacca' which arrived quite safely. Heaps of love and kisses to you and the Child from your ever loving son,

TOOTS.

G Ward, No 14 Casualty Hospital, Boulogne, France, 27 Jan 1917

Dearest Mateeboos

You will be a bit surprised to see where I have got to. I am quite alright though, having got hold of a nice dose of mumps. I had only been back from England one day before they appeared and I was sent away immediately and didn't stop until I arrived here. Of course, we are all isolated and so keep pretty quiet, but it is a great change from the line in the mud, snow and slush.

It has been bitterly cold here for days now with everything frozen hard, including the medicines and soda water in the syphons, so I can consider myself very lucky in not being out in it. We have a little stove in the ward which we keep going and which keeps us all nice and warm. The only thing I'm sorry about is that they didn't show up whilst over in England where I could have had a good time during convalescence.

There is no hope of getting over from here as mumps are not serious enough to send over. I don't know where I could have got them except in England and I hope I haven't given them to my nephew or his parents. The extreme cold over here seems to bring them on and chiefly amongst the Australians. I am in a ward of 13 all of whom are Colonials.

It is 12 years ago since we were all over here. Do you remember the meals we used to get? I don't remember much about the place, but so far we have not been out and the hospital is in a different part to where we were before. We are right on the beach in amongst all the little bathing huts that are used in the summer. I saw the big monument of Napoleon which I remembered. We will probably all go to a convalescent camp for a short time after leaving here. It is quite the best thing to catch don't you think.

I wonder if you have received my photos from Cousin Bess. They ought soon to be done and by the time you get this they ought to be well on their way. I hope they turn out well and are something like me.

When I was over there I bought £30 worth of Commonwealth War Loan as the money was standing to my credit in my pay book and I wasn't allowed to draw it all whilst on leave. So I thought I might just as well be getting the 4½% interest on it. The scrip will be held on my account in Safe Custody at the C'wealth Bank Sydney.

I suppose all my letters will be going astray now and will take some time getting to me now I have left my unit. I have left word for them to be sent on however.

Please give my best love to Gran and Aunt Mog hoping they are both keeping well and also the Child. I wonder if Cleon has left yet, and what are the arrangements. Goodbye now Mateeboos, with heaps of love and kisses from

Your loving son, TOOTS.

British attacks in the Ancre valley of the Somme resumed in January 1917 and forced the Germans into local withdrawals there, due to their acute manpower shortages and morale problems after the Somme battles of 1916. The Russian Revolution beginning in February 1917 allowed German troops to relocate from the Eastern Front to the Western Front, but on the Flanders section of the Western Front Germany proceeded with a strategic retreat of about 4 miles to their Hindenburg line of defence. They waited for their U-boats and aircraft to start turning the tide of war in their favour. The tactic straightened the German line of defence and allowed a greater concentration of troops per mile. The German withdrawal was made over roads still in relatively good condition but then deliberately destroyed, and made even more impassable for the advancing British troops because of a thaw, which turned the roads to bogs. It took a huge effort to move the artillery guns.

Moving the Artillery Guns, Western Front
Source AWM C00467

For the time being, Steve remained safe from the fighting. After hospital came convalescence, further medical checks and 10 days additional training before a sick soldier was returned to his unit.

No 1 Convalescent Camp, Boulogne, France, 14 Feb 1917

Dearest Mateeboos

You see I am still at the Conv. Camp but am now out of isolation. Am probably leaving here tomorrow or the next day for a Base Details camp where we will all be sorted out into our various brigades and divisions before going back up the line.

I had a post card from Cousin Bess saying she had sent my proofs out to me at the Battery but as I had left before they arrived I missed them. I have written to her asking her to order & choose them & send some out to you, so I hope they will eventually arrive & that they will be good & you will like them. There will be one each for Aunts Mog & Phoebus & Thea I expect, as Cousin Bess wanted to know if she should send some off to anyone I wanted.

Am very pleased to be able to tell you that the very severe & cold weather has let up a bit and now we are getting heavy frosts with sunny days – of course there is hardly any warmth in the sun, but it is better than nothing.

I heard today that my brigade of artillery has been broken up – I knew it was coming before I left. However we are still in the same division (the first) and you had best continue sending my letters to the same address as usual until you hear from me, when I get back to whatever battery I am going to. It is a bit of a 'noosance' as I left some good clothes behind me when I left, not being able to bring them away with me & I expect I shall lose them. However, such are the ways of the army.

I heard from Mona a couple of days ago, saying that Billy had not yet arrived, but expected to get over in a week or so. I expect he is over there now & feeling very proud of his son. Mrs Manser, a friend of theirs & Billy's in Parkstone, seemed to be making great preparations in the way of amusements for him, so I expect he will have a good time.

I had a walk into Boulogne yesterday afternoon & remembered a little of the streets & gates of the walls, but I think everything must have changed a lot since we were here before. The harbour of course is nothing but shipping now, very different from peace time. We are camped right at the foot of the big monument of Napoleon on the top of the hill outside the town. Do you remember going up to the top of it? I haven't the faintest notion as to where we stayed though.

Will you please give my best love to Gran, Aunt Mog & all relations at Coolah. I hope the photos arrive alright. With heaps of love & kisses for Matee from

Her loving son, TOOTS.

Stephen left his convalescent camp on 24 February and next writes from the 1st Australian General Base Depot on the French coastline at Étaples, about 20 miles south of Boulogne. This was the congregation and 'sorting out' point for Australians arriving in France or returning from hospital. Others had their base camps at Étaples too – the English, Canadian and Scottish forces – together forming the huge Étaples Army Base Camp. It was served by a network of railways, canals, and roads connecting the camp to the southern and eastern battlefields in France and to ships carrying troops, supplies, guns, equipment, and thousands of men & women across the English Channel.[169]

BASE CAMP, SOMEWHERE IN FRANCE, 3 MAR 1917

My dearest Matee

I have left behind me the hospital and corresponding details camp and am now in our base camp awaiting to go once more up the line. I have been here nearly a week now and it is not bad here, much better and cleaner than the awful mud.

I have not received any letters since leaving the battery, but I suppose some day they will catch me up in the form of a little bundle. You had better not address me to the old battery because it is no more now. When I go back up the line I shall have an altogether different address and will let you know when that happens, and what my new address is. Meantime my address is No. 3872, Cp S.P.B. 1st A.G.B.D, A.P.O., Section 17, B.E.F. France and all letters will be forwarded on to me after I leave here. So don't forget the address or lose this letter and tell the Child in case she is writing.

I am pleased to tell you the weather has greatly improved during the last week and although it is still a bit nippy we have had a little sunshine as well. I think

---

169 Information from http://throughthelines.com.au/research/etaples , accessed 17 Mar 2015

however, we must get another spell of bad weather, as this is only March, before the summer arrives properly.

All traces of the mumps have gone, but I am stone deaf in my left ear. I have seen the Specialist about it, but so far have had no treatment. He says I shall remain so most likely until the hot weather returns as it is all brought on by the cold. Meantime it is very awkward and a bit of a 'noosance' and if I go back on the gun it will not be long before I get deaf in both ears. However, the 'doctor man' may do something yet.

I haven't heard from anyone since I last wrote to you. I would like to get some news from Billy as to how things are going along. I expect any day to hear. I wonder if you have heard from Cousin Bess yet, and whether the photos have arrived. I haven't seen them myself yet, and am very interested to see what I looked like. She is sending you one of each positions and one each for the rest of the family.

The *Brisbane* has left Sydney I saw by the paper and I wonder what the Child is going to do. Perhaps some letters will come along soon and tell me of the various arrangements.

Please give Gran and Aunts Mog and Phoebus my love and also the Child. I hope my p.c. arrived safely last week and all my letters are reaching you in due course. With heaps of love and kisses to Matee boos, the spell in hospital has been a great relief and enables me to pick up a bit, from

Your ever loving son,

TOOTS.

Have written to Hal since he arrived in France, but don't know if he got my letter. Have not heard from him yet.

Hotel Windsor, Victoria Street, London S.W., 4 Mar 1917

Dearest Mum

Your letter of Jan 14th to hand about 2 days ago. It was a lovely long one and I much enjoyed getting it. You had just heard by letter from Mrs. Little of the young son, and, of course, were very keen to hear more of your grandson. You will have heard both from Mona and myself all about him by this time.

He is doing famously and Mona tells me he is becoming more and more like me; he has one of my traits particularly well-marked, and that is impatience! However, I shall be able to see him for myself shortly now, as you will see by the address of this letter that I have at last managed to get over to England.

I am very excited I can tell you. He was to have had his photograph taken last week, if he has and it is anything worth looking at I shall send you one as soon as they are ready as I know you will be keen to see what your new relation looks like.

I was very lucky to get leave. I had to put in for special leave, as ordinary leave has been closed permanently from March 1st. Only 2 officers per Division per week are being allowed leave now under special circumstances. I had a very tedious journey down from Bethune in France, the rail head to Boulogne. Travelled in a cattle truck on an empty supply train. It was bitterly cold, and the journey took me 9 hours - left at 4.15 in the afternoon and reached Boulogne at ¼ past 1 in the morning, however, one doesn't mind that at all.

Pleased to hear, Mum, that you have let "Ermo" again. I do hope the tenants pay up regularly and don't do you down as the vast majority of them seem to do. If you don't remain at Gladesville I suppose you wouldn't be able to return to the farm at Scheyville, now you have definitely resigned and had a send-off. I would have a try for it again, if I were you and you think it will suit you. You shouldn't have so much manual labour to do if you are the matron surely. Your job should be purely supervisory. You don't tell me much of Thea, what she is doing with herself, and if she is terribly depressed and moody at Cleon's departure.

I have just rung up Mona, and have asked her if she would care to come up for a night or two while I'm in London and see one or two of the theatres and then we could spend the rest of my leave (10 days) with Master Philip. She is to let me know in ½ an hour. The train fares are so terribly expensive now, they have all been increased for civilians, that it will cost her £3 I think, so it means a pretty big expense.

I had a post card from Steve a day or two ago, written from Étaples, quite near Boulogne, where he is at present in a base convalescent depot. His hearing has not recovered, and he thinks it possible he may be kept there for a few weeks yet. I expect he has a ruptured tympanum or ear drum, a common accident with gunners – it means loss of hearing for a few weeks usually and then the hearing recovers – tho' he may not be able to appreciate the finer sounds with that ear afterwards.

Things were very quiet in the line when I left, nothing much doing. Great preparations are being made for the offensive in a few weeks' time when the ground gets harder, I understand. The Germans are desperate now, and it will be a grim business before it is all finished. The casualties will be huge I am afraid.

Today was a beautiful sunny day with just a nip in the air. I do hope I shall get some nice weather for my leave.

Well, Mum, I must stop now - I shall be able to give you first hand details of Philip when next I write. Hope you are all well at home. Love to the Child, Aunts and Gran.

Yours in haste, NIGE

A big hug and a kiss.

Somewhere in France, 11 Mar 1917

My dearest Matee boos

Am still going strong, have not yet left for the line although I expect to get away sometime this week. Have had a fairly good spell in this camp which has been much appreciated. It has been a bit of a 'noosance' not getting any letters since I came away from the battery. I suppose they are held up somewhere and I shall get them in a couple of months' time, after I settle down in some new unit.

I haven't the faintest notion what battery or unit I shall go to, so at present I cannot tell you what my address will be. I think perhaps it would be best to send them to me to the following address:

No 3872, Cpl. S.P. Boulton. A.F.A. 1st Aust. Division C/o A.I.F. Headquarters, London.

I ought to be posted to some unit by the time I write next when I shall let you know where I am.

I had a letter from Cousin Bess a few days ago saying you had written and were again at Coolah. I expect you miss the life at the farm. She also told me she was sending off the photos by this week's mail which I hope you will like. The ones she sent me have disappeared in the usual way, for the time being only I hope.

Billy also wrote saying he had not yet been able to get over to England on leave. He will have a hard job now that the fine weather is coming on, but I hope he will get it, and be able to see his son who I hear is growing up more and more now every day and beginning to take an interest in things round about.

We had a couple of falls of snow during the last week, but today (Sunday) is beautifully fine and warm, too warm in fact to last, and we shall probably have rain tomorrow. It is a great change to see the sun again and very pleasant.

Please give my love to Gran and Aunt Mog, hoping everything is going on well and that Tyrone is keeping its end up still. I shall not know what has been happening at home until I get a letter and I don't know how long that will be. Cousin Bess told me that Cleon[170] had left, but didn't know where to.

Heaps of love and kisses to you and the Child from

TOOTS.

P.S. We are restricted to 2 sheets of paper whilst in this camp, only one side to be written on. There is not much news in any case.

Base Camp, Somewhere in France, 17 Mar 1917

Dearest Matee

I have just received 2 letters from you dated 10th and 17th Dec, both sent on from the battery. I was very pleased to get them as you can imagine, as it has been some time since I heard. The last one came when I was with the battery about the middle of January.

There is nothing in the way of news to tell you in this letter as I am still in the same camp and only ordinary camp life is going on. I don't know when I shall be going up the line, it may be any day. Meantime the weather is getting better every day and nearer summer which is a great relief in itself. We don't have a bad time whilst we are here, get up at 6 and during the day do a little training and route marching occasionally.

We are sleeping under canvas which I think provided they are not overcrowded are as comfortable as anything. There are 10 in mine so we cannot do with any more. I rather refrain from telling you any experiences whilst in the line as the censors are very strict and if there is anything in the way of military matter in it

---

170 Just before Christmas in 1916 Cleon sailed off from Sydney in the brand new *HMAS Brisbane* for the Mediterranean, but the ship was soon ordered back to the Indian Ocean to help hunt down several German raiders.

you wouldn't get the letter probably. I know the papers publish a lot of letters, some genuine and some not. After the landing at Gallipoli the stuff the papers put in as letters from the trenches kept the lads at Anzac amused for months. By the way, I suppose you know that it is the officers of your unit who censor letters.

And so you have left Scheyville and the farm. It is a great pity you could not accept the matronship, but I suppose you couldn't get away from Gladesville. I wonder if there is any chance of you getting it a little later on. Perhaps Gran might like to go and stay at Chatswood for a while. Am very glad you had such a good time there and you ought to go back and see them all whenever you get the chance of a few days holiday. They seemed to wish you to go and visit them occasionally.

I expect the whole family is once again assembled at Coolah. I wonder if the Child will be coming over here. She is apparently very keen on it by her last letter and wants you to come too. It sounds alright, but a bit of an undertaking. Does she know that Cleon has come over here?

I haven't heard from Hal for months and I wrote to his battalion but in a letter from Aunt Eleanor she tells me he has returned to England to do some chemical work in a munitions factory.[171] It is a good thing he got the job, as the infantry will get terribly chopped about this spring and summer, and it would have been a miracle if he came through it all.

And now goodbye Matee boos, give my best love to Gran, Aunt Mog and the Child, hoping you are all well and in good spurrits with heaps and heaps of love and kisses to Matee from

Your loving son, TOOTS.

During Steve's illness another reorganization of the Artillery saw batteries increased in size from 4 to 6 guns, to economise on the numbers of commanders needed. Thus the 21st FAB ceased to exist from 24 January 1917, with Steve's unit (the 22nd Battery) transferred a short distance from their regular wagon lines at Havernas to the wagon lines of the 1st FAB at Rainneville, north-east of Amiens. Around this time a formal photo was taken of the 22nd Battery, showing its size, but it's unlikely that Steve was present.

---

171 Hal resigned from the A.I.F. and worked in England in the Explosives Department of the Ministry of Munitions from early March, 1917.

22nd Battery, March 1917
Source AWM DAX1709A

On 29 March Corporal Boulton was posted to the 1st Battery of the 1st FAB and rejoined his old brigade mates, who had recently entered Bapaume north-east of Albert, after holding the line on the Somme through the bitterest of winters. Subsequently there was a long gap in Steve's letters.

Meanwhile, Nigel appeared to be based further north, in the Arras section of the front line, serving with the 1st Leicestershire Regiment, when he wrote his next few letters.

ADVANCED DRESSING STATION, SOMEWHERE IN FRANCE, 28 MAR 1917

Dearest Mother

Am back again in amongst it. Returned 4 days ago to the Ambulance after a most glorious holiday.

I found 2 letters from you, one from Aunt Mog, and 2 from Thea awaiting me on my arrival. A great treat. I shall answer Thea's and Aunt Mog's as soon as possible. I had rather a trying journey across and spent 2 days and nights en route. Leave having been closed there are no regular leave trains, and one has to do one's best to get what's going and it usually means several changes and waits.

The day after my arrival, Sunday, we were shelled pretty heavily by some 9.2's - heavy naval guns with armour piercing shells. Fritz dropped 30 or more into the town where we have our ambulance headquarters. There were a good number of civilian casualties, but strange to say no military ones, except 2 or 3 of a trivial character. We had 2 shells right thro' our hospital, one at each end. The 1st took 2 legs off and pulverized the 2 lower limbs of a poor old bearded chap. An old lady had her leg blown off below the knee, and a man had his taken off below the hip, he died almost immediately after he was dressed. The old lady and the other old chap are almost certain to die. There were lots of others, but of a less serious nature. They had collected round a woman who had been hit by a previous shell and who had been dressed, when the shell that hit the hospital landed right in the middle of them. Fortunately, we had evacuated all our patients before the second shell knocked out the other end of the hospital, the military part. I was only a few yards off when this shell struck, and it was distinctly disconcerting. Every window in the place was shattered. Owing to the fact of the shells being armour-piercing they travelled thro' the roof and walls of the building before exploding. In 2 or 3 cases they detonated in cellars - being high velocity there was no warning shriek, and the explosions occurred without notice. Very upsetting. The Huns frequently amuse themselves shelling towns on Sundays. This place altho' very close behind the line hadn't been shelled much before, and probably won't again for a bit.

I am now in charge of an advanced dressing station just behind the trenches. We have got it fixed up in the cellars of a brewery of which very little is left. The village we are in is nothing but a shambles. This is quite a comfy and roomy dressing station. I have only just taken over - last night from another F. Ambulance - so things are not quite ship shape yet but will be running smoothly in a day or two I hope. There is another M.O. here with me with some of his men. We are running it jointly, which is very unsatisfactory. He has only been out in the country a month, so is a regular greenhorn - quite a baby, but very willing to learn. I am supposed to be instructing him.

Nigel Boulton & Officers, France, c Feb 1917?

(Nigel Boulton is standing at left hand end of top row, Picture Courtesy Julia Woodhouse)

Your two letters were dated Dec 29th and Jan 18th. The mails seem to be very irregular and uncertain now. Took 2 months to arrive. So you think I have altered a great deal. The photograph is really supposed to be an excellent one by everyone who has seen it. A speaking likeness – I think the "mo" makes a great deal of difference - when I shave it off, I look like a parish priest! I tried it for a bit cleanshaven again, and everyone was woefully disappointed, so I grew it again.

I hope you get the photograph of Mona and Philip Hugh - it is excellent one of the young lad, very like him indeed, tho' not so good of Mona. He looks more like a 6 months old baby than 3½ which was his age when taken. I hope you will like his appearance. I took some snaps when I was over with the family, but it was rather difficult to get good ones owing to the bad light and having to take them indoors. However one or two are quite good and will give you an idea of him, his dad, his mother, etc.[172]

Nigel with Pip, March 1917
(Picture Courtesy Julia Woodhouse)

Well, dearest Mum, no more this time. I hope you are not being worn out with Gran and that some arrangement will be come to as to free you. Bestest love to Thea and your dear old self. Remember me to A. Mog and Gran. I will write to Thea and A. Mog as soon as possible.

A big hug and a kiss,

Yours always,

NIGE

The little chap who is called "Philip Hugh" was born on Novr 21st - 4 days before his Mother's birthday. Mona doesn't like the abbreviation "Phil" as she considers it a girl's name.[173]

---

172 The photo taken indoors of Nigel with his son has survived, bottom right.
173 The baby was known as Pip.

Advanced Dressing Station, Somewhere in France, 7 Apr 1917

Dearest Mum

Your letter of Feb 3rd came to hand yesterday, and very pleased I was to get it, also one from Thea.

I have just written to Aunt Mog, so I shan't be able to find very much to say I'm afraid - the weather here still continues cold and wet. It seems as if the winter will never end. How extraordinary it sounds to hear that the heat at home is almost unbearable. So Aunt Mog tells me in her letter.

Have not been up to the mark lately, another little go of malaria, I think, at any rate after 3 or 4 doses of quinine, I am much better again and feeling my old self again.

I am still up here at an Advanced Dressing Station, and in charge of it as I told you in my last letter. I rather like the job. Still it is very depressing at times as one is continually being confronted with ghastly, grim and heart rending spectacles. The poor fellows come in here straight from the trenches and are frightfully knocked about, some of them with awful wounds. I have 4 bearer posts in the trenches which I visit every other day; one of my bearers was hit in the abdomen this week when carrying a case down and died on being removed to the Casualty Clearing Station. I hope I shan't lose any more as it depresses the other chaps so much - it's always likely to happen tho'. A shell wounded about 8 just outside this place this week also, one chap will probably die, but I think the others will recover alright.

The little village where I am is nothing but a ragged heap of bricks and walls. One can see that there have been some very nice houses here once. This dressing station is fitted up in the cellars of a brewery, and very comfortable it is, and practically safe for all intents and purposes. One has to have lights night and day tho' as we are living in the dark pretty well.

No more just now, best love to all.

A kiss and a hug,

Yours ever,

NIGE

Allied spirits were lifted when the Americans finally and belatedly entered the war on 6 April, and the Canadians covered themselves with glory on 9-12 April at the Battle of Vimy Ridge (otherwise known as the Battle of Arras because the scene of the battle was just to the north-east of Arras). Australian troops were nearby: on 11 April the Australian 2nd Division fought the first Battle of Bullecourt south-east of Arras. Steve's unit was still located on the Somme but Nigel was working on this Arras section of the front line.

ADVANCED DRESSING STATION, SOMEWHERE IN FRANCE, 20 APR 1917

Dearest Mum

Your two letters of Feby 12th and 25th came to hand yesterday. It was a great treat getting them. I am still here where I was when I last wrote, things have been a bit busier, and Fritz has been much more active with his artillery this last week, and putting over a fair amount of stuff. Fortunately, however, he has done comparatively little damage. He certainly has the wind up to a certain extent, the offensive down south is getting on his nerves and he is wondering whether we are going to strike on this front or not. I think altho' his losses recently have been heavy though not crippling, his morale is depreciating.

The trenches here are in an appalling state at present, it is the very devil for my poor stretcher bearers. The slush which is over your knees is quite all-right, but it's the thick sticky mud, which is knee deep also, so that when you get your leg in it you can't pull your foot out. It almost wrenches your boots off. It takes them about an hour to do fifty yards. It's an extremely difficult sector to evacuate wounded from - these 12 and 13 stone men are back breaking. The bearers can't put the stretcher down to rest owing to the wet.

I have had one or two very narrow escapes this week, absolutely Providential. I was about 10 yards off a shell walking down the road not far from the dressing station, a 5.9 it was, which is a pretty hefty calibre and high explosive, when it landed. Ordinarily I should have been blown yards, but it proved to be a "dud" and didn't explode! There was an officer and another man nearer to it than me. They escaped unhurt too. It was a near shave. The next day a large fragment from a 5.9 again whizzed past my ear and shoulder and buried itself in the ground just by my foot. If it had hit me on the head, only a matter of inches, I should have been reported "killed in action". These squeaks tell on your nerves after a bit, but it is no good worrying. Everyone has them. I have been spared so far and the Almighty I trust will let me come thro' all right. I had a vivid dream the other night that I had been wounded by a machine gun, had 2 bullet wounds, one thro' the calf of the left leg and one thro' the foot. I was very pleased indeed, as it meant being sent home to England for 2 or 3 months, and seeing Cherry[174] and the boy again during my convalescence. However, I was awakened to the reality of things again by a voice at my elbow saying: "Bad stretcher case just in, sir, compound fracture of forearm, wound of head, leg, etc."

I had a Field Service P.C. from Steve 2 or 3 days ago. He had not had a letter from me for some time, so as I had addressed them to Étaples they evidently had not forwarded them. However, I had written to him at his new address with the 1st Battery, so that ought to reach him surely. The Australian Army postal arrangements are positively rotten. It takes 10 or 11 days for a letter from me to reach him, altho' we are in the same country. Damnable, isn't it? The British A.P.O. are quite good. The delay is on the Australian postal authorities' part.

We had a Bosch prisoner thro' here this morning. The poor devil had been very badly knocked about. He had a compound fracture of both bones of left leg, and a bullet thro' his left upper arm. He was suffering agonies, but he didn't murmur. He got caught on our barbed wire outside our trenches, and so one of our fellows put a bullet thro' him to stop him disentangling himself. He must have been out the major part of the night with his fracture. His leg was like a ram's horn, and the fracture a comminuted one. He may have to lose his leg. I gave him an anaesthetic, while the fellow working with me here straightened it for him and splinted it. He was well fed, but seemed to be anticipating torture on our part. Agreeably surprised and very grateful when he was so well treated.

I wish I was a combatant often, one feels it wouldn't be half so bad. I should love to have a go at them sometimes and feel extraordinarily bloodthirsty.

There was a vacancy for a M.O. in the 9th Norfolks, one of our Brigade, and I thought I was a dead cert for it, as Collins[175], or "Wilkie" as I have nicknamed him and it has stuck, is not too fond of me, and I felt sure he would send me to get rid of me, as I had applied for a heavy siege battery. However, much to my surprise he sent another fellow called Anderson[176], much to the latter's dislike instead. He had only been with the Ambulance 6 weeks. The Padre, a Baptist, but a thoroughly good chap and extraordinarily broadminded, quite a friend of mine, told Wilkie that Boulton thought he was sure to go, but Wilkie remarked that I was much too useful to lose! Still I daresay I shall have to go when another vacancy occurs, as it is my turn - I have been with the Ambulance longer than most.

---

174 Cherry was Nigel's pet name for Mona.
175 Identity unknown: several doctors named Collins served in R.A.M.C.
176 Identity unknown: several doctors named Anderson served in R.A.M.C.

The weather here is still very unsettled and wet. We had a nice sunny day yesterday, really a spring day. Oh! wasn't it a change and a treat! The winter over here has been hell - absolutely. Especially for the poor unfortunate infantry in the trenches. In spite of our successes I think the war will see this year out. Aren't some of the revelations from Germany sometimes appalling? The Offal Conservation Co. especially. Expect your papers are full of it - ours are.[177]

No more just now, dearest Mum. Love to all at home.

Mona is taking part in a small amateur theatrical display to amuse the Australian soldiers at Wareham Camp. Pity Thea couldn't get things like this to occupy her time and thoughts. Give her my best love.

With a big hug and kisses for your dear self

Always your loving, NIGE

I trust you get these letters of mine, they are quite long ones, aren't they. Am real proud of their length.

I have written to Mrs. Barton. Better late than never.

Filling in the long gap in Steve's letters, in the Spring of 1917 the 1st Division A.I.F. was involved in the fierce fighting of the Battle of Arras. Except for Canadian successes at Vimy Ridge, this was a costly and largely failed attempt to push the Germans back to the Hindenburg Line.

On 6 April the 1st FAB (except for one unspecified section) moved out of the Behencourt rest area north east of Amiens to a staging camp en route and next day moved into its position south-east of Arras and north-east of Bapaume where the Australian 1st Division was holding a lengthy (13,000 yard) section of the front line. A few miles to the north, at Bullecourt, Australia's 4th Division had no success in the attempted pushback in the First Battle of Bullecourt on 10-11 April.

The German infantry saw their opportunity to pounce without warning on 15 April, at Lagnicourt, and they broke through a section of the front line held by the Australian 1st Division. The Artillery had no rifles of their own to defend themselves and, while surviving unit war diaries do not specifically mention the 1st Battery in which Steve served, they did report that four 18 pounders of the 4th Battery and one Howitzer of the 102nd Battery were totally destroyed. The Germans were

---

177 The existence and role of the German Offal Utilisation Company was an anti-German propaganda horror story run by the British in 1917, alleging that the Germans were rendering down the bodies of dead soldiers for the fats needed in manufacturing essential war items.

quickly pushed back, but this incident dented the otherwise proud record of the Australian forces in France.

Steve's unit stayed in the line until 21 April, when the 1st FAB was withdrawn for a few days of rest in the wagon lines before going back into battle, but the Australian 1st Division was not used in the Second Battle of Bullecourt from 3-17 May.

The 1st FAB was relieved in the line by a British artillery unit on the night of 19/20 May and moved back to reach the Behencourt Camp by 22 May, for a rest spell before returning north to Flanders. The Australian infantry remained behind on the Somme.

The front line near Ypres had changed little in two years of fighting, with the German line heavily fortified and deeply defended. The British held the city of Ypres in a salient bulging into German lines, a salient overlooked by German artillery observers but offering few vantage points for the British. Accordingly, the latter's capture of Messines Ridge south of Ypres from 9-14 June was widely regarded as a British tactical and operational success.

Stephen was fortunate to miss all this action in Flanders in early June. He'd been selected for officer training in England and on 6 June 1917 he entered the Officer Cadet School for the Royal Field Artillery run at Lord's Cricket Ground in London. Artillery officers required certain character traits as well as an aptitude for highly technical training, of much longer duration than officer training in the infantry, and it kept him away from the front line for five months. However Nigel was based near or within the active Ypres battle zone.

In the Field, 17 Jun 1917

Dearest Mum

Haven't had a letter from you or Thea for an age, expect something has happened to the mails. However, I daresay a letter will turn up soon.

Am still in the trenches, and am not having such a bad time. The summer is well on us and the heat is quite considerable, didn't realize after such a bitterly cold winter it was possible to be so hot. It is very pleasant and I don't mind it a bit. There is a possibility of this division taking part in the next push wherever that is going to be. Everything however is quite unsettled yet.

Had rather a good 8 days in the front line trenches this time. We had raids and bombardments every night practically. Gave old Fritz quite an uncomfortable time of it. He got very "windy" towards the end, and only a few shots were necessary to make him quite jumpy. It is great getting the better of him, which we are undoubtedly doing now. He has always given us a rotten time of it up till quite recently, but oh! it is lovely to begin to feel that the boot is on the other leg. I don't mean to infer that the war is coming to an end yet; hope it won't in fact. Want it to go on for some time still, and I want us to give him "hell" more and more from now on, till he is absolutely thrashed to a jelly.

I think he is just starting to realize that he is now right up against it, and that his chances are starting to become desperate. We are taking all the offensives now, he is practically always defending, such a wonderful change.

Steve, you will be delighted to hear, is going for a commission and I don't think he should find any difficulty in getting it. His experience in the ranks will stand him in good stead. He is to be home in England for 5 months. I think he will be stationed mainly in London.

It will be a great comfort for you to know that he is well out of it for a bit at any rate, Mum. He ought to be able to see something of Mona and Pip now and then; also be able to look up the Albert Dixons[178], and run down to Harrow. I have given him the Dixon's address. Should like to know what John and Ken have done with themselves.

I didn't do any good at the horse show in the jumping. My gee got so terribly excited and upset at the crowd and the band that it was only after much difficulty I got him out into the ring. I got him over all his jumps, but he jumped badly, didn't judge them properly, was quite beside himself, so couldn't take off properly. However, I enjoyed myself greatly, and was supposed to have managed a very fractious horse with much skill – ahem!

Well, Mum, how are things with you? You will be in the midst of the winter when this reaches you, and will be very tired of the short days and the long nights. Wonder what the Child will do with herself during the long tedious winter months? Daresay things are getting very tight over your way now; they certainly are here. Shall be fairly up against it when peace breaks out.

Have not decided on a transfer to the A.I.F. yet. Doesn't seem to offer many advantages. Still the fare back to Australia is going to hurt very much. Steve saw Billy Metcalfe[179] in London the other day. He is a Major now. In fact the

---

178 Albert Dixon Snr was married to Nigel's mother's cousin Mary Frances Ashby, and they lived at Teddington near Richmond on the Thames. Their two boys John and Ken Dixon were second cousins of the Boulton brothers and when the latter were at school in England the four boys had been playmates.
179 Billy was evidently another nickname, for James Beverley Metcalfe. An old boy of The King's School, he died of wounds on Anzac Day, 1918. See the 'Beyond 1914' website of the University of Sydney for more details of him.

fellows of my year are all Majors or Lieut-Colonels by this time, while I shall remain a Captain till the end of the chapter. There are no regulars or territorials or special reserves in the Australian army, they are all volunteers and amateur soldiers, so promotion is extraordinary. Never mind, wonder whether I shall get a decoration or "a mention" before I finish, they are very scarce in this division, being a regular division, whereas in other non-regular divisions they are handed round broadcast. They are most unfairly distributed. No more now, dearest Mum. Trust all is well with you.

Bestest love, always yours, NIGE

Nigel's expressed hope that 'some arrangement will be come to as to free' his mother from the onerous care of his 82-yr-old grandmother was answered when she died suddenly at 'Coolah' on 2 May.[180] Nigel and Stephen did not hear the news for some time. The four month gap in Stephen's letters ended with his reference to her death.

R.F.A. Officer Cadet School, Lord's, 29 Jul 1917

My dearest Matee boos

Have just heard from Aunt Bee who I have just paid a visit that poor old Gran has passed away. She did not have any details, having just had a letter from Boja whom Aunt Mog cabled to. I haven't had a letter from you or anyone at home for some considerable time. Shall be glad to hear from you soon about it all. I hope she had a peaceful end without any pain. I wonder what has happened to the family now. Aunt Bee said something about Aunt Mog having gone to live in the next village, which I suppose would be her little Tyrone at Tennyson. You may have gone to Ermo with the Child and Coolah will probably have been done away with. I suppose you all miss Gran, as her cares and wants certainly occupied a tremendous lot of your time.

As I said I went down to see Aunt Bee at Hoddeston, and had a quiet and enjoyable day. I enclose you her letter, which I thought you might like to see. They were staying in a nice little lodge in a big property with good garden, with plenty of vegetables and fruit trees. I didn't remember anything about her or Dorothy.[181] I don't think I had ever seen Dorothy before, and I don't

---

180   SMH, Thur, 3 May 1917, p 6, col a
181   Dorothy was Aunty Bee's only child, and a daughter of Rev Alfred Havergal Shaw. She was his mother's much younger first cousin on the maternal side.

remember anything of Aunt Bee whom I had seen at Ascot once or twice. They were all very nice. Pa Shaw is of quiet disposition, being rather tame. Dorothy is a tall thin fine, not what you could call pretty, but a nice pleasant face. She looks a bit faded working indoors most of her time. She seems to be pretty capable being in charge of about a dozen girls at Vickers Aviation Works.

Next Tuesday we are having another exam and everyone is sitting round the room now swotting, and asking one another questions. My letter is, I am afraid, rather rambling in consequence, owing to the din going on. I shall have to do some, as soon as I have finished this.

On Friday next we are to get four days leave and holiday after finishing 2 months of our course. I have arranged with Mona to go down to Parkstone and stay there which I am looking forward to. This is a very strenuous time we get here and the four days spell will be very acceptable. Mona is looking forward to the time when Billy comes over again, sometime early in September.

It is a good job I am home in England now as I heard yesterday from a chap in my old battery that the scrap coming off in Flanders is pretty considerable. Also they had had a good number of casualties in the brigade, more than ever before. The Artillery is catching it now, owing to both sides having got all their guns massed against each other and doing counter-battery work, which means they are going for one another's guns and batteries preparatory to any advance of the infantry. So I am very lucky to be out of it all and I expect you are somewhat relieved. I hope Billy is out of it too. I haven't heard from him for a little while, I suppose he is being kept pretty busy.

Matee-boos I will not write any more, as there are numerous things I want to read up and revise, and after this afternoon, there won't be any time. It is Sunday afternoon now, and I have been to Church this morning. Give my best love to Aunt Mog, am very sorry about poor old Gran, but she had a pretty good spin right up to the end. I expect you have all settled down to a somewhat new life by the time this reaches you. Give my best love to the Child, I hope she gets good news of Cleon occasionally. I haven't heard anything of the *Brisbane* over here yet, but that doesn't say that she isn't over here all the same.

With heaps and heaps of love and kisses from your ever loving son

TOOTS.

Stephen refers below to the casualties of the Third Battle of Ypres, which commenced on 31 July and continued through to the end of autumn. As was still the norm for any major Allied offensive, a heavy artillery bombardment over some days preceded the launch of the first attack and the bombardment from 18 July made use of 3,000 guns which expended four and a quarter million shells. Steve was lucky to be out of it, safe in London.

The volunteers in the Australian artillery had received very little training in a very technical form of warfare. Steve refers to 'our Australian methods' in 'our ragtime army' being different from British artillery traditions (where his experience proves that many months of intensive training was given to artillery officers). Here's an English officer's description of an Australian Battery Commander serving on the Somme late in 1916: 'when an urgent order came through, his orders to the guns were: From the broken tree, side angle 90, and shoot like Hell, boys!'[182] The casualty rate for artillery officers was high, but by the end of the war the artillery guns and artillery tactics on all sides had become a very accurate and highly effective killing force.

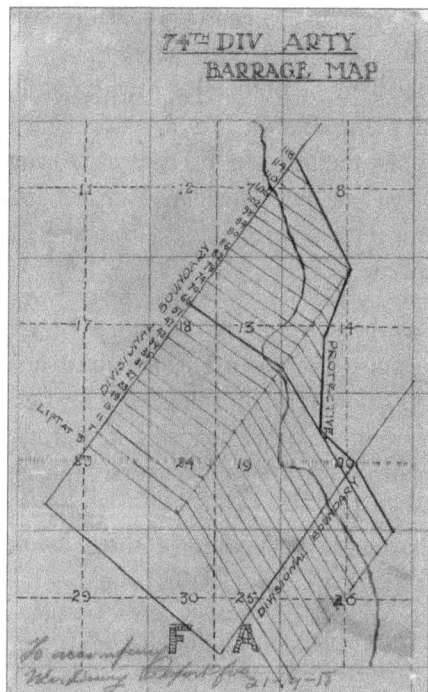

Creeping Barrage Map
Source AWM1 RCDIG1015670--2-

For example, the creeping barrage was perfected, whereby the artillery fired a wall of shrapnel at a set rate of progress ahead of their infantry advancing across No Man's Land. It was aimed at protecting the infantry from enemy fire by forcing the enemy to take cover. Timing and co-operation between infantry and artillery was crucial. Before and during the assault would come the counter-battery work, attempting to locate and destroy the enemy's artillery and other guns. It was very dangerous work for all concerned, as the supply of ammunition had been stepped up in 1916 at the expense of quality. Shells often exploded prematurely, did not fly accurately and failed to explode. The 1930 film 'All Quiet on the Western Front' contains unforgettable imagery of this form of warfare.

---

182 Tytler, *Field Guns in France*, p 131

R.F.A. Officer Cadet School, Lord's, 12 Aug 1917

My dearest Matee

I have successfully inamputated another exam which came off at the beginning of the month and so are now 2 months up with three more to go, provided I get through everything without a hitch. Things though are getting much more difficult as we go along and all our Australian methods have to be forgotten for the time being and replaced by the Tommy styles which seem such a waste of time as our ragtime army won't listen to all the English methods. However if I do miss a month or rather do a month extra it always means another month in England which at the present time is by far the best place to be in.

The Australian artillery have lost very heavily in the last Ypres battle and there three of my old officers and 2 other chaps who were in the old 22nd Battery and got commissions have all gone under. Also both doctors in the 1st and 2nd Brigades. The 1st Brigade doc. was Aspinall[183] – one of the Sydney family I expect although not Archie, but might have been Archie's son or some relation to him – was killed dressing wounded. He was a fine chap and greatly liked by us all. He got the Military Cross at Lagnicourt previously. He used to play footie with us when out of the line having a rest. So things are not too good over there just now.

Last week end from Friday night till Monday night we had leave and I took the opportunity of running down to Parkstone and staying with Mona and the son. I had a great time and enjoyed every bit of it, although it was only 3 days. Philip had grown tremendously since I last saw him in January and is going to be a strong and sturdy lad. He is an excellent boy and lies in his pram quite contentedly for most of the day, amusing himself with his dolls etc, doesn't mind being alone in the least and never squawks. He got used to his Uncle very soon and rather liked me amusing him. Mona took some photos of us. She will no doubt send you along some if they come out alright.[184] On Sunday we all went down to Sandbanks, a little place on the beach near Bournemouth and spent the day at a little hut on the beach. The nephew enjoyed it all I think and was able to get his fat legs well browned. Am sure Billy will be pleased when he sees him again, at the tremendous pace he is growing. I suppose he will

---

183 Captain William Robert Aspinall, son of Rev Arthur Ashworth Aspinall of Potts Pont, Sydney, killed in action at Ypres in Belgium on 20 July 1917. His older brothers Archibald John Aspinall, Arthur Martel Aspinall and Andrew Eric Aspinall also served as doctors in the Great War. See the 'Beyond 1914' website of the University of Sydney for more details.
184 None of the photos have survived.

soon begin to talk, or doesn't that come till later. He tries to imitate anyone humming now.

On Monday I was run in to playing tennis with a Mr. Manser; he and his wife are friends of Mona's, being brother to Capt. Courtney who lived with Billy and Mona in Egypt. I left Seafield soon after lunch and went over to Dean Park Tennis Club at Bournemouth. It wasn't so bad, but I wasn't playing at all well, being terribly out of form. I changed at the club and came straight on to London. Mona and Mrs. Little with the boy are off to Torquay tomorrow for a holiday and change. I don't know how long they are to be away. Billy is expected over from France again on Sept 8th or thereabouts. I wonder whether he will go on. Mona was saying he will if they give him his majority but not otherwise.

Cousin Bess and Aunt Julia are away at Eastbourne till about the 20th. I heard from Cousin Bess the other day who said they were enjoying the change and were feeling very well. Mona is due to go to them at the end of this month, but she wants to wait till Billy comes over, and go along together.

I wonder how you are all getting along now. The family is more or less split up now that Gran has gone. I suppose Aunt Mog is at Tyrone, and you I expect are out at Ermington with the Child. I haven't had any letters for a very long time now. I wonder where they are going; they should be forwarded on to me by this time. I have written to Aust. Base P.O. two or three times, but nothing much seems to happen. I am anxious to hear all about things that have happened the last few months. A good lot of mails have been lost lately too, having been torpedoed from submarines.

I think if you sent my letters C/- Mona it would almost be best as she always knows my whereabouts and could send them on to me and they would avoid going through the military authorities and so reach me much quicker.

And now Matee I will say good-bye this time, please give my best love to the Child and Aunt Mog, also Aunt Phoebe and Phil. I hope everyone is well and in good spurrits. Am afraid I have horribly neglected all my correspondence since coming here, as there is practically no time to write letters during the week at all. However you should have got one every week nearly. With heaps and heaps of love and kisses,

Your ever loving son

TOOTS.

R.F.A. Officer Cadet School, Lord's Cricket Ground, St. John's Wood N.W., 19 Aug 1917

Dearest Matee

Another week has gone and it is Sunday afternoon again and I have just finished a nice snooze after dinner, the only one I get during the week, which is therefore all the more enjoyable.

Last week I got & received a letter from you dated May 16th & addressed to A.G.B.D. in France. It was pretty old, but better than none at all. How glad you will be to get back to Ermo again & it ought to be very comfortable for the three of you. I can imagine you doing the 'outside man' and enjoying it all. I expect the garden will soon begin to look up again, and you will all be very happy there. It is about time you had a bit of a spell and you always did look forward to Ermo. Aunt Mog is going to Tyrone you say, which she will like, and it will not be so far to go to the wharf & much more convenient & comfortable for her & a maid I expect. It has turned out quite a good investment. I expect you will be as you are now when I arrive back, goodness knows when that will be though. This show is apparently going on for another year at the least from all appearances at present.

We are one week nearer our third exam, which we get every month, each one getting more difficult as we go on. It is a very strenuous life and I have lost a bit of flesh & weight since coming over here, but I expect I would have lost it just the same over the other side. I am about half way through the course now, provided I get through everything first go, and directly it is over no time is wasted before going out to France again. The usual thing is about 10 days leave in which time we have to get all our kit and equipment.

By the time I get out there the winter will be coming on again – it is sure to be pretty wet if not very cold. It is a miserable business to look forward to again. I don't know how I will get on, as I am still deaf in one ear (the left) and the cold weather usually makes it worse. It is very awkward even here and I am like Gran, 'you know I don't hear everything'. I don't want to see the quack about it yet as I may be turned down as unfit for a commission. However it will keep & I may do something if I get through this business.

Yesterday afternoon I went out to see Aunt Eleanor and Blanche. They had only just come back from a holiday at Oxford which they both enjoyed immensely. I thought Aunt Eleanor was not looking quite so well as previously, due perhaps to tiredness through travelling. She said she had been doing a lot since coming back in getting things straightened up after being away. Blanche appears to me to be almost useless – talks about getting indigestion if she does anything beyond dusting her room. The garden was looking very well & the fruit trees of which they have a few are thick with fruit. Plums, apples, pears, gooseberries & greengages. The pears are not ripe yet. Aunt Julia & Cousin Bess are still away at Eastbourne & come back tomorrow. They are all looking forward to seeing young Philip. Mona has put off going to them until Billy gets over which is the best I think, as it is an awful business travelling over here now, and she couldn't manage the luggage & the boy all by herself.

They are all down at Torquay now enjoying the sea breezes. I had a letter a couple of days ago telling me of their journey down there & that Philip was an excellent lad, all the time being very interested in everything and did not cry once. He is a wonderfully good child. She enclosed a little snapshot taken whilst I was down there and which I am sending you in case you don't get one, although Billy is sure to send you some. Anyway, mine might arrive first. He is rather enjoying being nursed by his uncle & seems quite happy.[185]

I expect I shall have to go out to Harrow to see Aunt Julia & Cousin Bess when they return but may wait until Billy & Mona go there & so make a sort of family party of it. It is rather an ordeal doing the job on your own.

Please give my best love to Aunt Mog, I hope she is quite settled & happy in Tyrone. And also the Child, it is ages since I heard from her, but I suppose there are some letters over here somewhere & there is very little time for me to write. I wonder if she knows where Cleon is yet!

And now with heaps & heaps of love & kisses to Mateeboos, hoping this letter doesn't go down as it has the little snap of Philip & myself which you will like to see. I wouldn't over do the outside man, not if I were you.

From your ever loving son,

TOOTS

How do you like the swanky paper & envelope?

---

185 The photo of Stephen with baby Pip has not survived, but Mona did send a photo of Nigel with his son, see page 297.

In the Field, 20 Aug 1917

Dearest Mum

Have not had another letter from you since I last wrote and don't suppose I shall for some time again.

I am lucky now if I hear from you every 6 weeks. It is pretty hard that the mails are so infrequent and uncertain.

I wonder if you get all my letters, or whether you are as destitute of news from Steve and me. Only the P. & O. boats go thro' the Mediterranean these days, so I suppose the majority of our letters go via the Cape.

Well, Mum, everything is well with me. We are still out at rest, but shortly expect to go into a "show" somewhere or other. We have all immensely enjoyed the rest from the line and have greatly benefitted by it.

My contract expires early next month, Sept 8th is the exact date. I have refused to renew my contract, so will be sent home in about a fortnight's time. The A.D.M.S. of the division wanted my reasons in writing for my refusal to renew, so I just stated that I was anxious to transfer to the Australian Medical Corps. I don't suppose I shall be able to do it, but I shall try by personally applying. There are no real advantages as far as I can see, as I shall have to start off scratch again, but I shall have my fare paid home again, which is a great thing. Also there are better chances of promotion, if this war is going to drag on for a year or so. Anyhow I shall see what the R.A.M.C. have to offer (by the way I shall miss my leave if I transfer) and they may perhaps find my fare back to Australia which is not an unreasonable request, if I sign on for another year. I shall tell you all about my interviews when I write next perhaps, or the letters afterwards more probably.

Mona is now down at Torquay, and having beautiful weather when she wrote. She wants me to go down there too when I go over and I hope to, as I should love to see Devon. Mona says she can't possibly manage the journey to Harrow alone, as she had a devil of a time travelling from Parkstone to Torquay with 4 changes. So we shall probably go up to Harrow together at the end of my leave, and I may stay a day or two with Cousin Bess before I go down, as I have one or two things to fix up in London and I have the War Office people to deal with too.

Steve went down to see Mona and the boy before she left for Devon. He was there for 3 days, and greatly enjoyed himself he told me in his letter. The lad was extremely good and loves being nursed by anybody, even his uncle. He had grown tremendously since Steve saw him last and is quite a big chap now.

Smiles and gooes all day long. I am very anxious to see him and his mother. Wish you could too, Mum. If only this war would soon come to an end.

What are you doing with yourself now? I expect you are living at Ermington now for good. Is Thea with you too? No more just now, dearest Mum. Do hope my letters reach you. Will write again soon and tell you how I get on with the War Office.

Bestest love to you and Thea. With a big hug and a kiss,
Ever your NIGE

Had a very nice letter from Cousin Bess. I won't miss visiting them this time I am over. Another kiss, NIGE

Undated Postcard from France

Dearest C, & P[186]

How do you like this group? It's a bit better than the other one, altho' from my point of view, nothing to rave about. All infantry officers except the motor machine gunner, myself & the staff captain, who belongs to our brigade. Will write tomorrow. Am in the line again. Had a v. good rest.

Best of love, yrs ever

NIGE

Nigel Boulton & Officers, France, c August 1917
(Nigel Boulton is in top row, second from right. Picture Courtesy Julia Woodhouse)

---

186 Nigel's pet name for his wife Mona was Cherry, and his son was Pip, hence the C & P. Card addressed to 'Seafield', Parkstone, Dorset.

R.F.A. Officer Cadet School, Lord's Cricket Ground, St. John's Wood N.W., 30 Aug 1917

My dearest Matee

I may have missed this mail as they are never advertised. Am 3 days late in writing this time as I was doing some severe swotting for another exam which came off yesterday and which I felt pretty hazy about. However, it is all over now, and I think I did pretty well getting a few questions which I did know. We do not know the results yet, but I am fairly confident that I did some good, which is a good thing in its way although it brings me one month nearer France and its winter months, which is not too pleasant a thing to look forward to.

We will know the results tomorrow and I shall let you know by my next letter how things went. If successful I shall be in my last month at Lord's provided I get through the next month. It is a very stiff month and the work is fairly crammed into you, so I may have to have two shots at it, if it is too much for me. After that month is over there is another 5 weeks to be put in at Larkhill Camp, which is down on Salisbury Plain and not nearly so pleasant as being up here. It is right in the centre of the big Military Camp and everything is beastly regimental and military. The work down there is terrific so I hear. The time over here at this School has gone like a flash. It is now nearly 3 months since I came over from France, and it seems only like yesterday.

After this course is over & I manage to get through I have some pretty expenditures. We don't get any £50 kit allowance in the A.I.F. but have to provide nearly all own stuff. £8 will be deducted for this uniform I have had made whilst here and which will be suitable for an officers uniform, but getting fairly worn by then. That will leave me £7 out of the £15 which we are credited with for kit and the rest I have to spar up for. I shall be getting about 15/- a day less deferred and allotment money which will help me along to make up any deficiencies that my necessaries for France will have cost.

Last Saturday I went out and called on Aunt Eleanor and Blanche.[187] I think I told you but may not have. They had just come back from a holiday at Oxford. Aunt Eleanor looked a bit tired and worn out I thought, but this may have been due to a lot of work she had been doing in the house after getting back. She said she had been very busy since they came back in getting everything straight again.

---

187 Aunt Eleanor by this stage was close to 80-yrs-old. Blanche Hitch was his mother's first cousin on her father's side. Blanche's mother died in 1860 when she was a newborn and she was raised by her maiden aunts Eleanor and Henrietta (who died in 1890). Eleanor and Blanche also lived at Harrow, a short walk from Kennet House.

Blanche seems to be almost no use at all in the house except to dust her room. She says she gets digestion if she tries sweeping. Cousin Bess and Aunt Julia were away at Eastbourne at the time, but have now since returned. Cousin Bess wrote to me a couple of days ago saying they had come back and asking me to go out and see them again. I shall run out as soon as I get a chance and see them.

Billy is due over here on the 7th of next month and is going to Harrow as soon as, or very soon after, arriving over from France. He is getting the job over before going down to Torquay to Mona and the boy. I don't know if they are going at some other time together as Mona was to have gone and taken Philip, but getting Philip and all the baggage along and over London was too much to expect, especially in these days of no taxis when you want them.

During the week I received the first letter from you for a very long while, which was very cheering. You wrote from Tyrone dated June 17th and addressed it C/o Mona which was quite a good idea. You had just received my cable, which no doubt gave you all a bit of a shock. However, I thought you would like to know quickly although I thought you would wonder what it was until it was opened.

I should think Aunt Mog would be very comfortable at Tyrone with all the good pictures and carpets on the floor. I hope the sarvint stays and helps things on in that way. You will enjoy your gardening at Ermo I expect, but I shouldn't go at it too strenuously and blow yourself out.

Please give my love to the Child, I should think you all will enjoy being at Ermo for a while altho' it will be very quiet, but you don't seem to mind that and there won't be many visitors calling. Also give my best love to Aunt Mog when next you go down to Tyrone. I hope she likes her little cottage.

Expect to run out to Harrow next Saturday afternoon and see them all at Kennet House. I may not be able to get out there when Billy arrives, so I had better get out when I can. This next month there won't be much time to do anything except swot.

And now good bye Matee boo with heaps and heaps of love and kisses, hoping you have sent all my letters to Mona from

Your ever loving son

TOOTS.

R.F.A. Officer Cadet School, Lord's, 15 Sep 1917

My dearest Matee

Received two letters from you this week forwarded on by Mona. They seem to come in fits and starts due no doubt to the irregular mail service. Was very surprised to hear that the *Brisbane* had arrived at Fremantle as I always had thought she was over here somewhere. Hope the Child arrived over there in time to see Cleon as it was a long trip to make for such a short time to see Cleon himself.[188]

Am glad to hear that Jean Herbert was with you, as you wouldn't be all on your lonesome whilst the Child was away. You must be very quiet in little Ermo, but no doubt that has its advantages. What a wonderful thing to have sold Concord. I think somehow it was wise as it was generally a source of worriting, what with repairs and cleanings up for new tenants and it wasn't profitable as it should have been. You didn't do so badly at £450 as it is war time and I don't suppose there is much sale for house property. If I remember rightly you gave about the same for it. I hope you get good solid shares which are safe and leave alone the "No bottom tin mines." I expect Uncle Frank[189] will put you wise to the best and surest things. Miss Business[190] seems to have done well for herself in the role.

Nothing much has happened during the week since I last wrote, excepting for the usual week's work. We are nearing our last exam at Lord's which is going to be a very solid one, and I feel a bit hazy on it. It comes off on Tuesday week; in the meantime I shall be swotting a good bit in any spare time and at night. This coming week is going to be a very busy one for me as I am to be Cadet Corporal i.e. in charge of the squad in which I am. Each Cadet takes it in turn for a week. It means a lot of extra duties and it has come at a bad time, just a week before the exam.

On Tuesday next I am going down to No 3 London General Hospital to see an ear specialist to see if he can do anything with it. Am afraid he won't be able to, but it is best to let him have a look at it anyway. If he gives me half a chance at having a little holiday I will make the most of it. Have heard he is a decent chap, so will keep my good ear open all the time.

I heard from Billy during the week. They are having a great time at Torquay and Billy is enjoying every bit of it. It was a good idea Mona being down there just

---

188 Thea travelled on one of the first trips of the transcontinental railway connecting Sydney and Perth, now known as the Indian-Pacific Railway, before the rails had bedded down.
189 Unfortunately, Uncle Frank's advice caused his mother to lose her money.
190 Apparently the family name for Jean Herbert

as he came over. It makes a great holiday and change for him. I am expecting 2 days holiday at the end of this month's course when I will try and get down to see them. It will be good being down there with Billy at home. I think he will be there, but am not quite sure when his month's leave is up.

We had our photo taken yesterday, the whole squad together in a group. Shall send you one along when they are done and you will be able to see what we are like. Colonials and all sorts are there. S Africans, Canadians, a Mexican, New Zealanders, Austns, Yankees and Englishmen all mixed up. Most of them are good chaps and we have plenty of fun when off parade.

Cadets, Royal Field Artillery School, London, Sep 1917
(Stephen Philip Boulton in middle row, second from right, marked with cross. Picture Courtesy Julia Woodhouse)

Was very sorry to hear about Tony Barton[191] going under. Mrs. Barton must feel it very much, losing both her sons. Will you convey my sincere sympathies when next you see her or perhaps the Child will as she is more likely to be about. I think I told you in my last letter that I had seen Jack Weedon[192] over here getting about on crutches. He was looking very fit and had put on a lot of weight in spite of his losing his leg. Jack Philips[193] wasn't looking very fit and hadn't changed much.

Please give my best love to Aunt Mog, am glad to hear she is being looked after and made comfortable by Hannah. Expects she likes Tyrone very much. And now with heaps of love and kisses to you and the Child, hoping you will get this letter safely and spite the submarines, from your loving son TOOTS.

---

191 This was Max Barton's brother Robert Anthony Barton, killed in Belgium on 9 June 1917.
192 Probably John Francis Warren Weedon, a 25-yr-old auctioneer of Sydney when he embarked in September 1915 as a Lieut with the 5th Infantry Brigade.
193 His identity and connection to Boulton family is unknown.

Stephen's postcard to his brother (now Captain N P Boulton RAMC), arranging to see Nigel at Seafield, Parkstone in Dorset, showed the impact of the relentlessly-pounding guns of the artillery. The postcard was in the form of a photo of Stephen and his fellow cadets at the Royal Field Artillery School in London.

ST JOHN'S WOOD, 26 SEP 1917

Dear Billy

Many thanks for yours received today. Will be very pleased to come down on Friday. There is a train that leaves Waterloo at 7 which I caught last time. I don't know of any other sooner, also cannot tell exactly at what time we will be finished. Saw the ear chap & he cannot do anything. One ear has gone to the clouds & I have got to look after the other one. Will bring down Mother's letter. Thea is over at Fremantle with Cleon. Best love to all from Billy.

Cpl Stephen Boulton & Capt Nigel Boulton, Sep 1917
(Picture Courtesy Sarah Dennis)

Cpl Stephen Boulton, Capt Nigel Boulton, Mona & Pip, Sep 1917
(Picture Courtesy Julia Woodhouse)

Durrington Camp, Salisbury Plain, 28 Oct 1917

My dear Auntie Bee,

Many thanks for your letter of 25th inst.

I have been down here for a month now and am just finishing off the course. We had our final exam yesterday morning and I think I will scrape through. We are shooting from today up till next Thursday which finishes everything. It is a pity in one way that it has all come to an end, as it is ever so much pleasanter in England now that the winter has arrived. If I get through, expect to be off to France again in about a fortnight.

Larkhill & Durrington Camp Buildings
Picture Courtesy Julia Woodhouse

We have been very comfortable down here in rooms with a fire every night which we shall miss very much I am afraid.

I have been down to Parkstone twice since I saw you. The last time Nigel was at home & so we had quite a family gathering. He went back about 3 weeks ago after having a month's leave.

Am glad to hear Dorothy came through the raids all right, they must be rather upsetting at times for the London people. We all came down here just after they started.

Am afraid Trowbridge will be a bit out of my direction after I go from here, as there will be a tremendous lot of kit & stuff to get before I go out again, but if ever I get over again I should like to come and see you all again.

With kindest regards to you all

Yours very affectly

Stephen
S P Boulton

Durrington Camp, Salisbury Plain, 30 Oct 1917

Dearest Matee boos

Have finished all our exams and am nearly at the end of the course, provided I am through. We don't know the results yet, but should do so tomorrow or the next day. We are doing our shooting now, but I don't think it has much bearing on the result. I have an idea that I will get through as I think I did fairly well in the exams, but there is no telling as to what is going to happen.

They don't often keep the Colonials back for another month, I only wish I could have a bit more here, as it is not at all bad and tons better than France. If I am through I will be leaving here on Friday morning for London to hand in some clothes to the Cadet School after which shall have to report to A.I.F. Head Qrs. There will be about 10 or 12 Australians going along all at the same time, and I don't suppose we will all get an extra bit of leave which we are after. Anyway we will have a good try. There will be all the kit and clothes to buy then to take out with me for the winter.

Am going to have a little holiday somewhere with another Australian chap. We haven't decided where to go quite, it may be Scotland or Devon. We get a ½ fare railway warrant to anywhere we like so it won't cost so very much and it is no good staying in London all the time. Shall spend a few days at Harrow after I come back or perhaps before I go while I am getting my gear.

I believe Mona and Mrs. Little are going to stay at Kennet House early next month which is the postponed visit that was put off on account of the air raids.[194]

You will get this letter about Xmas time I expect so I will wish Matee boos a very happy Xmas and also the Child in case she is home again. I hope you will have a nice little drop of stuff to warm you up a bit, and that 1918 will be a prosperous one for you all and that we will come back again before it is out.

I expect I will be out in France for this Xmas which will make my third away from home.

It is very late now Matee and there is nothing much more to tell you that has happened during the week so with heaps and heaps of love and kisses to Matee boos and all the family from

Your loving son,

TOOTS.

---

194 These were nothing new – they'd started at Dover in 1914.

P.S. I haven't heard from Billy lately, but Mona says he is living in a tent somewhere near the base, I think in a convalescent camp which must be pretty dull.

Stephen was successful in his exams and entered the officers' ranks as a 2nd Lieutenant on 3 Nov 1917. Although his and Nigel's letters no longer mention the Middle East, it should not be forgotten that the war continued there. On 31 October 1917, the Australian Light Horse rode into history at Beersheba, on the northern edge of the Sinai Desert, in the continuing struggle against the Turks. It was the last and probably the greatest cavalry charge in history. The Australian Light Horse played a significant role in the ongoing desert campaign in Palestine and Syria and the surrender on 1 October 1918 of the glittering prize of Damascus to the Commander of the Australian 10th Light Horse Regiment, ahead of the entry of Lawrence of Arabia and King Feisal's troops. The Ottoman Empire had been defeated.

In Europe, the next phase of the Third Battle of Ypres was about to get underway. Even more heavy artillery had been sent to Flanders from the armies further south. Compared with the battles in August 1917, much more emphasis was placed on the use of heavy and medium artillery, and aircraft for observation. The weather in late September helped too. The Battle of the Menin Road Ridge, the Battle of Polygon Wood and the Battle of Broodseinde were great successes and showed that German defences could no longer stop well-prepared attacks made in fine and clear weather. Australian forces played their part in all of these battles.

Then the weather turned bad. Frequent periods of rain and the destruction by artillery bombardments of the Flanders' lowlands drainage systems created waterlogged conditions. Mud made all movement difficult and limited the ongoing frontline use of artillery. Rain and mist made for poor visibility. Nevertheless the offensives continued in the hope of draining German manpower through attrition. The Battle of Poelcappelle on 9 October led to many casualties on both sides without much change in overall ground held. The First Battle of Passchendaele on 12 October was fought by exhausted troops and saw huge casualties, especially for the New Zealand troops. Army commanders agreed that attacks would stop until the weather improved and road access could be extended. Action by the French Army further south was successful but came too late to help with the Flanders campaign. Canadian troops relieved the ANZAC forces and were successful in the Second Battle of Passchendaele, capturing the village and the high ground north of the village and bringing an end to the overall campaign.

The Allies' grand plan of sweeping through to the German submarine bases on the Belgian coast failed. The front was pushed back by only a mile or so, without any breakthrough being achieved, while losses estimated at 310,000 for the British Army forces exceeded the German losses. Steve was lucky to be away from the front during the entirety of this Third Battle of Ypres.

BEDFORD HOTEL, LONDON, 13 NOV 1917

My dearest Matee boos

This is my last day in London and am packing up all my kit. I had to report to Head Qrs at 10 o'clock this morning which I did do for instructions and I go down to one of our camps at Salisbury Plain tonight and proceed overseas which means France on the 16th. So that gives me 3 days down there. There are a whole lot of us budding Officers going which makes it a bit better.

I spent 3 days at Harrow and had quite a good time. Very quiet and all that sort of thing and they were all very kind. You had better speak in glowing terms of my visit when you write to Cousin Bess. Aunt Julia gave me £3 to buy a valise[195] with and Cousin Bess told me to get a fleece lining for my trench coat which I did. The money £2.15.0 hasn't come to light yet, but I expect it will later on.

Cousin Kate[196] who was staying there at the same time presented me with another £1 to get a cardigan which I got at Selfridges. Have got most of everything I require now. Whilst at Harrow I had my photograph taken again which you will get in time.[197] Was done in about 4 different positions, one full size showing all my uniform excepting my cap and the others only head and shoulders and a small size. Cousin Bess will

Cousin Kate (Kate Mansfield) at her home 'The Warren', c 1915
(Picture Courtesy Julia Woodhouse)

be sending you out yours. She thought you would like the big ones. Also had 2 teeth stopped whilst I was there, by a Harrow dentist who seemed pretty good, so I was pretty busy all the time I was there.

---

195 A Wolsley Valise – see picture on page 32
196 Bessie Charles' younger sister Katharine Rachel Charles, married to the Hon. Henry William Mansfield.
197 See pictures on page 348 and page 349

Mona was to have been there at the same time which would have made it better for the two of us, but she couldn't get up on account of young Philip getting a cold. She is going up on the 15th as she previously arranged. Am sure they will all like the lad, who is growing up and developing quickly.

I had to leave Harrow and rush down to Parkstone to see them all down there before going out. I didn't have much time having rather depended on seeing Mona up at Harrow. Got down on Saturday afternoon and left again on Sunday night as I still had a few things to get in London on the Monday.

They were all looking very well and young Philip had quite recovered from anything he had had. He is a fine little chap and I wish you could see him. He looks very well in a pair of woollen breeches he has got and every inch a boy. He is already very talkative and doesn't miss much. He will be walking the next time I see him and will probably come running down to the door to meet me. Whilst he will be at Harrow he will have his birthday which ought to be good for him. Mona is starting a bank account for him to which we have all subscribed as our birthday presents. It is not a bad idea starting early and better than giving him toys etc which he has enough of. He gets all the amusement he wants out of Teddy Bear and a little rubber cat that squeaks.

I shall most likely be crossing over from Southampton to Le Havre so that I shall not be seeing anything of Billy on the way. Haven't any idea of where I am going or to what unit. Shall most likely be on the move for some little time before I get settled anywhere, so it will be best for you to always send my letters to Mona who will send them on. Whilst I was down there I got 2 from you dated about the 19th Sept which is not so bad. I shall let her know as soon as I get a permanent address.

Yesterday I went down to Head Qrs and made an additional allotment of 4/6 a day which now makes it 7/6 a day from the 16th of Novr. I wish you would find out if the money is being paid into my account alright and make sure the new amount is being credited. The account where the allotment gives payment is at the Savings Bank Dept. of the Commonwealth I believe. If the payments are made every fortnight they should be £5.5.0 each one at the new rate. It is advisable to make sure they are going in alright, as if time passes and it is not done it is difficult to get back any money afterwards.

Your friend Mr. Armitage would find out and let you know I should think. It wouldn't be a bad idea to let me know what is standing to my credit at these two places, the General Bank and Savings Bank Dept. Had pretty well forgotten all about them and they should be mounting up a bit. You have always got the use of them when you want to. You have the required authority.

And now Matee I will say adieu. Best love to the Child, Aunt Mog and Aunt Phoebe and Phil. Am glad the new maid at Tyrone is all that is required and that Aunt Mog likes the place so much.

I suppose the Child is back from the West by now, or is she still staying over there? Cousin Bess was much interested in the gale you had had. It is a good job that Ermo stood it so well.

Cousin Mary is away at Matlock so I haven't been able to see her before going out. I wrote and said good-bye. John is at Salonika or maybe Italy now.

And now with heaps of love and kisses to Matee, will let you know as I go along what is happening, from

Your loving son,

TOOTS.

£186.10.9 allots. 3/- per diem to Dec. 27. No change to that date.

Steve left England via Southampton for France on 16 November and was recorded at the Australian General Base Depot at Étaples next day. He was heading into the wettest winter in the northern France for 30 years. His mention of the vacancies in the batteries was his only concession to the impact of the heavy fighting of the last few months and the huge number of casualties.

Somewhere in France, 27 Nov 1917

My dearest Matee

Have arrived at my unit where I expect to be temporarily. Have been here now 3 days and am almost settled down. Am at the 1st Div Ammunition Column A.F.A. and as I say only expect to be here temporarily before being sent up to a battery.

It is quite a good unit to kick off with and get broken in by. Had a pretty fair trip over from England & spent 3 days at the base before coming on here. It took another 3 days to come up the line and find this outfit. You will be pleased to know that we are at present out of the line, having come out a few days before I arrived and I hope it will be a good spell for the lads who have just had a pretty rough time of it.

I am lucky in starting off like this and already I am quite settled. Naturally I am appreciating to the fullest the extra comforts etc. compared with all former experienced. There are 2 other officers in the outfit, both sports, and we hit it off well together and are quite happy. One of the other chaps is a cadet officer like myself so we have many things in common. We are in a billet which is much better than I have been used to, but at the same time it is not the best. Still it is great living in a house instead of the barns with the straw or floor as a bed.

1 have got Billy's old sleeping bag which keeps me nice and warm, also I am not confined to 2 blankets which is also a great boon. Up to the present it has been remarkably mild even up till now, the end of November. Tonight it is a beautiful moonlight night and not a bit cold, but quite like summer. Fritz is taking full advantage of it too, and scattering his bombs about, but a good way away from us.

Things are very quiet in front of us. Two nights ago we entertained some Australian Sisters to dinner and gave them a good feed, all turned out by our cook who is an excellent man for the job. We ably assisted him by providing a few extras from neighbouring villages. We started off with soup, followed by fish bought and cooked to a tee. Then a chicken which we bought off Madame who owns the farm where we are billeted. Then came some tinned apricots and custard finishing up with nuts and fruit. Also 2 bottles of champagne. After dinner we had the gramophone going which we borrowed from a neighbouring unit nearby. From this you would hardly think there was a war on would you? The Sisters came from a Casualty Clearing Station some little distance away. The other 2 chaps drove them home in a French cart with a donk in the shafts. In this show where I am, all the animals except the Officers and N.C.O.'s mounts are mules.

Haven't decided on my horse yet. Am afraid it will not be anything flash as there is not much to choose from. Haven't got a batman or servant yet either. Just at present we are a bit short handed, so I haven't worried much but am carrying on with one of the other chap's batman doing for both of us. Where we are now there is very little for them to do except clean boots and make the beds.

I don't think they will keep me here long as there are vacancies in the batteries and I expect I will be sent on to one of them sooner or later. In the meantime keep on sending my letters to Mona who will forward them on. I have written to her and told her my new address and expect to get some letters sooner or later.

(A day later.)

Have got hold of a batman now, he is quite a novice at the game, but that doesn't matter as there is very little to do. He will probably like the job as it means he will have a better time than if he stayed in the lines with the donks. Also have picked up my nag. He is a very pretty chestnut and ought to turn out a good hack later on, but at present he is lame, having got one of his fore feet pricked by bad shoeing. Have got the vet on to it and he says he will be able to fix him for me.

We haven't got anything to do except the daily routine of work such as exercising the donks each morning, grooming and harness cleaning. Another young one-star artist like myself arrived today at the unit so it makes it easier for all of us. Expect to go for one or two rides of an afternoon now there is a chance of getting away. There is nothing very much to do in the evenings. We generally play cards for a while and censor letters, and up till now play with the gramophone, but that is going back tomorrow and we shall miss it. We don't go to bed till fairly late, generally about 11 and have a good lay out till 8 o'clock in the morning.

Fortunately for us our acting O.C. is very fond of his bed and never gets up till breakfast is being put on the table. Each morning one of the 3 other subs is supposed to be on the early morning parade at 7 o'clock but so far we haven't come at it. It is plenty time enough when we go back into the line. Notice this Officer's life entails a great deal more in the expense line. The mess runs away with all the brass especially when we all have large appetites.

I haven't had any letters at all since arriving here and cannot expect any for about another 10 days I suppose. Am expecting to hear from Cousin Bess as to how the new lot of photos came out. She is sending yours along; I hope they will be good. Mona should also have a few to send on to me as soon as she gets my address, but it seems to take a long while for letters to go through military post offices.

I hope Billy is comfortable. He will appreciate this little spell of fine weather we have been having, it is wonderful weather for the end of November. I told you about my new increased allotment. Don't forget to find out as to whether it is being paid in alright.

The vote for conscription is to come off here amongst us all soon. Big proclamations are being distributed and posted up amongst all the Austn. units. I think more will vote "yes" this time than last; there will be heaps who will still vote "no". I think everyone would like to see the strikers pushed off over here and as there are a lot of Sydney mails with the strike pictures over here it will help matters on a bit for conscription.[198]

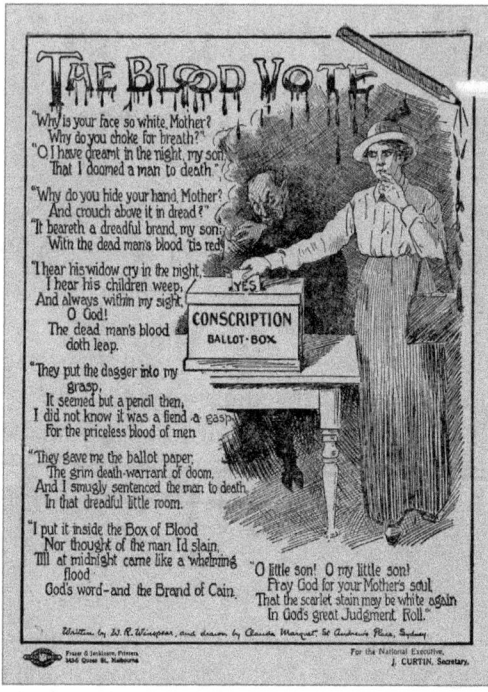

Source AWM RC00337

How is the Child getting on? I wonder if she has returned to her "mee-maw" yet. Please give her my love, I expect she sees all my letters to you so I don't write to both. Give my best love to Aunt Mog at Tyrone. You will all be living in your separate ovens now I suppose. I wish some of the sun could be transferred over here and dry up the ground. Although it hasn't rained for nearly a week the mud doesn't seem to get any better or ever dry up. The moisture seems to ooze up from the ground always.

And now with heaps and heaps of love, hugs and kisses to Matee boos, hoping she will keep up her spurrits and that she enjoyed her drop of stuff at Xmas time, from

Your loving son

TOOTS.

Stephen rejoined the 2nd FAB, in the 6th Battery, between 1 & 8 December. This Brigade was largely formed of men from Victoria, where Steve was born and spent the first five years of his life. No matter that he'd spent some years with the 1st FAB from NSW: as far as the Army was concerned, he was a Victorian. He fitted right in. As a new officer, his training was not quite complete and almost immediately he found himself at another course, near Calais.

---

198 Australian Prime Minister Hughes' second attempt to introduce conscription, at a referendum in December 1917, was lost by an even greater margin than his first attempt. The campaign was categorized by opponents as 'The Blood Vote' and featured a powerful poster.

Somewhere in France, 18 Dec 1917

My dearest Matee

Another little note to let you know that I have been sent away from the battery for 10 days to attend a Veterinary Course of Instruction at a big Vet. Hospital in a town some little way back behind the line. It is quite a holiday for us. There are 2 other officers here with me on the same job. They are out of the Infantry and look after the transport department for the different battalions. We are all billeted in a house in the town fairly close to the hospital.

There is not room for us to live with the officers belonging to the hospital and so we are billeted out. Personally we much prefer it as being with a large mob of strange Tommy officers. It is a pretty expensive job though, costing us 12 francs a day for 3 meals and this comes out of our own pocket. I think we will most likely get a ration allowance which amounts to about 4 francs per day so we will be a bit out of pocket. However that doesn't matter much. We are getting a nice little spell out of it.

The work we do only consists of a lecture at 9 o'clock for an hour and a half and then round the wards with some of the vets and watch them treat some of the horses. Strictly speaking it is rather a waste of time as when up the line each unit carries a veterinary man from the Vet Corps who is in charge of all the horses and no one is allowed to touch them but him.

It is a great hospital and very interesting seeing some of the operations. The horses must feel pleased when they arrive at a place like this after being in the line. They try and make them as comfortable as they can and they seem to have plenty of hay and stuff to chew, at all times.

After dinner we go down again and look round for a bit which is all we do. We are very comfortable in our billet and have a nice fire to sit alongside in between times. There is nothing to do after tea, as all the lights are put out in the town as it has suffered pretty considerably in the past by air raids and bombs. The people have all got the wind up and nearly everyone sleeps in their cellars now.

Last night the Gothes passed over but must have been bound for another town as they didn't stop over us, but went on. My 10 days will be up on the 24th, a day before Xmas, but I shall stay on here for Xmas Day and get something solid if not very tasty into my little Tummick. It will be better than travelling, and it doesn't make much difference when I get back. The battery was to have gone into the line about 2 days after I came away, but am not certain as to whether they went in.

I heard down here that they didn't, but were to stay out for a bit longer. They may still be out when I get back. It is going to be a very quiet spot where we are going in to, so I hope there won't be much doing for some considerable time. It is I believe to be our winter quarters so we ought to be as comfortable as can be expected.

Just before I came away I heard from Mona, who also sent on my mail which was quite good. There were six letters from you dated Sept and Oct telling me all the news. Am glad to hear you are getting some of my letters and that they are not all going down to the bottom. You want to know how to address me now. Just plain Lieut. S.P.B. 6th Battery A.F.A. A.I.F. France, but as I seem to get your letters more regularly although they take a little longer through Mona, I think it best to keep on sending them to her. It is a good idea keeping them apart from all the military letters as a lot must go astray in such quantities that come along.

It must be pretty lonely for you at Ermo just now with the Child still away and Jean Herbert gone. Miss Business I can quite imagine being a bit of a trial, but it is good to be able to get a cup of tea in bed occasionally and let her do some of the cooking. You seem to be always wiring in at the garden, but it is a big job doing it all on your own. Am glad to hear your pear trees are looking so well covered with their blossom. I wonder if they are old enough to have any pears or are they quite young ones you have put in. I think I remember some trees which had a big crop on down at the bottom of the garden. Eggs at 9d a dozen are cheap - over here now they are 1 franc each for the best fresh eggs, which is about tenpence, and all the little farms are trying to make as much as they can. You see the old Madames come out and count her fowls every morning to see that none have been pinched in the night.

Expect Tyrone will be making a good show of the garden with all the new soil and manure. Am glad Aunt Mog is so delighted with it all. Have got a lot of letters to get off now for Xmas time, so will knock off now with heaps of love to Aunt Mog and all the family. Do you see anything of Aunt Phoebe or Phil now?

With heaps of love and kisses to the Child and yourself hoping you will keep up your spurrits for a wee while yet, from

Your loving son TOOTS.

Have written a small note to the Child this mail.

Somewhere in France, 24 Dec 1917

My dearest Matee

This is Xmas eve once again and I wonder how many more I shall spend away. Am still away from my unit which is a bit of good luck as they have gone into the line since I left them.

So I am going to spend my Xmas in a French town in a billet or French house. There will be nothing in the way of big Xmas dinner, but I will be warm and get three good meals, which I might not be getting anywhere else.

The Veterinary course which I have been attending is finished. We finished up today so that tomorrow morning I will be able to have a good lay out with breakfast in bed if I want it brought up by my batman. I won't get any letters till I get back to the battery, where there ought to be some waiting for me sent on by Mona, and I expect Cousin Bess has written. Xmas however comes and goes much the same as any other day. The Xmas we are all looking forward to is the first one we get at home again, where we shall have to have a real bust up.

I went out and had a very nice dinner a few nights ago with the Officers of one of the Hospitals a few miles from here. An English Major invited three of us out (all Australians). He had previously met a lot of the lads at Malta when they were sent there from the landing at Gallipoli and thought a good deal of them. He had been out in China before the war and is now running the Chinese hospital where all the Chows[199] go. He speaks Chinese well and is probably about the only one who does here. The poor sick Chows worship the ground he walks on. There are a lot of cases of pneumonia amongst them. They are only used as Labour Corps here, making railways and unloading trains full of stores, timber etc. Anyway it was a very nice dinner with good wines and 5 courses. Of course they are a long way back and so can get anything they want. Not a bad sort of war for them eh?

As I said before I am putting in the day tomorrow here and the next morning I am going to push off for the battery once again. They have gone into the line since I came away, which saved me the journey in with them which is always a good thing to miss. You get deadly cold sitting on a horse most of the day going along the road, and more often than not it is usually raining and generally miserable. I think it is a quiet spot where we have gone this time so it won't be so bad.

---

199 Members of the Chinese Labour Corps, tens of thousands of men recruited by the British for manual labour to free up the front-line troops. The French also employed Chinese labourers.

I see by today's paper that Australia is voting "No" pretty solidly.[200] The paper says that you all expect an early ending to the war and that the men who are enlisting voluntarily will be enough to finish it. Doesn't look like ending when you see it over here. I wonder what is going to be done now by the Government.

I had a letter from Billy just before I came away. He seems to be getting along more comfortably now and is running whist drives for the men in his camp. I suppose you saw about Frizell's death in the paper.[201] I heard he was wounded and his wounds turned to blood poisoning.

And now Matee it is bed time. I haven't written very much as I only wrote a few days ago and nothing exciting is happening here thank goodness. Please give my best love to Aunt Mog, Aunt Phoebe and Phil, also the Child if she has arrived back from the West. I wonder if my latest lot of photos have arrived yet and what you think of them. Am off to my bed now and it is a good one too. A big French one with soft mattress and on which I put my sleeping bag and blankets and on the top of that goes an old eiderdown. It is pretty cold now at nights as you can easily imagine.

With heaps and heaps of love and kisses to my Matee Boos, from

Your loving son TOOTS.

According to later correspondence, Nigel moved to the No 10 Convalescent Depot at Écault around the end of September, but his letters for the last 4 months of 1917 have not survived. Écault was near the coast, just to the south of Boulogne. Convalescent depots or camps accommodated men who'd been discharged from hospital but were not yet fit enough for duty.

No 10 Convalescent Depot, B.E.F. France, 28 Dec 1917

Dearest Mother

As you see by the date above, Xmas is over, tho' there are still 3 days left of this year. I wonder what 1918 will hold in store for us all. 1917 has seen a lot of

---

200 He refers to the second referendum attempting to introduce conscription.
201 Major Thomas James Frizell, at university with Nigel Boulton, was wounded on 10 October and died in France on 2 December 1917. His brother Cpl Fredric George Frizell was there at his death and attended the funeral. For more details, see the 'Beyond 1914' website of the University of Sydney.

wonderful things happen, but nothing very vital that has made the end of the war seem very much closer. Still I think the worst of the war will be over this coming year, altho' it is going to be a fearful one, I'm afraid. The casualties will be very heavy, but I trust the Yankees will pay their share of the toll.

Well, Mum, we have had a very enjoyable little Xmas here. Real Xmas weather. The ground and country round is covered with a thick white mantle of snow – everything looks very pretty. The snow is still upon the ground and the thaw hasn't set in yet. It will be awfully sloppy when it does. I had my first go at tobogganing yesterday, and it was quite good fun. Also had a pretty strenuous snowball fight with the men. It doesn't sound very much like war, does it? However, we try and have as good a time as possible, as we all realize that we shall be returning to the line again sooner or later.

I gave all the Australians in camp, about 200 of them, a Euchre party. The Australian Red Cross gave £10 for the amusement of the "Ossies" as they are all called over here now, and I thought a Euchre party the best thing, instead of squandering it on eatables. They asked anyone they liked and they immensely enjoyed it, I think. Gave a lot of prizes, and made it as jolly as possible for them. They all feel the cold very much and so do I, so I can sympathize with them. It is not quite so cold now, only 1 or 2 degrees of frost, but 3 or 4 days it was tremendously severe, 40 degrees below freezing. The edge of the sea froze and the beach was littered with ice, a sight I have never seen before.

I haven't heard from Steve lately; he addressed 2 of my letters wrongly, but he should have my right address by now. The last time I heard from him, he thought he possibly would spend it at a Veterinary Show where he was having a fortnight's course, but Mona told me in her last letter that he told her he was spending it in the line. I hope he enjoyed himself as much as possible under the circs. He is very much more comfortable now as an officer and gets lots of comforts.

What do you think of the referendum result? I expect you are pretty sick. But it is hopeless to think that with a secret ballot people are going to vote against their own personal comfort, etc. If England had had a referendum, compulsory service would never have gone through. The only way to deal with a measure of this kind is to pass it thro' Parliament. I suppose Hughes[202] will be coming over here next to try his hand in Imperial politics. He made a great hit over here last time he was over. I trust that slippery snake Holman[203] doesn't try to take Hughes' place. I am disfranchised, altho' I was born and bred in the country. Only those Australians who are in the Australian Imperial Forces are

---

202 William Morris Hughes (Billy Hughes) was the Australian Prime Minister
203 William Arthur Holman was Premier of NSW and a rival of Hughes in Labor Party circles.

granted a vote, provided they have been 6 months at some time or other in the Commonwealth.

I tried to transfer, but I was informed that I should have to return to Australia to do so, pay my own fare out, of course, and get no credit at all for previous service. These politicians absolutely nauseate me. The English parliamentarians are much the same. All for their own selfish ends pretty well.

Well Mum, I wonder what sort of a Xmas you had. You must get Thea to read this if you can't manage it. The pen is not much of a one; neither is the writing.

Best love,

Ever yours, NIGE

1918

By 5 Jan 1918, Steve had rejoined his Battery, which was operating 'in the line' in the Oosttaverne area south of Ypres. He was soon sent for yet more training, to Pigeon School for 3 days at the end of January, learning about the use of carrier pigeons by the artillery. Just after he was confirmed as a full Lieutenant on 3 Feb, the 2nd FAB was relieved 'in the line' and he was sent to the Corps Gas School for a week.

Somewhere in France, 20 Jan 1918

My dearest Matee

I received 2 letters from you a couple of days ago dated about 13th and 22nd Novr. It seems quite a good idea sending them to Mona as I am now getting them regularly. Also received the scarf made by Mrs Jones before I left which will come in very handy although I have another good & warm one I paid 7/6 for in England.

Am glad to hear that the Child has got back to you safe & sound after being away for such a long time. Am sorry I haven't got your letters with me just now. Am again scribbling this off from Infantry Hqrs where I am doing the usual Liaison job tonight and I have got half an hour to spare. Have had to borrow this paper from one of the infantry officers who is also writing some letters alongside me.

Everything is going on much the same as usual in this part of the line. Last night I was up all night excepting for a couple of hours sleep from 12 till 2. From then on the battery was firing till daylight at various intervals. This is always the customary thing with every battery. The war and especially the Artillery go strong at night, the idea being to prevent the Hun getting his rations & stores up. We keep going on all his roads & tracks & trenches which he uses & which we are kept informed about from aerial photographs taken from the aeroplanes. At 7 o'clock I turned in till lunch time. After lunch I was busy round the battery most of the afternoon until I left for this place.

The day before I spent at our O.P. Usually this is a very cold job as I have said before, but am pleased to say lately the days have been fairly mild wih sun hanging about. We won't have much more winter to do soon & up till now it hasn't been a patch on last year when we were in the Somme. Of course we have had several falls of snow & everything frozen hard & stiff for a few days, but it has always been followed fairly quickly by a thaw and mild days. We will soon have to expect the rain now, which when it starts will probably last for a month or two, accompanied by gales which will not be very pleasant and will sure to be pretty chilly. We keep a fire going in our little dugout known as "the mess" all day & night which is very cheering & keeps us warm too.

I have taken over the job of mess secretary, which when I first came to the battery was pretty exhorbitant. We were then out of the line. It is not costing us nearly so much now, but of course we are only getting the ordinary plain food but plenty of it, with a few additions in the way of tinned stuff. I suppose when we get out it will increase in the way of expenses, when we will find it easier to get things & a greater variety. I am not too keen on the job as it is always a very thankless affair. I believe Billy was running his mess for a while at a loss to himself sometimes. The main thing is to get plenty to eat I reckon. At present the potato ration is very small & if it wasn't for us having a few acres of turnips, either self-sown or put in by the Bosche, we should not get many vegetables. As it is now we get turnips well-cooked for breakfast, dinner & tea which helps things along well. We are in country recently taken from the Hun – at least, a few months ago when the very heavy fighting was on & I was in England. He may have put in the turnips for his own use in which case it was very considerate of him & everyone round about is making the most of them. It doesn't do to dislike many things these days.

We will be going out for a spell in less than a month now, but don't go back to where Billy is as was rumoured a little while ago. It is hard to say how long it will be for, as no-one knows what is going to happen from one day to the next.

I received a bonzer Xmas cake from Mrs Barton at Hunter's Hill & it was greatly appreciated having been made in Australia with good flour & plenty of sugar. Things we don't get here now. It kept & travelled very well, having come in a sealed tin & sent on from St John's Wood & various other places.

Heard from Mona last night, who says that the young son has produced his first tooth & another one appearing. He also stands up now & crawls about all over the place. He seems to keep them on the go now & has to be watched all the time now that he can get about & get into mischief. Mrs Little is very fond of him & is a real worshipping grandma. She wishes you could have seen the young lad grow up. She is always very kind & looks after me well when I go there. She is always very busy looking after the boy & so lets Mona get out occasionally. They are leaving Seafield & going into some furnished rooms. Seafield has apparently been sold. Mona writes & says there is a spare room for me when I get over.

And now no more Matee. Give my best love to The Child, Aunt Mog, Phoebe & Phil. Hope everyone is well & that the garden will continue to look well at Ermo with plenty of vegetables on hand. With heaps of love & kisses to Mateeboos from your loving son

TOOTS.

Through these quieter winter months, the Germans were planning their Spring Offensive of 1918, transferring 500,000 men and equipment from the inactive Eastern Front with Russia to the Western Front. Germany was keen to make the most of its temporary numerical advantage before the Americans had time to contribute significantly to the Allied forces. The German Spring Offensive aimed to split the British and French armies at Amiens and advance to Paris, and also to break through the British section of the front line at Ypres and at last reach the Channel ports.

Germany launched its attacks and, in the Spring of 1918, it very nearly won the war.

On the last day of February, Steve's unit began the march overland to help shore up the defences south-east of Ypres. As they marched the weather was inclement, one day being 'a cold and wintry day, with snow and sleet falling'. His next letter, written from this new position, is dated 1917, but its context indicates that Steve made a slip of the pen and should have written 1918.

SOMEWHERE IN FRANCE, 4 MAR 1918

My dear Child

Just a hasty little note thanking you for your two letters of 22nd Dec & 8th Jany. Am very glad to hear you have been able to get a good writing desk and I will be able to look forward to getting some letters written from it.

Am in the line again and at this present moment at Battery HQrs away from the battery, doing a 48 hour liaison job with the infantry. I should be at one of the various O.Ps (observation posts) now but it is raining and misty, so nothing can be seen. I went round the line yesterday & this morning & incidentally strafed some Huns who rather foolishly showed themselves. It was otherwise quite quiet.

Have been very busy lately with the business of coming in & taking over. Haven't got any writing paper up here with me so am using the good old army stuff.

The Heads over here are beginning to get the wind up about Fritz's push. In consequence all leave has been stopped which is extremely pleasant just as I was beginning to look forward to it.

I'm glad to hear you all had a good Christmas though quiet. Am sorry I missed the drop of "stingo"[204] but hope to celebrate when I get back. It was bad luck Cleon did not arrive back in time.

Won't be able to write any more now. There are too many interruptions. There are 2 infantry officers in one corner discussing defence schemes and 2 more in another talking duckboards & sandbags which makes it very hard to write. Please give my best love to Mee maw, Aunt Mog, Aunt Phoebus & Phil & remember me to Cleon when next you see him. The tobacco etc has not yet arrived but I believe Mona has got it. She was expecting me to go on leave so didn't send it over until she heard from me. Very many thanks all the same. It will go well up here. We are a good way in & it is very difficult to get anything.

Show this letter to Mee maw in case hers doesn't arrive at the same time. I wrote to her just before coming in. Cheerio with heaps of love

Your loving brother

TOOTS.

Have got a pretty rotten cold as usual!

The 2nd FAB saw much action throughout the month of March, with enemy action very severe around the 6th Battery's position on 10-12 March. Some men were killed and wounded, and one gun was blown up during action at Verbrandenmolen Ridge. A number of men in the 6th Battery afterwards received awards for bravery. On 17 March they suffered a heavy gas bombardment and two days later they prepared themselves for anti-tank warfare. On 27 March, after nearly four weeks of solid fighting, the 6th Battery was relieved 'in the line' and Steve had the opportunity to write home.

---

204 A strong ale originating in north of England.

In the field, 29 Mar 1918

Dearest Matee

Just a hasty little note to let you know I am still going strong in spite of all the Hun advance. We are lucky in being out of it at the start, otherwise I might be over in Fritz land by this time. We are however expecting to go down there at any moment now and so am getting this off whilst I have a few spare moments.

At present I am down at our wagon line with the horses for one or two days for a spell and also to enable me to get back my voice, which has quite gone due to some of the Hun's gas. I got a whiff of it about 10 days ago up at the battery, but apart from that I am still feeling pretty well. He has been very free with it lately and quite a few have been evacuated to hospital from the effects.

Today I received from Billy a nice little tobacco pouch for my birthenday which is to be celebrated in two days from now. Also a small package containing cigarettes from Mona which were very acceptable. It is quite an occasion.

All leave has been stopped owing to the Hun offensive and goodness knows if it will ever open again. Let us hope so. Am afraid it will be some time though. I feel rather disappointed at not being able to get over and see the nephew who has come on considerably and is toddling about now. Billy is in the same boat and suppose is equally fed up.

We are cutting down all our kit to its lowest in anticipation of all the moving about which is in front of us. It doesn't sound very inviting and will be pretty uncomfortable especially as it is raining again and we shall have practically no shelter. However, it is no use meeting troubles half way and we are not down there yet.

I think I told you in my last letter that I had got my second star and am now a full Loot. However continue to send my letters to Mona as I get them nearly a week before the Austn mails arrive for the other chaps sent direct to the 6th battery. So much for the Military Post Office.

We are all turning in just now after a good day's work, so please give my love to Aunt Mog, the Child and Aunt Phoebe and Phil, and don't forget old Doos and keep up your spurrits Matee boos, with heaps of love and kisses, from

Your loving son

TOOTS.

No 10 Convalescent Depot, B.E.F. France, 31 Mar 1918

Dearest Mum

Am afraid I am a bit slow in writing to you this time, but we have been very busy here since this enormous offensive started, the biggest of the War. It is a terribly anxious time. Steve, I'm afraid, is in the thick of it, altho' I believe he escaped it at the commencement. So far as I've heard he is alright, altho' he had all his gear blown up some days ago. Today is his birthday, so I expect you are thinking of him a lot today and wondering how he is and where he is. I sent him a tobacco pouch the other day, which I trust he will get safely; he ought to as I registered it. He writes pretty regularly, either to Mona or myself. I have just written to him again today and asked him to let me have a P.C. whenever he gets a chance.

I feel I ought to be up there myself, instead of down here at the base. I have applied for a transfer to a Division, but I don't know whether I shall be moved at present. I haven't told Mona, it would only upset her if she knew I had applied, still I ought to be there. I've been down at the base now 6 months and with Steve up there it worries me my being here. Don't tell Mona if I am transferred to a Division that it was at my own wish. We are terribly busy here now; men are pouring in; we are going to expand up to double our present accommodation, which will make 5,000 in all. A huge camp. Still it is a very healthy place here and the men pick up very rapidly. We start pitching tents tomorrow.

Wonder what you all think of this huge offensive in Australia? When this reaches you, the most anxious time will be over. I think altho' we have lost a large amount of ground, we have to congratulate ourselves on our stand. We must have inflicted enormous losses on the enemy. The loss or capture of ground, in my mind, means very little; the only means of bringing the war to an end is to go on killing Huns and the faster we kill them off the speedier our chance of peace. We have undoubtedly accounted for 10's of 1000's this large colossal attack.

The Hun is getting very desperate now and is making gigantic efforts to force a decision. As long as he goes on attacking with his present mass formation, he is playing into our hands, our withdrawal has been carried out in a wonderful manner, and I think the German must be very disappointed at his results.

I don't know when I shall be getting leave; it is at present closed. Perhaps it will be re-opened in April some time. Expenses in England are tremendous. I hope this rationing will ease matters a little. It starts on the 8th of this month, Mona tells me.

The weather has been very beautiful, and the worst of the winter is undoubtedly over. It means continued fighting from now on. Do wish the Yankees would start and give us increased help; their man power is sorely needed.

Won't write any more now, dearest Mum. Hope you and the Child are both well. Don't worry too much, altho' it is a very anxious time. Steve and I have come thro' so far all right, our luck may stand right thro'. Little Toots is a full blown Lieutenant now! Lots and lots of love, a great big hug and a kiss,

Ever yours,

NIGE

Will write again soon. Tell the Child I will try and send her another letter. Thank her for hers. It is nice having them,

N.

In their Spring Offensive the Germans also struck heavily on the Somme. The British were forced back quickly as the enemy advanced steadily westwards under a heavy bombardment of high explosives and gas. The vital railhead around Amiens was under threat and once again Paris began to fear the enemy's long-range guns, as they had in 1914. In late March, Australian infantry were brought south from Belgium as reinforcements to help shore up the British line and attempt to push back the Germans.

Australia's official war historian records that move. On 25 March :

> *when, late in the afternoon, the lorries with the leading brigade, the veteran 4th, turned sharply off the main road at St. Pol into the countryside south-eastwards, it came into an atmosphere of suppressed excitement. This country had been twenty-two miles behind the line, and till now was practically untouched by the war; but now St. Pol lay battered with heavy, long-range shelling, and far ahead, Bapaume way, a pillar of smoke smudging the blue sky showed where some depot - probably the great dump at Bapaume - was being burnt as the operations reached it. At Barly the creaking lorries came on the old people of the village standing in groups outside their cottages, piling mattresses, beds, washstands, and other household goods upon carts, about to abandon their homes. Then occured a scene which was to be repeated - as the documents constantly record - many times in other villages*

during this and the next two days. As lorry-load after lorry-load of cheerful men bumped past, each crowd shouting and waving to the old folk, these paused in their loading. Australian infantry had never been stationed in that region, but before long - spontaneously, as it seemed - they were recognised. The gazing villagers could be heard calling from one house to the other, "Les Australiens." A few minutes later, as spontaneously, they began unloading their carts, and the furniture was carried indoors again. An old man said to one of the 13th Battalion, whose lorries halted there for a while, "Pas necessaire maintenant - vous les tiendrez." [It's not necessary now – you'll hold them.] "We'll have to see the old bloke isn't disappointed," said the digger, when the remark was translated to him.[205]

On 3 April, the 2nd FAB was relieved in the line near Ypres and, after a few days' rest, these men also set off for the Somme 'down south'.

IN THE FIELD, 7 APR 1918

Dearest Matee

Have just received your letter of 10th February, telling me of all your doings relative to the visit to Aunt Phoebe. It seems to have passed off very well.

Am glad to learn Cleon has arrived in Port at last. I suppose the Child and he will have a bit of a fly round whilst the time lasts. Should think the change at Mulgoa will do him a lot of good.

Nissen Huts, WW1
Source University of Newcastle, NSW, Cultural Collections, Dalton

You must excuse the scribble in this letter, but I am sitting on my bed trying to write, we are very crowded just now, 2 batteries living in a hut though it should only hold one. There are 12 officers all told in the hut, a Nissen. No doubt you have seen some pictures in some of the pa-

---

205 Bean, *Official History of Australia in the War of 1914-1918*, Vol 5, pp 119-120

pers of these affairs. They are quite good being waterproof and with a stove going in them are quite warm. I am fortunate enough to have a shakedown to sleep on whilst 6 other chaps get down on the floor of a night, in their valises of course.

For the last week we have been having a quiet time but busy. We have been getting ready for the show on down south and are now ready and are off now. It will be all new country I suppose at least not new, but not chopped about quite so much as the old Somme battlefield. The Hun made a wonderful advance, but did not meet with much opposition as far as I can gather. It was the Colonial Troops again that came to the rescue. One of our other divisions got a great reception from the French civilians and British Troops too, when they arrived down. Our chaps, also the New Zealanders, Canadians, S.Africans and Jocks seem to put the wind up the Hun more than anyone. It is a pity the British Troops that are fighting now haven't got more guts. It is more the fault of the staff tho' than the men. And now we are going to have our fling now.

My military address is Lieut. S.P.B., 6th Battery, 2nd A.F.A. Brigade, A.I.F, France, but it is better to send my letters to Mona as I seem to get them quicker and with more certainty than through the Military Post Office. When you send my letters to her leave out the Lieut. for her to put in.

I had quite a good mail today with yours, a letter from Harry Lloyd, Nora Barton[206] and Daisy Blomfield[207] which is not bad. Everything seems to be going on just as usual. Everyone seems to be going away for holidays surfing etc. I suppose over there you wouldn't know there was a war on.

Have been living this last week with Steve Friend[208] who is a Loot in the 102nd Battery (Howitzer). He got his commission a few months before me. His battery is in the same brigade, so we see a good deal of one another. I didn't know him before coming away except that he was a brother of Jimmy Friend who was at TKS[209] with me.

Shall look forward to the next letter from you telling me of my allotment money, also as to whether the photos arrived safely. I got your Xmas reminder quite safely and am at this minute using it. It is very useful and am taking it with me in spite of cutting down all our gear to a minimum.

---

206 Nora Barton was a cousin of Max Barton, and married to Dr Harry Lee of Wollongong.
207 Presumably the Daisy Blomfield who lived in the Wollongong area and later married Dr E F M Solling.
208 Stephen Gilbert Friend was a career military officer after the war, becoming a Brigadier. He died in 1960.
209 The King's School

Best love to the Child and Cleon, Aunts Mog and Phoebus, Phil and everyone at home. Keep up your spurrits and remember me to Doos or Whisky, with heaps of love and kisses to you Matee

Your loving son

TOOTS.

No 10 Convalescent Depot, B.E.F. France, 12 Apr 1918

Dearest Mum

Am afraid it is over a week since I last wrote to you, but the fact is I have been fearfully busy. We have now about 4,000 men here, and are expanding up to 5,000, so there is an enormous amount to be done, in the way of buildings, pitching of tents, detailing of staffs, etc. etc., in addition to one's ordinary medical work. There are only 3 M.O.s here so we are all three worked hard.

My application, I dare say you will be pleased to hear, has been turned down. I am to apply at a future day, as at present it is not considered advisable to shift me. I shall apply again I suppose when the new officers arrive, which ought to take place soon.

The weather we are having now is delightful. It started today, a real spring day; it ought to continue as we are right in spring now. I have applied for leave on top of the refusal of my application. I am due for it, as it is 6 months now since I left England, more in fact, and all the other officers here have had leave more recently, I don't suppose they will let me go until we are reinforced with more officers. I have arranged to go to Barnstaple in the N. of Devon, it is delightful country from all I've heard, and I am looking forward to seeing it. Shall only spend 4 or 5 days there, and see all we can in that time. I do hope the weather will be decent, if so we shall have a very happy time.

I have at present a brute of a cold coming on, sore throat, head, stuffed up feeling, etc. Hope I get rid of it before I go on leave. Mona is looking forward to seeing me very much. Poor little girl, am afraid she is getting tired of waiting, as she expected me over last month. However, perhaps I may manage it soon.

Well, the war is in a very critical stage at present, and I dare say fighting will still be taking place on a large scale when you receive this. This year will be crammed with fighting and battles and I think the eventful year of the war, and I do hope we manage to frustrate the Hun in his advance; he seems to be concentrating every man he has on one front, and is getting desperate at last. The casualties will be terrific. I heard from Steve last night, he has been fortunate so far in escaping the worst of the strafe. I hope he doesn't get into a hot spot. He seemed very cheery when he wrote and much better for a rest at the wagon lines after his dose of gas.

What do you think of the latest Man Power Bill? Raising the age to 50. It is ridiculous really, as only a limited number of men over 40 are able to stick front line trench work. Ireland with 120,000 men young and fit is allowed to escape. I wonder whether Government will have the 'guts' to tackle Ireland and introduce Conscription? It would put me right for a month at least!

Love to all at home,

Ever your loving,

PIGE.

Travelling on an overnight train, Steve's unit (the 6th Battery) reached Amiens on 9 April and marched overland to St Ouen, one of the villages surrounding the Allies' behind-the-lines rest town of Vignacourt. On 12 April they moved again to Allonville, north-east of Amiens, ready to move into the line to resist the advancing German forces.

Almost immediately after the Australian troops left for the Somme, Germany also targeted a section of the line back in Flanders, now held by two under-strength Portuguese Divisions. The latter promptly ran away in the face of the enemy. On 10 April the Germans broke through at Messines, which Australian troops had taken at great cost in July 1917 and had held since. Exhausted troops of the British Second Army and their newly-drafted recruits also retreated, although some British units held on tenaciously. This was a disaster for the Allies. On 11 April the British General Haig issued his famous 'Backs to the wall' message, exhorting all British forces in France to hold every position, to the last man, with no retirement. On 12 April the Germans began targeting Hazebrouck, an important railway junction that supplied half the British front with its daily supplies. (See 'Map 8: North East France, 1916-1918' on page 236.)

The Australians of the 1st Division, who'd just arrived on the Somme, were immediately ordered back to Belgium by General Haig, charged with stopping the Germans advancing any further. As they waited for their troop trains, for some hours German aircraft heavily bombed the stations where thousands of troops were gathering. The bombing caused huge damage and delays, but the troops were quickly moved to shelter under nearby tree cover and by some miracle they mostly escaped harm.[210]

When the 8th Battalion infantry arrived back in Flanders they were met by the Chief of Staff of the British Second Army, Lieut Genl Sir Charles Harrington, who described the situation as critical and told them that 'the 1st Australian Division is the only formed body now between here and the Channel Ports'. As they marched away from the station he described them as 'glorious fellows', but afterwards, in newspaper reports and British war histories, Australian troops weren't given the credit due to them for saving Hazebrouck and the Channel ports. Usually all that was said of their role, if anything, was that they arrived four hours late. The brilliant Australian General John Monash remonstrated with war correspondents and officialdom and eventually corrected some of the record, to the point where the English public then felt the Australians were getting too much credit.[211]

War unit diaries for the 2nd FAB at this time tell a rather panic-stricken tale. Having just arrived at Allonville on the Somme, next day they were sent back to Belgium, moving overnight by train to Cassell and then marching to the battlefront at Hazebrouck. Known as the Battle of the Lys, also known as the Battle of Éstaires or the Fourth Battle of Ypres, from 9-29 April the attack and defence campaign raged in fresh country which had previously been relatively peaceful farmland, held safely in Allied hands for almost four years.

As usual, although engaged in active firing, with the enemy shelling their lines, Steve minimised his dire circumstances.

In the Field [near Hazebrouck], 19 Apr 1918

Dearest Matee

Only a hurried scribble to let you know I am still well and going strong. There isn't much time for writing letters these days, however I must get this off tonight in spite of difficult surroundings and conditions. We have been moving up and down the line lately a good deal, wherever the Hun makes a bit of a stunt. So far we have not been in any of these many retreats, which is something to say these days.

However we are in the line again now, and have been very comfortable for the last 4 days. We have occupied an evacuated French farm practically intact after

---

210 Belford, *Legs Eleven*, pp 552-554
211 Joynt, *Saving the Channel Ports* 1918, pp 37-42

the Hun had pushed the Portuguese and Tommies back. So we are in quite fresh country with everything on the farm including cows, rabbits, a goat, plenty of potatoes and a good farm house with plenty of coal to burn in the stoves.

It is a shame for all the French people to have to clear out of all their homes with practically nothing except what they stand up in. It brings the war home, doesn't it. They all go back as fast as they can and leave everything, fully expecting never to see their home again. One shell is enough to finish all these sort of houses. We can all be very thankful that the war is not in Australia.

Tomorrow we move from our farm somewhere else. Most of the cattle and livestock are being driven back out of the battle area. The Australian troops have had a great time in this last business, milking all the stray cows and getting fresh milk, also living on poultry.

However, enough of the war. I am still well and have quite recovered from a whiff of gas I got hold of a month ago now. It affects your chest a bit, but I think I am all O.K. again. There is no leave now whilst all this business is on. It is out of the question for quite a while now. Heard from Billy and Mona a couple of days ago. He is very disappointed at not getting his leave too. He has a much better chance of getting his before I do.

Oh well, keep your spurrits up Matee, it is not bad here now, and am keeping well. Will write again as soon as I get time. Hope you are getting my letters alright. Yours are coming along fairly well and are always welcome and cheering.

Please give my best love to the Child and Cleon, hope they had a good time whilst the boat was in. Best love to Aunt Mog and Aunt Phoebe and Phil. Hope everyone is well. Did you see what John Bull said this week in a column "Things we want to know", when is the British army going to help the Australians to win the war? Not bad is it.

Heaps of love and kisses to Matee boos from her loving son

TOOTS.

The following letter from Nigel, in the British Army, proves that there was a conspiracy of silence about the work of the Australians at Hazebrouck. The Australians he mentions 'in reserve' were some of those down at Amiens.

No 10 Convalescent Depot, B.E.F. France, 23 Apr 1918

Dearest Mum

Well another week has gone by, and things are still in a very critical state. I think the fighting will go on on the present huge scale for the next two months, during which time the Hun will make the most desperate efforts, regardless of all casualties to force a definite decision in his favour. He is out after the Channel Ports, and we must defend them to the last as they are of vast importance.

I daresay when you receive this, things will have progressed a great deal and we shall be able to view the situation more clearly. I wonder what will have happened by then; if we are still holding him, the game is ours. I don't think there is much doubt now that this is the decisive year of the War. It may even usher in peace, but that is too ambitious an ideal to hope for almost.

I heard from Steve yesterday, the first letter I have had from him for a fortnight so I was pleased to get it and to learn he had escaped most of the big strafe so far. He had apparently been up north, and was rushed down to the Somme area when the big thrust started, and when he got there he was immediately sent up north again. He has so far been in reserve as the rest of the Australian forces have this time, as well as the Canadian, New Zealand, and other colonial troops. The English, Irish and Scottish troops have borne the brunt of the fighting this time, which is a comfort to know as it means our Australian casualties won't be as heavy as usual.

Two new Medical Officers have arrived here, so things are much easier. I have handed over the bulk of my work practically entirely to them, so I am at present having a pretty "cushy" time of it. However, I shall be busy again I dare say before long. 2 more M.O's arrived yesterday for temporary duty for a fortnight, each adorned with a Military Cross. Every M.O. one sees these days has a ribbon of some sort on his chest. I am absolutely out of it. I don't seem to have distinguished myself in the slightest during this war, although I have been in the army over 3½ years now. However, I suppose it is largely a question of luck. I must have a go at the front again before I finish. Shall re-submit my application in a week or so for a transfer. Leave is quite out of the question for some time to come I am afraid. I heard yesterday it was whispered that leave could not possibly recommence till the 1st of June, so I shall have to just grin and bear it.

Mona will be very disappointed too as she had been counting on my being over before this, and when my turn came to apply, leave was squashed. Still if

I manage it in June that will be something, as the weather and country ought to be delicious then. The railway fares are going up another 50% I believe on the 1st of May, so travelling will be practically prohibitive from then on. But we must see North Devon at all costs, it is one of the beauty spots of England I hear on all sides from those who have been there.

Well, dearest Mum, I won't say more now. I hope all is well with you at home. You will be having autumn or practically winter when you get this, with the long quiet uninteresting evenings. Cheer up, Mum, perhaps it will be the last winter we shall spend so far away from one another. Best love to the Child. I haven't managed to write her another letter yet.

A great big hug and a kiss,

Ever yours,

NIGE

Down south, on the Somme front, the Australian troops being temporarily rested were about to write themselves into history. The Germans had managed to advance their front towards the town of Villers-Bretonneux, south east of Amiens. The town held significant strategic value, as it was positioned on high ground that would have provided a line-of-sight for German artillery observers to target Amiens. In early April the Germans launched an attack to capture the town and succeeded after heavy fighting (the first Battle of Villers-Bretonneux). During the first night of the second Battle, 24-27 April, two Australian and one British brigade partly surrounded Villers-Bretonneux and on 25 April the town was recaptured. Australian, British and French troops restored the original front line by 27 April, with the first tank-versus-tank battle in history occurring around this town.

After the Anzac Day counter-attack, British and French commanders lavished praise upon the Australian soldiers for "perhaps the greatest individual feat of the war".[212] A relative lull followed in that section of the Western Front through May and June.

Steve was still fighting up near Ypres, away from the other Australian troops down on the Somme. As a component of Australia's 1st Division, his unit helped

---

212 Coinciding as it did with the third anniversary of the Gallipoli landing, the battle holds a significant place in Australian military history and is yearly commemorated by Australians, although it was a combined Allied effort. In the 1930s an impressive memorial was established at the top of the Villers-Bretonneux Military Cemetery to honour all Australian soldiers who fell in France in the war. The town's citizens still honour the Australian effort.

halt the German push at Hazebrouck, with no official recognition of their efforts at that time or over the next four months of active combat in Belgium. He wrote his next letter from a farmhouse somewhere near Caëstre, when his unit was active in shelling the Rouge Croix and Pradelles areas. By now he was an expert at compartmentalising the events in his life.

IN THE FIELD [CAËSTRE], 28 APR 1918

Dearest Matee

2nd Lieut Stephen Boulton, Harrow, Nov 1917
(Picture Courtesy Julia Woodhouse)

Have just received your little note of 25th Feb saying you had received the photos alright. Am glad you like them. I haven't seen the big ones, but I thought the small size quite good too. There was one of me sitting astride a chair which I didn't go much on. Am still well and going strong. We are having rather a peculiar time just now. We are living in a farm house recently evacuated by the French farmer and his family who all had to leave without any notice due to the rapid retirement of the Tommies, who have made a name for themselves more than once in that way lately.

Consequently we have had the house to live in with all its conveniences such as stoves, ovens and all the cooking gear. Besides this we are now running the farm in all spare moments and get good fresh milk every evening from a couple of cows and tons of pork from several porkers wandering round. Also a few fowls, plenty of potatoes, flour etc. We have been living like fighting cocks for the last week and carrying on the war at the same time, dealing out plenty of biff.

Our guns are a fair way away as all the houses round about get knocked by the Hun sooner or later. So far we have been lucky and ours is still O.K. It is all rather uncanny and unlike a war, living in a house with a carpet on the floor and a good fire going in the stove, table cloths, vases with flowers on the table.

Had a good mail from Aust. today. You have addressed mine to the battery this time. Had 5 letters all told, which is not bad. One from the C'wealth Bank saying that they have had no notification from the Defence Dept. of the increase from 3/- to 7/6 a day in my allotment. I hope it is going on alright now; the 7/6 was to start on the 16th Nov 1917 and the date of the letter from them is 22nd Feb. It is about time it was fixed up. I don't want to lose any of that money: 4/6 a day extra for 6 months is worth looking after. Am glad to hear that the Child and Cleon are having a good time at Leura and that the change is doing Cleon some good.

Heard from Billy the day before yesterday. He is good-oh still, but expects to be off up the line again soon. Mona and the boy seem well and happy. They are all very disappointed about the stoppage of all leave. The way things are going it doesn't seem if it will ever start again either.

Please give my bestest love to all at home. Hope Aunt Mog is keeping well and that the ramalinas are flourishing. Expect to hear from Aunt Phoebe when she gets my photo. With heaps of love and kisses to Matee boos and the Child and hoping you all are in good spurrits,

Your loving son, TOOTS.

2nd Lieut Stephen Boulton at Harrow, Nov 1917
(Picture Courtesy Julia Woodhouse)

2nd Lieut Stephen Boulton, Harrow, Nov 1917
(Picture Courtesy Julia Woodhouse)

On 29 April Steve's Brigade Headquarters was heavily shelled and an officer and 11 men were killed, with others wounded. In the first week of May around Caëstre, all batteries of the 2nd FAB maintained harassing fire on the enemy by day and night, concentrating on enemy roads and hedges, with prisoners captured by the infantry reporting the fire as very effective. Some units were wearing gas helmets. A new Observation Post (OP) was opened at Flêtre church, and Farm Serbie was set on fire. As usual, Steve was the master of under-statement.

In the field, 8 May 1918

Dearest Matee

Your letter of 8th March to hand yesterday. It came along direct to the battery and so I got it a bit earlier and sooner than if it had gone to Mona. However I think the safest way is always to address them to Mona first, whose new address is "Highclere", Dane Court Rd, Parkstone. The English letters from Australia go by a different boat to the troops' letters I think, because I generally seem to get my letters a few days before the big Australian mail for everyone else arrives.

Re the P.O.O.[213] you sent along last Xmas. It arrived alright and I have I think told you several times that it purchased for me a writing case which has been in use ever since Mona sent it over. You probably have forgotten. It arrived before Xmas I think so it didn't go down after all.

I think Billy and Mona must have written too, and thanked you for their share. Anyway it was very kind of the Mee Maw and the writing case is in use now.

Am glad to hear that the young people had such a good time at Leura and no doubt greatly benefited by the change. By now I suppose the ship has gone out again, taking Cleon with it, and the Child is once again with you at Ermo, saving up for his next spell ashore. I wonder how the Nellie Herring[214] visit went off. It appeared to be a bit of a blow which had to be.

Am so glad to hear you all like the photos. I don't know why Cousin Bess didn't put one in for Aunt Mog. She was told to.

Things have been fairly quiet here lately with 2 days rain. It is fine again now and things are a little livelier. I am down at the Wagon lines for one or two days having a bit of a spell away from the guns. Every 4th night I go up to do a 24 hour job, observing day and night: during the day for any movement or enemy targets which show themselves, and at night for S.O.S. rockets[215] and general enemy attitude. It is a pretty deadly game and thank goodness only comes every 4th night. No sign of any leave yet and I don't suppose there will be much likelihood of any for some time to come. Could do with a bit of a holiday now. It is 6 months since I came over from England and the time has gone very quickly.

---

213 Post Office Order
214 Nellie was presumably Ellen Bell Herring, an older sister of Jack Herring who'd died of his wounds in 1915.
215 Fired by the Infantry, calling for urgent Artillery support

Did you ever get another sort of Anzac Book which I had sent out soon after Xmas? You have never mentioned any word of it yet and I wonder if it arrived. I hear pretty regularly from Cousin Bess. She generally has some news from you to tell me. She and Aunt Julia have gone down to Oakham for a change to stay with Cousin or Uncle Jim[216], the Parson chap.

And now good-bye Matee boos, please give my best love to the Child and Aunt Mog, Aunt Phoebe and Phil. I hope everyone is keeping well and in good spirits. Am having orderly room tomorrow which means I try a chap for being drunk etc. Shall not punish him myself but remand him to the O.C. Some boy now eh!

Heaps and heaps of love and kisses to Matee. Am glad to hear that old Whisky is going strong and such good company,

Your loving son

TOOTS.

Unit war diaries for the 2nd FAB tell a tale of very active warfare in May, working with the 5th Infantry Battalion. The artillery made many direct hits on targets believed to be enemy OPs. On 14 May the 6th Battery made a direct hit on a farm near Merris Church, set it on fire and heard 3 loud explosions. On 18 May, the 6th Battery moved forward and engaged, destroying a farm with incendiary shell and targeting a large building in Oultersteene believed to be an OP. The building was set on fire, resulting in a large explosion and a dense column of black smoke. The term 'moved forward' indicates that the 2nd FAB was supporting the new strategy of 'peaceful penetration', spontaneous and independent initiatives by small groups of Australian infantry, aggressively patrolling and sneaking forward into German lines, catching the enemy by surprise and capturing prisoners, equipment and positions.

Bombing by the enemy's planes was very active for several hours from 10.15 pm on 18 May, with the planes passing by in relays, using their machine gun fire a good deal as well. Steve had another near-miss when bombs were dropped on Flêtre and on the Caëstre to Cassel road.

---

216 Rev James Hamilton Charles, Aunt Julia's eldest son.

In the field, 19 May 1918

Dearest Matee

Haven't had any letters from Australia for about a fortnight now, so I suppose there will soon be a mail in bringing a letter from you.

Am still going well and at present it is beautifully hot, quite like Australia. All the chaps are getting about with just the minimum amount of clothes and enjoying the fine summery spell of weather.

We are still in the same place and I am back with the guns again. Our farm house has not been found yet or touched, for which it is unnecessary to say we are very thankful. Our 2 cows are still giving plenty of milk which keeps the battery supplied, so all the diggers are in their element. Last night being very clear and fine there was a good deal of aerial activity and Fritz dropped a small bomb in our paddock which had the wind up us for a bit.

The last 3 mornings I have been partaking of a cold bath before breakfast. There is no bathroom. However 3 buckets of water out in the sun go very well and all the other officers are now doing the same. Not a bad sort of war is it? The main thing is not to think about it all, but make as good a time as you can while you can.

Yesterday I was "O.P. ing" all day. Fritz hunted us with iron foundry's just at the end of the day. We however had given him a bad time all the afternoon with some incendiary shell. Blew up one of his ammunition dumps for him, much to the glee of all the diggers.

Had a letter from Cousin Bess a few days ago. She has ordered the *Weekly Times* for me and the first copy arrived yesterday. It is good getting the paper although the news is a bit behindhand. Have had no letter from Billy for a little while. The last thing he seemed to expect was going up the line again. No sign of any leave yet. It would be great to get over to England now during the summer weather. Did you see that Billy Metcalfe had died of wounds quite recently? I saw him whilst over in England and he must have come over about the same time as me.

How is the Child getting on now? Haven't yet heard whether Cleon has gone with the ship. I expect he had by now and she is once again with you at Ermo.

Mona and Mrs. Little seem to be very well and happy looking after Pip, who keeps them amused all day long. He must be a bit of a trick now and rather interesting.

Please give my best love to Aunt Mog and the Child, also Aunt Phoebe and Phil. Aunt Eleanor tells me that Hal is expecting to be called up again. He won't like the life after his present job.

And now good-bye Matee, with heaps and heaps of love and kisses, hoping Ermo is looking well and as comfortable as ever, from

Your loving son TOOTS.

Am enclosing a bit of a souvenir. Had dinner at this place several times. Now in the hand of the enemy.

Although no AIF unit was at full strength from May 1918, the Australians held their front line positions and the German attack faltered. For the rest of May, the unit war diaries for the 2nd FAB made many more references to the Australians moving forward, the infantry assisted by the artillery's fire. For example, on 22 May the 6th Battery moved forward and engaged several targets 'with splendid results', including destroying with incendiary a farm which was strongly held by machine gunners. Next day the 6th Battery set fire to two farm houses. On 24 May harassing fire was directed by all batteries upon all enemy roads, houses, tracks and trenches, although visibility was very bad all day. On 25 May their tank gun position was heavily shelled and all batteries reported heavy gas bombardment all along the front. Next day they retaliated, firing gas cylinders towards the enemy, and the 6th Battery moved forward & destroyed four houses with incendiary fire.

Steve took all of this in his stride in his next letter.

IN THE FIELD, 27 MAY 1918

My dearest Matee

The mail came in last night and brought me 3 bonzer letters from you dated 19th and 24th March and 1st April. The last one has come along very quickly. I suppose a fair time will elapse before the next lot arrives, as after getting a lot together there is generally a bit of a break.

I am still very well and going strong. The weather is beautiful now with daylight from 3.30 in the morning till about 9 at night. Also plenty of sun lately. It has in fact been quite hot, and like home. Lately we have been having a bath every morning with 3 buckets of cold water and feel much the better for it. Needless to remark there is no bathroom, which perhaps is an advantage as it is beautiful in the sun in the mornings.

Goodness knows what I am going to do after the war. I have a servant or batman now who gets everything ready, cleans boots and all my gear, does my washing, in fact, does the valet stunt. After this is over I shall have to clean my own boots again I suppose. Oh well I have done it before, so I suppose I will be able to do it again.

We are having a pretty busy time of it now and dealing out plenty of "biff". The Hun is expected to attack again at any minute, but we are quite ready for him and hope to give him a very bad time when he comes. Our infantry are in great nick and very confident. Up to the present they have always been too good for him and are waiting for him to come. The Australians have done some wonderfully good work lately and all the English papers are full of praise etc. All the Colonial troops stand out alone from the Home troops and are quite the best in the field.

I heard from the Commonwealth Bank by this mail, advising me that the increase of allotment has not commenced being paid in yet, but that they will let me know as soon as it does. When you or the Child are in town again, could you call and ask them if they have advised me yet about the increase to 7/6, as mentioned at the end of their letter. Am sending you the letter along. You will also see my address which will always find me.

There is great excitement at Kennet House just now, as Rachael Campbell[217] some relation of theirs whom I met when over there has just had twin sons. These are the first great grandchildren for Aunt Julia. Hence all sorts of rejoicing. Hubby is out in Palestine now. He was the chap who was taken prisoner in Germany and afterwards escaped. Cousin Bess is sending me the *London Weekly Times* every week now which is good of her and is much read and appreciated. It is jolly hard to get papers here sometimes and we don't know what is happening on the other parts of the front.

Am sending you along one of the small photos of myself. I didn't send one because you were getting a large size one. I thought you would like a big one better. However, here is one of the little ones. They are not bad. I don't think anyone can say they are flattering. Quite a good likeness I think, although I look as if I was going to win the war off my own bat.[218]

Am glad to hear of the Child and Cleon having a good time while it lasts. I suppose Cleon will be convoying some of our reinforcements over a part of the way. See by the papers that recruiting is booming in Australia. They must

---

217 The Rev Uncle Jim's daughter
218 See Pics on page 348 and page 349

all think the war is going to end soon, and are getting away in time, so as to be able to say they went to the war.

I heard from Billy yesterday. He seems to be pretty fed up with his job now, and badly wants his leave whilst the good weather is on. There doesn't seem any chance of leave starting though.

It seems a pity for you to leave Ermo now that it is running along so well and everything is so comfortable. Also if you let it furnished it will get knocked about again and all the furniture broken. Am looking forward to the time when I can sample all the home made jam and bottled fruit etc.

I wonder how Colby[219] is getting along. Hope she settles down there as she ought to be a great comfort to Aunt Mog at Tyrone. And now good-bye Matee boos, give my best love to Aunt Mog and Aunt Phoebe and Phil, with heaps of love and kisses to Matee boos and the Child, from

Your loving son

TOOTS.

No 10 Convalescent Depot, B.E.F. France, 4 June 1918

Dearest Mum

Well, there is not much to tell you this time, as usual, I'm afraid. I have not had an answer from Nina Boulton[220] yet, so I can't tell you any news of the genealogical tree yet. I hope that it hasn't got much aphis on it! That doubtless tho' will be concealed.

There is a chance of my getting over on leave this week! My application has gone into Hd. qrs. but up to now has not come back. It is 8 months since I left Mona, and Pip has altered out of all shape since then, and is walking and talking now. Mona tells me in every letter now that I am missing the best of the son, and to come over soon. Also all her new clothes are getting worn out, and that I had better hurry up before she becomes too shabby. It is very hard not

---

219 The unidentified Colby was Aunt Mog's new maid or companion.
220 Another first cousin, being the youngest sister of Harold Boulton. Nina was about 30 years old at this time. Nigel's widowed mother was obviously keen to know more of her husband's family connections in England.

being able to get over and to miss practically all of the son's babyhood. Perhaps tho' I shall get leave this week, I half expected it to come through last night, but no such luck. I sillily wired to Mona telling her I should probably be over today and she wired back to say she would meet me in London, so the poor little girl will be terribly disappointed when she finds the train empty as far as she is concerned. It is no use trying to make any arrangements. I had hoped to save a day if she met me in London, as we could then go straight down to Devon, instead of waiting in London for a day while she came up from Dorset. There are not very many trains running now.

The weather has been absolutely delightful, just the very best time of the year for leave. Am afraid Toots won't get his yet awhile, as leave has not been open yet, only for those officers and men at the base and on lines of communication who can be spared - I come under this category.

The Huns seem to be revealing their desperate savagery more and more each day. Bombing churches and hospitals now. The churches on Sundays, of course. Several of the hospitals only a few miles from here have had a very awful time with 100's of casualties among the patients, doctors and nurses. The German Squadron responsible went over here and were subjected to a heavy anti-aircraft gun barrage. The shell fragments from these were dropping round this camp like hail stones for a bit. I expect you will see the account of it in the papers.

The offensive at present going on is on huge lines, and the position at present is critical and anxious. We shall know in a week's time better how things are. The Hun certainly makes big advances, but the cost is very large. Well, dearest Mum, I have practically no more to say this time. I hope when I write next I shall be able to tell you of the family. Love to Thea. Trusting you are both well. With a big hug and a kiss,

Ever yours,

NIGE

The 2nd FAB's unit war diaries in late May record much satisfaction with successful days of shooting and destruction of enemy targets. High morale was indicated with the following entry for 29 May: 'summer weather has set in, a glorious Australian sunny day. Health of the men is excellent.' Into June, enemy artillery was very quiet during the day and very active at night. All batteries in the 2nd FAB maintained harassing fire, shelling Meteren at intervals, and firing on Bailleul and

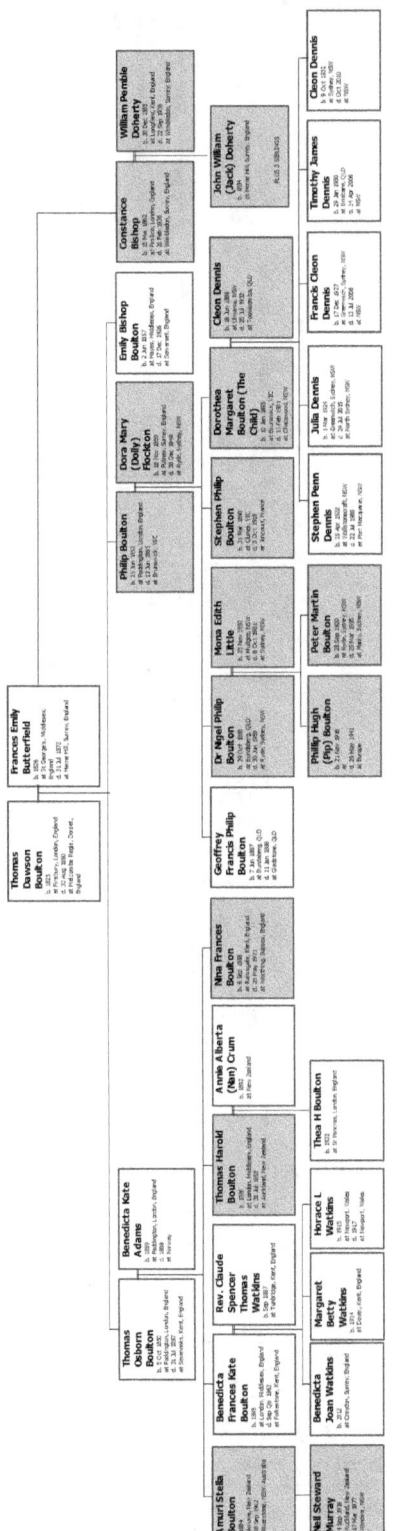

Boulton Relatives

People in the boxes highlighted are mentioned in the letters

This family tree image maybe too small to read. Please go to the author's website to download a larger format PDF for viewing at: www.louisewilson.com.au

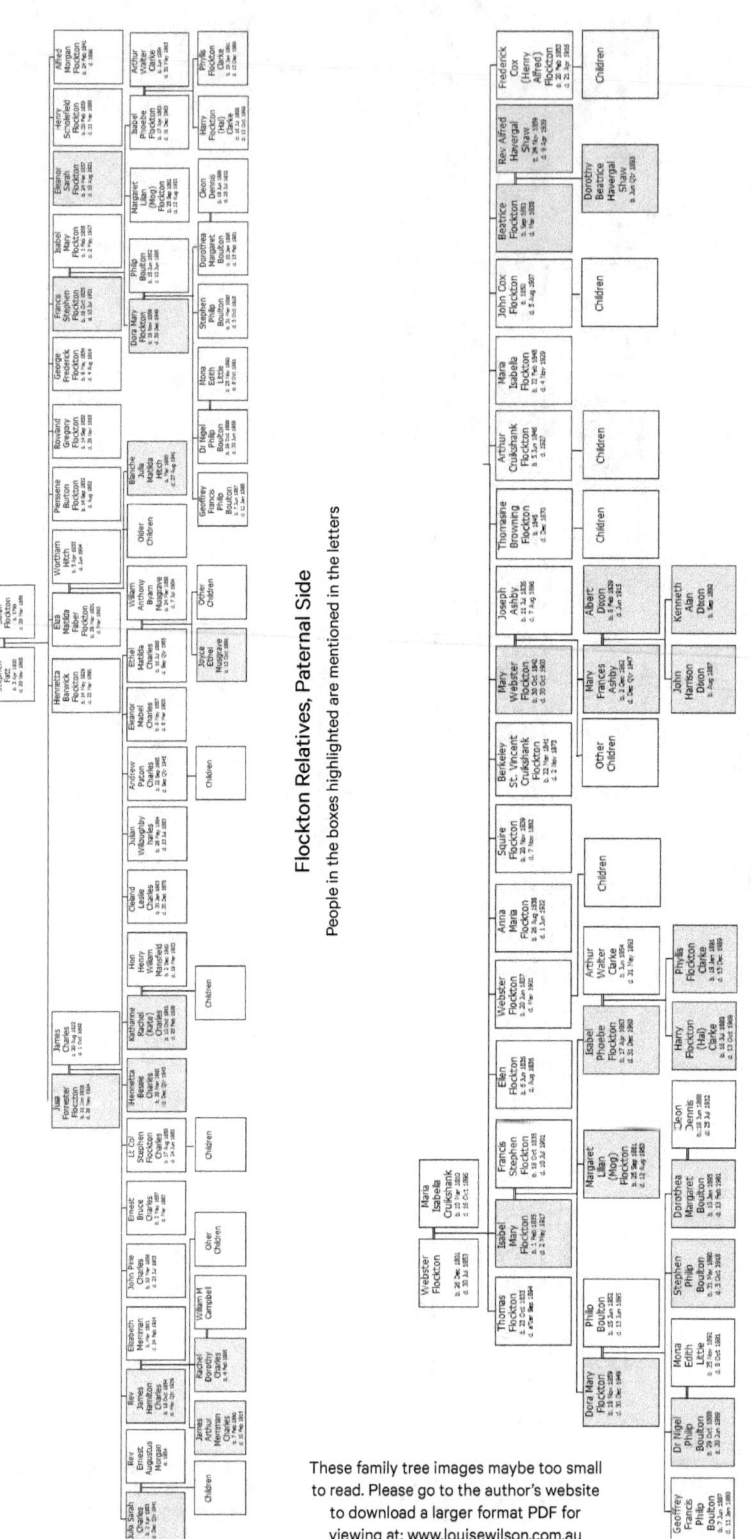

Oultersteene. Flêtre and Merris were also mentioned. The enemy returned fire on battery positions around Caëstre and Rouge Croix and increased its activity in rear areas by shelling roads and the routes to the 2nd FAB's battery positions and wagon lines, mentioned by Steve in his next letter.

In the field, Somewhere in France, 11 Jun 1918

Dearest Matee

Haven't had any letters for several days now, so I suppose there will be some arriving any day now. I think it averages about once a fortnight. I expect your mails are about the same too. In the meantime am still well and everything is going on much as usual.

Since I last wrote we have moved out of our farm house, which turned out to be a good thing afterwards, as Fritz has commenced strafing it. We have once more got down to our army rations again as everything else has been finished off including the 2 cows which were reclaimed and driven back to be claimed by the French owners. We still get plenty of potatoes and a few lettuces from which are made some good salads for lunch. They go well these warm days too.

We have been lucky so far in not being up against any of the Hun pushes, but I am touching wood as it is hard to say where he will start next. Most of our work is done at night now. Things quieten down a lot during the day and as soon as it gets dark both sides commence going at one another. So during the day we are not doing much and once every third night one of us stays up and shoots the battery till after daybreak. We are always very late in getting up in the mornings and so make up for any time lost out of bed. We have got back once more to the dugout stunts and have got a very comfortable one fixed up.

There are four of us who live inside, of course somewhat cramped for room, but we each have got our little shakedown and so are pretty well fixed up. We have just got another gramophone, a Decca this time, and some of the latest records which is going to cheer us up considerably. The last one died a natural death as they all do over here, getting terribly knocked about with all the travelling about the country, being chucked into wagons and out again.

Yesterday I had an afternoon away from the war and took a run into a small town a bit back from the line. Had a look round the place which was most interesting and made several small purchases in the way of magazines and tobacco etc. Had dinner at the only hotel in the place and a jolly good one too, and then hopped on our horses and came back home again. It was quite a good outing and we both enjoyed ourselves. Have got a good horse now, as strong as a lion and he can go some. The only thing wrong with him is his personal appearance which is somewhat spoilt by the absence of a tail. Some Tommy unit must have had him previously and docked it. He is known as "Bobtail" now.

Please give my love to Aunt Mog, and Aunt Phoebe and Phil. I suppose the Child is back again with you at Ermo or have you gone to live somewhere else and let it furnished. Heard from Mrs. Little tonight. She is in great form and enjoying her grandson's company by herself. Mona had just gone up to London to meet Billy who was expected over but had not arrived up to the present.

Heaps and heaps of love to you Matee and the Child,

Your ever loving son

TOOTS.

P.S. Sent you a copy of the *'Aussie'* which is run by the troops over here. Some of it is amusing.

Have just heard that our April mail has been sunk. Cheerful isn't it?

June and July near Hazebrouck

Another gap of several months in Steve's letters is filled by the unit war diaries for his Brigade. As June progressed, the German Spring Offensive was in its closing phases but the presence of as many as 16 enemy planes flying low over their lines prompted the 2nd FAB to expect and prepare for an enemy attack at any minute. Fears eased on 16 June when two escaped British prisoners walked in to the Australian line with news that German troops in this area were very sparse, and they had heard nothing of an imminent attack. That day, Steve was released for a 10 day break at the Officers' Rest Hotel, Boulogne. Presumably he visited Nigel, if Nigel was not in England. On the day he returned, enemy planes dropped three small bombs near the 6th Battery.

From July 1918 the Allies launched offensives which once again created a war of movement instead of attrition. Down south, the Australians captured Le Hamel on 4 July, in an operation meticulously planned by General Monash. The attack incorporated all the lessons of war learned so painfully and utilized all available forms of the military for the first time. After the Battle, the French Prime Minister visited the troops and said 'When the Australians came to France, the French people expected a great deal of you … We knew that you would fight a real fight, but we did not know that from the very beginning you would astonish the whole continent.'

Up north, Steve's Brigade reported carrying out much good shooting as they supported the move forward by the infantry in their continuing campaign of 'peaceful penetration'. There was even time for some rest and recreation on Saturday 13 July, which kept up the men's spirits. The 6th & 102nd Batteries of the 2nd FAB combined and played a game of cricket with the 3rd FAB, the latter winning by 7 runs. A tug of war was held, in fancy dress, adding much humour to the afternoon. The Sergeant's messes of all groups entertained the 'Sentimental Blokes' concert party to tea and visiting officers including the C.R.A.[221] were entertained to dinner.

The process of 'shoving back' continued, despite enemy shelling and aerial bombing. The village of Meteren, north east of Hazebrouck, had been captured by the Australians and the Scots by 22 July, when the 2nd FAB was relieved in the line. Next day the Brigade moved out of the Caëstre area to lines on the bank of the Canal de la Fosse, Blaringhem. Rain fell during the whole of the march but cleared in the afternoon. Generals Glasgow and Anderson inspected the Brigade after it had moved about 5 miles over dirty roads and in pouring rain and appeared very pleased with the whole turn out. The Brigade bivouacked and all men were got under cover of trench shelters or canvas of some sort.

For the next week, the men enjoyed many opportunities for swimming in the canal and aquatic sports competitions. On Sunday 28 July a Church Parade was held and many men attended. On Wednesday the concert party from the 31st Division came down and gave a most successful concert. The stage was arranged in a marquee tent with one side rolled up. Audience members, consisting of practically the whole Brigade and many visitors, were seated on the canal embankment. A successful sports afternoon, with foot and mounted events was arranged on Thursday, followed by a concert given by the 27th American Division Party, the first such concert played to this Brigade. The breezy attitude of the performers brought forth much applause from the audience.

Their short period of rest ended. General John Monash, who'd taken over as Commander of the Australian Corps on 31 May 1918, was finally permitted to move his reliable Australian forces out of Flanders to join his planned offensive on the Somme. It would be the first time all five Australian Divisions would operate under an Australian commander. Now honed into a highly disciplined and highly effective killing machine, on the Somme battlefront the Australian Corps became spectacularly successful in bringing about the final end to the war.

---

221 Commander, Royal Artillery

As they departed Flanders, the British General Plumer 'gathered some of the senior members of the Division together and told them that perhaps 'no division … in the whole British Army' had 'done more to destroy the morale of the enemy than the 1st Australian Division.'[222]

Major General Glasgow was told by Lieut General De Lisle:

> *Before your magnificent division leaves my corps, I wish to thank you and all ranks under your command for the exceptional services rendered during the past four months. Joining this corps on April 26, during the Battle of the Lys, the division selected and prepared a position to defend the Hazebrouck front, and a few days later repulsed two heavy attacks with severe losses to the enemy. This action brought the enemy's advance to a standstill. Since then, the division has held the most important sector of this front continuously, and by skilful raiding and minor operations has advanced the line over a mile, on a front of 5,000 yards, capturing just short of 1,000 prisoners, and causing such damage to the troops of the enemy that nine divisions have been replaced. The complete success of all minor operations, the skill displayed by the patrols by day as well as by night, the gallantry and determination of the troops and their high state of training and discipline, have excited the admiration and emulation of all, and I desire that you will convey to all ranks my appreciation of their fine work and my regret that the division is leaving my command.*[223]

AUGUST 1918 ON THE SOMME, THE BATTLE OF AMIENS

Monash was brilliant at outsmarting and surprising the enemy and gave orders accordingly. The preparations reported in the unit war diaries of the 2nd FAB were repeated throughout the Australian forces. From 2 to 4 August, the 2nd FAB moved south to Glisy, on the eastern outskirts of Amiens. Playing its part, overnight on 5/6 August, the 2nd FAB prepared in secret for the coming battle, doing all the work possible without giving away the positions of the guns. Since the guns were about to be placed in a wheat field, the men stacked ammunition in the field and camouflaged it very effectively with straw. The Batteries bivouacked for the night at Saint Sauveur, near Villers-Bretonneux. Overnight on 6/7 August, the guns were brought forward and left in the sunken road near their intended positions. Ammunition work was completed. Overnight on 7/8 August, the guns were pulled into position and laid out on their attack lines.

---

222 Joynt, *Saving the Channel Ports 1918*, p 41
223 Belford, *Legs Eleven*, p 606

Camouflaged Gun,
Western Front
Source AWM E02800

At 4.20 am on 8 August the attack began. It was ever-afterwards described by the Germans as their 'black day' and signified the beginning of the end for Germany.

With no prior bombardment to alert them, the Germans were taken completely by surprise and overrun by the Australian infantry. Very pleased with the efficiency of the barrage, by 8.20 am the infantry had advanced so far forward that the Australian guns were out of range. Overnight on 8/9 August, the batteries stayed in the reserve to the left of Villers-Bretonneux, and in the morning moved forward to Harbonnières, which had now been captured. Next night the batteries moved forward again, to Rosières, but their guns were practically silent up to 15 August, apart from occasional firing at the request of the infantry. Despite suffering thousands of casualties, the Battle of Amiens was a major Allied victory as, along a section of the front 20 kilometres long, it pushed the Germans back eastwards by 11 kilometres.

Meanwhile, unaware of his brother's involvement in Monash's pivotal campaign, Nigel continued to serve as a doctor at Écault, near Boulogne.

No 10 Convalescent Depot, B.E.F. France, 17 Aug 1918

Dearest Mum

Your 2 letters, one dated 24th May, the other 3rd June, to hand last night, nearly 3 months on the way! It's pretty hopeless, isn't it? However, one ought to be thankful, I suppose, that we can communicate with one another at all; it is a stupendous distance when one comes to think of it.

Thank you for the cuttings, they are always interesting. It's all very well for the people out there like Andy Stuart[224] to talk about the 1,000s of men Australia ought still to send, but in spite of the fact that there are no doubt a lot of rotters at home we could easily be without, I don't see how Australia can afford to send any more men. All the cream of the country have come pretty well, and of these 50,000 have been killed, not taking into consideration the 1000's who have been rendered permanently unfit, and who will be a big drain on the State to a large extent in coming years. There is still Ireland who can supply 600,000 of the best fighting material at England's left hand, if she only had the guts to conscript them. No, I think Australia, considering her population has done her duty and has little to reproach herself with, in this respect at any rate. Now America has come in, I think they can afford to keep up our man power. We don't want the British Empire bled absolutely white.

The story about the shortage of doctors is greatly exaggerated. The Australian forces are at present very well off for medicos, even better than the British Army, and it is not really short, altho' the politicians at home are always raising this cry. The Yankees again are bringing over big reinforcements in this branch of the service.

Well, Mum, my 4th year's service as I have previously told you terminates very shortly now, the 8th September to be precise. The British Government want me to sign on for the duration of the war! The Military Service Act now embraces the medical profession as well as the rest of the community. I have refused, on the ground that I am an Australian domiciled in Australia. I have written to Andy Fisher[225] for particulars of my passage back; they are very difficult to get now and have to be sanctioned by the Government. I have also applied for permits for Mona, her mother and the wee son. I have not had an answer yet. It probably will be very unsatisfactory and depressing when it comes - however, I shan't leave it at that, but interview him in London when I am sent over to the War Office next month. If I remain in England for 3 months, I become naturalized now under the Conscription Scheme, and am therefore liable to service for the termination of the present emergency. So if I cannot get a boat,

---

224 This was Sir Thomas Anderson Stuart, Dean of the Faculty of Medicine at the University of Sydney. In an article in the Sydney Morning Herald on 30 May 1918 he argued that young doctors-in-training should not be sent to the war and that there were thousands of men loafing at street corners and at racetracks who could be sent. A week later Stuart forecast a looming shortage of trained war doctors.
225 Andrew Fisher, Australia's High Commissioner in London

I shall have to sign on again, but I am only going to do so on the stipulation that it is for 6 months.

It will be extremely difficult to get permits for the family I know, altho' I see Hughes[226] brought his wife and baby over. But I suppose that is a different story. Mona is very loath to travel at present, as it certainly is very precarious, the U boats being still alarmingly active. However, I think I shall decide to come back if it can be arranged as I must start to think of beginning a practice and furnishing a home for my belongings. Things will not get any easier by waiting, in fact, probably increasingly difficult, which I know is your opinion. Have done 4 years now and have given the Hun many opportunities of killing me, so I think I have done a fair whack, altho' these ultra-patriots probably would maintain I am a shirker. I have thought the thing over and over; if I were single, of course, it would be different and I really then would have very little excuse for pulling out. But I have other responsibilities to look to. Don't count on my coming too much, Mum, there are difficulties in the way, and I know boats are extremely difficult to get. I shall cable probably if I am coming.

Am very sorry to hear that you didn't get that £2 I sent you, it is ages and ages since I instructed Holts and Co. to send it. I shall write to them and ask them what has happened to it. I haven't sent you the £10 for the pigs, as I hadn't heard whether the scheme I suggested was practicable from your point of view. But I will also instruct them to forward that too. It's very annoying the £2 not having arrived. I know lots of mails go astray; there are notices frequently appearing in the paper about the loss of Australian mails. Many thanks for sending the Havelock[227], I know I shall enjoy it if I ever receive it. But it is so seldom anything ever gets thro'; either lost or appropriated en route. That pair of tan woollen socks you made me, and a tin of cigarettes from the Child, are the only things I have ever received. It's pretty maddening, isn't it?

I haven't heard from Steve lately. I am expecting his next letter to tell me that he has proceeded home on leave, as he told me in his letter he hoped to get it soon. Aunt Julia and C. Bess are well. I owe the former a letter.

I am feeding up now, and taking cod liver oil and malt, a promise I made to Mona when last on leave, and am getting a little fatter. Haven't had any malarial attacks now for several months. Am all right in the hot weather so Australia ought to suit me!

No more now, dearest Mother,

---

226 The Australian Prime Minister
227 A cloth cover for a military service cap, with a flap to protect the back of the neck, reportedly named after Sir Henry Havelock

Bestest love to you, and the Child. Also to Aunt Mog.

I do hope I shall be able to come home soon. Don't despair, I long to come back. It would be lovely to see you waiting on the Ermo Wharf to see the prodigal's return, altho' I expect you would venture as far as Circular Quay when you heard I was coming.

A big hug and a kiss,

From yours ever,

NIGE

After the Battle of Amiens, the 2nd FAB was relieved 'in the line' on 15 August and the men moved back to rest positions on the banks of the Somme Canal at Aubigny. That day, Steve was released to go on leave.

TORBAY HOTEL, TORQUAY, 21 AUG 1918

Dearest Matee boos

You will see I am in England once again. My leave suddenly came along a bit sooner than I expected and away I came from the line on the 15th. It is just the thing getting over here again, especially at this time in the fine and summery weather. I managed to get over here too, 6 hours sooner than I should have which all counts.

I spent a couple of days in London doing a fair amount of shopping which had to be done. Stayed at the Bedford Hotel again where I had been before. Didn't like it so well this time, it was more crowded and there are all sorts of food restrictions now which make it hard to get a good feed. Everything is terribly expensive and dinner anywhere runs into half a guinea before you know where you are and then you hardly feel as if you have had anything.

Before coming over we are issued with a ration book containing various tickets or coupons for meat, sugar, tea, jam etc. which have to be forked out each time. Whilst in London I went out to Kennet House where my suitcase and some of my clothes were and saw Aunt Julia and Cousin Bess and also Cousin Jim, the Parson chap. They were the only people there, which was a bit of an escape. Aunt Julia was very well and quite recovered from her poisoned foot which she had just got over.

Cousin Bess was much as usual and very well. They were all very pleased to see me again. I was only there a couple of hours during which time I had dinner and came away afterwards. Promised I would go there again before I went back and perhaps stay the night, which I suppose I shall have to do. They wanted me to stay this time, but I didn't bring anything with me and was coming away to Torquay the next morning to Mona, Mrs. Little and young "Pipen."

It took me best part of a day to get down here from London and another to go back, so I have given up ideas of getting up to Scotland this time and shall probably stay here for a few more days and then go back to London afterwards and see some of the theatres before going back to France. I found everyone at Manstow[228] looking very well and it is very healthy and bracing for young Pip. He is looking very fit and enjoys himself all day long. He has grown tremendously since I last saw him. When I was over last he wasn't even crawling and now he is stumping about everywhere and walks back from the beach every day, being greatly admired by all and sundry. He persists in calling me Dady, having a bit of a job in remembering his Unkie. However, we are good friends, and he didn't take 5 minutes to get used to me. He is a very good boy and never squawks. He calls himself Pipen Boulton and sometimes Boulton Pipen Boulton which will probably stick to him.

Pip Boulton with toys, July 1918
(Picture Courtesy Julia Woodhouse)

We take him down to the beach nearly every day where he delights in getting into the water with his uncle and thoroughly enjoys it. After that he stumps home on his big fat legs so you can imagine he is a pretty sturdy lad. He has his own bucket & spade and various other toys but only plays with them at odd times before going to sleep. He seems to amuse himself stumping round the place picking up anything that is about. Just now he is having his morning sleep after a bit of a walk down the village. He has got a fine big cot with wooden rails instead of iron and a net which goes over the top that prevents him from climbing out.

It is pretty dull down here as far as having a lively and exciting holiday, but there is plenty of swimming and one or two amusements. Yesterday Mona and I went over to a little place called Oddicombe where I had swim while she

---

228 Manstow was apparently a hotel or boarding house at Torquay.

sat on the beach. She rather wanted to come in, but the accommodation in the way of bathing machines was very limited. I got into one which was being used by several N.Z. Officers who made room. It was great in the water and I enjoyed it very much.

Afterwards we had tea and then sat about for a bit until another girl from Manstow turned up who was to meet us. She is a Canadian and the wife of a Canadian R.A.M.C. chap out at the front. We all went and had dinner at the Royal Hotel and afterwards walked home round the cliffs. So although it is not a wild whirl of excitement here it is doing me some good I suppose.

Mrs. Little is looking very well and helps look after the boy when Mona is out. We all went to a bit of a show here the other night as a bit of an outing called 'Eliza comes to stay'. The show was very second rate and poorly acted, but could be made a good play. There wasn't any room for me at Manstow so I am staying at the Torbay Hotel where I sleep and have breakfast. It is a very flash place, but rather quiet now that the war is on. So I generally come up and see the family after breakfast and have lunch and dinner with them, or go out together somewhere. There is no Devonshire cream or apple dumplings going now. All the cream is being made into butter unless you have a doctor's certificate whereby you are allowed to have and buy some. Mona gets some for Pipen, but somehow he doesn't seem to care for it much. The apple season is a very poor one this year I believe. This afternoon we are thinking of going over to Paignton to give the lad a bit of a swim and an outing.

Mona tells me that Billy is coming over again in September and is thinking of giving up his Army job. Haven't heard from him for some time. It seems that all temporary M.O.s have got to sign on for the duration of the war now, or resign and be conscripted or clear out of England. Don't quite know what Billy is to do. He may go back to Australia but Mrs. Little won't go back yet and thinks it is too risky to take the young son on the water.

Mona wants him to carry on with his army job until the end, now that it looks like finishing within another 12 months. He may have told you what his plans are, but so far nothing much has been decided definitely. I think if he went back to Australia he would soon want to come over again after being there for a little while.

My leave is up on the 29th so almost half has already gone. It doesn't take long to go once you get over here. I believe all the Australians are to be given a bit of a spell some time perhaps in the winter for 2 or 3 months, which will be good-oh. That was the latest rumour when last I left. I hope it comes true; although I don't suppose it will be much of a spell, it may be out of the line.

I won't write much more now Matee, as lunch is nearly ready and punctuality has to be observed at these places or you will miss. I received a letter from you this morning dated the 17th June and addressed to Mona; got the Abdulla cigarettes you speak of quite alright. Am glad to hear you got some of my letters. I thought of sending you a cable when I got over on leave, but thought perhaps better not, as you would prefer hearing in the usual way.

I brought a few little souvenirs over from France for the young son when he grows up - 2 German bayonets, a German cap, some bullets and a few other odds and ends. Had a bit of a job in getting them over, but managed it somehow.

Please give my love to Aunt Mog and Aunt Phoebe and Phil. Hope everything at Tyrone and Hillcrest[229] are going on well.

Aunt Phoebe's Home, Hillside, View St, Chatswood, c 1916
(Picture Courtesy Julia Woodhouse)

How is the Child now, you said in Mona's letter that she was looking very pale and peaky. Have you heard any more about the lung? Hope it was nothing serious. I got a letter from Cleon by the last mail in answer to the book I sent over.

And now good-bye Matee Boos, with heaps and heaps of love and kisses from

Your loving son

TOOTS.

P.S. Hope this letter doesn't go down, as it is a long one.

---

229 He meant Hillside, the name of Aunt Phoebe's house in View St, Chatswood.

France [Boulogne], 29 Aug 1918

Dearest Matee

You will see that I am once more back in France. Am writing this little note from Boulogne before going up the line again. Crossed over today at about 11:30 after leaving London at 7:30 a.m.

I had a great time on leave, the only drawback being that the time goes so quickly, however I suppose it is better than no leave at all. I told you in my last letter about going down to Torquay and staying with Mrs. Little, Mona and Pip.

I came up to London for the last 3 days to see some of the theatres in town and do some shopping. I went out to Harrow for a night, and so did my duty in that respect. Arrived out there about 4 o'clock in the afternoon. They had some visitors who had just called. Cousin Kate was staying; also Joy Musgrave[230] who however didn't turn up till nearly dinner time as she has got a job in town, typewriting etc. at the Air Board. She is quite young, about 19 I should think. I don't know if you ever saw or remember her. She was only staying the night and left the next morning directly after breakfast for her office.

However it saved the situation a bit as she is a bit lively. We played the gramophone in the evening and amused ourselves by putting on all the lively music. Everyone departed for bed shortly after 10 o'clock which made it a short evening.

Aunt Julia seemed well, but she no longer walks about as much as she used to. She has taken to a stick now, and only climbs the stairs once a day. She still occasionally gets out round the garden, when it is fine only. She feels the cold very much and is kept well wrapped up now in summer. She had quite recovered from her poisoned foot and appeared as well as ever.

Cousin Bess was as usual very well, also cousin Kate and all her family. I went down and saw Aunt Eleanor and Blanche the next morning before going back to town. They were very pleased to see me and are going away soon for a holiday with the Morgans.[231]

Aunt Eleanor keeps very fit and is still as energetic as ever. Blanche hasn't altered at all. Mona stayed a week with them a little while ago whilst waiting for Billy to come over from France. She said it was pretty awful and Blanche

---

230   A granddaughter of Aunt Julia
231   Aunt Julia's eldest daughter married a Rev Morgan.

absolutely got on her nerves. She was to have gone to Kennet House, but they were all away at the time.

I came away from Harrow in the afternoon and had the last night in town. Stayed at the Austn. Officers Club in Piccadilly which is quite good, as other chaps were there who were returning to France from leave, and were doing the early morning act.

Had dinner at the Regent Palace Hotel with another Aussie I met whilst cadetting. He had just come over on leave. Whilst having dinner there, Gerald Christoe[232] strolled in from hospital where he has been for a couple of months. He seemed well and I was pleased to see him. He hadn't altered a bit and was just the same as ever. He had been wounded in the leg somewhere. The second occasion. He is also a full Lieut., but in the infantry – 3rd Battn. Had a bit of a yarn to him, but he didn't have much news that I didn't know. He will be coming back to France later.

After dinner I went and saw 'Yes Uncle' at the Shaftesbury Theatre and enjoyed it very much. It is one of the best shows on in town now and I laughed nearly the whole time. Some very good music. Previously I had seen 3 other things, all of which were good with the exception of one, "Tails up". They were all musical plays which I like, being cheerful and lively.

Everything is terribly expensive in London now and theatre tickets run you into 13/- now with amusement tax added, about 10/6 in the dress circle, so you can imagine how the money goes. Can't get a feed under 5/- anywhere, so it is not the place to live in peace time.

Whilst in London l went down to the Commonwealth Bank and saw a whole lot of chaps I knew who were in the Sydney Office with me, also a lot of ex-union chaps who left the C.B.A. too before me. They were telling me all about the show. It seems to have turned out a wonderful concern and the staff are well paid and looked after. The Governor Denison Miller is over here on a visit now, so I called in and saw him. He is a very decent chap and was pleased to see me and hear how I had been getting on. He didn't talk about the Bank at all or ask if I was going to chuck it or not after the war. The lads told me there was another bonus for the staff last year which I didn't know of.

I saw the *New Yorker Magazine* when in there waiting to see the Governor, with photos of all the Sydney offices and rooms and latest contrivances etc. It seems to be a very fine place. The lads were telling me that the Governor was

---

232 Gerald Blood Christoe, a bank officer with the Bank of NSW, enlisted in Sydney as a 2nd Lieut on 30 Aug 1915, aged 26. He died in Hay in 1944.

very good to all the returned chaps belonging to the bank and their screws were all increased pro rata for the years they had been away and were given the choice of all the branches they liked to go. I thought it just as well to go and see the old boy whilst I was there and had the chance, in case nothing else turns up and I have to carry on.

Have had a day and night here in Boulogne, waiting for my train up the line, so I went out and saw Billy at his convalescent camp. He was acting O.C. of the place whilst the other chaps are away on leave. He has already told you of resigning his job and going back I suppose. He is still very undecided as to what to do, as Mona and Mrs. Little don't want to risk taking the boy on the sea just now. They also all want to go back together, if possible, and so don't quite know what is going to happen.

However, they are all waiting for Billy to get over there which he expects to do about the 7th or 10th of next month. They may have some difficulty in procuring passages and may not be allowed the travel. Billy should be able to go alright, but the women part may get knocked back. Stayed the night out at the camp with Billy, who is very comfortable out there, with nothing much to do.

Am off back to the Somme area again where my Division is and where I left them. The war news has been pretty good lately and the Hun ought soon to begin to feel the pinch. Now that my leave is all over it is not too pleasant going back again. The next spasm takes in all the winter again. There is a faint possibility of us being out of the line during a part of the winter I should think, but there is no saying what we will do.

You ought to get a few letters by the next English mail from the Harrow people, telling you of my visit. You had better send my letters direct to me at the battery now, as there is a possibility of Mona not being over here to forward them on.

Hal has moved from Gretna[233] to another place in Derbyshire. Cousin Bess had a letter from him whilst I was there. They have got a bit of a joke there amongst themselves about Hal's letters, as he generally writes about the beautiful birds etc. which tickled them all immensely.

How is Aunt Mog getting on at Tyrone? The house has got another name now I believe, but I have forgotten it. Please give her my love and also the Child. I wonder if she is with you now or away at the Lido.[234] Am expecting to find

---

233 Gretna, on the English border with Scotland, housed the UK's largest cordite factory during WW1.
234 Thea's boarding house.

some letters waiting for me when I get back to the battery. In this moving about warfare, advancing etc, there is very little opportunity for writing letters as we all only travel with what we stand up in, with a couple of blankets for a bed.

So cheerio Matee boos, with heaps and heaps of love and kisses for all and yourself from

Your loving son TOOTS.

From 15 August the 2nd FAB had about a week of rest on the banks of the Somme Canal at Aubigny, then it went back into action. Once again, Steve's leave meant that he missed the secret preparations made for the barrage on Morcourt on 23 August, and the advance made by the infantry at Proyart and Foucaucourt on 27 August 1918, continually pushing the German line back. This was part of the softening up process before the Australian Corps' brilliant move which earned praise from British General Henry Rawlinson as the greatest military achievement of the war.

The artillery of the 1st Division was then pulled out of the line, not needed for General Monash's new strategy of attacking without providing the enemy with the standard warning signal of a preliminary heavy artillery bombardment. On the night of 31 August, Australian infantry crossed the Somme River and stormed, seized and held the key height of Mont Saint-Quentin (overlooking Péronne), a pivotal German defensive position. The German forces quickly retreated to the Hindenburg Line along the Saint Quentin Canal, the point from where they had started in the Spring of 1918.

While the Australian infantry covered themselves with glory in this battle, the 2nd FAB enjoyed the first week of September out of the line, bivouacked near Sailly-Laurette, following the usual camp routines and disciplines but also enjoying several concerts, band music and sports activities.

In the field [Sailly-Laurette], France, 6 Sep 1918

Dearest Matee

Am scribbling this off tonight before going to bed. Tomorrow morning we are off into the line again after a very short spell.

I arrived back from leave and found the battery had just come out the previous day. I think I told you this in my last letter. We have had quite a good time out

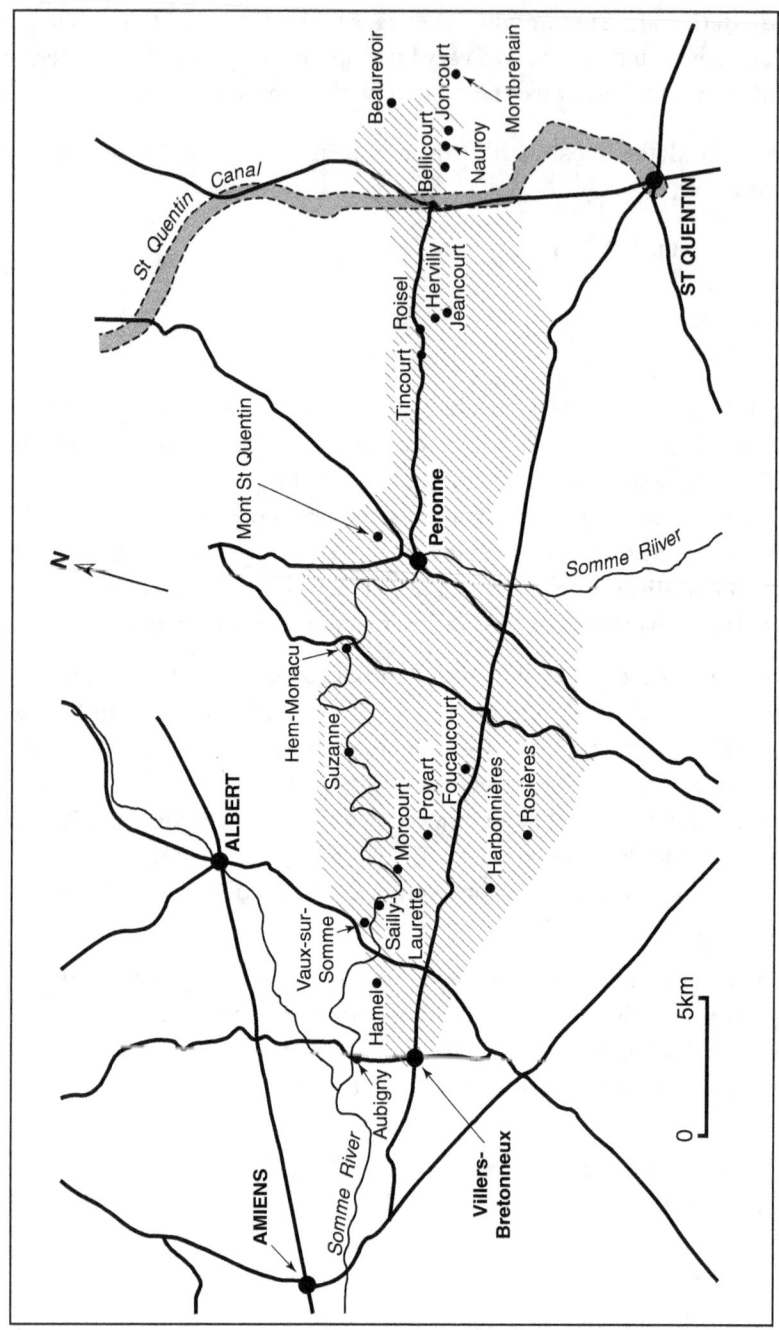

Map 11: Breaking the Beaurevoir Line, 1918

Map © John Newland, 2015

resting for these few days and the weather has been great. Fine, sunny and hot so that we have been able to enjoy some swimming in the river which is quite close to our camp.

After coming back from leave it is natural to feel a bit fed up after the stay in London and Torquay. However, I was lucky in finding the battery not in action I suppose, as I have had a few days of fair comfort in which to get broken in again.

Yesterday we had a sort of an impromptu sports meeting which went off very well and was much appreciated by all ranks. There are also a few concert parties which come round occasionally and give us shows which are sometimes very good and help pass the time.

I haven't heard from Billy or Mona for some time. Billy ought to be getting over to England any day now and then some decision will be come to as to what is going to happen. When I passed through Boulogne on my way up here I went out to see him and stayed the night there. He seemed very well and was at the time acting as O.C. of the camp whilst the Colonel was away on leave. He seemed very undecided as to what to do and I thought rather wanted to get back home to Australia, but Mona didn't like the idea of him pulling out just as the war seemed to be finishing, also Mrs. Little doesn't like to risk letting Mona and the young son travel on the water during the submarine campaign, but at the same time wouldn't interfere with any arrangements that Billy and Mona had come to.

So that was how it was, and they all await Billy's arrival to discuss the matter. If Billy gets a majority he will carry on out here again.

And now Matee I must be off to bed. Up early in the morning to get away early and must make the most of our last night out of the line.

Give my best love to the Child, Aunt Mog, Aunt Phoebe, and Phil, hope everyone is keeping well, with heaps and heaps of love and kisses from

Your loving son

TOOTS.

On 7 September Steve's Brigade left the Sailly-Laurette area and marched eastwards to Suzanne, reaching there by midday. Batteries went into bivouac and guns and horses were concealed in the trees and undergrowth. More concerts

followed, on 8 & 9 September, before the men moved forward and bivouacked in the Hem-Monacu area.

On 11 September, the 2nd FAB continued to help with the Australian pushback of the German forces, and moved forward to Tincourt area. The guns were brought up and engaged in a barrage. They remained in action through to an attack on Hervilly on 18 September, before reaching Jeancourt on 19 September. The area between Bellicourt and Nauroy was continually shelled by day and night, with harassing fire on 20 September, the Germans retaliating by dropping many bombs on the batteries. Next day, 21 September, the 2nd FAB's barrage on Jeancourt started. Somehow Steve managed to write to his mother.

IN THE FIELD [JEANCOURT], FRANCE, 22 SEP 1918

My dearest Matee

Have just received your letter of July 13th in which you say you have just received three of mine. Am glad to hear you are getting them alright. Thanks so much for enclosing the Comm. Bank letter saying that they are getting my increased allotment now alright. Am so glad it is now going on properly. Was getting a bit anxious about it myself, and when on leave in England last, went along to our Head Quarters and got them to write to the Defence Dept. about it. Now it is being paid in everything will be right. There is no use to worry about taking it out of the Bank and putting it in the Union.[235] It is quite safe where it is and getting more interest than if I transferred it.

Haven't had any time for letter writing lately as we have been in some pretty big stunts and in the line all the time. We are all wondering when we are going to be relieved and get a bit of a spell. We have been in now for a long time and the whole Australian Corps are in a bad need of a rest. Our chaps always do so well and never fail, they almost seem afraid to take us out. But still we ought to go out soon and it should be a fairly long rest this time. Billy Hughes[236] has just been over here from England and is doing a pretty shrewd political move in getting all the 1914 men returned to Australia. Quite a lot of chaps have already gone amidst great send-offs from all the other chaps although they all felt very envious. I know I felt that way and wished I had been one.

Something may be done for the early 1915 men like myself, but I don't think so. I don't see how it can possibly be done. The 1914 chaps are going home for

---

235 The Union Bank of Australasia, where his father had once been a manager and where 'Uncle Frank' was now a senior manager.
236 The Australian Prime Minister

six months furlough and are all to be back again in France by next spring. Billy Hughes is going back with them and I suppose when he gets home will make a big speech and say 'Here you are I have brought them all back with me'. In the meantime we are wondering how things are going to be carried on over here. There will have to be a lot of changes made.

Am glad to hear you are still at Ermo with no sign of a tenant. Can quite understand you not wanting to leave it and let somebody else come in and knock it about. It is a pity all the crops are being spoilt by the frost. We have had a most wonderful summer over here with the minimum amount of rain. Hope it will not be an extra wet winter to make up for it.

What a good thing Aunt Mog is so comfortable at Tyrone or whatever the name of the place is. Am glad to hear she is looking so much better now. The Child does not seem to be too well from your letters. She ought to go and see the doctor man and find out if anything is wrong with her.

We are having fine and clear nights now with a full moon and the Hun is pretty busy in bombing us every night with his planes. We don't see too much of him through the day but as soon as it gets dark he starts out. We are getting plenty of our own back though. I don't think he will ever make any more pushes as he has been having a deuce of a time lately and the Yanks are getting stronger and better every day. We shall most likely continue to push him all the winter.

Had a letter from Harold Boulton who is out in India now. He must have joined the Indian Army as they were calling for volunteers some time ago amongst the A.I.F. They go straight from France to India and so are finished with all fighting. They however take up the army as a profession and stick to it after the war is over. Wouldn't care much for the life although they get plenty of furlough from India and good pay, but at the same time it is all spent in living expenses I believe. Haven't had time to answer his letter yet. He is also in the Artillery.

Won't write any more now Matee. Give my best love to The Child and Aunt Mog and Phoebe & Phil and remember me to Cleon. There was a sailor up here the other day sightseeing off the *Yarra* which was in Genoa. They will no doubt be escorting these 1914 men going back. Heaps and heaps of love and kisses Matee, from

Your ever loving son,

TOOTS.

In constant action to 29 September when the Hindenburg Line was finally broken, the 2nd FAB withdrew next day to their forward wagon lines. General Monash's next bold move and stunning victory did not require artillery support until 3 October. On that day, the 2nd FAB and all other artillery in the vicinity launched a barrage. Monash's aim now was to breach the Beaurevoir Line, a well-defended series of barbed-wire entanglements and gun bunkers east of the main Hindenburg Line. There was very little trench protection for advancing infantry. The village of Beaurevoir and the high ground of Montbrehain were securely taken by 5 October, at the cost of 430 casualties.

2ND AUS F A BGDE [JEANCOURT], 6 OCT 1918

Dear Mrs. Boulton

It is with the very greatest regret that I write to inform you of the death of your son Lieut. S. P. Boulton of our 6th Bty who was killed in action on the morning of the 3rd inst. during heavy enemy shelling of the Bty position.

We buried him, side by side with 3 other Officers of the Brigade who were killed the same morning, in the military section of the Civil Cemetery at Roisel (East of Péronne) and the Unit will erect substantial crosses over the graves.

I know how miserably inadequate all expressions of sympathy must seem to you at such a time, but I do want to assure you that we all feel very deeply for you in your sorrow.

Throughout the Brigade your son was highly respected and well liked and we who were privileged to be his comrades very deeply mourn his loss, and can imagine something of what his death must mean to his loved ones in far off Australia.

Please accept our deepest sympathy with you all

Yours faithfully,

T. Theodor Webb.[237]
Chaplain
2nd Aus. F.A. Bgde

---

237 Thomas Theodor Webb was a 31-yr-old Methodist Minister from the Melbourne suburb of Surrey Hills when he left Australia for the war in September 1916.

The Unit's war diary reports the bare facts:

> *Jeancourt 3rd. At 6.5am a barrage was put down by all batteries of the Bde as well as all in the vicinity & a stunt started. The 2nd Div A.I.F. "hopped over", everything went according to plan & as far as can be ascertained the attack was quite successful. Lieut S.P. Boulton was seriously wounded by a gas shell and died a few hours later. Capt H.E. Kirkland A.A.M.C. at 5th Bty was killed, direct hit by a 5.9. Capt N.S. Hollis O.C. 6th Bty received gunshot wounds in the chest and died several hours later. Lieut H J Fisher received gunshot wounds in the head & died a few hours later. Capt Kirkland, Capt Hollis & Lt Fisher were all killed by the same shell. Major A W Dodd M.C. was severely gassed while attending to Lt Boulton but remained on duty.*

> *About midday orders were received for the Brigade to pull out of the line & return to wagon lines in the Jeancourt area. The move was completed without mishap.*

Next day Steve was buried:

> *Jeancourt 4th. Lieut W.T. Watson D.C.M evacuated gassed, results of yesterday's work. The C.O. and C.R.A. visited all Batteries & everything was apparently in order and satisfactory. At 5pm the bodies of Capt Kirkland, Capt Hollis, Lieut Fisher & Lieut Boulton were buried in the 'Roisel' Cemetery (K 16 b 3.7 sheet 62C 1/40,000). The C.R.A. and all the 2nd Aust F.A. Brigade officers were present, also a large party of men.*

Burial Site, Roisel Cemetery, 5 October 1918
(Picture Courtesy Julia Woodhouse)

If only Steve had lived for six more hours.

The action in which Steve, his fellow officers and the other Australians were killed was the last battle fought by Australian infantry during the Great War. Exhausted by continuous fighting for most of 1918, the Australians were withdrawn from the Front. The 2nd FAB trekked back 15 miles to Hem on 5 October, 18 miles to Vaux-sur-Somme on 7 October, 18 miles to Saint Sauveur on 8 October and next day trekked another 10 miles to their final rest point at Condé-Folie, a village west of the main congregation point of Vignacourt, where the following letter was written by the commanding officer of the 2nd FAB, in pencil, on army issue paper. It did not reach Steve's mother until December.

Condé-Folie, France, 14 Oct 1918

Dear Mrs. Boulton

I am writing to you to express my sincerest sympathies in the death of your son, killed in action near Nauroy early on the morning of 3rd inst. It will be consoling for you to hear from me as his Commanding Officer and to know that everything was done that could be done from a medical point of view to save him.

It was on the morning of our attack on the Beaurevoir Line, subsequent to our successful operation on the Hindenburg Line, that the Germans subjected our Battery positions to a heavy shell fire, with both gas and H.E. Very little cover was available and the officers, three in number, your son included, had constructed a small place to sleep by digging into the side of a railway embankment. For the time being this dugout had proved comparatively safe, although the shelling had gone on for some time. Eventually a gas shell fell and exploded on the parapet, filling the dugout with a deadly cloud of gas.

At the time your son was standing up and three pieces from the bursting shell entered his back. He fell, seriously wounded. Lieut. Watson[238], one of the other two officers who were lying down at the time, seeing his helplessness at once adjusted your son's gas respirator. It was apparent the wound was serious as he was almost unconscious.

He received immediate attention and was then taken to a Field Ambulance Station close by, where he died some few hours afterwards when every effort made to save him had failed. He was buried the day following in a Military Cemetery at Roisel by Capt. Webb, C of E. Minister attached to this Brigade. The Divisional General, myself, several of your son's brother officers and men from his Battery were present at the burial.

I would ask you to kindly accept my sincerest sympathy in your sad loss. Your son was a sterling boy with many good qualities. He was loved by his brother

---

238 Lieut William Thornton Watson was a young New Zealand-born Australian and member of the Wallaby Rugby team prior to the War. In action on the Western Front he was in November 1917 awarded the Distinguished Conduct Medal for "gallantry and coolness in going to the assistance of wounded men under heavy fire". In May 1919 he was awarded the Military Cross for gallantry as forward Observation Officer at Faucoucourt on 27 August 1918. He earned a bar to his MC for conspicuous gallantry displayed in heavy bombardment near Bellicourt on 2–3 October 1918 when although badly gassed, he tried to save the life of a wounded officer and stayed in command of his battery until withdrawn from the line. That wounded officer was Steve. Watson had a colourful life after the war and served with distinction in WW2.

officers and respected by his men, and his death has been a serious loss to the Brigade.

I am,

Yours very sincerely,
David H. Moore
Lt Col.[239]

Condé-Folie, France, 26 October 1918

Soon after the arrival of the Brigade at Condé-Folie an epidemic of influenza broke out amongst the men – about 60 officers & men were affected altogether.

They were victims of the 'flu' epidemic which started in October 1918 and quickly became a world-wide pandemic, infecting about 500 million people of whom 20-50 million died, many more than the casualties of the Great War. One of the deadliest natural disasters in human history, it was nicknamed the 'Spanish flu' but there is no evidence of its source.

At Condé-Folie all, with the exception of the more serious cases, were treated by the M.O. who established a hospital and isolated all cases in a billet in the village. The men's rations were added to by the purchase of vegetables from local farmers out of the Brigade Funds.

The surviving members of the 2nd FAB mourned their fallen comrades. With the passing of the influenza epidemic, on 26 October an 'In Memoriam' Service for the Officers, N.C.Os and men of the Brigade who had fallen in action since 1 April 1918 was held in the Factory at Condé-Folie. The Service was conducted by the Brigade's Chaplain, the Rev T. T. Webb, and attended by the C.R.A. (the senior artillery officer in the 1st Division) and Staff.

Lt-Col Moore had concern for the welfare of his men. At the end of September 1918 he wrote:

> The morale of the Bde has always been good. The tasks they have been set at various times recently have appeared almost impossible of accomplishment. That the infantry have appreciated the good work done by the Artillery and have thanked them for it has encouraged the men immensely. The morale of the personnel has been improved by the return to Australia on leave of all

---

239 When he sailed off to war in November 1915, Lt Col David Henry Moore was a 37-yr-old bank official, and Major, of the Melbourne suburb of Armadale.

> *1914 men becoming an accomplished fact. Seventy from this Bde left during this month. No reinforcements have arrived in their place. The consequence has been the work has fallen exceedingly heavy on the weak-manned batteries. If the men had not been buoyed up by the latter fact and the continual successes we have met with, they could not possibly have carried out the work. The clothing of the men is good and plenty is procurable. There is some little feeling about the cutting down of rations, especially as the winter is approaching.[240]*

At the end of October 1918 he wrote:

> *The month of October will ever be remembered by all ranks in the Brigade as a period of a maximum of work with a minimum of strength in Personnel. Practically 25% of the strength of the Brigade were withdrawn for furlough to Australia even before we were withdrawn from the line, in the vicinity of Nauroy. Not a single reinforcement arrived & with this reduced strength the Brigade still carried out successfully its part in the operations of the Beaurevoir Line. Subsequently it was withdrawn to the rear areas but with difficulty, as there were hardly enough men even to man the horses. As for officers, three of the Batteries were commanded by Subalterns & the other by a Captain.*

> *A week after settling down in our rest area at Condé-Folie about 50 reinforcements arrived, but they only compensated for the extra leave allotment to the U.K. With this reduced strength the Brigade had an enormous amount of work to do, such as re-equipment, cleaning of harness, painting of vehicles &, as the Engineers did not direct the building of houses & sheds, as a result the men had little or no time for the rest & recreation which they deserved.[241]*

It is of little comfort to the Boulton family that such sadly-depleted ranks contributed to a beautiful young man being taken from their midst. Comparing Stephen's photo taken early in 1915 with a photo taken two years later, the war strengthened his physical condition. Stephen clearly would have made a wonderful father and family man. He might eventually have become a 'somebody' in the Commonwealth Bank, as he was fully aware of financial matters and on familiar terms with the most senior executives in the bank.

But the family can take comfort in the good work that his artillery unit accomplished. And comfort in the knowledge that he had a proper burial in a

---

240 From AWM RCDIG1015037 images 18 and 19.
241 From AWM RCDIG1015038 image 14.

marked grave, escaping the fate of so many thousands of Unknown Soldiers of the Great War, lucky to be remembered by a name on a wall.

Steve's relatives in England, where he had so recently stayed, noticed his name in the casualty lists published in the *London Times*. Cousin Bessie wrote to the Australian Red Cross, asking for particulars of her young relative to send to his mother in Australia. 'He was an Anzac', Bessie said proudly. Anxiously she wrote: 'Could you kindly tell me how he was wounded? & where? & if he died in hospital? & which day he was wounded? was he conscious when he died? was the chaplain with him? is it known where his grave is? & was the funeral service read over his body?'

Relatives always hanker to know the last words of a dying person and Bessie was no exception: 'We should be so glad to have any of his last words or possibly messages if he was able to give them.'

She received the following response, written from the Western Front, in pencil:

France, 29 Oct 1918

Dear Miss Charles

In reply to your letter asking for particulars of Lieut S. P. Boulton's death, I will give you all the particulars I can gather at present, and if I can find out anything further I'll be only too glad to let you know.

On the morning of Oct 3rd he had just got out of bed, and was preparing to go forward on Observation Duty. Just then a gas shell burst very close to him, and badly wounded him in the shoulder and back. He was carried to an advanced dressing station and received medical attention almost immediately. He was conscious for a very short time, but did not appear to be suffering any pain. He soon lapsed into unconsciousness, and died shortly afterwards. These are about all the facts I can give you.

The officer who was with him when he was hit is at present in hospital at Welwyn, and I am sure if you could spare the time, he would gladly give you any information he knew. His name is Lieut. W.T. Watson, M.C. D.C.M., also the then Bty commander Major A W Dodd is in Wandsworth Hospital. Either of these officers could give you more information than I can. At the time of the occurrence I was adjutant of the Bgde. Mr. Boulton was buried with full military honours in Roisel Cemetery by Chaplain T.T. Webb. A large number of officers and men were also present including our Divisional Commander.

Please allow me to offer my deepest sympathy. I knew him very well, in fact he was a pal of mine, and I personally regret his loss very, very much. His quiet unassuming manner made him generally liked, and his death was a deep blow to us all. You can rest assured that everything possible was done for him.

I expect to be on leave very soon, and if convenient for you, would like to tell you what I've tried to write.

Yours sincerely,

(Major) A. McMullin.[242]

Cablegram, 31 Oct 1918

Cable No 55 via Pacific

From France 11.40 31st

12 words

Dora Boulton, Ermington NSW

Just heard Steve's Death. Sincerest sympathy. Writing. Captain Boulton

Received 10.15am 5th Nov 1918

Throughout October, the Allies recaptured a number of Belgian and French towns and kept pressing forward.

Somewhere in Belgium, 5 Nov 1918

My dearest Mum

I have been meaning to write to you every day, but I have put it off hoping that I shall have had an answer from Steve's C.O., but so far he hasn't answered. Letters take so long these days of advance, that the position of the various units is continually changing and so the Post Office has difficulty in keeping track of them. However, I ought to hear any day.

---

242 Alfred Oswald McMullin was a 29-yr-old grazier of Aberdeen NSW with 8 years of military training behind him when he joined up in August 1914. He had recently been promoted from Captain to Major when he wrote this letter.

Cousin Bess has written, I've written and Mona I think wrote too, so we ought to have news before long. I will write the moment I hear, and Cousin Bess has promised to let me know as soon as she learns anything definite. She has also communicated with the Australian Red Cross Society who have a special department for dealing with all casualties and they are setting the wheels in motion too.

So it's just a question of patience, Mum, we shall get all particulars shortly, I shall endeavour to visit his grave, and have a photograph taken of it, and get hold of his little personal belongings. His C.O. or the 2nd in command, if anything has happened to the former, will be able to give us the information we seek all right.

It would have been so much worse if Steve had been missing, and we had been left in an awful state of uncertainty as to his fate, like poor Mrs. Barton. He was buried by his own people, and attended to by them, whereas he might so easily have fallen into German hands, like so many others to die there. Dear C. Bess wrote me a charming letter of sympathy, and so did Aunt Eleanor. They were all so fond of poor little Tootie at Harrow. Mona too is greatly upset, as she and Steve were such good friends, and he used to make little confidences to her, that I never heard. The wee son too, whom Steve took such a fancy to, and whom he reckoned was "a great lad" has lost his only uncle. He will treasure I know tho' in after years the silver mug which his Uncle gave him before he gave his life for his country in the greatest war of all history.

Poor dearest of Mothers, how I feel for you being so lonely and so far away and how I wish I could have been with you in this your sorest of trials. It will age you terribly I'm afraid. Still you will be brave and proud of little Tootie, won't you, Mum? He couldn't have had a more glorious death.

His name will go on the Roll of Honour at The King's School. I should write to the Headmaster there and give him the particulars he requires. Steve died on Oct 3rd. I shall be able to tell you in what part of France later on. I have had 2 letters from you recently, both written in September, you had just heard about the possibility of Steve's getting furlough to visit Australia, and were so looking forward to it. It did hurt reading about your hopes of seeing him again, but you had heard the sad news, when I received it.

Well, we are still out at Divisional rest, and are receiving reinforcements daily, which are busily being trained. We have got 4 new M.O's for the ambulance, so are now up to strength. One of them is an American. I expect we shall be going into action again soon, but we think it will be another part of the line.

The division is being reviewed by the King of the Belgians today. It is pouring with rain so it will be a ghastly business. Fortunately I have escaped it.

Mona and the boy have postponed their visit to Harrow as the "flu" epidemic has been raging in England lately, especially round London. 400 Harrow boys are down with it, Mona informs me, so she thinks perhaps it would be wiser to wait a little. It has been attended by a big mortality, being followed by a septic pneumonia of a virulent type. We have had a large number of cases among the troops too, but the mortality over here hasn't been anything like as bad as with the civil cases.

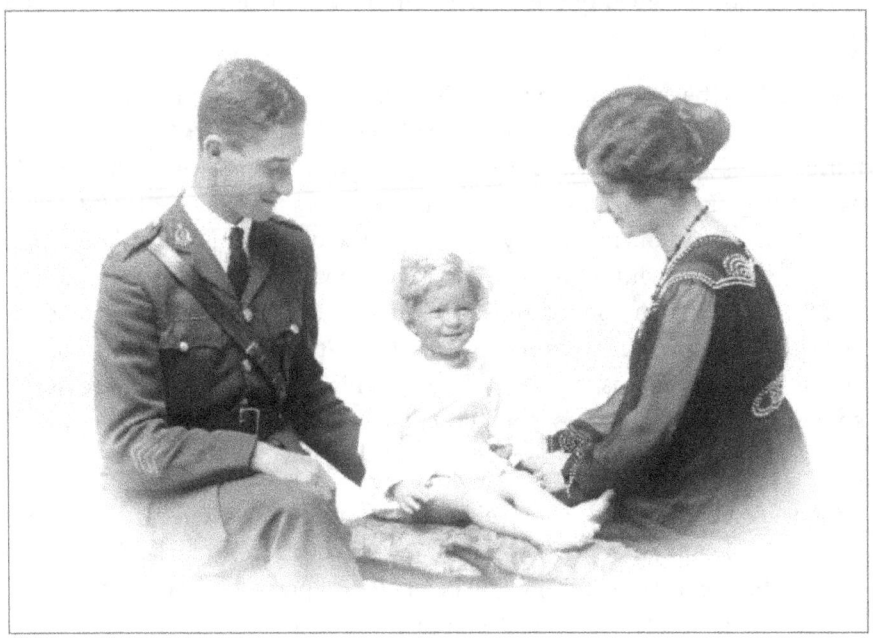

Nigel, Pip & Mona Boulton, mid 1918
(Picture Courtesy Julia Woodhouse)

I sent you off a photo a few days ago, which I hope will reach you safely, it is a paltry Xmas present, still I know you will like having it, altho' it's only a cheap one. How I should love to have one of you: I've only got a very small one taken a good many years ago of you. No more now, darling Mum, lots and lots of love to you and Thea. With a big hug and a kiss,

Always your loving, PIGEE

The Germans faced the reality that they were defeated and agreed to an Armistice to take effect at the eleventh hour of the eleventh day of the eleventh month of

1918. The slaughter was over, the guns fell silent, and countries around the world mourned the deaths of 15 million people. Of that momentous world event, the war diary for Steve's old unit says only 'Received news of the Armistice.'

When Nigel next wrote to his mother he was unaware that Steve's C.O. and Padre had already written to her in Australia. He enclosed the letter written by Major McMullin to Cousin Bess on 29 October.

Somewhere in Belgium [Harlebeke], 12 Nov 1918

Dearest Mum

Not a long letter this time, but as I have some news from you of Steve, I thought I would write straight away. The enclosed letter which was sent to me by Cousin Bess will give you all the particulars we have so far. As Steve's C.O. was on leave at the time, I don't know whether he will be able to give anything further. But I shall write to the padre who buried him and find out all he has to tell me.

Well, Mum, peace is now at hand and the Armistice terms have been signed. We are all anxiously waiting to see what they are. I do trust they will be satisfactory, but I think Foch will see to that. The excitement over here when the news came thro' the night before last was indescribable. Church bells going, cheer upon cheer rending the air for hours - fires, rockets, and lights, motor horns, and processions all over the place. We are at present billeted in a large town called Harlebeke, which was only evacuated by the Bosche 3 weeks ago. It is more or less intact.

We don't quite know what is going to happen yet. Hostilities ceased at 11 o'clock yesterday morning. Demobilization won't start till the peace terms are signed, which will probably take one or two months at least perhaps - we shall probably enter Germany before long. I don't know how soon I shall be freed, as I foolishly signed on again till September next; they can still keep me till then, but I may be liberated before then. I think they ought to let the fellows with the longest service go first. I am at present attached to the 9th Battalion of the Seaforth Highlanders, who are a very decent crowd. I don't know whether I told you in my last letter.

Oh, dearest Mum, it is so sad little Tootie going right at the end of the War like that. However, you still have Pigee, altho' he felt latterly as if he didn't much mind if he went too. Love to Thea, I trust she is fit again. I suppose she will see a great deal of Cleon, now peace is here. Lots and lots of love, dearest Mum, with a great big hug and kisses. Perhaps I shall be seeing you again next year! What a sad Mum she will be.

Your NIGE

Very many thanks for the 10 bob, Mum. Poor Toots won't have his now. What would you like me to do with it? Your birthday in 6 days' time now.

The next letter indicates that Major McMullin asked his wife back in London to visit the No 3 London General Hospital in Wandsworth and speak to Stephen's injured unit commander Major Arthur W Dodd.[243] Once recovered, Dodd wrote to Cousin Bessie (Miss H.B. Charles) on 17 November 1918 and she sent his letter back to Stephen's mother in Australia, finishing with *I sent him your address. Again so much love, Yours lovingly, Cousin Bess.*

C/O Sir W. Napier, Cherton Hangar, Chart, Farnham, Surrey, 17 Nov 1918

Dear Miss Charles

I am afraid you will think it very rude of me for not having written you before but I must plead my inability to do so was due to a bad right arm which was operated on and necessitated my lying up for another fortnight. However all is well now & I hope to be well on my way to Australia soon.

I am afraid I am unable to tell you much more about the sad death of my dear friend and fellow Officer Stephen Boulton than Mrs McMullin has already told you. I informed her of the full particulars just in case anyone should write. However in case she has not outlined the occurrence quite clearly I will let you know herein.

We were in action in rear of the village of Joncourt, and were under very heavy bombardment from 77mm, 4.2 & 5.9 shell when a message came that Steve was to report for O.P. duty. He was in the act of putting on his jacket when a shell entered the dugout we were occupying, and he got 4 pieces in him. One in the right arm, one in the back, one in the left groin & one near the heart. Lieut Watson immediately put on Steve's gas mask & after adjusting our own

---

243 Major Arthur William Dodd, of Kew in Melbourne, was already a 2nd Lieut when he joined up in August 1914, aged 20. He was wounded a number of times during the war and received the Military Cross and the D.S.O.

we pulled him out on to a stretcher and got him away to the dressing station. Just before he left us he lost consciousness although for 20 minutes after he was hit he put up a wonderful fight. His pain was so bad that he did not feel it & he never spoke again & died without recovering consciousness.

He was buried alongside Capt Hollis, Capt Kirkland & Lieut Fisher of our brigade who were killed the same day. Crosses are being erected and all necessary precautions taken to ensure that his grave is looked after.

I wish you all to accept the heartfelt sympathy of the Officers, NCOs & men of the Battery on the loss of one of the bravest and best gentlemen it has ever been our chance to meet & as he was so long with us I assure you he was sorely missed by all. His kit will be forwarded to his mother through the A.I.F. Kit Stores. Hoping you will forgive me for not having written before,

Believe me,

Yours Truly,

Arthur W Dodd, Major

Nigel now served with the 28th Field Ambulance, Army of Occupation.

Somewhere in Belgium, 18 Nov 1918

Dearest Mum

This is your birthday, and I fear it will be the loneliest and saddest you have had. Let's hope tho' that it will be followed by better ones, and that at all events you will have Pigee and the small grandson, whom I know you will love very much, with you next year. It certainly looks extremely likely now, as I think peace is assured beyond doubt now. Germany from the reports that keep coming thro' is going to break up completely, and the Government at home is rather worried as a revolution seems to be on the cards, tho' now the House of Hohenzollern has been got rid of perhaps it may not go to the same lengths as in Russia.

I have rejoined the Ambulance, and we are about 20 to 25 kilometres from Brussels at present. We hope to be in the Belgian capital next week. I shall be extremely interested to see it again, as I was there about 6 weeks before the War broke out, and remember it quite well.

Enclosed letter I forward on, Mum, as I know you will like to have it. It is a great comfort to know that Steve had a proper burial, and was so appreciated by those who knew him. It was a great honour to have the Divisional Commander present, and it shows that Steve was a great loss to the Division. He had been with them such a long time, and had been thro' a very great deal. I do hope you will get all these latter letters of mine, as I can well imagine how anxious you will be after weeks of waiting to learn what actually happened to Steve, and whether there were any messages. I suppose the poor little chap was really only semi-conscious before he lost consciousness, so evidently did not have any clear thinking moments.

It is a tremendous relief that all this awful fighting is over; it's scarcely comprehensible that after nearly 4 years of failure and disappointment we have crushed the awful tyrant that looked like oppressing the world. I had some pretty narrow squeaks latterly since I've been with this division, and thought several times that I would stop something. Mona was very anxious, but I didn't let her know how dickey things were at times. Anyhow Pigee is safe and sound, for which he is truly thankful.

The winter is right on us now, and we've had 3 or 4 days of hard freezing - the first snow yesterday, but it was only a light shower.

Things are very uncertain at present. I don't think demobilization will take place for some time yet, this year at any rate. No more now, dearest Mum, Xmas will be over when you receive this, and probably 1919 has begun. Let's hope and pray that 1919 will be a much happier year than 1918; altho' 1918 has seen the end of the War, it has been unhappy for us.

Bestest love to Thea and you, dearest Mum, with a big hug and a kiss,

Ever your, NIGE

C/O Sir W. Napier, Cherton Hangar, Chart, Farnham, Surrey, 20 Nov 1918

Dear Mrs. Boulton[244]

---

244 Mona Boulton

In the first place I wish to apologise for not having written you the news of your brother-in-law's sad death, but believe me when I say it was entirely due to my own indisposition that I have been unable to write.

As you no doubt know, poor old Steve was in action with us near Joncourt and had just been detailed for the duty of F.O.O.[245] for the attack which was taking place at 6am. He was in the act of putting on his coat when a shell came into the dugout we three (Watson, Steve and myself) were occupying and severely wounded Steve in four places, burning and gassing Watson and I.

After adjusting his gas helmet we managed to drag him into another shelter which was close by, and found he was wounded in the left groin, back shoulder and right arm - all bad wounds. He put up a gallant fight and although suffering intense pain he was so bad he could not feel it.

We said good-bye to him just before he left for the C.C.S. and he then became unconscious and never regained consciousness, passing away on his way to the C.C.S. (advanced). He was buried at Roisel Cemetery along with Lieut. Fisher, Capt. Hollis and Capt. Kirkland who were also killed on the 3rd inst.

It was a terrible blow to me to know that poor old Steve had gone and I can assure you he was a real man in all the dealings I had with him during our year's acquaintance. He was a fine officer, capable, and lived the clean life of a brave gentleman.

Please accept on behalf of myself, the Officers, NCOs and men of the 6th Battery their heartfelt sympathy on your sad loss. I feel that whenever I look at his photo that it will always remind me of one of the best pals I ever had.

His kit and all belongings must be forwarded to his next of kin and I am afraid I am unable to help you in any further way with regards to this as A.I.F. Headquarters are naturally very strict on nobody touching any effects of deceased Officers.

Please accept for your husband and yourself my sympathy and believe me to be

Yours faithfully

Arthur W Dodd, Major

---

245 Forward Observation Officer

Somewhere in Belgium, 26 Nov 1918

Dearest Mum

Not a very long letter this time, as we are continually on the move, and one can't find much time for letter writing. We are trekking across Belgium towards the German frontier, and are due at the latter place in 5 days' time. When one gets into one's billets at night one is dead tired, and goes to bed early to be fresh to start again the next morning.

I received your cable 2 days ago, but have not answered it, because the details you ask for are already on the way. C. Bess has sent everything she has been able to collect and so have I. My news is practically all derived from her. Poor little Tootie didn't suffer and died shortly afterwards. He apparently was not sufficiently conscious before dying to give any intelligible message at all. His effects have been sent on to you by the Australian authorities direct. Now hostilities have ceased, they ought to reach you, Mum, safely. He was buried with the M.O. of the regiment, a Dr. Kirkland[246] from Lithgow, I dare say it's one of the same family who took the Mackensie's house at Gladesville. They have only temporary crosses, but better ones are being made if they have not already been done. Poor old Mum, I am afraid the appalling long wait for details of his death will be terribly wearing. However, you will have got them all by the time this letter reaches you. I am afraid you won't have them by Xmas, but you ought to shortly afterwards.

1919 will be with you when you receive this. I trust it will be a happier year for you, and that it will see us with you once more. But there will be a big blank when Steve doesn't appear. Aunt Julia wrote me a v. nice letter, she said she was writing you one too, so you will probably have received it.

The Belgian population are overjoyed and frantic with excitement when we arrive at each village and township, as we are the first British troops thro' and we are hailed as deliverers everywhere. From what they tell us they have had a very bad time and the Germans seem to have used a system of terrorization to absolutely cower them, and thus relieve him of having to use many troops to occupy the captured territory. They never lost hope though and were always confident that they would be delivered from their bondage eventually. I witnessed the entry of the King and Queen of the Belgians into Brussels, the Capital.[247] It was a wonderful affair, and, of course, of great historical interest

---

246 Hugh Edward Kirkland. See the 'Beyond 1914' website of the University of Sydney for more details of him.
247 On 22 November.

which will be a date for evermore in the Belgian future history books. Albert is a fine big chap, very short-sighted. His wife looked very frail and delicate. They both rode in on horseback. One of the English princes was also there in a flying uniform. Brussels had not been knocked about at all, and seemed exactly the same as it was when I saw it in 1914.

No more now, dearest Mum, we are looking forward to getting into Germany. Oh, what hard luck it is that all the brave fellows who have fallen are not here to reap the fruits of victory and see that accomplished for which they gave their all. One almost feels ashamed that one is alive sometimes, but I must be thankful to God for my life. It would have broken your heart completely if we had both been taken. Let's hope that Master Pip will be a comfort to you when he gets back to Australia, and may remind you sometimes a little of your Toots.

Lots and lots of love to you and Thea. I wonder if Cleon will have more time ashore now the German Fleet has been surrendered.

A great big hug and a kiss for you both.

Always your own NIGE

I shall certainly make a point of visiting Steve's grave before I leave Europe and will bring you back a photo of it.

An Army Chaplain visited Steve's grave in December 1918.

130 HORSEFERRY ROAD, LONDON, 3 DEC 1918

Mrs. D M Boulton,
Coolah, Ross St
GLADESVILLE.

Dear Madam:

It has been my privilege recently to visit the little Cemetery at Roisel where the mortal remains of your dear Son have been laid at rest. I went to see the grave of my own Boy[248], and he lies with over twenty other lads side by side, and one of them is your Boy. I thought you would like to have a line from somebody who had stood with bared head at the Grave, and had reverently

---

248 Gunner Norman Gladstone Holden, an 18-yr-old student of Kew in Melbourne, Victoria, when he sailed off to war in July 1916, killed in action with 11th F.A.B. on 29 Sep 1918.

read the loving inscription placed upon the central wooden Cross that has been erected at the head of each Grave.

Roisel is about nine miles east of Péronne. The town has been completely destroyed, not one habitable house being left. Strange to say, however, beyond two or three shell holes, that of course have done a little damage, the ancient little Cemetery is unharmed. It is almost in the middle of the town, or what used to be the town, within 200 yards of the railway station, so that the lad rests not out in No Man's Land, but in an old established Cemetery (Roman Catholic of course), that has around it a brick fence, and that contains some really fine monuments. Right in the very centre of the Burial Ground is a steel Crucifix, some twenty feet high. It represents our Saviour as looking out upon the desolation on all sides, but as protecting God's Acre whose soil has been made sacred by the bodies of our brave dead. On the day that the Armistice was signed, whilst shouts of rejoicing could be heard in every direction, I stood alone, with a lump in my throat, feeling in no mood to wave flags, though deeply grateful that hostilities had ceased and that no more precious human lives would have to be sacrificed.

Please pardon these few lines, but I thought you would like to have them. I write as one who has been bereaved like yourself, and who, like you too, is sustained through God's grace, by the memory of a noble lad who has died for me.

With sincere and prayerful sympathy,

Sincerely yours,

A T HOLDEN[249]

Senior Chaplain, (Meth), Australian Imperial Force

Near Verviers, Belgium, 3 Dec 1918

Dearest Mum

I guess it's about time I wrote to you again, as it is a week since I last did so. I got the Child's letter written on Sepr 23rd this morning, which I must answer some time. Thank her for it in the meantime.

---

249 Rev Albert Thomas Holden, Methodist Minister of Kew in Melbourne, hence AIF Met (for Methodist).

As you see by the above address we are right up close to the German frontier, which we expect to cross tomorrow. The cavalry have already gone across and were received by the population, chiefly women and children, with boohs and hissing! However, they are extremely comfortably ensconced. Rumour has it, for which I believe there is considerable grounds, that 2 Canadian cavalrymen were shot by the Bosches the other day, and 6 Germans were despatched yesterday in Verviers as a reprisal.

The Belgians have been having some trouble in Aix la Chappelle and these are some of the regulations now holding in that town. No civilian is to be out of doors between 7 p.m. and 5 a.m. No soldier is to be allowed about at all in uniform. No one is to carry arms or have them in their possession. A light is to be shown in all ground floor windows between 4 p.m. and 8 p.m. The whole of every house is to be placed at the disposal of the Belgian Army at any hour of the day or night with the exception of one room. All civilians are to step off the pavement when a Belgian officer passes. No theatres, cinemas, or public amusements to be allowed. No public meetings or demonstrations of any kind to be held. And traffic and vehicles are to be restricted in their use.

That's the stuff to give them, Mum, isn't it, there's nothing like making them eat dirt. I don't suppose our authorities will be up to things like this. They're too soft, and namby pamby. However, we're all to carry revolvers always; never to go about alone; no soldier or officer is to be billeted alone.

Xmas is approaching, I don't think there is the slightest doubt about my spending it in Germany now. The last 6 Xmases I have spent respectively at sea, in England, in Egypt, 2 in France, and now the next in Germany. So it's 6 years now I have been away from home. I do hope I shall spend the 7th with you, Mum; if I can't get over to you I shall send your fare over. Travelling will be safe enough then, so there won't be any excuses.

   I have bought you a lace collar which I hope you will receive safely. I shall send it off tomorrow probably. I have to get a registered envelope. It was purchased at Liege, and is pure Bruges lace, and is supposed to be very good, and I am also supposed to have got it wonderfully cheap. I shall try and get Thea a collar of Brussels lace if I get another chance, but it's pretty expensive and I can only buy it bit by bit! I suppose it will wash. I thought it would look very nice round your dear soft neck.'

Forgive me for not writing a longer letter, dearest Mum, but I shall write again next week. I mustn't miss now there is no poor little Toots to write. It's hard to realize he's gone.

Best love to Thea, with heaps for yourself, with a big hug and XX's

Your NIGE

Dolly wrote to her surviving son Nigel, on paper edged with black to signify mourning.

Fernleigh, Kiama, 24 December 1918

My dearest Pige

I was very glad as usual to get two letters from you this mail, the last one the 17th September – written from the advanced dressing station. I was surprised to find you were in the line, as the former letters by the same mail held out no hope of it. Anyway I am sure you are very glad of the change to more exciting life and the open air will be good for you, if it is not too horrible from the weather point of view.

I also had a letter from Bess and Kate, full of sorrow and loving sympathy; they seem to have been very fond of our dear Toots, and deeply grieve for his loss. I also had a letter (a very kind one) from Lt Col Moore of Steve's Brigade, written on the 14th Oct. I expect you will have had particulars of his death, either from the Battery or perhaps from Bess, who says she is trying to find out all she can for me. Col Moore says he and two other officers had made themselves a dug out in the side of a railway bank and had been safe for some time, but:

> *Eventually a gas shell fell & exploded on the parapet, filling the dug out with a deadly cloud of gas. At the time your son was standing up & 3 pieces from the bursting shell entered his back. He fell seriously wounded. Lt Watson, one of the other two officers who were lying down at the time, seeing his helplessness at once adjusted your son's gas respirator. It was apparent the wound was serious, as he was almost unconscious. He received immediate attention but died some five hours afterwards when every effort made to save him had failed.*

He was buried the day following in a Military Cemetery at Roisel, etc.

Poor poor Lil Toots, it seems as if it had to be, and he was picked out from those 3 boys in the dugout, to go from this world: and so it was God's will and intention to take him. I wonder if he was quite unconscious, or if the gas fumes had prevented him from speaking again, during the 5 hours he lived? Perhaps you may have had more particulars, my Pige.

Yesterday I received from Mona a delightful photo of the Boulton family group and one for Thea too. We are both delighted with them as they seem such good likeness of all three of you. Pippen is an out & out darling – we all say (Aunt P. & Phil too) he is the sweetest thing we have yet seen – no wonder everyone is so charmed with him. Mona looks very well we think: she is quite a young matron isn't she – and is there another little Boulton expected – or is it the dress she is wearing responsible for that effect? [250]

I wonder if you will go to Berlin my Pigee, it would be a rather exciting way of filling up the rest of your Army Career, as I dare say you will have to stick it till your term is up in Sept & no doubt there is plenty for the military doctors to do still, with all the sick and wounded.

As you see we are at Kiama and find "Fernleigh" a very comfortable house indeed to stay in. We are 4 in a room but are quite comfortable as it is large. The house is a mile out of town on the Jamberoo Rd – very lovely surroundings on all sides. About 25 in the house. Edith & Bert are at Shellharbour, at the Royal; they are coming over for a picnic on Boxing Day. The surf is an awful distance for the girls.

Thea heard today from Ceylon, from Cleon. It has been a long time coming and we don't know where he is now, perhaps in England.[251] You might be able to meet some time, if he is going to be over there for a while. I suppose you would write to the Australian Navy.

I expect we shall be here for a fortnight, as it is a very pleasant change, but 35/- a week is rather expensive. If I knew you w^d be in Europe till Sept I would come over as I so much want to go to France and especially I should like to see our dear boy's grave. Having no particular resting place, I could put in some time in England, & perhaps return to NSW later on.

I think I told you I had applied for a military pension. Well to my intense surprise they have allotted me £7 a month!! Wonderful isn't it? They say until further notice, I suppose that means as long as the bankrupt Government can pay it? Anyway it is just lovely, I should have been very hard up, after Aunt Julia's death, as if I had lived in Ermo, the rent of Concord, which is only 19/- a week, w^d have been my income, and out of that nearly £20 a year comes out

---

250 See picture on page 386. Mona would not have been pleased with the last comment!
251 HMAS *Brisbane* reached Portsmouth, England, in Jan 1919, for a refit. See pic on page page 24.

of it for rates of one kind and another. So you can imagine how relieved and thankful I am for it, as long as it lasts.

I can imagine my dearest Pigee what a shock dear Toots death must have been to you and Mona, having seen him so lately in health and happiness, tho' I still have the feeling that he had a premonition of his death, judging from his letters after he returned from his holiday.

And now my dear the bell is just going to ring & so must say farewell my dearest Pige. It cheers me up so much to hear from my one and only son.

Much love dear to you all, if you are together when this reaches you.

Yours ever, Mums

POST WAR

Solingen, Germany, 15 Feb 1919

Dearest Mum

This is the last time I shall probably write to you from this country. A wire came thro' when I was on leave to the effect I was to be demobilized at as early a date as possible. I returned here to the unit to collect my kit, and to return the Colonel's bag which I had borrowed, only to learn that my kit had been sent off the day before! Well, I am leaving the day after tomorrow for England, where I shall be released from the army and then find myself on my beam ends, as I shall have to wait a month or so for my berth. What little capital I have will be eaten up I'm afraid, however, I shall have to try and get some locums, so as to make it eke out as long as possible.

Mona is going up to Harrow on the 18th and while in town is going to see the Orient people about her berth, she and her mother having return tickets. I have secured the promise of my passage back by a transport, and Mona's and Pip's too, but Mona cannot let her mother travel back alone, she being such an appallingly bad sailor. Mrs. Little has offered to pay my fare back, if I will travel back with her and forego the Government transport. It certainly will be far more comfortable but I hate placing myself under obligations and haven't made up my mind altogether yet, altho' Mona thinks it very foolish of me to refuse, and that it's not a question of an obligation at all. Well, things aren't settled yet.

I shall be reaching England again about the 19th so Mona ought to be installed at Kennet House, if she hasn't had to postpone her visit again. I left her mother rather poorly at Bournemouth with a cold on her chest, but it may have cleared up and not been severe.

I haven't heard from Mona since I left, as a letter hasn't had time to reach me, and I may miss it, leaving here before it arrives.

Well, Mum, there seems every likelihood of our returning now this year, and let's hope we shall be on our way in 2 or 3 months' time. I shall arrive back an impoverished doctor, without a practice and with probably not much in the way of a prospect of getting one - it's going hard with us fellows who have been away at the war for so long; the chaps who stayed behind have collected all the plums. However, that's the way of the world. We must just buckle to and do our darnedest. I'm not looking forward to the struggle ahead. Still things may turn up all right; I've been usually rather lucky in falling on my feet in the long run. I must try and get over to France to see Toots' grave before I leave, but passports are very difficult to get, when once again one becomes a civilian.

I shall probably no longer be in the army when I write next! 4½ years in uniform; it's a long time. My civilian clothes are going to cost a bit. Still it's no use whining, I'll come thro' all right. Hal, I expect, is nearly home by now. He will have been back some weeks when you receive this. He had a pretty easy war in a way, altho' rather an uninteresting one. Still no doubt he did valuable work.

Lots of love, dearest Mum. Trusting you are all fit.

A big hug and many X's,

Your,

PIGEE

On reading this letter thro', it sounds a frightfully depressing one. Somehow or other tho', I get bad attacks of depression every now & then since Billy's death. They're hard to shake off. I expect you feel it terribly too. I've never realized what he meant to me till I lost him. Still Pip cheers me up a lot & Cherry too. It will be great seeing you again Mum, but not the same as it would have been with Toots. I feel I've no right to be coming back at all. Cheer up Mum, it's rotten my writing in this depressing strain. I'll write a very cheerful letter next time, & tell you what my plans are.

The Legacy

The army must have been drowning in correspondence related to the tens of thousands of war dead. The Australian War Memorial website reminds us:

> For Australia, as for many nations, the First World War remains the most costly conflict in terms of deaths and casualties. From a population of fewer than five million, 416,809 men enlisted, of which over 60,000 were killed and 156,000 wounded, gassed, or taken prisoner.

In other words, around 10% of the population went to war, all volunteers, and almost 52% were casualties of one kind or another. Australia paid a huge price and the war changed the country forever.

Early in 1919 Steve's mother obtained copies of his death certificate from the army and she sent the Army proof of probate of his Will on 30 June 1919. In return she received his Commission document, black kit bag and its contents, valise and its contents and an envelope containing his Commonwealth Bank cheque book. Another parcel sent from the field and received in August 1919 contained personal effects apparently recovered from his uniform and pockets before he was buried – an emotionally-wrenching moment for his mother. These items must have been saved by 34717 Private W Calder, who helped to get him ready for burial and saw the grave ready at the Cemetery but was not actually present at the burial.

The items were two discs (his identification tags), four stars (on each shoulder a full lieutenant wore two stars), a whistle (officers carried a trench whistle), five badges (presumably the set of 'Rising Sun' and 'Australia' hat and collar badges he was wearing), two brass 'A's' (signifying Anzac, from the sleeves of his uniform), two coins, two metal watches (damaged), a style pen (ie a fountain pen) and a nail clipper.

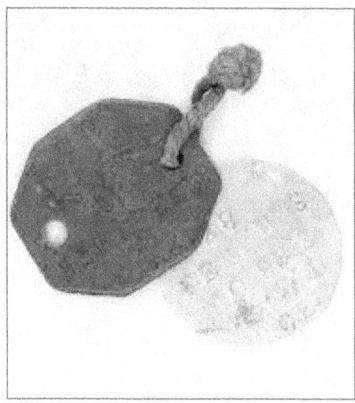

Identity Discs
Source AWM1 REL25339

A for Anzac Badge, for service at Gallipoli
Source AWM REL30226

His Memorial Scroll and King's Message arrived in 1921 and Victory Medal in 1922.

Rising Sun Badge
Source AWM REL29538

Australia Badge
Source AWM REL36564

Lieutenant's Shoulder Pips or Stars
Source http://www.thefullwiki.org/Lieutenant

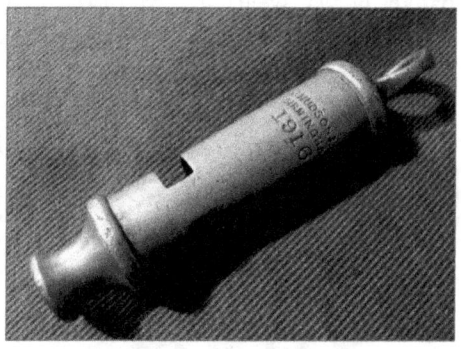

Officer's Trench Whistle

Example of a Black Kit Bag
Source AWM REL41503

Australian Imperial Force.

AK.18.

A.I.F. KIT STORE,
110, GREYHOUND ROAD,
HAMMERSMITH,
LONDON, W. 6.

Inventory of Effects of - Lieut. S.P. Boulton, 2nd. F.A.B.
Forwarded to - Mother,
Mrs. D.M. Boulton,
"The Hutch",
Ermington,
Parramatta River,
New South Wales.

Deposited at Kit Store, 2.8.18.
ONE BLACK KIT BAG (sealed) Containing:-

1 Cardigan Jacket, 2 Suits Pyjamas, 1 Housewife, Handkerchiefs, 1 Belt, 2 Devotional Books, 1 Pack Playing Cards, 1 Pr Braces, 1 Pipe & Case, 1 Towel, 1 Singlet, 1 Shirt, 1 Writing Pad, 1 Tie, 1 Letter, 1 Lead Pencil.

D/S.47396 in Case No. 1758.
No. of Package   Checked by

List of Contents of Kit Bag
Source NAA B2455, BOULTON S P p 59

Australian Imperial Force.

17.

A.I.F. KIT STORE,
110, GREYHOUND ROAD,
HAMMERSMITH,
LONDON, W. 6.

Inventory of Effects of - Lieut. S.P. Boulton. 2nd.F.A.B.

Forwarded to - Mother,
Mrs. D.M. Boulton,
"The Hutch"
Ermington,
Parramatta River,
N.S.W.

Received from the Field. 31/10/18.
One Valise (sealed) containing :-

2 suits pyjamas, 1 sleeping bag, 1 suit case containing 2 pair slacks, 1 tunic (Officer's Pattern) 2 handkerchiefs, 4 collars, 1 tie, 1 diary, 1 writing case, photos, letters, 1 Sam Browne belt, 1 pair spurs, 1 soap box, 1 cigarette case, 1 pair field glasses, 1 holdall, 3 razors, 1 razor strop, 1 housewife, 1 shaving brush, 1 safety razor in case, 1 sponge, 1 fountain pen, 1 haversack.

No. of Package   D/S. 47399 in Case No. 1758.   Checked by

List of Contents of Valise
Source NAA B2455, BOULTON S P p 55

1925

In March 1925 the French Government decided to close the Roisel Communal Cemetery (a general cemetery in the middle of the village) and move all the graves elsewhere. The Imperial War Graves Commission, forced to act, stepped in and exhumed the military bodies, moving them to the nearest suitable British Cemetery. Steve's remains now lie at Plot 1, Row M, Grave 4 of the Roisel Communal Cemetery Extension. His grieving Anglophile mother had his headstone engraved with the following message:

> Au Revoir darling Toots
> Our Loving
> Brave True-hearted Boy
> An ANZAC

Roisel Communal Cemetery Extension, France, 2001
(Picture Courtesy Cathryn Gillespie-Jones)

Inscription, Roisel, Plot 1, Row M, Grave 4, 2001
(Picture Courtesy Cathryn Gillespie-Jones)

A plaque at this Cemetery says Roisel was captured from the Germans in April 1917, lost in March 1918 and finally retaken in the following September. The Cemetery contains the graves of 737 British, 6 Canadian, 107 Australian, 29 South African and 514 German soldiers and airmen who fell in these actions.

The Commonwealth War Graves Commission continues to maintain the Roisel Communal Cemetery Extension, among the dozens of war cemeteries serving as a permanent memorial to the men who did not return home from the Great War.

During 1928, Dora Mary Boulton made a selection from her sons' war letters, had them typed and presented a copy to the Australian War Memorial in Canberra.

She subsequently donated the originals to that body, upon request. She gave a copy of Nigel's letters to him for his 40th Birthday on 29 October 1928. Shortly afterwards, she set off on the long journey to Europe to visit Stephen's grave.[252]

GREENWICH RD, 28 OCTOBER, 1928

Dearest Pige

This is to wish you much happiness on your birthday and all through your new year! Which will I hope include health, prosperity, absence of anxiety and that feeling of 'well done' that bestows such a pleasant glow upon us.

I don't know if you would rather have had something else, my Pige. Anyway I am sending you a copy of some of your war letters. They are full of memories of those poignant, but dear years, when you and dear lil Toots were seldom out of my anxious thoughts. The rest of your uncopied letters (many more) I am keeping till I depart, and after that you may like to hand them on to your boys, who when they are men, and understand life, should be interested to read of those eventful days in their Dad's youth.[253]

How full you were of enthusiasm, patriotism, the cause of duty, love of work, forgetfulness of self, & affection. No wonder I felt so proud of my two boys, and hoped great things for them: a pale reflected light even seemed to rest upon me, when I thought of the small part I had taken in your earlier years. I have put in a few photos too, which you may like to have Pige.

I have been thinking the 29th was on Wednesday - & meant to have taken the parcel over, or posted it, for that day, but now it will have to go by hand, perhaps by car tomorrow.

The Moles, Con, Amurie & Neil have gone to Manly for afternoon tea.[254]

Well dear old Nige, wishing you every good thing with my love and happy thoughts of you.

Ever thine, Mums

---

252 Her return journey has been identified. Dora M Boulton, born c 1860, Ticket No 1445, departed Southampton on 16 October 1929 for Brisbane, where Thea and her husband and children now lived.
253 They do not survive, as Dolly's belongings were later burnt in a house fire.
254 'The Moles' was a nickname for Cleon & Thea Dennis. Con was their friend Constance Huggins of New Zealand. Amurie Murray was a sister of Harold Boulton and Neil was her son, both also from New Zealand.

More than 70 years later, proving he is not forgotten by those with living memory of that generation, in May 2001 Steve's niece Julia Woodhouse, great-niece Cathryn Gillespie-Jones and great-great-niece Helen Gillespie-Jones journeyed from Paris to stand at his graveside and mourn his loss and his sacrifice for his country. The three Australian women were driven by a young French friend, Guillaume Calligaro, who had never before visited the Great War memorial gravesites. He was unaware of the impact of the Great War on Australia, and was overwhelmed at the extent of the losses suffered by faraway Australia in defending his homeland.

In 2011 Steve's Australian great-nephew Frank Dennis visited the grave, followed by Frank's son Andrew and his wife and children in 2012. Tears were shed. Andrew felt that Stephen's spirit was present, saying 'G'day Matee, it's good to have visitors from home.'

Amelia (Millie) Dennis, Roisel, 2012

(Picture Courtesy Andrew Dennis)

Lest We Forget

Always slightly inclined to depression, Nigel paid an ongoing price for his confronting and stressful wartime service and suffered lifelong feelings of guilt over the loss of his brother. As the eldest child of his family he somehow felt that it should have been him who paid the ultimate price for the freedom of others. He also felt that he had not achieved anything himself during the war.

The term Post Traumatic Stress Disorder did not exist, and the men returning from the war received minimal treatment for their various issues, but he did benefit from one token effort made to help the men who served. In March 1919, before returning to Australia, he was sent south to the pleasant Mediterranean climate of Menton on the French Riviera, a place used for recovering the health of demobilized troops. He left Menton on 3 April 1919, heading for London via Paris, Le Havre and Southampton, to rejoin his family at Kennet House, Harrow.

Here Nigel received a token letter of thanks from the War Office, dated 19 May 1919:

> Sir, On the occasion of the completion of your service in the Royal Army Medical Corps, consequent on the demobilization of the Army, I am commanded by the Army Council to convey to you their thanks for the services which you have rendered to the country during the War, and for the excellent work which you have done.

He'd already departed England when this letter arrived at Harrow. Needing urgently to find a source of income for his family, Nigel returned to Australia ahead of them, leaving Portsmouth on 17 April 1919 aboard *HMAS Brisbane,* the ship on which his brother-in-law Cleon Dennis was Engr. Lieut. An impoverished doctor without a practice and little likelihood of acquiring one, somehow he managed to purchase a Dr Sharp's practice in the old Bank House at Ryde in Sydney.

In October 1919 Mona returned separately with her mother and young Pip, who arrived home calling his mother Mona, to the astonishment of the family in Sydney. The family story goes that on the ship (*Niagara*) Mona made Pip call her Mona so that she could pass him off as a young relation, not acknowledging him as her son.

Nigel and Mona's second son Peter was born in September 1920.

Good time girl Mona ran off with another man in 1923, a Queenslander named Jimmy Dee who was the Municipal Engineer of Mosman Council and did not serve in the Great War. Nigel returned home from work to find an empty house.

His mother moved in with him for a period, bringing some of her furniture, and acted as his housekeeper until he found the time and money to re-establish himself. Divorce followed in 1924 and he was granted custody of the two boys until they were 14. They attended their father's old school, The King's School at Parramatta.

Fascinated by motor cars and flying machines in the war, Nigel took up flying in June 1927. He learned to fly a 'Moth' aeroplane and he piloted a B J Monoplane in the first leg of the East-West Air Race of 1929.

Nigel married his second wife Marie Ellen Tofield (née Memory) in 1927. Despite the photograph on page 407 indicating otherwise, it was an unhappy marriage

Mona & Nigel Boulton with Thea Dennis, Sydney, c 1920
(Picture Courtesy Julia Woodhouse)

Mona, Peter & Pip Boulton, c 1925
(Picture Courtesy Julia Woodhouse)

P H Boulton, at The King's School, c 1928
(Picture Courtesy Julia Woodhouse)

and she ran off with a poet in the later 1930s. Around this time he was the driver of a car which knocked down and killed a man at a conditional tram stop at Gladesville. The verdict was accidental death, but Nigel later paid compensation to the man's family.

After many years on his own, Nigel divorced Marie in 1950 and found happiness from 1951 with his third wife Thelma Attwood née Robertson, a widow and well-known antiques auctioneer.

When Second World War broke out, history repeated itself. Nigel's elder son Pip had travelled to England aboard SS *Ormonde* in May 1939 and so was in England when the war commenced, as his father had been 25 years beforehand. He joined the RAF as a fighter pilot, Australian Pilot No 907098. He also followed in his father's footsteps in his personal life:

> Here's a little surprise for you, and I hope not too much of a shock. I was married on 30 January 1940. Her name was Eileen Sellars, and her father is an Electrical Engineer. I have known her for about six months, so it is not quite one of these wild fancies.

Nigel Boulton & second wife, Marie Tofield née Memory
(Picture Courtesy Sarah Dennis)

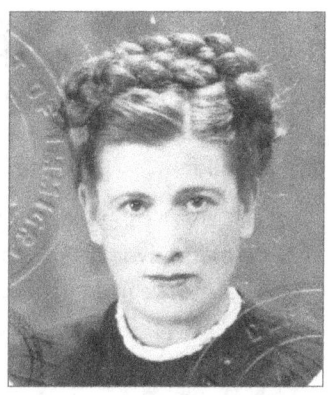

Nigel's third wife, Thelma Attwood
(Picture Courtesy Julia Woodhouse)

Philip Hugh Boulton (Pip),
England, Winter 1939
(Picture Courtesy Julia Woodhouse)

Eileen Boulton née Sellars, c 1939
(Picture Courtesy Julia Woodhouse)

Pilot Officer Philip Hugh Boulton of the R.A.F. was killed in action on 29 May 1941 on a special mission just after the Battle for Britain, and is buried in the so-called 'Hero's Corner' of Alperton Cemetery in London (the section maintained by the Commonwealth War Graves Commission). After the war, Eileen sent back to the family in Australia several pictures of her tending Pip's grave, accompanied by her young son. The family always assumed that this must be Pip's son, but research indicates he was her son by her second marriage of 1945. Contact with Eileen then ceased.

After the war Nigel was a caring father to his other son Peter and to his daughter-in-law Doris née Brentnall, both of whom called him 'Father'. Peter met Doris when she nursed him after he was so severely injured in a wartime plane crash that he was left for dead. Peter and Doris lived at Manly and enjoyed a long marriage but had no children.

Nigel was also a caring brother to his sister Thea Dennis. After her husband Cleon died prematurely in 1932, leaving her with five young children, he visited her every week for years to offer support and comfort. Not having any grandchildren of his own to hold, Nigel took a great interest in Thea's grandchildren.

Eileen Boulton and her son, c 1951
(Picture Courtesy Julia Woodhouse)

Peter Martin Boulton, c 1944
(Picture Courtesy Julia Woodhouse)

Nigel Boulton & Great Niece Jennifer, 1947
(Picture Courtesy Julia Woodhouse)

He also looked after his ailing mother and had her admitted to the Home for Incurables where he worked so that he could supervise her care and visit her frequently. She died there on 30 December 1949, aged 90.

Nigel's wartime experiences and awareness of the sufferings of so many soldiers led him to a lifetime of service. During the Great Depression he looked after the poor patients in his practice without charge, although some of them paid him 'in kind', with eggs and so forth. He served as the Repatriation Department's LMO (Local Medical Officer) for almost fifty years, from August 1920 to 24 June 1969, six days before his death on 30 June. He also served concurrently as Honorary Medical Officer to the Royal Ryde Homes (NSW Home for Incurables), from 26 July 1920 to 26 June 1969. Cerebral thrombosis (a stroke) took him away at the age of 80.

His sister Thea Dennis died at Chatswood in 1981, aged 86. Unlike Nigel and Stephen, she has many descendants. They have not forgotten her brothers in the Great War and the price they paid for others.

Sources

Original Letters

The letters of Dr Nigel Philip Boulton, R.A.M.C. and his brother Stephen Philip Boulton, A.I.F., typed copies held within the author's family, original copies held at the Australian War Memorial, Canberra, with Copyright granted to Louise Wilson. Stephen Boulton's letters are accessible online via website https://www.awm.gov.au/collection/1DRL/0138/. Most of the letters were written as one continuous flow of thoughts, as if speaking. Accordingly, paragraphs and punctuation marks have been added to aid the reader. The wording remains as written. Footnotes have been added to give context to the people and places mentioned in the letters.

Online Material

Stephen Boulton's Personal Service Records are on the National Archives of Australia website http://recordsearch.naa.gov.au/SearchNRetrieve/Interface/DetailsReports/ItemDetail.aspx?Barcode=3100567&isAv=N His brother Nigel's service records with the RAMC, held in England, were not accessed, but his wartime movements are fairly clear from his letters.

Stephen Boulton, always anxious to receive letters, regularly provided his military address to his family at home, but he usually glossed over his actual locations, movements and scenes of battle. Fortunately these could be traced via the official unit war diaries for his various artillery units on the excellent website of the Australian War Memorial. See https://www.awm.gov.au/collection/AWM4/13/. For example, the details of the final battle fought by Australian infantry in WW1, on the Beaurevoir Line, can be viewed on https://www.awm.gov.au/military-event/E125/ with the role of Stephen's unit in that battle on https://www.awm.gov.au/collection/RCDIG1015038/?image=3&fullscreen=true#display-image

Confirmation of Nigel Boulton's pre-war place of employment in London came from Jonathan Evans, Trust Archivist, Barts Health NHS Trust, Trust Archives, Lower Ground Floor, 9 Prescot Street, London E1 8PR. Email jonathan.evans@bartshealth.nhs.uk. Further details of the East London Hospital for Children were found on the website http://www.ncbi.nlm.nih.gov/pmc/articles/PMC1912742/?page=3, accessed 22 Mar 2015

Details of many school friends of the Boulton brothers are sourced from the website of The King's School at Parramatta, NSW, http://kings.edu.au/ANZAC/profiles.php

Details of many of Nigel Boulton's medical colleagues are sourced from the 'Beyond 1914' website of the University of Sydney, http://beyond1914.sydney.edu.au/

Digitized newspapers on the TROVE website of the National Library of Australia were used for much cross-checking of names, dates and places, http://trove.nla.gov.au/

Details of the hospital setup on Malta in 1915 from the website 'British Army Medical Services and the Malta Garrison, 1799-1979', http://www.maltaramc.com/ramcoff/1910_1919/ramcoff1915.html , accessed 9 Nov 2014

Use of chemical weapons in WW1 from Wikipedia's website, https://en.wikipedia.org/wiki/Chemical_weapons_in_World_War_I , accessed 15 May 2015

Royal Army Medical Corps of 1914-1918 website, http://www.1914-1918.net/ramc.htm

A number of websites have been established to commemorate World War 1, the Great War. These websites were consulted to assist the author to fill in the gaps in the story told by the Boulton brothers. For example, see 'Australians on the Western Front 1914-1918, the Australian Remembrance Trail in France and Belgium', http://www.ww1westernfront.gov.au/ and website of Imperial War Museums, http://www.iwm.org.uk, World War One Cemeteries website, http://www.ww1cemeteries.com/ and Curry & Marchment, Research Family War Diaries website http://www.curryww1.com/default.asp

The website 'The Great War, 1914-1918' cites the book *Military Operations: France and Belgium 1914,* Vol II: Antwerp, La Bassée, Armentières, Messines and Ypres, Oct - Nov 1914, compiled by Brigadier-General Sir James E. Edmonds, 1925 when explaining the role of 'Ypres in the Great War of 1914-1918'. See http://www.greatwar.co.uk/ypres-salient/town-ieper-history-1418.htm , accessed 15 May 2015

Background details of Vignacourt, the region of the Allies' base camp near Amiens on the Somme, from https://www.awm.gov.au/wartime/58/vignacourt/

Jonathan Kinghorn's website http://www.atlantictransportline.us was the source of the photographs of several ships used as troop carriers.

Boulton family history research of Louise Wilson, including the blog posts on http://boultonfamilyhistory.blogspot.com.au/

Books

James W. Barrett & Percival E. Deane, *The Australian Army Medical Corps in Egypt*, published in 1918, online as a Project Gutenberg EBook at http://www.gutenberg.org/files/41911, accessed 17 Mar 2015

Charles Edwin Woodrow Bean, *Official History of Australia in the War of 1914–1918, Volume V – The Australian Imperial Force in France during the Main German Offensive,*

1918 (8th edition, 1941), online at https://www.awm.gov.au/histories/first_world_war/AWMOHWW1/AIF/Vol5/

Capt. Walter C Belford, *Legs-Eleven, Being the Story of the 11th Battalion (A.I.F.) in the Great War of 1914-1918,* (Imperial Printing Company Limited, Perth, 1940)

Anne Dobbs, Judy Files & Les Pitt, Compilers, *Letters from the Front: the Experiences of Daylesford District WW1 Soldiers, Told Through Their Letters,* Daylesford & District Historical Society Inc, Daylesford VIC, 2015)

Peter G. Griffin, *A Story of Four Brothers in the Great War,* (Self-published, Melbourne, 2005)

David Horner, *The Gunners, A History of Australian Artillery,* (Allen & Unwin, Sydney, 1995)

W D Joynt, VC, *Saving the Channel Ports 1918,* (The Dominion Press, North Blackburn VIC, 1975)

K M Lyall, Compiler, *Letters from an ANZAC Gunner,* (Lyall's Yarns Pty Ltd, East Kew, 1990)

Serjeant-Major, RAMC, *With the R.A.M.C. in Egypt,* (Cassell & Co, London, 1918), online at https://archive.org/stream/withramcinegypt00serjuoft/withramcinegypt00serjuoft_djvu.txt

Albert G. Mackinnon, *Malta: the Nurse of the Mediterranean,* (Hodder & Stoughton, London, 1916)

Alison Miller, Editor, *Death Sat on a Pale Horse,: the World War One Diaries, Letters & Sketches of Harold Stephens & W. "Billy" O'Neil,* (Midland Heritage Press, Newstead, VIC, 2008)

Edward L Moore, *Gallipoli to the Somme: the WW1 Diaries of Sapper Edward L Moore MM,* (Neville & Virginia Moore, Harkaway VIC, 2010)

Monica Sinclair, Editor, *Dear Ad, Love Ron: the Complete Collection of the Handwritten Letters and Diary Entries of Ronald Augustine Sinclair, Australian Inmperial Forces, Fifth Division Artillery, 14th Field Artillery Brigade, 114th Howitzer Battery on Active Service in Egypt, France and Belgium, 1915-1919,* (M T Sinclair, Neutral Bay NSW, 1997)

Lieut Col Neil Fraser Tytler, *Field Guns in France,* (Hutchinson & Co, London, 1922)

Louise Wilson, *From Buryan to Bondi, the Dennis Family of West Penwith, Cornwall & Some Australian Descendants,* (Self-published, South Melbourne, 2008)

Louise Wilson, *A Fragrant Memory: Margaret Lilian Flockton,* due for publication in 2016

Acknowledgements

Nigel and Stephen Boulton were my grandmother's brothers. Some years ago I was happily surprised when Pamela Lloyd, the niece of Nigel Boulton's daughter-in-law Doris, contacted me out of the blue and presented me with her typed copy of Nigel Boulton's set of letters and his family photos.

More recently, cousin Sarah Dennis provided her typed copy of Stephen Boulton's set of letters, and several photos.

In 2014 I had both sets of letters converted by OCR scanning to digital format.

It took time to do justice to this historical treasure trove. With the book now completed, I'd like to acknowledge with thanks the moral support of my sister Cathryn Gillespie-Jones throughout, her knowledge of the stories my grandmother liked to tell, her assistance when cross-checking the typed letters against their digital version and her valuable feedback on the first draft of the manuscript.

My sister Stephanie Arbuthnot helpfully read and commented on the second draft and John Timlin was encouraging about the third draft.

John Newland prepared a series of maps to help readers understand the geography of the Great War.

Andrew Dennis, son of my cousin Frank, worked with his young son Ben on ideas for the cover of the book and also provided photos of his visit to France in 2012.

Various friends and relatives had input into the 'blurb' for the back cover of the book.

To conclude, I appreciate the contribution made by everyone involved in this community effort to pay tribute to two memorable men who served in the Great War of 1914-1918.

My big regret is that my mother Julia Woodhouse died this year, before she could read this longed-for book about her very special uncles.

Index

A
Achi Baba, Gallipoli 147
Aden 108
Advanced Dressing Station 271, 295, 296, 298, 299, 302, 383
Afternoon Tea 22, 26, 37, 183, 223, 233, 284, 405
A.I.F.. *See* Australian Imperial Force
Air Board 370
Aircraft 43, 47, 53, 56, 58, 60, 102, 107, 243, 333, 351, 352, 360, 376, 377, 407, 410
Air Raids 58, 60, 302, 318, 319, 324, 327, 361
A.J.S. Bank 79
Albert 260
Alcohol 51, 140, 142, 148, 167, 175, 183, 275, 319, 324, 326, 329, 336, 351
Aldershot 20, 62, 66, 67, 89
Alexandria 74, 76, 79, 80, 86, 89, 91, 92, 93, 94, 95, 96, 99, 104, 108, 110, 112, 113, 114, 119, 122, 123, 124, 125, 128, 132, 134, 138, 143, 146, 150, 151, 156, 157, 160, 161, 162, 165, 168, 169, 174, 175, 176, 178, 179, 182, 183, 184, 186, 188, 189, 191, 198, 199, 200, 204, 206, 208, 211, 212, 214, 220, 222, 223, 228, 230, 233, 240, 270
Americans 102, 129, 299, 316, 331, 335, 339, 361, 364, 377, 385
Amiens 249, 274, 280, 294, 335, 339, 347, 362, 363, 366
Ammunition 55, 56, 77, 99, 105, 108, 113, 114, 115, 131, 139, 193, 220, 237, 275, 352, 362
Anderson, Dr 300
Anderson, General 361
Anglo Egyptian Bank 104
Anzac Book 239, 263, 351
Anzac Buffet 190

Anzac Club, London 190, 208
Anzac Cove 140, 142, 159, 193, 194, 206, 209, 237, 239, 243, 261, 294
Anzac Day 303, 347
ANZAC Troops 39, 44, 63, 76, 91, 96, 103, 106, 115, 143, 147, 148, 152, 154, 164, 180, 197, 204, 206, 263, 320, 341, 346, 404
Armentières 242, 249, 257
Armistice 387, 394
Armitage, Hugh Trail 179, 219, 240, 322
Army & Navy Stores 281
Army of Occupation 392, 395
Army Service Corps 43, 56, 153, 241
Arras 272, 295, 299, 301
Artillery Barrages 299, 333, 356, 363, 373, 376, 378, 379
Artillery Bombardments 35, 90, 115, 193, 255, 257, 302, 306, 320, 336, 339, 351, 353, 363, 373, 380, 388
Artillery Comparisons 43, 237, 243
Artillery Duels 273, 305
Artillery Reorganised 224, 238, 288, 294, 320, 373
Artillery Role with Infantry 54, 105, 381
Artillery Training 87, 100, 285, 305, 307, 309, 313, 315, 319
Ashley Hall
  John (Jack) 25
  Marion Louisa 25
  Philip 25
Ashmead-Bartlett, Ellis 180
Aspinall
  Andrew Eric, Dr 307
  Archibald John, Dr 307
  Arthur Ashworth, Rev 307
  Arthur Martel, Dr 307
  William Robert, Dr 307
Attitude to British Troops 149, 259, 341, 345, 348, 354
Attwood, Thelma Alice 408

Aubigny 366, 373
Aunt Bee. *See* Beatrice Shaw
Aunt Eleanor. *See* Eleanor Sarah Flockton
Aunt Julia. *See* Julia Charles
Aunt Mog. *See* Margaret Lilian Flockton
Aunt Mog's Cottage. *See* Tyrone
Aunt Mog's Job 46, 103, 110, 150, 165, 223, 271, 349
Aunt Phoebe. *See* Isabel Phoebe Clarke
Australian Attitudes 25, 35, 77, 100, 106, 131, 148, 152, 171, 195, 237, 261, 307, 329, 354, 376
Australian Casualties 93, 96, 100, 106, 111, 146, 152, 164, 190, 244, 247, 255, 257, 286, 305, 307, 346, 349, 378
Australian General Base Depot, Étaples 289, 323
Australian Imperial Force 54, 76, 224, 292, 294, 301, 303, 313, 319, 328, 341, 377, 379, 389, 391, 394
Australian Light Horse 63, 70, 98, 138, 140, 199, 320
Australian Medical Corps 311
Australian Navy 39, 44, 137
Australian Officers Club 371
Australians 122, 168, 172, 186, 198, 209, 211, 213, 222, 239, 252, 276, 289, 316, 319, 331, 353
Australians, drunken hordes 227
Australians, unspeakable human refuse 228
Australian Troops 35, 49, 343, 368
Australian Victories 44, 259, 320, 347, 351, 361, 363, 373
Authieule 260
Awards System 41, 282, 304, 346

B

Bapaume 274, 276, 295, 301, 339
Barton
    Alan Sinclair Darvall 89
    Francis Maxwell 89, 98, 101, 155, 270, 316, 341
    Mrs Cecelia 101, 155, 212, 215, 270, 301, 316, 334
    Robert Anthony 316
Base Camp, Alexandria 217
Base Camp, Étaples 232, 289, 293
Batman 324, 325, 329, 354
Battle of Amiens 366
Battle of Arras 299, 301
Battle of Broodseinde 320
Battle of Bullecourt 299, 301, 302
Battle of Éstaires 344
Battle of Fromelles 247
Battle of Gallipoli 100
Battle of Le Hamel 360
Battle of Lone Pine 145
Battle of Messines 302
Battle of Passchendaele 320
Battle of Poelcappelle 320
Battle of Polygon Wood 320
Battle of Sari Bair 145
Battle of the Lys 344
Battle of the Menin Road Ridge 320
Battle of the Somme 218, 269, 276
Battle of Verdun 218
Battle of Villers-Bretonneux 347
Battle of Vimy Ridge 299
Battle of Ypres 306, 320, 344
Beastly Irregulars 197
Beaurevoir Line 378, 380, 382
Bedding 32, 41, 87, 88, 125, 168, 173, 181, 186, 187, 195, 197, 218, 237, 243, 275, 324, 330, 341, 359, 373
Beersheba 320
B.E.F.. *See* British Expeditionary Force
Behencourt 301
Belgians 34, 42, 49, 237, 386, 392, 395
Bellicourt 376, 380
Bethune 272, 291
Bifrons 33
Billets 20, 47, 57, 176, 177, 184, 232, 235, 237, 239, 243, 249, 251, 252, 259, 262, 272, 274, 281, 324, 327, 329, 392
Billy. *See* Stephen Philip Boulton
Birch, Dr 181
Birdwood, William, Genl 72
Bishop, Constance 241
Blackwell, Major W R 27
Blaringhem 361
Blomfield, Daisy 341
Boja 71, 304
Bosch 243, 246, 251, 255, 271, 300, 334, 387, 395
Boulogne 271, 274, 275, 286, 288, 289, 291, 330, 360, 370, 372, 375
Boulton
    Amurie Stella 405
    Dora Mary 18–410
    Dorothea Margaret 26–410
    Mona Edith 19–408

Nigel Philip, Dr 18–410
Nina Frances 355
Peter Martin 407, 408, 410
Philip 18, 19, 241
Philip Hugh 279–409
Stephen Philip 18–404
Thomas Harold 234, 241, 263, 268, 355, 377, 405
Bournemouth 274, 279, 307, 308, 399
Brazier, Mr 192
Brentnall, Doris Louisa 410
British Army 20, 25, 43, 52, 163, 164, 218, 221, 287, 289, 302, 321, 341, 345, 347, 354, 364, 392
British Empire 35, 77, 106, 176, 364
British Expeditionary Force 20, 23, 76, 90, 289
British Navy 20, 25, 28, 29, 37, 40, 44, 48, 50, 66, 71, 90, 111, 159, 180, 183
British Orphan's Asylum 61
British Pride 29, 49
Brothers Meet Up 119, 121, 124, 127, 129, 131, 132, 214, 228, 316, 317, 318, 322, 360, 372, 375
Brussels 389, 393, 395
Bryant, Francis Egerton 78, 121, 150, 154, 156, 158, 179, 244, 315, 376

C

Caëstre 235, 238, 239, 348, 349, 351, 359, 361
Cairo 76, 80, 84, 86, 87, 90, 91, 92, 95, 96, 98, 104, 166, 176, 183, 191, 207, 211, 213, 214, 215, 217, 218, 220, 222, 225
Calais 28, 35, 37, 45, 53, 235, 237, 239, 326
Calder, Pvte W 401
Calendar events away from home 38, 51, 190, 209, 230, 278, 280, 319, 329, 331, 338, 395
Cameras 63, 80, 90, 129, 285
Campbell, Rachael 354
Camp de Caesar, Alexandria 222, 228
Campion, Rowland Burnell, Dr 79, 93, 94, 129, 163
Canadians 47, 145, 289, 299, 316, 320, 341, 346, 368, 395
Carrier Pigeons 333
Cars 122, 172, 208, 241, 277, 285, 405, 407, 408
Carson, Herbert William (Capt) 135, 136, 221
Casualty Clearing Station 261, 298, 324, 391
Cavalry 57, 63, 107, 395
Cemeteries 255, 259, 267, 347, 378, 379, 380, 383, 391, 393, 394, 404, 409
Censorship 48, 51, 67, 68, 80, 94, 102, 121, 125, 131, 136, 146, 214, 226, 229, 251, 294, 325
Champion, Arthur Handasyde 100, 106
Champion, Mr
 264
Charles
 Henrietta Bessie 24, 29, 37, 52, 164, 167, 207, 221, 226, 241, 277, 279, 281, 282, 283, 284, 285, 287, 288, 290, 292, 293, 308, 310, 311, 312, 314, 321, 323, 325, 329, 350, 351, 352, 354, 365, 366, 367, 370, 372, 383, 385, 387, 388, 392
 James Arthur Merriman 29
 James Hamilton (Rev) 351, 366
 Julia Forrester 24, 29, 207, 226, 229, 277, 281, 283, 308, 310, 314, 321, 351, 354, 365, 366, 370, 392
Chatswood 49, 158, 221, 294, 369
Cherry. *See* Mona Edith Boulton
Chinese 329
Chocolate 152, 161, 182, 187, 192, 208, 209, 277
Cholera 137, 178, 184
Christening mug 283, 285, 385
Christoe, Gerald Blood 371
Churchill, Winston 52, 111, 180
Church Services 22, 26, 64, 73, 124, 165, 172, 244, 284, 305, 361, 381
Clarke
 Harry Flockton 158, 261, 265, 271, 274, 277, 290, 294, 353, 372, 400
 Isabel Phoebe 49, 54, 118, 125, 150, 158, 201, 221, 261, 262, 263, 266, 268, 269, 271, 278, 279, 280, 290, 308, 323, 328, 330, 336, 337, 340, 342, 345, 349, 351, 353, 355, 360, 369, 375, 377
 Phyllis Flockton 118, 158, 221, 261, 263, 265, 278, 279, 280, 308, 323, 328, 330, 336, 337, 342, 345, 351, 353, 355, 360, 369, 375, 377
Cleopatra Camp 114, 119, 120, 124, 127, 183, 222, 241

Collier, W T, Dr 71, 90, 94, 163
Collins, Dr 300
Colonial Troops 106, 113, 180, 197, 286, 316, 319, 341, 346, 354
Commonwealth Bank 104, 179, 219, 240, 246, 263, 287, 322, 348, 354, 371, 376
Commonwealth Offices 19, 62, 67, 94, 110, 122, 128
Commonwealth War Loan 287
Concept of home
   Back in Australia 25, 29, 100, 203, 209, 213, 234, 261, 303, 311, 368, 375, 376, 382, 388, 393, 399, 407
   Home to England 91, 111, 144, 145, 148, 155, 178, 197, 219, 274, 300, 303, 305, 365
Concord 71, 86, 96, 110, 113, 116, 131, 141, 148, 162, 248, 315
Condé-Folie. *See* Vignacourt & Environs
Conscription 191, 235, 257, 264, 325, 326, 330, 331, 343, 364, 368
Convalescent Camps 171, 172, 173, 176, 178, 180, 181, 183, 186, 188, 190, 195, 196, 211, 286, 288, 289, 320, 372
Coolah 65, 71, 88, 92, 110, 120, 121, 125, 128, 155, 165, 168, 175, 186, 188, 204, 246, 247, 251, 270, 278, 286, 289, 292, 294, 304
Cordonnerie Farm 244
Cost of Living 24, 32, 37, 38, 50, 53, 58, 92, 119, 161, 187, 190, 196, 197, 201, 214, 223, 235, 291, 313, 321, 325, 327, 328, 334, 338, 347, 371, 400
Courtenay, A R, Capt 241, 308
Cousin Bessie. *See* Henrietta Bessie Charles
Cousin Kate. *See* Katharine Rachel Mansfield
Cousin Mary. *See* Mary Frances Dixon
Creeping Barrage 306
Cricket 98, 265, 266, 309, 313, 361

D

Damascus 320
Dancy, J H (Dr) 93, 94, 123, 125, 129, 181
Dardanelles 66, 71, 76, 77, 79, 87, 90, 91, 93, 100, 105, 106, 107, 110, 111, 114, 119, 120, 124, 125, 128, 130, 131, 132, 133, 134, 135, 136, 138, 139, 143, 144, 145, 152, 153, 180, 189, 214
Darracq 285
Deafness 253, 267, 290, 291, 309, 315, 317
Dee, Alphons James 407
de Lepervanche, Sgt Major 259
Demobilization 387, 390, 399, 407
Dennis, Cleon (Engr Lieut) 39, 44, 46, 122, 158, 216, 218, 223, 230, 244, 246, 247, 251, 252, 253, 255, 260, 262, 269, 270, 283, 287, 291, 293, 294, 305, 315, 317, 336, 340, 342, 345, 349, 350, 352, 354, 369, 377, 387, 393, 405, 407, 410
310
Dentists 61, 79, 163, 241, 321
Depression 387, 400, 406
Dermatology 157
Details Camp, Alexandria 183, 217
Details Camp, France 288, 289, 292
Devon 127, 130, 133, 166, 311, 319, 342, 347, 356
Dicky 88, 129, 134, 135, 139, 170, 179, 192
Diggers 340, 352
Dinner Party 163, 324, 329
Diptheria 178, 181, 185, 187, 192
Discipline 74, 77, 152, 227, 361, 362
Dixon
   Bob 285
   John Harrison 230, 285, 303, 323
   Kenneth Alan 230, 285, 303
   Mary Frances 26, 229, 280, 283, 285, 303, 323
   Mrs Albert H 285
Dodd, A W (Major) 379, 383, 388, 389, 391
Doherty
   John William (Jack) 241
   William Pemble 241
Dolling, Charles Edward (Dr) 163
Dolly. *See* Dora Mary Boulton
Doullens 260, 262
Dover 27, 28, 29, 34, 37, 42, 47, 53, 58, 60, 61, 67, 145
Dover Castle 30, 31, 37, 55, 60, 89
Dug out life 137, 140, 142, 155, 156, 193, 259, 277, 359
Dug outs 131, 134, 136, 137, 138, 149, 151, 154, 159, 161, 164, 182, 192, 242, 272, 380, 388, 391
Dunkirk 19, 35, 56
Duty Visits to Family in England 226, 270,

Index | 419

277, 280, 283, 310, 314, 367, 370
Dysentery 42, 94, 130, 140, 146, 148, 157, 158, 159, 160, 164, 166, 167, 169, 171, 173, 176, 177, 178, 189, 192, 204, 205, 209, 211, 213, 262

E

Easterling, Frederick George 137
Eastern Front 246, 287, 335
Egypt 40, 47, 49, 66, 71, 74, 79, 92, 95, 103, 110, 124, 126, 131, 138, 146, 150, 163, 169, 173, 176, 197, 200, 202, 204, 206, 207, 208, 209, 211, 212, 213, 214, 219, 220, 222, 224, 227, 228, 229, 234, 253, 255, 262, 265, 308, 412, 413
Emden 33, 39, 44
England 19, 26, 27, 29, 34, 40, 45, 66, 142, 169, 179, 239, 270, 279, 283, 286, 347, 399, 408
Enteric 126, 189, 202, 211
Entertainment 60, 65, 86, 119, 127, 129, 159, 190, 192, 195, 197, 209, 214, 217, 220, 223, 270, 283, 284, 285, 291, 301, 303, 324, 325, 331, 359, 361, 367, 368, 370, 371, 373, 375, 395
Epidemic Jaundice 189
Ermington (Ermo) 71, 86, 96, 110, 112, 116, 131, 133, 134, 139, 141, 143, 145, 147, 148, 149, 150, 151, 155, 156, 157, 158, 162, 165, 167, 175, 177, 179, 188, 192, 195, 198, 200, 201, 204, 208, 209, 217, 234, 243, 246, 247, 248, 260, 262, 263, 264, 266, 291, 304, 308, 309, 312, 314, 315, 323, 328, 335, 350, 352, 353, 355, 360, 366, 377
Erzerum 227
Espionage 33, 34, 43, 52
Éstaires 247, 248
Étaples 289, 291, 300, 323
Evans, Dr 94

F

Family Home. *See* Bifrons & Coolah
Farm House Life 243, 245, 345, 348, 352, 359
Fatigue camp 161, 162
Field Ambulance 90, 145, 163, 273, 380
Fisher

Andrew 364
H J (Lieut) 379, 389, 391
Lord 40, 111, 180
Flanders 32, 246, 260, 262, 264, 266, 268, 287, 302, 305, 320, 361
Fleas 197
Flêtre 349, 351, 359
Fleurbaix 235
Fleurbeau. *See* Fleurbaix
Flies 87, 127, 147
Flockton
    Dora Mary. *See* Dora Mary Boulton
    Eleanor Sarah 24, 25, 58, 294, 309, 313, 353, 370, 385
    Isabel Mary 38, 66
    Margaret Lilian 46, 262, 309, 310
Food 64, 65, 68, 72, 87, 102, 103, 108, 119, 124, 127, 129, 137, 140, 142, 146, 148, 149, 154, 155, 156, 159, 160, 161, 164, 167, 173, 175, 182, 186, 187, 195, 196, 197, 207, 208, 209, 211, 215, 217, 231, 237, 239, 245, 255, 259, 279, 324, 329, 334, 366
Fowler, Cosmo William, Dr 20, 21
France
    Australians move to 217, 221, 222, 224, 226, 229, 230
    cf Gallipoli 147, 148, 161, 197, 245
    Civilians 49, 124, 132, 231, 237, 296, 298, 324, 328, 329, 341, 345, 359, 381
    Forces 42, 52, 56, 79, 209, 218, 320, 347
    Navy 72, 229
    Nigel's hopes 33, 37, 51, 62, 63, 72, 145, 224, 234, 265, 267, 271, 400
    Weather 60, 229, 231, 232, 237, 239, 243, 245, 251, 263, 264, 267, 270, 274, 275, 277, 278, 279, 280, 282, 286, 288, 289, 292, 293, 298, 323, 325, 331, 333, 339, 342, 356, 375, 377
Fremantle 315, 317
French Language 166, 176, 184, 189, 214, 277
French, Sir John 32, 101
Friend
    Jimmy 341
    Stephen Gilbert, Lieut 341
Fritz 295, 299, 302, 324, 336, 337, 352, 359
Frizell, Thomas James (Major) 330
Fromelles 235, 247, 257

Frost bite 199, 202, 204, 209, 268
Funerals 126, 153, 330, 378, 379, 380, 383, 385, 387, 390, 391, 392, 409

G

Gallipoli 86, 90, 91, 93, 96, 101, 111, 113, 115, 121, 122, 131, 136, 138, 139, 142, 143, 146, 159, 167, 172, 177, 180, 206, 221, 239, 242, 257, 294, 329, 347
Garbett, Alan Montague 138
Gas Attacks 239, 243, 337, 345, 380, 383
Gas (Chemical) Warfare 238, 333
    Gas Warfare 353
Gas Helmets 239, 240, 243, 349, 391
German East Africa 234
German Navy 32, 50
Germans 28, 29, 31, 32, 33, 34, 35, 36, 37, 38, 40, 43, 44, 50, 52, 54, 56, 60, 90, 98, 100, 111, 113, 144, 152, 169, 206, 247, 264, 273, 276, 287, 292, 301, 335, 339, 343, 347, 363, 376, 380, 392, 395. *See also* Boch, Fritz, Goths and Huns
Germany 395
Ghain-Tuffieha Convalescent Camp 196, 198, 203, 205, 208
Gifts sent home 39, 175, 194, 205, 209, 216, 217, 247, 395
Gladesville 33, 46, 65, 86, 98, 101, 122, 158, 165, 178, 217, 244, 259, 282, 291, 294, 392, 408
Glasgow, General 361, 362
Global War 19, 108, 111, 238
Goths 327
Gran. *See* Isabel Mary Flockton
Gran's Ill Health & Death 64, 107, 110, 122, 170, 217, 220, 243, 251, 262, 264, 278, 286, 297, 304, 305, 308
Granville, Alexander (Dr) 184, 206
Groppi's 223
Gueudecourt 274, 276, 279
Gunner's work 99, 131, 137, 142, 154, 192, 194, 218
Gun noise 102, 103, 104, 137, 253, 271, 273, 290
Guns
    18 pounder field guns 193, 194, 224, 225, 235, 238, 242, 255, 348, 362, 375
    Anti-aircraft 47, 53, 356

    Anti-tank 353
    Artillery 37, 54, 56, 110, 137, 139, 155, 237, 251
    Howitzers 56, 193, 224, 238, 242, 255, 341
    Machine 299, 351
    Mobile 242
    Naval 102, 228, 295
    Rifles 43, 56, 132, 183, 194, 206, 253
    Siege 56, 339

H

Hamilton, Ian (Sir) 103, 106, 130, 149, 180
Harrow 24, 58, 280, 282, 283, 284, 285, 303, 311, 313, 314, 319, 321, 322, 349, 370, 371, 372, 385, 386, 399, 407
Havernas. *See* Vignacourt & Environs
Hazebrouck 235, 249, 344, 348, 360, 361
Heliopolis 210, 211, 213, 214, 215, 216, 222
Hem-Monacu 376, 379
Herbert, Jean 315, 328
Herring
    Edward Edgar (Jack) 98, 101, 137, 140, 142, 149, 155, 350
    Ellen Bell 350
    Sydney Charles Edgar 101
Hervilly 376
Hindenburg Line 287, 301, 373, 380
Hitch, Blanche Julia Matilda 24, 309, 313, 314, 370
HMAS *Brisbane* 244, 269, 290, 293, 305, 315, 397, 407
HMAS *Sydney* 33, 39, 44, 46, 216, 244
HMAS *Yarra* 377
HMAT *Marere* A21 63, 68, 229
HMHS *Aquitania* 265
HMHS *Essequibo* 210
HMHS *Grantully Castle* 170, 171, 172
HMS *Formidable* 54
HMS *Speedy* 29
HMT *Knight Templar* 228, 231
HMT *Minneapolis* 102, 228, 229
HMT *Minnewaska* 71, 72, 90, 93
Holden, Albert Thomas (Rev) 394
Holland
    Austin George Selwyn 222
    George Henry (Col) 222, 223
Hollis, N S (Captain) 379, 389, 391
Holloway, Rupert Arthur 244
Holman, William Arthur 331
Holt's, London 265, 272, 365

Homesick 79, 176, 366
Horse Boat 63, 68, 70
Horses
    Artillery 55, 64, 65, 68, 87, 104, 107, 108, 114, 115, 119, 120, 124, 194, 209, 218, 228, 233, 251, 260, 287, 327, 337, 375, 382
    Australian Light Horse 199
    Civilian 122, 151
    Officers' 128, 272, 303, 324, 325, 359
    Transport 271
    Walers 63
Hospitals. *See* Military Hospitals
    East London Hospital for Children, Shadwell 19, 81, 157
    St Mary's Hospital, Paddington 157
Hospital Ships 111, 153, 161, 170, 171, 190, 211, 212, 214, 265
Huggins, Constance 405
Hughes, William Morris 264, 326, 331, 365, 376, 377
Huns 296, 333, 334, 336, 337, 338, 341, 343, 344, 345, 346, 348, 354, 356, 359, 365, 372, 377

I

Imbros 159, 160, 164, 165, 167, 168, 170
Infantry 55, 94, 98, 101, 105, 107, 134, 193, 239, 249, 255, 257, 259, 268, 275, 276, 294, 301, 305, 312, 316, 327, 333, 335, 336, 349, 351, 354, 361, 363, 371, 373, 379, 381
Influenza 28, 41, 89, 170, 231, 381, 386
Inoculations 28, 31, 49, 88, 104, 123, 126, 130, 137, 145, 178, 184, 189, 221, 232
In the Field 55, 90, 163, 222, 251, 260, 262, 354, 362
In the Line 52, 242, 243, 245, 251, 252, 259, 268, 271, 272, 274, 280, 292, 293, 312, 325, 327, 328, 329, 331, 333, 335, 336, 344, 361, 366, 373, 376
Italian Forces 40, 111, 113, 323

J

Jacob
    Harry Alan 138
    Maude Eliza 138
James, H E R, Col 135, 156, 163, 177, 189, 207
Jeancourt 376, 379, 388

Joncourt 388, 391
Jones
    Dr 20, 21, 23
    Jack 120, 154
    Miss 120
    Mrs 333

K

Kaiser 34, 45, 48, 55
Kanowna 213
Kennet House 24, 283, 284, 313, 314, 319, 354, 366, 371, 399, 407
King Albert Enters Brussels 392
Kirkland, Hugh Edward (Captain) 379, 389, 391, 392
Kirkwood, William Russell Barton 259
Kitchener, Lord 24, 56, 130, 149, 188

L

Lagnicourt 301, 307
Lane, Dr 45
Larkhill Camp 313
La Valentine 230
Lawrence of Arabia 320
Leave in England 245, 280, 282, 284, 291, 292, 311, 321, 366
Lee
    Frank 153
    Harry (Dr) 89, 122, 153, 235
    Mrs Nora 37, 51, 89, 122, 220, 341
Le Havre 232, 235, 322, 407
Lemnos 76, 93, 94, 96, 114, 115, 119, 124, 159, 160, 168
Little
    E Graham (Dr) 157
    Mona Edith. *See* Mona Edith Boulton
    Mrs Edith Elizabeth 22, 25, 29, 33, 34, 37, 38, 43, 48, 53, 166, 179, 207, 209, 217, 224, 255, 261, 269, 282, 284, 290, 308, 319, 334, 352, 360, 367, 368, 370, 372, 375, 399
Lloyd, Henry (Harry) 118, 120, 154, 251, 267, 268, 341
London 19, 261, 277, 283, 284, 285, 291, 292, 302, 303, 308, 311, 319, 321, 322, 356, 360, 364, 366, 370, 371, 375, 407, 409
Lucas, Major 128
Luna Park 211, 213, 214, 215, 216, 218

M

Macansh, Stirling 98, 137, 140, 142
Magnificent men 100, 106, 152
Maids in Sydney 125, 192, 217, 314, 316, 323, 355
Mail Sunk 160, 308, 328, 360, 365, 369
Malaria 262, 266, 269, 298, 365
Malta 71, 171, 172, 173, 174, 176, 180, 183, 186, 188, 199, 201, 204, 206, 209, 211, 212, 214, 215, 216, 219, 229, 265, 267, 269, 270, 273, 329
Manser, Mrs 284, 285, 288, 308
Mansfield, Katharine Rachel 321, 370
Manstow 367, 368
Marseilles 166, 190, 229, 230, 231, 233
Matee. *See* Dora Mary Boulton
Maternity Nurse 282
McLaughlin, Geoffrey (Mjr) 226
McMullin, Alfred Oswald (Major) 384, 387, 388
McMurray, W (Dr) 157
Medic 284
Medical Board 162, 165, 199, 203, 204, 205, 206, 211, 213
Medical Cases 19, 60, 79, 93, 96, 114, 123, 133, 135, 157, 167, 169, 189, 202
Mee Maw. *See* Dora Mary Boulton
Mena Camp 76, 84, 87, 90, 92, 96, 215, 218
Menton 407
Merris 351, 359
Mesopotamia 222, 234
Metcalfe, James Beverly 303, 352
Methuen, Lord 197
Military Hospitals
    25th Casualty Clearing Hospital 164, 168
    No 1 Auxiliary Hospital 211, 213, 215, 216
    No 3 London General Hospital 315
    No 10 Convalescent Depot, Écault 330, 338, 342, 346, 355, 363
    No 14 Casualty Hospital 286
    No 15 General Hospital 62, 74, 79, 82, 89, 93, 96, 99, 104, 110, 112, 122, 125, 128, 132, 134, 138, 143, 146, 151, 156, 160, 162, 165, 168, 172, 175, 179, 186, 188, 189, 200, 206, 220, 223, 233, 240, 261
    No 19 General Hospital 189, 203
    Section Hospital, Dover Castle 30, 37, 40, 42, 44, 46, 48, 50, 51, 55, 57, 60
    Stationary Hospital, Imbros 165
    St. John's Military Hospital 172, 174, 178, 181, 187, 192, 195
    Western Heights, Dover 28, 31
Military Units
    1st Aust Field Artillery Brigade 142, 225, 230, 235, 238, 294, 301, 302, 326
    1st Battery 295, 300, 301
    1st Divisional Ammunition Column, No 1 Section 55, 63, 87, 91, 113, 158, 183, 212, 216, 217, 218, 220, 222, 237, 323
    1st Leicestershire Regiment 295
    2nd Aust Field Artillery Brigade 218, 238, 259, 333, 336, 341, 344, 349, 351, 353, 361, 362, 366, 373, 376, 378, 379, 381
    6th Battery 326, 328, 336, 337, 341, 351, 353, 360, 378, 391
    9th Seaforth Highlanders 387
    17th Field Ambulance 271, 295
    21st Aust Field Artillery Brigade 238, 242, 247, 249, 252, 257, 260, 268, 269, 274, 276, 279, 280, 294
    22nd Battery 225, 227, 230, 238, 242, 247, 252, 274, 294, 295, 307
    28th Field Ambulance 389
    Brigade Ammunition Column 87, 142, 158, 192, 193
    Divisional Ammunition Park 140, 142, 147, 154, 193, 216
Milk on Malta 182
Miller, Denison 371
Ministry of Munitions 294
Minnett, Charles 151
Monash, John (General) 344, 360, 361, 362, 373, 378
Mont Saint-Quentin 373
Moore, David H (Lt Col) 381
Mosquitos 134, 158
Mouquet Farm 257
Mudros 159, 160, 161, 162, 165, 170, 171, 186, 265
Mud, Western Front 232, 269, 272, 275, 276, 280, 286, 287, 289, 299, 320, 326
Mules 72, 108, 115, 120, 124, 193, 194, 324, 325
Mumps 286, 290
Murray, Neil Steward 405

Musgrave, Joyce Ethel 370
Mustafa Pacha 74, 75, 79, 94, 128, 129, 170

N

Naours. *See* Vignacourt & Environs
Napier, Sir W 388, 390
National D'Escompte de Paris 132
Nauroy 376, 380, 382
Near Misses 259, 260, 267, 296, 299, 338, 352, 360, 390
Nerves 62, 159, 241, 260, 267, 299
Neutral Bay 266, 268, 270
Newcastle, NSW 64, 65, 68, 70, 124, 165
Newcomb, Miss D 263, 268
New Oases Camp 212
Newspaper accounts 154, 162, 180, 259, 264, 294, 364
New Zealanders 143, 203, 209, 263, 268, 316, 320, 368, 405
Niagara 407
Nigel's Contract with R.A.M.C. 27, 144, 154, 311, 364, 368, 387
Nissen Hut 340
No Man's Land 272, 394
Nurses 47, 133, 135, 145, 171, 172, 182, 186, 188, 194, 195, 199, 209, 211, 215, 324, 356

O

Observation Posts 302, 335, 347, 349, 350, 351, 352, 383, 388
Oultersteene 351, 359
Owen, Robert Haylock (Col) 139

P

Parcels from home 112, 143, 155, 157, 159, 164, 167, 178, 182, 183, 186, 187, 188, 190, 192, 201, 204, 215, 217, 237, 253, 277, 333, 365
Parcels from home - Billys 201, 208, 212
Parcels from home - Xmas 208, 209, 274, 279, 280, 281, 334
Paris 43, 52, 166, 190, 339, 407
Parkstone 279, 282, 284, 285, 288, 305, 307, 311, 312, 317, 318, 322, 350
Parmiter, Bernard Rayne (Dr) 163
Paterson, Alan 'Banjo' 89
Peaceful Penetration 351, 361, 362
Péronne 373, 378, 394
Pets 103, 108, 110, 116, 128, 150, 246, 337, 342, 351
Philips, Jack 316
Phillip, Laurance 170
Phillips, William James Ellery (Dr) 98
Picquet Duty 68, 88, 199, 218
Pigee. *See* Dr Nigel Philip Boulton
Pilcher, Dr 212
Pitt Town 266, 268, 270, 275
Ploegsteert 247, 248
Pneumonia 93, 96, 113, 167, 202, 329, 386
Port Macquarie 19, 51
Port Said 166, 206
Postal Service 128, 131, 134, 139, 143, 174, 179, 182, 186, 216, 225, 226, 232, 300, 325, 337, 341, 384
Pozières 249, 252, 255, 256, 257, 259, 267
Prisoners 33, 106, 349, 351, 360
Promotions 66, 133, 135, 144, 225, 226, 229, 260, 263, 269, 270, 274, 304, 308, 311, 320, 321, 324, 333, 337, 339
Public Health Department, Egypt 176, 184, 185, 202, 206
Purdie, John Smith (Major) 88
Pyramids 87, 121, 215, 218

R

Ragtime army 307
Ramalinas & Fungi 110, 349
Rates of Pay 20, 58, 119, 136, 153, 168, 172, 184, 196, 197, 199, 201, 202, 235, 270, 313
Rationing 339, 366
Rawlinson, Henry (General) 373
Red Cross 34, 47, 166, 167, 190, 209, 331, 385
Regimental M.O. 47, 57, 128, 261, 267, 273, 300
Reminiscences of Earlier Trips 26, 151, 181, 241, 283, 285, 286, 288, 305, 370, 393
Retreat from Gallipoli 206
Retreat from Mons 43, 58
Return to Australia 53, 163, 166, 224, 235, 332, 381
R.F.A. Officer Cadet School 302, 304, 307, 309, 313, 315
Rheumatic Fever 93, 186, 202
Rheumatism 167
Richards, Archdeacon 143
Richmond, Surrey 23, 135, 190, 285, 303

Roberts, Dr 133, 135, 169
Roberts, Lord 24, 56
Roisel 378, 379, 380, 383, 391, 393, 394, 404
Route March 87, 161, 230, 239, 251, 252, 262, 272, 274, 280, 293, 329, 335, 344, 361, 375, 379, 392
Royal Army Medical Corps 25, 27, 30, 38, 42, 52, 57, 125, 128, 133, 144, 152, 153, 172, 184, 195, 265, 311, 368, 407, 413
Royal Edward 153
Royal Garrison Artillery 47, 56
Runic 284

S

Sailly-Laurette 373, 375
Saint Sauveur 362, 379
Salonika 172, 198, 199, 209, 222, 234, 261, 262, 265, 323
Sanitary Officer 281
Sari Bair, Gallipoli 145, 180
Savings 22, 104, 201, 240, 287, 322, 323, 349, 376
Scarlet Fever 135, 169, 174, 178, 186
Scheyville 282, 291, 294
Scottish Forces 40, 111, 126, 195, 289, 341, 346, 361, 387
Seafield 279, 308, 312, 335
Sellars, Eileen Mary 408, 409, 410
Sentimental Blokes 361
Sewell, Evelyn Pierce (Lt Col) 169
Sexton, Michael John (Dr) 154, 163
Shakedowns 243, 341, 359
Shaw
    Alfred Havergal (Rev) 305
    Beatrice 26, 304, 305, 318
    Dorothy Beatrice Havergal 304, 318
Shelley, Mac Robert 259
Shrapnel Gully, Gallipoli 193
Sliema 172, 174, 178, 181, 185, 187, 192, 195, 199, 209
Slough 61
Smallpox 178, 184, 221, 231, 232
Smoking 98, 101, 151, 172, 186, 209, 253, 277, 286, 336, 337, 359, 365, 369
Snipers 100, 105, 137, 193, 273
Social Change 55, 125, 126, 157, 364
Soldiers Home, St Paul's Bay 197, 205
Somme 247, 249, 260, 264, 271, 274, 276, 283, 287, 295, 339, 341, 346, 347, 348, 361, 362, 366, 372, 373
South Africans 341
Southampton 28, 48, 57, 66, 322, 323, 407
Souvenirs 155, 182, 253, 353, 369
Spring Offensive 335, 339, 360, 373
St Léger les Domart. *See* Vignacourt & Environs
Stoops
    James 267
    Mary 267
    William 267
St Ouen. *See* Vignacourt & Environs
St. Paul's Bay 197, 205
St. Pol 339
Stuart, Thomas Anderson (Sir) 364
Submarines 32, 54, 56, 72, 108, 115, 207, 228, 229, 287, 316, 320, 365, 375
Sudan 153
Suez 98, 138, 200, 207, 211, 212
Sunderland, Dr 170
Surgical Cases 19, 20, 47, 57, 60, 106, 111, 114, 123, 126, 167, 169, 189
Suvla Bay 177, 209
Swimming 64, 80, 92, 94, 98, 119, 120, 124, 127, 140, 142, 150, 201, 265, 286, 307, 341, 361, 367, 368, 375
Sydney 54, 63, 79, 88, 104, 121, 132, 156, 158, 162, 171, 213, 223, 244, 290, 307, 371

T

Taylor, Mick 267, 268
Tel-el-kebir 213, 219, 222, 223, 225, 228, 253
Tenedos 115
Tennis 25, 98, 126, 201, 308
Tent Life 87, 88, 121, 124, 125, 127, 129, 163, 198, 208, 219, 229, 233, 259, 293
Territorials 21, 40, 304
Thea's Marriage 244, 248, 251, 253, 255
The Child. *See* Dorothea Margaret Boulton
The King's School, Parramatta 100, 138, 141, 190, 303, 341, 385, 407, 408
The Oven 65, 88, 103, 269, 326
The Pops 220, 245
Tilney, Leslie Edward (Lt Col) 98
Tincourt 376
Tofield, Marion Ellen 407
Tommies 102, 152, 155, 164, 168, 171, 187, 195, 197, 204, 209, 237, 259, 261,

263, 307, 327, 345, 348, 360
Tonbridge, Lt Col 119
Torpedoes 28, 32, 44, 54, 153, 190, 229, 230
Torquay 166, 308, 310, 311, 314, 315, 366, 367, 370, 375
Tothill, Col F W G 61
Toulon 228, 229, 230
Trains 34, 68, 87, 199, 210, 211, 215, 220, 228, 232, 233, 249, 262, 271, 274, 285, 291, 295, 315, 329, 344, 356, 372
Trench foot 202, 268, 281
Troop Ships 64, 68, 70, 71, 102, 108, 153, 228
Turkey 40, 53, 66, 76, 90, 104, 110, 121, 132, 147, 149, 177
Turks 47, 90, 100, 105, 106, 107, 110, 111, 113, 115, 136, 137, 140, 142, 147, 149, 155, 177, 180, 182, 200, 213, 320
Turnips 334
Twynam, Edward (Major) 98
Typhoid 28, 49, 123, 125, 126, 127, 130, 133, 135, 144, 145, 146, 147, 157, 169, 177, 178, 181, 184, 185, 189, 211, 255
Tyrone 293, 304, 308, 309, 310, 314, 316, 323, 326, 328, 355, 369, 372, 377

U

Uniforms 21, 24, 88, 100, 105, 168, 201, 215, 232, 269, 277, 313, 319, 321, 352
Union Bank of Australasia 78, 244, 376
Union Club, Alexandria 183, 201
University of Sydney 19, 20, 39, 89, 98, 138, 202, 303, 307, 330, 364, 392

V

Valletta 172, 178, 181, 186, 195, 196, 199, 204, 205, 209
Vaux-sur-Somme 379
Verbrandenmolen Ridge 336
Verdun 52, 276
Verviers 394, 395
Veterinary Care 325, 327, 329, 331
Vickers Aviation Works 305
Vignacourt & Environs
    Condé-Folie 379, 381, 382
    Havernas 252, 280, 294
    Naours 280

St Léger les Domart 259
St Ouen 343
Vignacourt 249
Villers-Bretonneux 259, 347, 362, 363
Voluntary Aid Corps 130, 133, 135, 139

W

Wacher, Harold, Dr 135, 136
Waddy, Richard Granville (Dr) 202, 207
Wagon Lines 259, 275, 276, 294, 337, 343, 350, 359, 378, 379
Walers 63
Wallace, Bessie 203
War Office 21, 22, 24, 27, 30, 32, 51, 57, 62, 77, 80, 177, 202, 311, 364, 407
War Strategy 27, 35, 41, 43, 45, 52, 54, 55, 66, 90, 107, 111, 113, 130, 138, 139, 144, 146, 152, 180, 200, 218, 246, 247, 264, 276, 287, 333, 335, 339, 347, 360, 373
Washing 30, 140, 155, 209, 233, 280, 281, 352, 353
Watson, William Thornton (Lieut) 379, 380, 383, 388, 391
Waugh, Dr Arthur John 20, 21, 23
Webb
    Dentist 163
    Thomas Theodor (Rev) 378, 380, 381, 383
Weedon, John Francis Warren 316
Western Front 61, 101, 111, 137, 139, 148, 152, 224, 225, 247, 255, 287, 335, 362, 380
Williams, Mrs 192
Wilson, Dr 163
Wollongong 19, 21, 34, 89, 98, 122, 139, 153, 166, 203, 341
Wren, Miss M 253, 277

Y

Ypres 35, 235, 240, 262, 274, 302, 307, 321, 333, 335, 347

Z

Zietoun 138, 216, 218, 222, 225

www.ingramcontent.com/pod-product-compliance
Lightning Source LLC
Chambersburg PA
CBHW051828230426
43671CB00008B/879